BANKRUPTCY

CARL FELSENFELD

Professor of Law
Fordham University School of Law

THE PROFESSOR SERIES

emanuel®
a divison of Aspen Publishers, Inc.

Aspen Law & Business
Legal Education Division
New York   Gaithersburg

About Aspen Law & Business
Legal Education Division

Aspen Law & Business is proud to welcome Emanuel Publishing
Corporation's highly successful study aids to its list of law school publications. As part
of the Aspen family, Steve and Lazar Emanuel will continue their work on these popu-
lar titles, widely purchased by students for more than a quarter century. With the addition of the Emanuel titles, Aspen now offers the most comprehensive selection of
outstanding publications for the discerning law student.

ASPEN LAW & BUSINESS
A Division of Aspen Publishers, Inc.
A Wolters Kluwer Company
www.aspenpublishers.com

Introduction

This is largely a book about one long, complex statute. In discoursing about the statute, one is never sure whether to quote its words directly, in which event the book will be too long and less than useful to the student, or to discuss its provisions, in which event — in failing to use precise statutory language — the book will be less than accurate. The author has tried to steer equidistant from Scylla and Charybdis. He warns the reader, however, that in interpreting a statute it is the statutory language that is dispositive. In giving legal interpretations based upon this book, or in answering questions on an examination, the statute itself must always be consulted.

SUMMARY OF CONTENTS

TABLE OF CONTENTS

Chapter 1

SOURCES OF BANKRUPTCY LAW

Chapter 2

THE BANKRUPTCY CODE:
AN OVERVIEW

Chapter 3

COMMENCING A CASE —
INITIAL STEPS

Chapter 4

THE DEBTOR — GENERAL RULES

Chapter 5

THE TRUSTEE

Chapter 6

THE CREDITOR — GENERAL RULES

Chapter 7

THE BANKRUPTCY ESTATE

Chapter 8

THE TRUSTEE'S AVOIDING POWERS

Chapter 9

FILING UNDER CHAPTER 7 — LIQUIDATION

Chapter 10

FILING UNDER CHAPTER 9 — MUNICIPAL BANKRUPTCY

Chapter 11

FILING UNDER CHAPTER 11 — REORGANIZATION

Chapter 12

FILING UNDER CHAPTER 12 — FAMILY FARMER WITH REGULAR ANNUAL INCOME

Chapter 13

FILING UNDER CHAPTER 13 — INDIVIDUAL WITH REGULAR INCOME

Chapter 14

JURISDICTION AND VENUE

CAPSULE SUMMARY

This Capsule Summary is intended for review at the end of the semester. Reading it is not a substitute for mastering the material in the main outline. The order of topics is occasionally somewhat different from that in the main outline; that's because this Capsule Summary is meant to be a separate outline for night-before-the exam review, not just be a summary of the main outline.

CHAPTER 1
SOURCES OF BANKRUPTCY LAW

I. FEDERAL BANKRUPTCY POWER

A. Bankruptcy law under federal power: The bankruptcy power appears in Article I, Section 8 of the Constitution — "The Congress shall have Power...to establish... uniform Laws on the subject of Bankruptcies throughout the United States." It is clear that the federal law of bankruptcy, emanating from the power in the Constitution, preempts inconsistent state law. In 1898, Congress enacted a statute which established bankruptcy law as a permanent part of our federal legal structure. The 1898 statute was amended by the Chandler Act in 1934. This was the last major bankruptcy law until the enactment of the present Code.

B. The Bankruptcy Code (Title 11 U.S.C.): In 1978, after years of study, Congress replaced the then-existing bankruptcy law with the "Bankruptcy Code," codified as Title 11 of the United States Code. Since 1978, the Bankruptcy Code has been unchanged in its essential conception and structure. For convenience, we generally refer to the pre-1978 law as the "Act" and today's law as the "Code."

  1. Focus on rehabilitation: *Rehabilitation*, or a "fresh start," *is the central underlying philosophy of the Code*. The United States has led the way among the major commercial nations in this evolution. In general, the United States bankruptcy laws are more debtor-oriented than those in the rest of the world.

  2. Studies leading to the Code: The studies leading to the Code stressed three major events that changed our views of bankruptcy law after the 1934 Chandler Act:

    a. The Uniform Commercial Code: The Uniform Commercial Code, which fundamentally changed the law of secured transactions (in Article 9), came about in the 1950s. The Bankruptcy Code embodies a treatment of secured creditors that reflects the policies of the U.C.C.

    b. Consumer credit: The monumental growth in consumer credit introduced a new body of debtors. Many of the provisions in the new Code were developed with consumer debtors in mind.

    c. Social acceptance of bankruptcy: Increasingly, the American public has grown to accept the debtor in bankruptcy as a sympathetic figure. The essentially unlimited invitation to debtors to file in "voluntary" bankruptcies reflects the public's acceptance of bankruptcy as a social need. The use in the Code of the term "debtor" instead of the term "bankrupt" reflects this attitude.

II. RELATIONSHIP OF FEDERAL AND STATE LAWS

A. Federal bankruptcy supremacy: With its enactment of the first enduring bankruptcy law in 1898, the federal government effectively *preempted any state action on bank-*

ruptcy cases. This preemption has continued and expanded under the various amendments to the bankruptcy laws. Despite this federal preemption, the individual states have continued to enact laws dealing with related topics, such as assignments for the benefit of creditors.

B. State statutes—assignments for benefit of creditors: All states have some statutory scheme for dealing with insolvent entities. Often called "assignments for the benefit of creditors," these statutes may, in their simplest form, call for the sale of an insolvent debtor's assets, with the proceeds going to creditors. Normally, in the case of a corporate or partnership debtor, the sale will be followed by liquidation. However, an individual debtor cannot secure a discharge from debt in a state proceeding and will typically remain subject to whatever debts are left after sale of his assets.

III. BANKRUPTCY RULES AND OFFICIAL FORMS

A. Bankruptcy rules: Supplementing the Code are the Bankruptcy Rules. The Rules are written and proposed in the first instance by the Judicial Conference of the United States. The Supreme Court has the power to prescribe by general rules "the forms of process, writs, pleadings and motions, and the practice and procedure in cases" under the Code. The Supreme Court then reports the Rules to Congress. In many cases dealing with procedure in the bankruptcy courts, the Rules simply refer to the Federal Rules of Civil Procedure. Each district court is authorized to provide its own local rules of bankruptcy.

B. Bankruptcy forms: The Bankruptcy Rules contain a set of forms for use in bankruptcy cases. The forms may be modified as necessary for particular situations. The forms not only provide procedural guidance but are useful in interpreting statutory language.

CHAPTER 2

BANKRUPTCY CODE OVERVIEW

I. EQUITABLE NATURE OF THE BANKRUPTCY CODE

A. Bankruptcy falls under equity jurisprudence: Courts of bankruptcy are essentially courts of equity; the themes of equitable jurisprudence underlie the Bankruptcy Code. In addition to the commitment to equity that attaches to the bankruptcy courts through their placement in the federal court system, the courts have an independent tradition to prevent abuse of the bankruptcy process.

B. Concern with good faith: A duty to act in good faith is imposed under most provisions of the Code (as, for example, the duty to propose a Chapter 11 reorganization plan in good faith). The bankruptcy courts regard the exercise of good faith as a pervasive underlying requirement that causes them to examine all transactions for their integrity, motives and general good faith prior to granting bankruptcy relief.

II. STRUCTURE OF BANKRUPTCY CODE

A. Chapters 1, 3, 5 — general application to other chapters: Chapters of the Code are generally designated by odd numbers. The first three chapters establish a series of general rules that apply to filings under the latter five chapters. Chapter 1 contains definitions and some basic rules of construction. Chapter 3 deals with the administration of a bankruptcy case. Chapter 5 establishes rules relating to the major bankruptcy players — creditors, the debtor and the estate.

B. Chapters 7, 9, 11, 12 & 13 — cases which can be "filed": There are five basic types of bankruptcy cases provided for by the Code. The cases are traditionally given the names of the chapters that describe them.

1. **Chapter 7 cases – liquidation cases:** This chapter deals with liquidation of the debtor and the distribution of its assets among its creditors. In the case of corporate or partnership debtors, liquidation under the code is generally followed by dissolution under state law. In the case of individual debtors, liquidation is followed by a fresh start, free of most debts.

2. **Chapter 9 cases – municipalities:** This chapter covers filings by municipalities which can no longer meet their debts.

3. **Chapter 11 – business reorganization:** This chapter concentrates on business reorganizations. The debtor goes through a period of consolidation and emerges with a reduced debt load and a renewed existence.

4. **Chapter 12 – family farmers:** This chapter deals with filings by family farmers, who are especially vulnerable to fluctuations in the markets for their products.

5. **Chapter 13 – consumer reorganizations:** This chapter offers a simpler form of reorganization than Chapter 11. It is used by individuals with fixed incomes.

6. **Foreign proceedings; § 304 cases:** In addition to the five basic "filing" chapters, this section deals with a special kind of "case," which is generally a Bankruptcy court extension of a foreign proceeding.

III. DEFINITION OF DEBTOR

A. **Broad definitions of "debtor" and "person":** A "debtor" is defined in the Code as a "person" (or a municipality) concerning whom a case has been commenced. "Person" is in turn defined to include an individual, partnership or corporation.

B. **United States connection required:** Any person that resides or has a domicile, a place of business, or property in the United States (or a municipality) may be a debtor.

IV. CASES ANCILLARY TO FOREIGN PROCEEDINGS — § 304

A. **Cases involving U.S. assets of foreign debtors:** A case under § 304 is called a "case ancillary to a foreign proceeding". It deals with the American assets of a debtor in bankruptcy in a foreign jurisdiction. Only a foreign representative, essentially the foreign equivalent of our trustee, may start a § 304 case. The Code gives the bankruptcy courts virtually unfettered power to handle the United States assets as they see fit, in order to best assure an economical and expeditious administration of the estate. They may enjoin other proceedings, stay the enforcement of judgments, order the turnover of property, or order other appropriate relief.

B. **Law and procedure drawn from cases:** The courts usually attempt to assist the foreign proceeding rather than enforce the specific rules of the Code. To the extent that the foreign law resembles the Code, the task is easy. However, where foreign law is radically different from the Code, they may resort to the remedies of the Code in order to justify the reasonable expectations of United States creditors in assets located in the United States.

V. GENERAL DEFINITIONS — § 101

A. **"Claim":** "Claim" is very broadly defined in order to include the greatest possible kinds of economic obligations by a debtor in a bankruptcy case. It means a *right to payment* "whether or not such right is reduced to judgment, liquidated, unliquidated, fixed, contingent, matured, unmatured, disputed, undisputed, legal, equitable, secured, or unsecured."

1. **Must be capable of reduction to money damages:** Because the Code is concerned with economic obligations rather than behavior, the definition of "claim" goes on to pro-

vide that a right to an equitable remedy for breach of performance is not a claim unless it can be translated into money damages.

    2. Relationship of "claim" and "interest": The Code frequently refers to "interests" along with its references to "claims." The word "interests" is not defined in the Code, but it is used to mean that relationship between the holder and the debtor which entitles the holder of the interest to assert the right or opportunity to receive a payment, though he may not be owed a debt. The most common example of "an interest" is the ***equity participation*** in a corporation.

B. "Debt": A "debt" is the liability side of a claim. If D owes C $1,000, C has a claim against D for $1,000; D has a debt to C of $1,000.

C. "Insolvent": Under the Code's so-called "balance sheet" test of insolvency, a debtor is insolvent if debts exceed assets. The Code does not always employ the balance sheet insolvency test. For example, there is an alternate "equitable" test of insolvency that looks to the ability to pay current debts in order to establish whether an involuntary bankruptcy may be begun.

VI. RULES OF CONSTRUCTION — § 102

A. "Notice and hearing": There is frequent reference throughout the Code to the phrase "after notice and a hearing." This phrase requires notice and the *opportunity* for a hearing. Thus, a hearing need not actually be held if it is not requested by a "party in interest" or if the court authorizes action without a hearing. However, in some instances, a hearing is specifically required by particular provisions of the Code or the Rules.

B. "Party in interest": This undefined phrase is used frequently throughout the Code. It clearly includes the debtor, the creditors and the trustee. It may include appropriate third parties, as determined by the court.

C. "Includes" and "including": The use of the term "include" and "including" is specifically defined to be "not limiting." In other words, where specifically enumerated categories follow the term "include" or "including" in a statutory provision, the court may find that the inclusion of additional categories is warranted.

VII. BACKUP POWER OF COURT — § 105

A. Backup power of court generally: The bankruptcy courts and the district courts have extremely broad power to "issue any order, process, or judgment that is necessary or appropriate to carry out the provisions" of the Code. The courts may do this on their own motion or on the motion of a party in interest.

B. Status conference: Under the backup power, the court may also hold a status conference regarding any case or proceeding and issue any order it deems appropriate to ensure that a case is handled expeditiously and economically.

CHAPTER 3

COMMENCING A CASE — INITIAL STEPS

I. THE VOLUNTARY CASE — § 301

A. Filing a voluntary petition; the order for relief: Under the Code, voluntary bankruptcies make up the bulk of all cases. A voluntary bankruptcy case begins when the debtor files a petition. The debtor need not satisfy any prescribed standard of insolvency in order to file a voluntary petition. The ***filing of the voluntary petition constitutes the "order for relief;"*** no actual adjudication occurs. By comparison, in an involuntary case, the court issues the order for relief when it grants the petition for bankruptcy.

B. **The joint voluntary case — § 302:** A joint case may be filed by an individual and the individual's spouse. The petition constitutes an order for joint relief. If the assets were used to satisfy the obligations of both spouses, the court is more likely to consolidate them. If the assets were used separately by each spouse, the two estates may be administered and disposed of in the same case, but consolidation is less likely.

II. THE INVOLUNTARY CASE — § 303

A. **Filing an involuntary petition:** An involuntary case begins when a creditor, or a group of creditors, files a petition against the debtor. Involuntary cases represent less than one-half of one percent of all bankruptcy cases. An involuntary case may be brought only against persons that qualify as debtors under either Chapter 7 or Chapter 11. An involuntary case may not be brought against a farmer or charitable corporation.

B. **Requirements for an involuntary petition:** An involuntary petition must meet the following minimal criteria.

1. **Aggregate claims:** The claims by those joining in the petition must aggregate at least $10,000 more than the value of all liens held to secure those claims. No claim may be contingent or the subject of a bona-fide dispute.

2. **Aggregate claim holders:** In involuntary cases which have 12 or more claim holders, at least three of these claim holders must join in the § 303 petition. In the infrequent case involving fewer than 12 claim holders, one or more claimants may file the § 303 petition. In determining whether there are 12 claim holders, holders who are employees, insiders, and transferees of the debtor with voidable transfers are excluded.

C. **Debtor may answer or contest petition:** The debtor, or a general partner of a partnership debtor that did not join in the petition, may file an answer to a petition to contest it. If the involuntary petition is answered, the case has begun, but an order for relief does not issue immediately. The petitioner must generally prove that, unless such debts are the subject of a bona-fide dispute, the debtor is not paying debts as they become due. The court may examine such factors as: whether a large portion (not necessarily 50%) of the debtor's debts is unpaid; the periods of time over which the debts have been unpaid; and even the degree of care taken by the debtor in managing the payment of its debts.

D. **Period between the petition and the order for relief — the gap:** ***In involuntary proceedings, the period between the petition and the order for relief*** (i.e. the finding by the court that the petitioner has proved its case for bankruptcy), ***is called the "gap" period***. The debtor may continue to operate its business during the gap.

1. **Appointment of a trustee:** A party in interest in a Chapter 7 case who believes operation by the debtor will harm the estate may ask the court to appoint an interim trustee. The interim trustee will take possession of the business and operate it for the benefit of all. A Chapter 11 trustee may be appointed for similar reasons.

2. **Filing a bond:** The debtor may file a bond to regain control of the estate from the trustee; the creditors may be required to file a bond indemnifying the debtor against damage to its business caused by the involuntary petition.

III. ABSTENTION; DISMISSAL; SUSPENSION

A. **Court may dismiss or suspend case:** A bankruptcy or district court may dismiss a case or, in the alternative, suspend all proceedings in a case. It may do either if the interests of the creditors and the debtor would be better served by the action. Considerable discretion is given to bankruptcy courts in this regard because they are courts of equity. The court may abstain or suspend where the only real dispute among the parties is already under consideration in a state or foreign court and the bankruptcy would only complicate matters. The court may also abstain from acting if there are active settlement discussions in progress.

IV. LIMITATIONS IN CONSUMER CASES

    A. Provisions to curb increase: Provisions added to the Code in 1984 were designed to make it more difficult for consumers to file in bankruptcy. No individual may be a debtor if he was a debtor in a case pending during the previous 180 days *and* either of two situations exists: (1) the prior case was dismissed by the court as a result of debtor's misconduct; or (2) the debtor obtained voluntary dismissal of the prior case after a request by a creditor for relief from the automatic stay. The second ground creates a presumption of misconduct in situations where a debtor files a case knowing that he is not entitled to the automatic stay and asks for a dismissal when a creditor petitions the court for relief from the stay.

CHAPTER 4

THE DEBTOR — GENERAL RULES

I. DEBTOR'S INITIAL DUTIES

    A. Schedules produced by debtor: The debtor is required to file certain lists and forms with the court, including a list of creditors; schedules of assets, liabilities, income and expenditures; a statement of financial affairs, including financial history, source of income, pending lawsuits, payments to creditors, recent transfers of property, and prior addresses; and with respect to secured consumer debts, a debtor's statements of intention to either retain the property and reaffirm the debt, claim the property as exempt and redeem it, or surrender it to the secured creditor.

    B. Free flow of information: The creditors must have notice at once that a bankruptcy has begun to avoid violating the automatic stay. The automatic stay requires that they abstain from certain acts as soon as the bankruptcy begins.

    C. Other duties of the debtor: If a trustee has been appointed, the debtor must cooperate with the trustee and, in general, turn over all property of the estate and all records pertaining to the estate. (In Chapter 11, 12 and 13 cases, the debtor usually retains extensive management over estate property.)

    D. Hearings, examinations, and other duties: In his central role in the bankruptcy proceeding, the debtor is required to appear at various hearings and must perform various duties. The debtor is required to appear and submit to examination under oath at the first meeting of creditors and is required to appear at the discharge hearing.

II. THE AUTOMATIC STAY — § 362

    A. Automatic stay enjoins creditors: *Upon commencement of the case (the filing of the petition), the automatic stay is imposed, which prevents creditors from taking any action to enforce their claims.* The stay is applicable to all "entities," including government bodies. A creditor is subject to the stay whether or not it knows of the bankruptcy. Actual and punitive damages are available for breach of the stay.

    B. Duration of stay: The stay of an act against property of the estate continues until the property is no longer property of the estate. All other stays (including stays against property other than of the estate) remain in effect until the earliest of the following events: (1) the case is closed; (2) the case is dismissed; or (3) a discharge is granted or denied.

C. Situations in which the stay applies: There are eight instances in which the automatic stay applies.

   1. Stay of actions, proceedings, and claims: The stay applies to the commencement or continuation of any legal action or proceeding to recover a claim that arose before the petition.

   2. Stay of enforcement of judgments: A judgment obtained before the commencement of the case cannot be enforced against either the debtor or property of the estate.

   3. Stay of acts against property of the estate: Any act to obtain possession of property of the estate, or to exercise control over property of the estate, is stayed.

   4. Stay of acts to effect liens against estate: The stay prevents the creation, perfection, or enforcement of any lien against ***property of the estate*** after the petition is filed. An exception applies as to the perfection of liens that relate back to the time the lien was obtained.

   5. Stay of liens affecting property of the debtor: If a lien secures a ***claim against the debtor*** that arose before the petition, the lien may not be created, perfected, or enforced against the debtor's property after the petition. Note that this provision deals with property of the debtor and that the previous provision deals with property of the estate. The debtor's property will be outside the estate if it is exempt or the debtor earned it or received it as a gift after the petition.

   6. Stay against acts to collect claims against debtor: The sixth situation to which the stay applies is to stay any act to "collect, assess, or recover" a claim against the debtor that arose before the commencement of the case. For example, if a debtor requests a college transcript after filing a bankruptcy petition and the college refuses because of a policy of not releasing transcripts where a tuition bill is unpaid, the stay has been violated. Not releasing the transcript is an effort to collect a bill during the period of the stay.

   7. Stay against asserting setoffs: In bankruptcy, if A owed B money before B's petition, A is stayed from setting that debt off against what B owes A. The debt from A to B is property of the estate, and A may not use it without court supervision.

   8. Stay of proceedings in the Tax Court: A special provision applies the automatic stay to proceedings before the Tax Court. This provision indicates that a bankruptcy is given precedence over a Tax Court proceeding.

D. Acts excepted from the automatic stay: There are a number of exceptions to the automatic stay. The most important of these are:

   1. Criminal actions: The stay does not affect criminal actions or proceedings against the debtor.

   2. Alimony, maintenance and support: There is no stay (1) against an action or proceeding for paternity, or (2) against the collection of alimony, maintenance, or support from property that is not property of the estate.

   3. Liens that relate back: Despite the general prohibition on perfecting liens, perfection is permitted for liens that are perfected after the lien is obtained and that relate back to the date of obtaining the lien.

   4. Police and regulatory powers: The commencement and continuation of an action or proceeding by a governmental unit under its police or regulatory powers is permitted. For example, an action by the United States to enforce or to obtain reimbursement of costs under an environmental cleanup order is not stayed.

   5. Enforcement of governmental judgments: The government, acting under its police or regulatory powers, may enforce a judgment for remedies such as specific performance, but is stayed from collecting a money judgment.

6. **Tax deficiencies:** The IRS is permitted to conduct an audit to determine tax liability, to issue notice of a tax deficiency, demand unfiled tax returns, assess a tax, and issue a demand for payment.

7. **Lessors of real property:** A lessor of real property may take action to dispossess a lessee under a nonresidential lease, if the stated term of the lease expires before or during a case. A consumer lessee filing under Chapter 13 is protected against such action.

8. **Negotiable instrument notices:** The holder of a negotiable instrument may present it and give notice of protest and dishonor under Article 3 of the Uniform Commercial Code. These acts are not stayed because they do not involve the payment of money and are necessary to keep promissory notes and checks alive and to preserve the remedies of parties to the instruments.

E. **Relief from stay:** Of critical importance is the fact that the automatic stay can be modified or terminated before it expires.

1. **Modification for cause:** The stay can be modified for "cause." The elements of cause are fact-sensitive and are decided on a case-by-case basis.

   a. **Injury to collateral:** *Relief from the stay for cause generally applies when the creditor's collateral is being diminished.* The prime example of diminished collateral is the normal depreciation suffered during the period that the collateral is held by the debtor and, the creditor is prevented from receiving payments on its obligation by the stay.

   b. **When creditor is undersecured:** Cause for relief may be found where a secured creditor is undersecured (that is, the value of its security is less than the amount of its claim) and the debtor has no continuing interest in the property.

   c. **Other elements of cause:** Cause may also consist of fraudulent behavior by the debtor, failure of the debtor to care for or to insure the collateral, or failure of the debtor to fulfill the terms of a reorganization plan.

2. **Payment of adequate protection:** For a secured creditor, cause includes a lack of "adequate protection."

   a. **Definition of "Adequate Protection":** *Adequate protection refers to the benefit to the creditor* (e.g., payments in money) *that ensures that the protection that the creditor gets from its collateral will not diminish while it is being held by the debtor and depreciating in value.*

   b. **Right to immediate possession by creditor:** The doctrine is usually applied when the creditor has an immediate right to take possession of the collateral under the terms of the security arrangement with the debtor, but the debtor continues to hold the collateral under the stay.

   c. **Time value of money:** Although money not paid over a period of time usually bears interest, the Supreme Court has held that the *time value of money need not be included in compensation for adequate protection.* Compensation will be measured only by the actual reduction in the value of the property during the bankruptcy. *United States v. Timbers of Inwood Forest*, 484 U.S. 365 (1988).

3. **Protection of creditors in reorganizations:** In reorganizations, the debtor often remains in business for a prolonged period of time and may attempt to use the creditor's collateral for its operations. Under these circumstances, the creditor may need to be protected from the acts of the debtor. The creditor may obtain *relief from the stay* and recover its collateral *in reorganizations* if (1) *the debtor has no equity in the collateral* (that is, the collateral is worth less than the debt), and (2) *the debtor does not need it for an effective reorganization.*

4. **Single asset real estate cases:** In 1994, the Code was amended to include special relief from the stay for creditors in "single asset real estate" cases. In such cases, the debtor fre-

quently files for bankruptcy in order to prevent or delay foreclosure proceedings in state court. This special relief is limited to single asset real estate cases where the property generates substantially all the income of a debtor and there are secured debts of no more than $4 million. In such cases, the real estate may be released from the automatic stay unless, within 90 days after the order for relief (or such longer time as a court may order) either (1) the debtor has filed a feasible plan of reorganization, or (2) the debtor has started making interest payments to the creditors for their secured interests in the real estate.

III. EXEMPTIONS — § 522

A. **Exemptions in general:** Under an exemption, a debtor may select a limited amount of *property that is needed for personal use*. Property that is exempted is removed from the estate and is not liable for any debts that arose, or that are determined to have arisen, before the petition. *Exemptions under the Code are available only to individuals* — not to corporations, partnerships, or other entities. The debtor may not claim an exemption with respect to property that was transferred voluntarily or concealed.

   1. **Exempt property reachable for certain debts:** Exempt property remains liable for certain debts even after it has been returned to the debtor, including: certain tax debts, certain alimony and child support debts, debts secured by liens on the exempt property, and certain debts of individuals involved in bank fraud.

B. **Duties and rights of the debtor:** The debtor must file a list showing all property claimed as exempt. Some debtors facing bankruptcy will gather non-exempt assets, sell them, and then buy exempt assets with the proceeds. The courts must determine whether the assets claimed as exempt serve the function of the exemption design — the debtor's right to make a fresh start — or, instead, whether they represent a device to defraud creditors out of what is rightfully due to them.

C. **Choice of exemption scheme:** The debtor is theoretically given a choice between the exemptions available under the Code, or those available under state and federal (nonbankruptcy) laws.

   1. **Exemptions under the Bankruptcy Code:** As permitted by the Code, 36 states have passed opt-out legislation, leaving only 14 states in which the debtor may utilize the exemptions choice provided by the Code.

   2. **State law and federal (nonbankruptcy) exemptions:** The debtor may use the exemptions allowed to him under the law of his state, plus all federal nonbankruptcy exemptions (i.e., exemptions under federal laws other those provided for in the Code scheme, such as under the Civil Service, veterans, and Social Security laws). Because a majority of states have opted out of the federal scheme, most debtors must utilize this scheme.

   3. **Single election for joint cases:** In joint cases, both debtors must agree on a single election. If they cannot agree and they live in a state which has not opted out of the option of selecting the exemptions under the Code, they are deemed to have elected the Code exemptions.

D. **Power to avoid liens on exempted property — § 522(f):** The debtor is granted limited rights to avoid certain types of liens on exempt property. *Liens are more likely to be voidable if they are not "reliance liens," such as security interests or mortgages.* A "reliance lien" is generally given to the creditor as a security interest at the inception of a transaction. Because they are closer to traditional property rights, the Court has not generally allowed the rejection of a reliance lien without the awarding of just compensation to the holder of the lien as required by the Fifth Amendment. *Louisville Joint Stock Land Bank v. Radford*, 295 U.S. 555 (1935).

1. **Application to two kinds of liens:** The debtor is permitted to *avoid two kinds of liens against exempt property — judicial liens and nonpossessory, nonpurchase-money liens.*

   a. **Judicial liens:** A judicial lien is defined as a lien established by a state procedure, such as attachment or execution, that is used to enforce an unpaid judgment or to restrain assets of someone who may disappear with those assets. It is the typical "non-reliance lien." To constitute an avoidable judicial lien, the property must be owned prior to the time that the lien is imposed. Judicial liens for alimony and child support as prescribed by the Code are not avoidable under this provision.

   b. **Nonpossessory, nonpurchase-money liens:** A *nonpossessory* (i.e., the creditor has not taken possession of the collateral), *nonpurchase-money lien* (i.e., the loan was not made for the specific purpose of purchasing the asset) *upon exempt assets* such as household furniture and health aids, *is avoidable*. Such liens are commonly used by some creditors as arm-twisting devices to force repayment of a loan. They are not really intended as security devices.

      i. **Liens avoidable:** Nonpossessory, nonpurchase-money liens are avoidable for three types of exempt property of the debtor or a dependent of the debtor: (1) *household furnishings and goods* held primarily for personal, family, or household use, including animals and crops, (2) *professional books or tools of the trade*, or (3) *professionally prescribed health aids*.

      ii. **Certain business liens retained:** Creditors' lien interests in professional books, tools of the trade, farm animals, and crops are protected if they resulted from consensual security interests given by the debtor before bankruptcy and exceed $5,000 in value. This provision only applies in cases in which the debtor is utilizing state exemptions (i.e., the debtor is in a state that has opted out of the exemption scheme under the Code or the debtor voluntarily chose the state rather than the Code system).

E. **Effect of § 522(f) on impaired exemptions:** A debtor may *avoid judicial and non-possessory, non-purchase money liens* on an interest in his property *to the extent that such liens impair an exemption to which the debtor would have been entitled.*

   1. **Judicial liens that affect exempt status:** Where state law defines as non-exempt, property that is otherwise exempt even if it becomes subject to a judicial lien, the Supreme Court has held that the lien may nevertheless be avoided and the exemption allowed. *Owen v. Owen*, 111 S.Ct. 1833 (1991).

   2. **Mathematical approach to determining extent of impairment:** A lien may not impair an exemption where the debtor has limited equity in property. Under a formula added to the Code in 1994, a lien is considered to impair an exemption to the extent that the sum of all liens on the property and the amount of the exemption that the debtor could claim if there were no liens on the property *exceeds* the value of the debtor's interest in the property without counting for liens. If the result is zero or a negative number, the exemption is unimpaired.

F. **Waiver of exemptions restricted:** The *debtor's exemptions* (under either the state or Code schemes) *may not be waived in a transaction with an unsecured creditor*. However, a waiver of exemptions may be included in a secured transaction. Thus, a waiver of exemptions in a mortgage on land or a security agreement on personal property will be valid in favor of the secured creditor.

IV. EXCEPTIONS TO DISCHARGE — § 523

A. **General definition of discharge:** If a debt is discharged, whatever the creditor receives comes only from the bankruptcy estate and the creditor has no further right of collection against the debtor. The times at which discharge occurs and the particular debts are discharged differ from chapter to chapter. Certain debts are not dischargeable, including for such reasons as public policy and the actions of the debtor when the debts were incurred.

B. Exceptions from discharge: In general, exceptions from discharge occur automatically. However, creditors for certain debts must ask the court to determine that the debts are excepted from discharge. Where a particular claim is not discharged, the creditor may pursue its legal remedies against the debtor after the general discharge as though the bankruptcy had never occurred.

C. Principal exceptions from discharge: There are eleven principal exceptions from discharge.

1. **Certain tax claims:** Tax and customs duty debts that are excluded from discharge include (1) those arising in the ordinary course of the debtor's business during the "gap" period in involuntary cases; (2) taxes for which returns were due for the three years before the petition; and (3) taxes due, as to which a return was not filed or was fraudulent.

2. **Fraudulent representations:**   Upon application to the Court, discharge for debts for money, property, services or credit may be denied if obtained through fraud.

   a. **Presumption of fraud:** There are two rebuttable presumptions of fraudulent conduct that cause the underlying debts to be non-dischargeable. The first applies where a consumer aggregated debts of more than $1,000 to a single creditor for luxury goods or services within 60 days of the petition. The second applies where the consumer obtained cash advances under an "open end credit plan" (typically a credit card or overdraft checking plan) of more than $1,000 within 60 days of the order for relief.

   b. **Fraudulent credit statements:** In order for a fraudulent credit statement by the debtor to be excepted from discharge, the credit statement must: be materially false (not false in minor particulars), deal with the debtor's or an insider's financial condition, have been reasonably relied upon (the creditor must in fact have relied upon the false statement itself and not discovered it later in an effort to avoid the discharge), and have been made by the debtor with intent to deceive (e.g., the debtor did not make a reasonable and good faith attempt to disclose his financial condition).

3. **Debts not listed, scheduled, or known:** An undisclosed or unlisted debt will be exempt from discharge. Although lack of notice and of actual knowledge will prevent a creditor from participating in the case, it will be able to pursue the individual debtor after the discharge. This can often be of greater value than participation in the bankruptcy. However, if the creditor was able to timely file a claim or, where this is required, request an exception from discharge, the debt will be discharged.

4. **Fraud, defalcation, embezzlement, and larceny:**   Upon application to the Court, a debt will be denied discharge if it was incurred though fraud or defalcation while the debtor was acting in a fiduciary capacity, or if it was incurred through embezzlement or larceny.

5. **Obligations for support or alimony:** If a debt is for alimony, maintenance, or support stemming from a separation agreement, divorce decree, or court order, it will not be discharged.

6. **Willful and malicious injuries:** Debts resulting from willful and malicious injuries to person or to property are, subject to the court's review, excepted from discharge.

7. **Fines, penalties or forfeitures:** If owed to a governmental unit, a fine, penalty, or forfeiture that is "not compensation for actual pecuniary loss" is not dischargeable. Under a special Code provision, fines owed on delinquent taxes are dischargeable unless the tax itself is of a sort that is nondischargeable.

8. **Educational loans:** Debts for educational loans, made, insured, or guaranteed by a governmental unit, or made under any program funded in whole or in part by a governmental unit or nonprofit institution are not dischargeable unless the debtor can show the debt imposes an *undue hardship* on her and her dependents.

9. **Drunk driving exception:** Liability for death or personal injury caused by the debtor's operation of a motor vehicle while drunk or under the influence of drugs is nondischargeable.

10. **Further on divorce and maintenance obligations:** If the debtor has obligations incurred in connection with a divorce or separation agreement or court proceeding, different from those covered in paragraph 5 (such as an obligation to pay over earned royalties), they are discharged only if (1) the debtor can not make payments beyond those necessary for his support, or (2) such a discharge results in a benefit to the debtor that outweighs the detrimental consequences to a spouse, former spouse, or child.

11. **Condominium and cooperative fees:** A fee that becomes due to a cooperative or condominium association after the order for relief is not discharged if the debtor physically occupied the dwelling unit or leased it to a tenant during the applicable period.

V. EFFECT OF A DISCHARGE — § 524

C
A
P
S
U
L
E

S
U
M
M
A
R
Y

A. **Discharge affects personal liability:** Discharge annuls unsecured obligations but leaves intact liens against both real and personal property. A judgment with respect to a debt that has been discharged is also discharged.

B. **Discharge enjoins future action:** Discharge will operate as an injunction against the "commencement or continuation of an action, the employment of process, or an act to collect, recover, or offset" any personal liability that was discharged.

C. **Reaffirmation agreements:** Reaffirmation agreements are agreements between debtors and creditors that bind the debtors to the terms of obligations that are dischargeable in the bankruptcy. A *reaffirmation agreement* is valid if it is (1) *made before the discharge*; (2) *contains a statement that the debtor can rescind it at anytime before the discharge or within 60 days* after being filed with the court, whichever occurs later, and that the agreement is not required by law or by any other agreement; and (3) is filed with the court together with an affidavit of the debtor's lawyer that the *agreement is voluntary, does not impose an undue hardship on the debtor or a dependent of the debtor, and that the debtor is fully informed*.

D. **Voluntary payment of debts:** A debtor who has been discharged may voluntarily repay any debt.

VI. THE DISCHARGED DEBTOR — § 525

A. **Prohibitions on discriminatory and other acts:** To sustain the positive effects of a discharge, certain acts may not be executed against a discharged debtor under the Code.

B. **Prohibitions applicable to governmental units:** Most of the prohibitions are with respect to acts of governmental units. In broad outline, a government unit may not "deny, revoke, suspend, or refuse to renew a license" or a similar grant, discriminate with respect to such a grant, or deny or discriminate with respect to employment, "solely" because the individual has been a debtor under the Code, was insolvent before a case was begun, or has not paid a debt that is dischargeable.

C. **Prohibitions applicable to private employers:** The restrictions on private employers are limited to prohibitions against discrimination in employment.

D. **Student loans:** Neither a government entity that makes or guarantees student loans, nor a private business that makes loans guaranteed or insured under a governmental student loan program, may discriminate against an applicant solely because the applicant has been a debtor under the Bankruptcy Code or because the debtor has failed to pay a debt dischargeable or discharged under the Code.

CHAPTER 5
THE TRUSTEE

I. ROLE OF TRUSTEE — § 323

A. The trustee represents the estate: A trustee — generally someone who manages assets for their true owner — is present in varying capacities throughout the Code. A trustee is always a part of any bankruptcy case under Chapters 7, 12 and 13 and, although not required, may be appointed under Chapters 9 and 11.

B. Trustee's right to sue and be sued: As with corporate management, the trustee may sue and be sued on behalf of the estate. The trustee may also be sued personally for mismanagement of the estate. Most courts hold that negligence by the trustee in the conduct of his fiduciary duties is enough to sustain his liability; others require an intentional or willful act.

C. Relationship to Chapter 9 and 11 debtors: A Chapter 11 reorganization enables the debtor to continue the operation of its business protected by the automatic stay. To enable it to carry on its business, the Chapter 11 debtor is given the same powers as are ordinarily available to a trustee under the Code. Whenever we discuss the powers of the trustee, it should be noted that the debtor in a Chapter 11 case can exercise these same powers when no trustee has been appointed.

II. ELIGIBILITY AND QUALIFICATION TO SERVE AS TRUSTEE

A. Individual as trustee: A trustee may be any individual who is competent to perform the duties of trustee. Although a corporation may also act as trustee, most bankruptcy trustees are individuals. To qualify as trustee in a case under Chapter 7, 12, or 13, the individual must reside in or have an office in the judicial district where the case is pending or in an adjacent judicial district. To qualify, the trustee must normally file a bond to secure faithful performance.

B. Corporate trustee: A trustee may be a corporation, so long as it is authorized by its charter or its by-laws to act as trustee. In a case under Chapter 7, 12 or 13, the corporation must have an office in the judicial district where the case is pending or in an adjacent judicial district.

C. United States Trustee: If necessary, the United States Trustee for the judicial district in which the case is pending may serve as the trustee in the bankruptcy case. However, the United States Trustee is really designed to serve as an administrative officer of the court, not as the trustee who acts for the estate.

III. FUNCTIONING AS TRUSTEE

A. Employment of professionals: The trustee is permitted to employ lawyers, accountants, appraisers, auctioneers, and other professional persons to assist him in carrying out his duties. The persons employed by the trustee must be disinterested and cannot represent an interest adverse to the estate. With court approval, the trustee may also be counsel or the accountant for the estate.

B. Compensation of professionals: The trustee may fix the compensation of professionals who are hired. The court may review this compensation and revise it if it proves improvident or if the professional person has an interest adverse to the estate.

    C. Lawsuits against the trustee: Lawsuits may be brought against trustees for various acts. In general, a trustee may be sued in state or federal court concerning an act in managing property subject to his control.

IV. THE UNITED STATES TRUSTEE

    A. History and scope of office: The United States Trustee is an administrative officer and, although he may often assist parties in mediating disputes among themselves, he cannot perform any judicial duties or intervene to resolve disputes. *The United States Trustee maintains a panel of private trustees that are available to serve as trustees in cases under Chapters 7 and 11.* The United States Trustee is under the supervision of the Attorney General of the United States. Each district has a United States Trustee, except for the states of Alabama and North Carolina.

    B. Duties of United States Trustees: The United States Trustee is given the generalized duty to supervise the administration of cases and trustees. The United States Trustee's basic duties include: scheduling and holding creditors' committee meetings; monitoring plans and disclosure statements in Chapter 11; reviewing applications for compensation and reimbursement; taking such action as may be appropriate to ensure that all reports are filed; monitoring Chapter 11 creditors committees; taking action to prevent undue delay; and reporting to the United States Attorney when necessary.

CHAPTER 6

THE CREDITOR — GENERAL RULES

I. FILING OF CLAIMS — § 501

    A. Proof of claims or interests: A creditor files a proof of claim; an equity security holder (i.e., a shareholder in a corporation or a partner in a limited partnership) files a proof of interest. "Proof" of claim or interest simply means that a formal submission of a claim or interest is made. Ordinarily, a claim against the debtor will have arisen at the time of or before the order for relief. Certain kinds of claims are deemed by the Code to have arisen before the order for relief, even though they actually arise after it. These latter claims arise from such events as the termination of a contract, or the reclaiming of property under the avoiding powers of the trustee.

    B. Filing of proof on behalf of creditor: The debtor or the trustee is permitted to file a proof of claim for a creditor and can thus force a creditor's participation in a case. This power is important where a creditor has not filed a proof of claim and the creditor's interest, such as an unperfected lien, may be avoidable by the trustee.

II. THIRD PARTY CLAIMS

    A. Guarantors and sureties: There are situations where a creditor has no incentive to file a proof of claim against the debtor in bankruptcy because he has been made whole by a third party, usually called a guarantor or surety. If so, the guarantor or surety is allowed to file a proof of claim. A similar situation arises where one tortfeasor pays the entire liability and looks for contribution from another tortfeasor who is a creditor of the debtor.

    B. Contribution or subrogation claim: *A surety has the option of filing a contribution claim* (arising from the right to recover from a co-debtor for payment of a debt) *in its own right*, or *filing as a subrogee of the prime creditor*. In subrogation, the surety steps into the shoes of the prime creditor of the co-obligor and its claim dates as of the date of the creditor's claim. The surety must actually have made payment to the prime creditor in order to assert its rights in bankruptcy against the debtor.

III. DEFENSES TO CLAIMS AVAILABLE TO THE ESTATE

A. Debtor's defenses available to estate: A defense available to the debtor before bankruptcy is available to the estate in bankruptcy. This is particularly significant since the estate is a separate legal entity from the debtor.

B. Debtor's ability to waive a defense: A waiver of a defense made before bankruptcy will be given effect; a waiver by the debtor after bankruptcy is ineffective.

IV. ALLOWANCE OF CLAIMS OR INTERESTS — § 502

A. Allowance of claims generally: If a proof of claim or interest is properly filed, it is deemed allowed unless a party in interest objects. Parties in interest include the trustee, the debtor, and other creditors. The terms *"allowed"* and *"allowable"* are used in various sections of the Code to mean that *a claim has been accepted as a debt of the estate*.

　1. **Time of petition controls:** The amount of a claim is its amount at the time of the petition.

　2. **Estimation of unliquidated claims:** When an unliquidated claim of great complexity is asserted against the bankrupt estate, the court is required to estimate the ultimate amount of the claim if waiting to fix it exactly would "unduly delay the administration of the case."

　3. **Claims may be barred by defenses of debtor:** The trustee may assert any defenses available to the debtor, including statutes of limitations, the statute of frauds, and usury.

　4. **Court will evaluate defense:** If an interested party objects to a proof of claim, the court will determine whether to allow the claim in full, modify its amount, or disallow it entirely.

B. Claims arising after the petition: There are several instances where claims will arise after the petition and will be allowed.

　1. **"Gap" claims in involuntary cases:** In involuntary cases, a "gap" in time occurs after the filing of a petition but before the order for relief or the appointment of a trustee. In this *gap period, claims can arise against the estate in the ordinary course of the debtor's business or financial affairs. These claims are permitted to relate back to a period before the petition and thereby become allowable.*

　2. **Claims arising from actions by the trustee:** As authorized by the Code, certain parties will have claims that arise due to the rejection of an executory contract by the trustee. Also, the trustee is authorized to undo certain transfers made by the debtor before the bankruptcy and recover the assets transferred. In both cases, these postpetition claims will be allowed.

C. Grounds for disallowance of claims: The court may deny a claim entirely in the following instances:

　1. **Claims unenforceable under agreement or applicable law:** A claim will be denied if it is unenforceable either by virtue of an agreement between the creditor and the debtor or due to applicable law.

　2. **Claims for unmatured interest:** Claims will not be allowed for unmatured interest, which is interest that accrues after the date of the petition. However, in a Chapter 7 case, the creditor may recover interest accruing after the petition if there are sufficient funds available in the bankruptcy estate.

3. **Taxes against property in excess of value:** Taxes in excess of the value of the estate's interest in the property will not be allowed.

4. **Charges by an insider or attorney in excess of reasonable value:** Charges for services by an insider or an attorney which exceed the reasonable value of those services will be disallowed.

5. **Unmatured family debts:** A claim for unmatured alimony, maintenance, or support that is excepted from discharge will be disallowed. The concept is that these debts will continue as obligations of the debtor after the bankruptcy.

6. **Limitations on claims for rent under leases:** Because lease terms, particularly for commercial leases, may stretch many years into the future, the amount of unmatured rent that may be claimed in a bankruptcy is limited, generally to from one to three years.

7. **Limitations on claims arising from employment contracts:** A claim for breach of an employment contract may not exceed the wages due for one year following the earlier of the date of the petition or the date the employment ended, plus any unpaid compensation due under the contract on the earlier of these two dates.

8. **Claims resulting from reduction in federal tax credit:** Claims for a reduction in the federal tax credit for late payment of state unemployment insurance taxes are not allowed.

9. **Claims not timely filed:** If a claim is not timely filed, it is generally not allowable. There are exceptions for Chapter 7 claims that are tardily filed within a specified time and for claims by governmental units that are filed before 180 days after the order for relief.

V. TREATMENT OF SECURED CLAIMS — § 506

A. **Secured claims generally:** *Bankruptcy recognizes two types of secured claims: those secured by a lien under state law* (including judicial liens) and *those with a right of setoff against property of the estate under the Code.* Almost all properly perfected liens remain in effect in bankruptcy.

1. **Liens under state law:** The usual lien is a mortgage on real estate of the debtor or a security interest under Article 9 of the Uniform Commercial Code in the debtor's personal property.

2. **Setoffs as secured claims:** A creditor may owe money to the debtor. It will have a claim against the estate if the amount such creditor owes is less than what is owed to by the debtor. Such a creditor is deemed secured to the extent of the amount that is available for setoff, i.e, the amount that the creditor owes the debtor.

B. **Valuation of security interests:** *A claim is secured only to the extent of the value of the security.* If the security is worth less than the amount of the claim, there is a secured claim equal to the amount of the security and an unsecured claim to the extent by which the debt exceeds the value of the security. The unsecured portion of the debt is often called the "deficiency." Valuation of security is made by the parties and court with the help of whatever expert witnesses or other evidence the court can obtain.

1. **Consequences of valuation:** Valuation of the security, in addition to determining whether the creditor is fully secured, will have several important consequences in the bankruptcy. It can affect all of the following: the amount of the debtor's equity and thus the ability of the debtor to keep property subject to the automatic stay, the amount of adequate protection that must be paid to the secured creditor, the best interests of creditor test (which ensures that a creditor receive under a Chapter 11 reorganization plan an amount that is not less than would be received in a Chapter 7 liquidation), and whether the creditor is oversecured and thus whether interest must be paid.

2. **Expenses can affect value of collateral:** If a trustee (or a debtor in possession under Chapter 11) incurs expenses in caring for or disposing of collateral that is in his possession

and those expenses benefit the holder of the claim that is secured by the collateral, the expenses may be charged against the value of the collateral.

C. Interest on oversecured claims: If a creditor is oversecured, the Code allows interest, fees, costs and charges up to the amount of the excess security and until the oversecured claim is paid. The Supreme Court has held that the language of § 506(b), "[T]here shall be allowed to the holder of such claim, interest on such claim, and any reasonable fees, costs, or charges provided for under the agreement . . ." provides for interest on all oversecured liens (including judicial as well as consensual liens). However, fees, costs, and charges are only available where they have been provided for in an agreement that gives rise to the claim. *United States v. Ron Pair Enterprises, Inc.*, 489 U.S. 235 (1989).

D. Voidability of liens generally: If a secured claim is disallowed, the lien is generally void because there is no longer a debt to which the lien can attach. There are two exceptions:

   1. Failure to file proof of claim: A lien will not be voided if it is disallowed merely because the creditor did not file a proof of claim.

   2. Disallowed unmatured family and reimbursement claims: Liens with respect to unmatured family claims and claims for reimbursement or contribution are not voided.

E. Voidability of liens on undersecured claims: If a debt is undersecured (the value of the property subject to the lien is less than the debt owed), the unsecured portion of the debt, or the deficiency, is handled like any other unsecured claim. The creditor may file a proof of claim as to the deficiency if it wishes to share in the distribution and typically will receive only a modest recovery. The Supreme Court has held that, despite the division of a claim between secured and unsecured portions, no portion of the lien is voidable (i.e., the lien can *not* be stripped down to the value of the collateral). If the property is foreclosed at a later date, any increase in value belongs to the secured party. *Dewsnup v. Timm*, 112 S.Ct. 773, 116 L.Ed.2d 903 (1992).

VI. PRIORITY OF CLAIMS – § 507

A. Priorities: Because the money available for payment to creditors in a bankruptcy is typically less than the total of their allowed claims, a system for payments is essential to bankruptcy administration. The distribution of proceeds is not pro rata; the Code has adopted a system of priorities under which some obligations are deemed of greater social significance than others and will be paid ahead of others. There are some 14 levels of priority in the Code.

   1. Priorities vs. liens: Priorities are matters of federal law as prescribed by the Code. Liens, on the other hand, are almost always (except when some special federal law applies) matters of state law, determined principally under laws relevant to real estate mortgages or under the Uniform Commercial Code. When a lien is dealt with in bankruptcy, its validity as a lien is generally measured by state law.

B. Order of priorities: Under § 507(a), the following order of priorities is established in a bankruptcy proceeding:

   1. Administrative expenses: The first priority is for *administrative expenses*, which must *benefit the debtor or the debtor's business after the commencement of the case*. However, this priority can drop into third place in the course of the bankruptcy if there are secured claims that have not been given adequate protection or with respect to new credit to the estate. Administrative expenses include: most taxes levied or incurred after the bankruptcy; administration fees and expenses due to the trustee, examiners, professional advisors, and the debtor's attorney; costs associated with administering and preserving estate property; and certain actual and necessary expenses incurred by creditors.

      a. Preservation of estate: The most significant administrative expenses are the expenses incurred in preserving the estate after the bankruptcy has begun. These cover a broad range of items, including the wages of employees who work for a business in bankruptcy, rent, and debts for purchases or money borrowed.

   b. **Certain expenses rendered before petition:** If services rendered entirely before the bankruptcy have benefitted the estate after the petition, they may be given administrative priority despite the statutory language requiring the services to have been performed after the petition. Courts may also divide the expense between services performed before and performed after the petition.

2. **"Gap" claims:** The second priority goes to "gap" claims made in the ordinary course of the debtor's business. These are claims incurred after an involuntary petition and before the earlier of the order for relief or the appointment of a trustee.

3. **Priority for wage claims:** A third priority status is given to certain wages and commissions, including vacation, severance, and sick leave pay. These are limited to the amount earned by an employee (and certain independent sales representatives) within 90 days before the petition or the cessation of the debtor's business, whichever occurs first, but not exceeding $4,000 per employee.

4. **Claims for contributions to employee benefit plan:** The fourth priority is for contributions to an employee benefit plan, arising from services rendered within 180 days before the petition or before the date of cessation of the debtor's business, whichever occurred first. This priority is limited to $4,000 per covered employee, less the priority wage claims paid to the employees under the wage claim (third) priority.

5. **Grain storage and fishermen claims:** The fifth priority is for claims by grain farmers against grain storage facilities and claims by fishermen against fish processors in the maximum amount of $4,000.

6. **Claim resulting from consumer deposits:** The sixth priority is designed to protect consumers who made deposits before the bankruptcy case in connection with the purchase of goods or services for personal, family, or household purposes, in those instances when the goods or services were not delivered. These claims are limited to $1800 per person.

7. **Alimony and support claims:** The seventh priority is for allowed (i.e., matured) alimony and support claims for spouse or child, but only to the extent embodied in a property settlement agreement, separation agreement, divorce decree, or other order by the court or a governmental unit. In order to be valid, the claim must not be assigned to a third party.

8. **Certain tax claims:** The eighth priority gives governmental units, both state and federal, a priority tax claim for a designated list of taxes. The most significant among the dozen items listed are income taxes due within three years of the petition.

9. **Bank and savings and loan claims:** The ninth and last priority was added to the Code to cure certain problems experienced by banks and savings and loan associations. If a debtor has made a commitment to a bank regulatory agency to sustain the capital of a bank or an S&L, the regulator has a priority claim.

VII. SUBORDINATION OF CLAIMS — § 510

A. **Definition of "subordination":** Subordination in bankruptcy is a legal concept meaning that one creditor will not be paid until another creditor is paid. A creditor may accept subordination in order to earn greater interest. A new investor may agree to make funds available to a business only if its other creditors agree to subordinate themselves to the new money. The existing creditors may be willing to accept the risk of a subordinated position in order to obtain the new investment. In accepting subordination, the Code defers to the agreement of parties, as interpreted under the law of the state where the agreement was made.

B. **Equitable subordination:** Under certain circumstances, the bankruptcy court will apply the concept of equitable subordination to create a priority of one creditor over another. Equitable subordination is often applied where the claimant engaged in some type of inequitable conduct (such as lending money to a corporation when some or all of that money should have been invested as stockholder equity), the conduct resulted in injury to the creditors of the bankrupt or conferred an unfair advantage on the claimant, and the subordination would be consistent with the Bankruptcy Act.

   C. Liens on subordinated claims: If an underlying secured claim is subordinated to another claim, the court will annul the lien on the secured claim.

CHAPTER 7

THE BANKRUPTCY ESTATE

I. NATURE OF THE ESTATE — § 541

   A. Creation and formation of the estate: The "estate" consists of those assets of the debtor that are available for distribution to creditors and, in the case of reorganizations, that form the basis for the reorganized entity. The estate is a new legal entity distinct from the debtor. Upon its creation at the time of the filing of the petition, the debtor's assets are transferred from the debtor to the estate.

      1. Importance of state law: Bankruptcy law determines whether or not an interest is property of the estate. *State law determines the nature and extent of the debtor's ownership interest in an item of property.*

      2. Treatment depends upon bankruptcy Chapter: How the assets will be handled depends upon the bankruptcy Chapter under which the petition is filed. In Chapter 7, the estate will be liquidated and the funds paid to the creditors. In Chapter 11, the estate will be operated by the debtor-in-possession or the trustee in an effort to yield funds for the creditors and at the same time, preserve the debtor.

      3. Relation of exemptions to determination of estate: In consumer bankruptcy cases, the debtor can regain some of the assets that are part of the bankruptcy estate through the system of exemptions. Because Congress allowed states to opt out of the federal bankruptcy exemption scheme in preference for their own scheme, exemptions vary greatly according to the state in which the debtor resides.

   B. Property in the estate: Subject to special modifications established in the particular bankruptcy Chapters, the estate generally consists of the following property.

      1. All property interests of the debtor: The estate consists of all legal or equitable interests of the debtor in property as of the commencement of the case. Included are such assets as: real estate, rights in intangibles, such as contracts and movie scripts; rights under leases; rights in lawsuits; equitable rights to redeem collateral from lienholders or to receive income from trusts; contingent interests and future interests, whether or not transferable by the debtor; and certain property that a debtor owns communally with a spouse.

      2. Recovered property: A number of provisions throughout the Code provide for the return to the estate of property that was transferred by the debtor before the filing. Examples of recovered property that are included in the estate are: excessive payments made by the debtor to lawyers; sales of estate property in which the bidders in the sale controlled the price by agreement among themselves; turnovers by a custodian to whom the property had previously been transferred; and the return of property recovered by the trustee under one of his avoiding powers.

      3. Interests debtor acquires after filing: Certain interests that the debtor acquires, or becomes entitled to acquire, within 180 days after the petition are made part of the estate. These after-acquired interests include interests acquired: by bequest, devise, or inheritance; in a settlement with the debtor's spouse or in a divorce decree; and as a beneficiary of a life insurance policy or death benefit plan.

4. **Interests flowing from assets of the estate:** Interests that flow from assets already in the estate become property of the estate. However, except for filings under Chapter 12 or 13, earnings from the services of an individual debtor following the petition belong to the debtor, not to the estate.

5. **Interests estate acquires after filing:** Any interest in property that the estate acquires after the commencement of the case is property of the estate.

C. **Items not included in estate:** Several assets are specifically excluded from the estate even though they would seem to fall under the broad definition of the estate. The most significant exclusion is any power that the debtor may exercise solely for the benefit of another, such as where the debtor has the power of a trustee.

D. ***Ipso facto* clauses invalid:** In bankruptcy, an ***ipso facto* clause** is a restrictive clause relating to an interest in property that ***provides within its own terms*** (*ipso facto*) ***that the interest may not be included in the bankruptcy estate***. With the exception of certain restrictive trust interests, including spendthrift trusts and interests in qualified pension plans, any provision in an agreement or provided by law that restricts or conditions the transfer of a debtor's assets upon a bankruptcy, or that is triggered by on the insolvency or financial condition of the debtor, is invalid.

II. ABANDONMENT OF ASSETS

A. **Right of trustee to abandon property — § 554:** The trustee may abandon any property of the estate that is burdensome or of inconsequential value. Some property can have a negative value to the trustee. One example is property that is completely burdened with a lien and is of no use to the debtor. Another is property that requires cleanup under pollution regulations or other circumstances when the value of the property is less than the cost of cleanup.

B. **Conflicts with other laws:** A proposed abandonment can sometimes result in a violation of laws governing the property. The Supreme Court has held that the right of abandonment may be restricted by other laws where necessary to protect the public health or safety from imminent and identifiable harm. *Midlantic Nat. v. New Jersey*, 474 U.S. 494 (1986).

III. USE, SALE, OR LEASE OF ESTATE PROPERTY

A. **Management of estate property generally:** The estate consists of the assets of the debtor at the time the petition is filed, with some additions (for example, property returned to the estate by avoiding a transfer made by the debtor) and some deletions (for example, property returned to the debtor under the exemption provisions). The assets in the estate, protected by the automatic stay of § 362, are retained by the debtor or trustee free from the claims of adverse interests, including lienholders who wish to take possession of them to cover their debts.

B. **Operating a business:** In some cases, the debtor or trustee will need to operate a business whose assets are part of the estate. In Chapter 7 cases, the need may be over a relatively short time because the goal is liquidation; in Chapter 11 reorganization cases, the need is more difficult to predict. For the operation of a business during bankruptcy, the Code makes a critical distinction between two classes of action by the trustee or debtor: (1) those in the ordinary course of business, and (2) those *other* than in the ordinary course of business.

1. **Actions in the ordinary course of business:** If the debtor's business is authorized to be operated during the bankruptcy, actions in the ordinary course of business — the usual and regular practices of running a business — may be taken by the debtor or trustee without intervention by the Court.

2. **Actions other than in the ordinary course:** After notice and a hearing, the debtor or trustee may take actions other than in the ordinary course of business.

C. **Adequate protection to creditor for use:** The court can require a debtor or trustee who is using an asset to give adequate protection to those, usually secured creditors, who have an interest in that asset. *Adequate protection ensures that the lienholder will not lose the value of the security in the hands of the debtor and is also extended to lessors of personal property for unexpired leases.*

D. **Sale of asset free of lien:** The property rights of a lienholder are generally protected in bankruptcy. Property in which creditors have interests may not be sold free and clear of those interests unless their rights are protected, particularly the rights of lienholders, whose liens are generally protected in bankruptcy. There are five situations, however, in which sales free of third party interests are permitted.

   1. **Sale permitted by law outside Code:** The court will respect an applicable nonbankruptcy law that permits the sale of property free and clear of a lien.

   2. **If the creditor consents:** The creditor may voluntarily join in the arrangement made by the debtor, the trustee, and/or the court for the sale of the property free and clear of its interest.

   3. **Sale for price greater than all liens:** If all liens on the property are covered by the sale price, the court will normally permit the sale, provided the sale proceeds are held by the debtor or trustee to cover the liens.

   4. **Bona fide dispute:** If there is a genuine dispute as to whether a third party really has an interest in the property, sales free of that interest may be made.

   5. **Release in exchange for cash:** This alternative enables the debtor to sell property free and clear of a third party's interest if it pays the third party the price required by law for a release of the interest.

E. **Sales of property subject to dower and curtesy:** The trustee may sell estate property free of any interests created under the rights of dower or curtesy in that property. The holders of the interest will be paid the value of the interest from the proceeds. Any balance will revert to the estate.

F. **Sales of co-ownership interests:** Property that the estate owns in co-ownership as defined by state law, such as a tenancy in common, joint tenancy, or tenancy by the entirety, may also be sold free of the co-owner's interest. Before a sale will proceed, the debtor or trustee must show that: partition would be impracticable, sale of the estate's interest alone would realize significantly less for the estate than sale of the entire undivided property, and the benefit to the estate would outweigh any adverse consequences to the co-owners. The co-owner will be paid the value of her interest after the sale.

G. *Ipso facto* **clauses invalid:** In the same way that *ipso facto* clauses imposed by creditor instruments are invalid to prevent the debtor's estate from using or assuming control over assets, any contract or statute that by its terms attempts to tie the return of assets to an event of insolvency or bankruptcy is invalid to prevent a sale of assets by the debtor or trustee.

IV. EXECUTORY CONTRACTS & UNEXPIRED LEASES — § 365

A. **Overview of debtor's executory contracts:** *The trustee has a statutory right to assume or reject the class of contracts called "executory" contracts.* If rejected, the other party has a claim against the estate that dates back to the moment before the petition was filed and gives that party a right to file a proof of claim for damages in the bankruptcy.

B. **Definition of executory contract:** The most widely accepted definition of an executory contract is a contract where the obligations of both the bankrupt and the other party to the contract are so far unperformed that the failure of either to complete the performance would constitute a material breach excusing the performance of the other. If, at the time of the petition, performance is due only from the debtor and that performance is the payment of money (rather than a physical act), it is usually held that the contract is not executory and the debtor does not have the right to assume or reject.

C. Leases as executory contracts: With some modifications of the basic rules, ***unexpired leases are considered the equivalent of executory contracts***. The rule is applicable to leases both of personal property and real estate and to debtors in their capacities both as lessors and lessees.

D. How contracts are rejected: Permission to assume or reject a contract must be obtained from the court. The standard for decision is the "good business judgment" of the debtor or trustee. The court must only find that the debtor or trustee has exercised sound judgment and that the decision was not the result of bad faith, whim, or caprice.

E. Rejection constitutes breach: The rejection of an executory contract or an unexpired lease annuls the contract or lease and releases both parties from all its provisions but it also constitutes a breach of the contract or lease and gives the non-debtor party a cause of action in damages.

　　1. Claim relates back: Upon rejection of an executory contract, the creditor is given an opportunity to file a proof of claim in the bankruptcy as if the claim had arisen immediately before the petition.

　　2. Measure of damages: The measure of damages is usually whatever is allowed under the state law dealing with breach of contract. Until a contract is rejected, the usual rule is that the estate is liable for the value it received from the other party's performance, rather than for strict performance of the contract.

F. Defaults occurring before bankruptcy: Frequently there will have been a default by the debtor under an executory contract or an unexpired lease before the bankruptcy begins. In order to assume and continue the contract, the trustee must fulfill three conditions: (1) cure the default or give adequate assurance that it will be promptly cured, (2) compensate any other party to the contract or lease for losses resulting from the breach or provide adequate assurance that losses will be compensated, and (3) give adequate assurance that there will be future performance under the contract or lease.

　　1. Adequate assurance: *"Adequate assurance,"* which should not be confused with adequate protection (the protection of the value of property while held by the estate), ***implies a satisfaction or confidence that the obligations due to the creditor are likely to be performed.***

　　2. Not applicable to *ipso facto* breaches: An executory contract or lease may contain an *ipso facto* clause under which a party who declares bankruptcy, becomes insolvent, or manifests a severe decline in its financial condition would be in default as a result of these events. Clauses containing these or similar provisions are not enforceable and their breach does not entitle the non-debtor to the adequate assurances described immediately above if the debtor is actually performing the terms of the contract.

G. Assumption followed by assignment: If an executory contract or an unexpired lease has substantial economic value, the debtor or trustee may wish to sell the contract or lease to a third party. The Code requires first that an assumption of the contract or lease be made before an assignment to the third party.

　　1. Unassumable and unassignable executory contracts: There are three types of executory contracts and leases that may neither be assumed nor assigned: (1) personal service contracts; (2) underwriting and credit accommodation contracts (contracts to lend money, to extend other forms of debt financing, or to issue a security); and (3) expired nonresidential leases.

　　2. Procedures for assumption and assignment: A trustee may sell rights in executory contracts and unexpired leases after assuming the contract or lease.

    a. Adequate assurance by the assignee: Before the contract or lease may be assigned, the assignee must give adequate assurance of future performance. This is separate from the adequate assurance that must be given by the trustee who wishes to assume where there has been a default previous to the filing. Adequate assurance here is required whether or not there has been any default.

    b. Prohibitions against assignment invalid: Except for the three types of executory contracts and leases that may not be assumed or assigned, a contract or lease may not by its terms or by reference to any law, prohibit or restrict assignment to the trustee. Essentially, this is another application of the *ipso facto* doctrine.

    c. Release of the assignor: Upon assignment of contract or lease, the trustee and the estate are relieved of any liability for breach of the contract or lease that may occur subsequent to the assignment.

  3. Timing of assumptions and rejections: The Code sets forth rules controlling the timing of the assumption and rejection of executory contracts and leases. The court has discretion to shorten or extend these time periods and will usually act to retain the status quo for a reasonable time in order to enable the trustee to make a reasoned decision.

    a. Chapter 7: In a Chapter 7 case, if the trustee does not assume or reject within 60 days after the order for relief, the contract or lease is deemed rejected.

    b. Cases under other Chapters: In cases under Chapters 9, 11, 12, or 13, assumption or rejection of an executory contract or unexpired lease of residential real estate or of personal property must occur before confirmation of a bankruptcy plan.

    c. Unexpired lease of nonresidential real estate: If an unexpired lease of nonresidential real estate is neither accepted nor rejected within 60 days after the order for relief, it is deemed rejected.

    d. Status of contract before assumption or rejection: During the time before an executory contract or lease is either assumed or rejected, a party receiving benefits under it must pay reasonable value for these benefits. The price set by the agreement or lease will not necessarily control.

  4. Assumption followed by breach: If a contract is assumed after the case has begun and then is breached during the course of the case, an administrative claim is likely to arise.

H. Leases and sales of real property and timeshare interests: If a bankrupt lessor terminates a real property lease, the lessee has the option either to treat the lease or interest as terminated or to remain in possession. If the lessor's termination causes any damage to the lessee, he may offset the damages against future rent, but he does not have an affirmative claim against the lessor. If a bankrupt seller terminates a sale of real property or of a timeshare interest, the buyer, if it is in possession, may treat the contract as terminated or may remain in possession and pay the price. It will have a like offset, but not an affirmative claim for damages. If the buyer is not in possession, it will have a lien on the property to secure its recovery of payments made.

I. Rights to intellectual property: There is a special provision to protect licenses of intellectual property. Intellectual property is defined to include trade secrets, inventions, processes, or designs protected by the patent laws, patent applications, plant varieties, works of authorship and certain materials relating to semi-conductors. If the executory contract at issue is an intellectual property license, the debtor licensor may affirm or reject the contract upon its bankruptcy. However, upon rejection, the licensee has the option to continue to enforce its rights instead of simply treating the license as terminated.

CHAPTER 8

THE TRUSTEE'S AVOIDING POWERS

I. INTRODUCTION

The avoiding powers enable the trustee to set aside certain transactions by the debtor that were entered into before the bankruptcy petition, in order to bring property back into the estate for a more equitable distribution to creditors.

II. PREREPETITION TRANSFERS & OBLIGATIONS – § 544

A. Scope of the power: The trustee is given several powers to avoid certain transfers made and obligations incurred by the debtor prior to the filing of the bankruptcy petition. The trustee exercises these powers in two ways: (1) as a *hypothetical creditor or purchaser under the so-called strong arm power*, or (2) *in the place of actual creditors or purchasers*. Transfer is very broadly defined to mean every mode of parting with an interest in property and includes both voluntary and involuntary transfers.

B. The "strong arm clause" — § 544(a): The so-called "strong arm clause," § 544(a), is one of the most potent and most used of the trustee's avoiding powers. The clause allows the trustee to avoid a prior transfer or obligation incurred by the debtor by giving the trustee the powers of a lien holder on the property and, with respect to real estate, the same position as a good faith purchaser of the property.

    1. Three powers — three hypothetical entities: The strong arm clause provides the trustee with powers that would be available to three hypothetical entities: (1) a *judicial lien creditor*, (2) an *execution lien creditor*, and (3) a *good faith purchaser of real estate*. In establishing the rights of each of the three hypothetical entities, the Code defines the entity, but does not tell us its rights. Those are established by state law. Similarly, the property rights established in the prior transfer or obligation that the trustee is looking to upset are also established by state law.

        a. Hypothetical judicial lien creditor — § 544(a)(1): The trustee is given the power of a hypothetical creditor who at the same time — *at the commencement of the case* — both (1) *extends credit to the debtor*, and (2) *obtains a judicial lien on property* of the debtor with respect to the credit. If a transfer of property or an obligation made before the bankruptcy petition (for example, an unperfected security interest) could be upset by a hypothetical unsatisfied judicial lien creditor, it can be upset by the trustee acting for the estate. Since normally a judicial lien first requires that a judgment be sought, won, and not satisfied by the debtor, it is obviously a legal fiction that all of this can happen at the same moment. The creditor whose rights are given to the trustee is hypothetical — that creditor does not actually exist except as a device to define the power of the trustee. The hypothetical creditor is also free of any actual knowledge of a prior transfer or obligation.

        b. Hypothetical execution lien creditor — § 544(a)(2): The trustee is also given the rights of a creditor who, under exactly the same conditions as a hypothetical lien creditor, *gives credit to* and *obtains an unsatisfied judgment execution against* the debtor.

        c. Hypothetical good faith purchaser of real estate — § 544(a)(3): With respect to prior transfers of real estate, the trustee is given the power of a hypothetical good faith purchaser, in addition to the powers of a lien creditor and an execution creditor. As with the first two hypothetical powers, the hypothetical good faith purchaser's powers are *exercised without regard to actual notice*; however, *if the hypothetical purchaser has constructive notice, he cannot be a good faith purchaser*. Actual notice depends on what is actually known by the purchaser; constructive notice depends on what should be known based on a reasonable inquiry.

2. **Unperfected security interests in personal property:** The most common use of the strong arm clause is in voiding prior liens that are not perfected. Where all the legal formalities have not been followed, either deliberately or through a mistake, the creditor may be in a position where it would lose that security interest to a subsequent lien creditor, an execution lien creditor or, in the case of real estate, to a good faith purchaser, and, therefore, to the trustee. Even if there is actual knowledge of unperfected security interests, they may be upset by other creditors who achieve the status of judicial or execution lien creditors.

C. **Rights of actual unsecured creditors — § 544(b):** In addition to the powers of hypothetical entities, *the trustee is invested with the rights of actual creditors*. Thus, the trustee has the right to avoid a prior transfer of property or a debt that could be voided by an actual unsecured creditor with an allowed claim.

1. **Rights of creditors:** Where the applicable state Fraudulent Conveyance Law provides that a transfer may be voided by creditors, the trustee acquires the rights of the creditors and may void the transfer. Where a debtor sells all of its inventory without giving notice to its creditors as prescribed by a state Bulk Sale Law, state law generally provides that any unpaid creditor of the seller who does not receive such notice may void the sale. Where such a creditor exists in a bankruptcy, the trustee acquires its rights and may void the sale.

2. **Charitable exception:** Rights given to creditors as a result of charitable gifts that would be exempt from fraudulent transfer restrictions under §548 are also exempt from the avoidance powers of §544(b). Any claim for a recovery under federal or state law as a result of such a gift shall be preempted by the Bankruptcy Code upon the commencement of a case.

III. POWER TO AVOID STATUTORY LIENS — § 545

A. **Scope of power:** Statutory liens (liens that arise by virtue of a statute for the benefit of otherwise unsecured creditors) are generally valid under state law. The trustee has the power to avoid a statutory lien if it is: (1) *created under a statute that operates "in contemplation of bankruptcy,"* (2) *not perfected or enforceable against a hypothetical good faith purchaser of property* (who is considered to have made the purchase at the commencement of the case); or (3) *for rent or of distress for rent*.

B. **Definition of statutory lien — § 101(53):** Not every lien provided for by statute is a statutory lien within the meaning of the Code. *Statutory lien is defined* as: (1) *liens arising solely by force of statute upon the occurrence of specified circumstances or conditions* and (2) *liens of distress for rent* (power in a landlord to take a defaulting tenant's property) whether by statute or common law. The definition of statutory lien excludes, regardless of whether provided for or only made fully effective by statute: (1) judicial liens, which are those liens typically obtained to enforce an unpaid judgment and which are also available in unusual situations to attach a debtor's property even before judgment, and (2) security interests. Examples of statutory liens include: artisan and repairman liens, which give one who repairs an object a lien upon it to secure his unpaid price; storageman liens, which give one who stores property a lien upon it for payment of the storage cost; and liens for unpaid taxes.

IV. POWER TO AVOID PREFERENCES — § 547

A. **Scope of power:** The trustee is given the power to avoid "preferential" transfers (transfers that "prefer" one creditor over others) made by the debtor during the 90-day period prior to the filing of the bankruptcy petition. Critical to the use of the power to avoid preferences is ascertaining the date of transfer, which is subject to specific rules. The statute sets forth specific rules for how the date of perfection affects the date of transfer.

B. A preference involves a transfer of a debtor's property — 547(b): The trustee is given the power to avoid "any transfer of an interest of the debtor in property" that has certain preferential qualities. A transfer includes selling goods, making a money payment, and giving a security interest in goods to stand behind an obligation. A transfer can be involuntary as well as voluntary. A transfer for § 547 purposes is not made until the debtor acquires rights in the property transferred.

C. Relationship of perfection of a security interest to date of transfer — § 547(e): Where a transfer involves the perfection of a security interest, specific rules are set forth in the statute to determine the date on which a transfer will be considered to have been made.

   1. When perfection occurs — general rule: With respect to a transfer of real property, perfection occurs when the transfer is valid under state law and will stand up against a subsequent good faith purchaser. For a transfer of personal property, perfection occurs when it is valid against a subsequent judicial lien creditor.

   2. Date of perfection fixes date of transfer: There are three basic rules under which the date of perfection of a security interest affects the date of transfer of the security interest.

   a. Perfection within 10 days: If perfection occurs at, or within 10 days after, the actual transfer (20 days for a purchase money security interest), the transfer occurs for § 547 purposes at the *time of the actual transfer*.

   b. Perfection after 10 days: If perfection occurs after the 10 days (20 days for a purchase money security interest) but before the case begins, the transfer occurs for § 547 purposes *at the perfection date*.

   c. Perfection after filing of bankruptcy petition: If perfection occurs after the case begins, the transfer for § 547 purposes is deemed to occur *immediately before the filing of the petition*. An exception from this rule is that, if perfection occurs after the case begins but within the ten (or 20) days permitted above, the transfer occurs at the time of the actual transfer.

   d. No perfection: If perfection does not occur at all, the transfer is deemed to occur *at the beginning of the case*. The effect of this is that, if the transfer is of a security interest that secures a debt, the transfer will be for an antecedent debt, which is one of the requirements for an avoidable preference.

D. The five requirements of an avoidable preference: In order for the trustee to avoid a prior transfer as a preference, the transfer must satisfy all five of the following requirements:

   1. Transfer must benefit the creditor: A transfer can benefit a creditor even though the actual transfer is not to it. For example, if G guarantees the debt of D to C and D pays C, the payment (by letting G off the hook) was to the benefit of D's other creditor, G.

   2. Transfer must be for an antecedent debt: The requirement that the transfer be on account of an antecedent debt, as opposed to a contemporaneous debt, is essential to support the concept of preferring one creditor to another.

   3. Transfer must be made while the debtor is insolvent: For purposes of § 547, there is a rebuttable presumption that the debtor was insolvent for 90 days before the petition is filed.

   4. Transfer must be on or within 90 days before petition: To be considered an avoidable preference, a transfer must have occurred on or within 90 days before the date that the petition was filed. If the creditor to whom the assets were transferred or who entered into an obligation with the debtor was an insider of the debtor, the period is extended to a year.

   5. Transfer must allow creditor to receive more than it otherwise would: The position of the creditor is improved if it receives more than it would have received if the transfer had not been made and the creditor had gone through an ordinary Chapter 7 liquidation.

E. Exceptions from the voidable preference rule — § 547(c): Some transfers satisfy the five conditions, described above, but for policy reasons they are specifically made not avoidable. To test these exceptions, the trustee has the burden first of proving the existence of a preference; the creditor then has the burden of proving nonavoidability. The eight exceptions are as follows:

1. **Substantially contemporaneous exchanges for new value:** This exception from the voidable preference rule applies to a transfer that (1) was intended by the parties to be a contemporaneous exchange for new value — a subjective test, and (2) was in fact a substantially contemporaneous exchange — an objective test.

2. **Ordinary and regular transactions:** In order not to upset ordinary payments, there is an exception that applies to transfers that are: (1) in payment of a debt incurred in the ordinary course of business or financial affairs between debtor and transferee, (2) made in the ordinary course of business or financial affairs between debtor and transferee, and (3) made according to ordinary business terms.

3. **Enabling loans:** There is an exception from the voidable preference rule for "enabling loans", also known as a "purchase money loans." Under this type of loan, a creditor lends money to a borrower to enable the borrower to buy specific property. The loan must be: (1) made at the time of or after a security agreement describing the property as collateral is signed; (2) made by the secured party to enable the debtor to acquire the collateral under that agreement; and (3) actually used to acquire the property. Equally important, the security interest in such loans (purchase money security interest) must be perfected within 20 days after the buyer receives possession of the goods bought.

4. **The "net result" rule:** Under the fourth exception, an otherwise preferential transfer may be reduced by amounts coming back to the estate after the transfer; a complete offset is not permitted.

5. **Floating liens on inventory and receivables:** The U.C.C. enables a secured creditor to establish a so-called floating lien on a debtor's inventory or accounts receivable and have that lien apply to every item of inventory and every individual account receivable as it flows in and out of the debtor's possession or ownership. Under the fifth exception, two dates are selected: the first 90 days before the petition is filed, the second, the date of filing. As of both dates, the amount by which the debt exceeds the inventory (or receivables) collateral is computed. To the extent that the amount is reduced from the first date to the second, there is a voidable preference. If transactions had not begun between debtor and creditor at least 90 days before the petition was filed, the first date for the comparison is the date on which they did begin.

6. **The fixing of a statutory lien under § 545:** The sixth exception provides that, if a statutory lien is not avoidable under the tests of § 545, it is also not preferential.

7. **Bona fide payment of debt to spouse or child:** Under the seventh exception, a transfer that is a bona fide payment of a debt to a child, spouse, or former spouse for alimony, maintenance, or support is not avoidable. However, the debt is avoidable to the extent that it is assigned, voluntarily or otherwise, to another entity.

8. **Certain consumer transfers:** For an individual debtor whose debts are primarily consumer debts, the eighth exception provides that the aggregate value of a transfer totalling less than $600 is not avoidable.

V. POWER TO AVOID FRAUDULENT TRANSFEROR OBLIGATIONS — § 548

A. Scope of power: A trustee has the power to avoid fraudulent conveyances occurring within one year before bankruptcy. The fraudulent act may consist of a transfer, or the incurring of an obligation. There are two alternative tests under this section. A transfer of interest may be avoided by the trustee under this section where the debtor made a transfer or incurred an obligation either: (1) **with actual intent to hinder, delay, or defraud**, or (2) that meets the criteria for **constructive fraud**.

B. **Charitable Gift Exception:** Gifts made by natural persons to charities by cash, check, or equivalent instrument that do not exceed 15 percent of the debtor's gross annual income for the year in which the gift is made or, if more than that amount, are consistent with the practice of the debtor in making charitable contributions, will not be considered fraudulent transfers even if the other tests are satisfied.

C. **Applicable to transfers made within one year — § 548(d):** By its terms, the power to avoid fraudulent transfers is limited to those transfers made within one year of the filing of the bankruptcy petition. The transfer will be deemed to occur when it is perfected to the extent that the interest of the transferee will stand up against a good faith purchaser. If the interest is not perfected at all before the bankruptcy, the transfer is deemed to occur immediately before the date of the filing of the petition, clearly within the one-year period. This power applies to voluntary and involuntary transactions.

D. **Intent to hinder, delay, or defraud test of § 548(a)(1):** Voidability is premised on the debtor's intentional act to hinder, delay, or defraud some or all of the creditors. Through the centuries, acts by debtors from which intent to defraud can be inferred have become known as "badges of fraud".

E. **Constructive fraud test:** In view of the difficulties inherent in proving that an act was intentional, there is a second test for a fraudulent transfer. Under this provision, the trustee must prove that: (1) the transfer was made in exchange for **less than a reasonably equivalent value, and** (2) one of the following three situations applies: (a) the **debtor was insolvent** on the date that the transfer was made or became insolvent as a result of the transfer; **or** (b) the debtor was engaged, or was about to engage, in **business** or in a **transaction** for which it was left after the transfer with **unreasonably small capital; or** (c) the debtor intended to incur, or believed that it would incur, **debts beyond the debtor's ability to pay as they matured**.

F. **Rights of one to whom property is fraudulently transferred —§ 548(c):** Assuming that a transferee took in good faith, it may keep what was transferred to the extent that it gave value.

G. **Transfers occur upon creation of lien and *again* upon enforcement of lien:** Even though a transfer is certainly made when a lien is originally created, a second transfer occurs upon a foreclosure, because then the debtor's equity of redemption (including its rights to pay off the loan and get the property back, and to receive a surplus if the property is sold for more than the debt), is transferred.

VI. POWER TO AVOID SETOFFS — § 553

A. **Setoffs generally valid:** Setoffs, under which a creditor sets a debt it owes to the debtor off against a claim it has against the debtor are generally valid in bankruptcy; they are invalid in specific situations that would give one creditor an unfair advantage over other creditors. Although setoffs are generally valid in bankruptcy, the automatic stay must first be lifted for a setoff to actually be carried out. Until the stay is lifted, adequate protection must be supplied. However, financial institutions are able to place an administrative hold on the portion of the debtor's depository accounts equal to the amount of a loan, thus temporarily preventing a debtor or the debtor's estate from gaining access to those funds. *Citizens Bank of Maryland v. Strumpf*, No. 94-1340, 1995 LEXIS 7408 (1995).

B. **Presumption of insolvency — § 553(c):** For purposes of § 553, there is a presumption that the debtor was insolvent during the 90-day period before the petition is filed.

C. **Avoidable setoffs:** The trustee may avoid a setoff by a creditor in the following situations:

    1. **Disallowed claims — § 553(a)(1):** Disallowed claims cannot be set off.

    2. **Claims transferred within 90 days — § 553(a)(2):** The trustee may avoid a debt by the debtor if it was transferred by a prior claimant to the creditor either (1) after the case has

begun or (2) after 90 days before the petition was filed and while the debtor was insolvent.

3. **Debt incurred to obtain setoff — § 553(a)(3):** The debtor may avoid a debt if it was incurred by the creditor within 90 days of the petition while the debtor was insolvent and was for the purpose of creating a right of setoff.

4. **Insufficiencies — § 553(b):** An "insufficiency" is the amount by which a claim by a creditor against the debtor exceeds a claim by the debtor against the same creditor. If D diminishes the insufficiency by making a payment to the creditor, the creditor has benefitted at the expense of D's other creditors. If a creditor offsets an obligation within 90 days before the petition, then the trustee may recover from the creditor the amount offset to the extent that any insufficiency is less than the insufficiency that existed either 90 days before the petition, or the first time that an insufficiency existed within the 90 days before the petition, whichever is later.

VII. LIMITATIONS ON AVOIDING POWERS — § 546

A. **Statute of limitations:** Actions under the avoiding powers must be brought before a case is dismissed or closed and not later than: (1) two years after the order for relief, or (2) one year after the appointment or election of the first trustee, provided such appointment or election is made within two years of the commencement of the case.

B. **Relation back of perfection affecting rights of trustee:** The avoidance rights of a trustee, all of which generally accrue at the time of the bankruptcy, may be cut off by a "generally applicable law" that causes an act of perfection to relate back to an earlier point in time.

VIII. ENFORCEMENT OF AVOIDING POWERS —§ 550

A. **Enforcement powers overlap:** The avoiding powers contain authority for the trustee to avoid certain transfers, all of which could be construed as self-executing. However, for various reasons (including the enumeration of rights of subsequent transferees), § 550 contains provisions for the enforcement of avoidances.

B. **Initial and subsequent transferees — § 550(a):** The trustee has the right to recover property from the initial transferee (or the entity for whose benefit the transfer was made) and from subsequent transferees of the initial transferee (see below).

C. **Limits on recovery from good faith subsequent transferees —§ 550(b):** While the trustee may recover from the initial transferee, the trustee may not recover property from a subsequent transferee that takes for value and without knowledge of the voidable transfer. This second transferee is generally known as a "good faith purchaser." The trustee is also prevented from recovering from later transferees of the good faith purchaser who take simply in good faith (irrespective of whether they also took for value).

D. **Rights of transferee to recover for improvement costs — § 550(e):** If a transferee, immediate or subsequent, has improved the property taken from him under the avoiding powers, he has a lien on it for the lesser of the costs incurred to make the improvement or the increase in value of the property as a result of the improvement. Improvements include not only physical changes but the payment of taxes and the satisfaction of superior liens.

E. **Statute of limitations — § 550(f):** A separate statute of limitations provides that a § 550 enforcement action must be commenced within one year after the avoidance, or before the case is closed or dismissed, whichever occurs first.

CHAPTER 9

FILING UNDER CHAPTER 7 — LIQUIDATION

I. INTRODUCTION

Chapter 7 of the Bankruptcy Code provides for the ***total liquidation of a debtor's estate and distribution of the proceeds to creditors***. In the case of an individual, the debtor achieves a "fresh start." If the case involves a business entity, such as a partnership or corporation, the entity generally dissolves under the state law under which it was organized. Chapter 7 is by far the most widely used of the five chapters in the Code providing for bankruptcy filings.

II. WHO MAY BE A DEBTOR IN CHAPTER 7 — § 109(b)

A. **Debtor must be a "person":** Subject to certain limited exceptions, any "person" may be a debtor in Chapter 7. "Person" is, in turn, defined to include individuals, partnerships, and corporations.

B. **Entities excluded:** Insurance companies are primarily state regulated and have their own forms of relief under state law. Domestic banks and related insured institutions have their own forms of relief under both federal and state banking laws. Foreign banks and insurance companies that are subject to domestic regulation are also excluded from filing under Chapter 7.

III. CONVERSION FROM CHAPTER 7 TO ANOTHER CHAPTER — § 706

A. **Debtor conversion:** The debtor has the ability at any time to convert from a Chapter 7 case to a case under Chapter 11, 12 or 13, provided that the debtor is eligible for the relief under the given chapter and that the case was not previously transferred to Chapter 7 from one of those chapters.

B. **Interested party conversion:** A party in interest other than the debtor may ask to transfer a Chapter 7 case to Chapter 11 but not to the other Chapters. Court approval is required where the debtor is not the moving party.

IV. DISMISSAL BY THE COURT — § 707

A. **Dismissal generally:** Chapter 7 cases may be dismissed ***for cause***. Included as justifications for dismissal are unreasonable delay, nonpayment of required fees, and failure of the debtor to honor its responsibilities to give information as required by the Code.

B. **Dismissal of consumer cases — § 707(b):** There is a presumption of non-abuse by the debtor, but the bankruptcy court has the ability to dismiss a case filed by an individual whose debts are "primarily" consumer debts if the court finds that the granting of relief would be a substantial abuse of the provisions of Chapter 7.

   1. **"Primarily" consumer debts:** Consumer debts are defined as debts incurred by an individual primarily for personal, family, or household purposes. Debts may be found to be "primarily" consumer if there is a substantial number or amount of consumer debts, even if the debts are fewer than 5 percent of the total.

   2. **"Substantial abuse":** Chapter 7 can be abused by a consumer in many ways. There may be fraudulent statements in the papers submitted to the court; the debts may have been incurred through living beyond one's means; the case may have stemmed from no more than anger with one's creditors. The prevailing view is that the ability to pay debts in the future is the best single measure of whether Chapter 7 is being appropriately used.

C. Effect of dismissal — § 707: The dismissal of a Chapter 7 case is without prejudice. Therefore, unless the court mandates otherwise, a dismissal does not prevent a debtor from refiling in bankruptcy and discharging its debts in the subsequent case. There is a 180-day prohibition on refilings by individuals and family farmers in certain circumstances.

D. Comparison between § 305 and § 707: Under § 305(a) (a *general provision* authorizing dismissal), a court may dismiss a bankruptcy case if *dismissal is in the interests of both the creditors and the debtor.* Under § 707, which only applies to Chapter 7 cases, the court may dismiss: (1) for cause, and (2) for substantial abuse in consumer cases. § 305 is usually used at the inception of a case; § 707 after it matures.

V. SELECTION OF THE TRUSTEE

A. Interim trustee — § 701: Promptly after the order for relief, the United States trustee appoints one disinterested person to serve as the interim trustee in the Chapter 7 case. The interim trustee has all the powers of a permanent trustee and serves unless and until the permanent trustee is chosen

B. The permanent trustee — § 702: *Unsecured creditors may elect a permanent trustee,* if, at the § 341 meeting (meeting of creditors and equity security holders), eligible creditors holding at least 20 percent of the amount of the claims request an election. A candidate is elected trustee if eligible creditors holding at least 20 percent of the amount of the claims actually vote and the candidate receives a majority of those votes. If no permanent trustee is elected, the interim trustee becomes the permanent trustee.

VI. DUTIES OF TRUSTEE

A. Duty to liquidate and close estate: The trustee's primary duty under Chapter 7 is to "collect and reduce to money the property of the estate. . . and close such estate as expeditiously as is compatible with the best interests of parties in interest." If the trustee during the course of the case seeks to sell assets of an estate other than in the ordinary course of business, the approval of the court is required.

B. Trustee's other duties: In addition to the duty to liquidate and close the estate, there are several other duties of the trustee.

1. **Property received:** The trustee is accountable for all property received.

2. **Debtor's intentions:** In the case of an individual with consumer debts, the trustee must ensure that the debtor performs his intention with respect to the retention or surrender of consumer property.

3. **Debtor's financial affairs:** The trustee must investigate the debtor's financial affairs.

4. **Claims:** Where appropriate, the trustee must examine proofs of claims and object to allowances that are improper.

5. **Discharge:** If advisable, the trustee must object to the discharge.

6. **Information:** Unless the court orders otherwise, the trustee must furnish information as requested by parties in interest.

7. **Taxes and reports:** If the business of the debtor continues in operation, the trustee must handle taxes and file reports concerning the debtor's business.

8. **Final report and accounting:** The trustee must make a final report and accounting of the administration of the estate.

C. Duty to examine creditor — § 341: Prior to the conclusion of the first meeting of creditors or equity security holders, the trustee is required to examine the Chapter 7 debtor orally to ensure that the debtor is aware of: (1) the potential consequences of a discharge in bankruptcy, including the effects on credit history; (2) the effect of receiving a discharge of debts;

(3) the ability to file a petition under a different Chapter of the Code; and (4) the effect of reaffirming a debt.

VII. REDEMPTION OF ASSETS BY DEBTOR — § 722

A. **Nature of redemption:** "Redemption" is the right of an individual debtor to procure the release from lien and the retention or return of property that is intended primarily for personal, family, or household use. The property must be either exempt or abandoned by the trustee. Where the debtor has an exempt interest in portion of property, the right to redeem extends to the entire property, not just the debtor's exempt interest. In order to effect the redemption, the ***debtor must file a statement of intention*** and then has 45 days in which to make the redemption.

B. **Making a redemption:** Property is redeemed by the ***debtor's payment to the creditor of the amount of the allowed secured claim***. Essentially, assuming that the asset has been accurately valued, the debtor is given a right of first refusal to buy the exempt assets. The amount of the allowed secured claim is determined as follows:

   1. **Even exchange; oversecured claims:** In a so-called fair or even exchange (i.e., where the value of the security is equal to the amount of the debt) or where the debt is oversecured (i.e., the security is worth more than the dollar amount of the debt), the ***amount of the allowed secured claim is the same as the debt***.

   2. **Undersecured claims:** If the debt is undersecured (i.e., the value of the security is worth less than the amount of the debt), the amount of the allowed secured claim is ***limited to the value of the security***.

VIII. DISTRIBUTIONS — § 726

A. **Division among creditors:** The basic distribution system is that the assets, which by the time of distribution have usually been reduced to money, are allocated in the order specified by § 726. Assets go first to the first in line; to the extent there are any left over, they go to the second in line; then to the third; and so on until the assets are exhausted. There will generally be more than one entity at each place in line; the distribution among those of equal rank is handled pro rata.

   1. **Priority claims:** First in line for distribution are priority claims, which must be paid in the order specified in § 507.

      a. **Time for filing:** The proof of a priority claim must be either: (1) timely filed (generally within 90 days of the first date set for the meeting of creditors) or, (2) under a special provision that is applicable only to priority claims under Chapter 7, filed before the date on which the trustee commences distribution.

   2. **Ordinary claims:** Most of the claims in a bankruptcy will fall into the second category — ordinary claims. With one set of exceptions (claims for fines, penalties or forfeitures or for multiple, exemplary, or punitive damages, which are subordinated to fourth position), this is the general catch-all for allowed unsecured claims.

      a. **Time for filing:** Generally, these claims must be filed within 90 days after the first meeting of creditors.

      b. **Excusable tardy claims:** Tardy second-category claims may also be paid if the creditor originally did not have knowledge of the case but then learned of it and managed to file the claim before all payments were concluded.

   3. **Late-filed claims:** The third distribution position is given to non-priority claims that are filed late when the creditor knew of the bankruptcy and, therefore, presumably was itself at fault in filing late.

4. **Fines, penalties and forfeitures:** Filed claims for fines, penalties or forfeitures, or for multiple, exemplary or punitive damages — that are not compensation for actual pecuniary losses — are reduced to a fourth position. In general, it is unlikely that fourth position claims will be paid in the usual Chapter 7 case because payment is contingent upon the existence of a surplus of estate assets after the general creditors in the prior categories have been paid in full.

5. **Post-petition interest:** Interest earned after the petition on any claim paid under the previous four orders of distribution is fifth in the order of distribution. The interest accrues from the date of the filing of the petition.

   a. **Unmatured claims:** Interest on a claim that is unmatured as of the filing of the petition is in the first instance disallowed. However, to the extent that the estate has funds after payment of prior claims, it may pay interest that matures after the petition.

6. **Remainder, if any, to the debtor:** If the estate still has assets after paying off the above five levels of distribution, any remainder will be returned to the debtor.

B. **Impact on other Chapters:** The order of distribution for purposes of Chapter 7 has an effect in Chapter 11, 12 and 13 cases. In testing plans under the other Chapters, one standard that must be met for the protection of creditors, known as the "best interest of creditor" test, is that creditors must receive at least as much as they would have received under a Chapter 7 liquidation.

IX. DISCHARGE — § 727

A. **Importance of discharge:** The discharge from debt is the pot of gold at the end of the debtor's rainbow and the basis of the "fresh start." It is effective as of the time of the order for relief and comes as one of the earlier events in a Chapter 7 case.

B. **Right to a discharge — § 727(a):** A debtor has a right to a discharge unless any one of 10 reasons for denial is proven. Presence of any one of the reasons will cause a discharge to be denied in full.

1. **Only individuals:** In Chapter 7 cases, discharge is restricted to individuals. This is because corporations, partnerships, and other business entities do not need discharges from their debts; they simply dissolve.

   a. **Comparison with other bankruptcy Chapters:** As we shall see, entities other than individuals can receive discharges in Chapter 9, 11 and 12 reorganizations. This is because reorganization is designed to continue the existence of the entities, usually with a reduced debt burden, and a discharge is required to free them from the debts they have incurred.

   b. **Denial of discharge to individuals:** If discharge is denied to an individual debtor, the debtor's obligations to creditors remain intact except to the extent that the creditors receive distributions from the estate.

2. **Fraudulent transfers by debtor:** A discharge will be denied if either the debtor (with intent to hinder, delay, or defraud creditors), or an officer of the estate charged with custody of property, has transferred, removed, destroyed, mutilated or concealed property, or has permitted any of those events to occur. This provision applies to transfers of the debtor's property made within one year before the filing and transfers of estate property after the filing.

3. **Inadequate records:** Discharge may be denied if the debtor conceals, destroys, mutilates, falsifies, or fails to keep or preserve any recorded information from which the debtor's financial condition or business transactions may be ascertained, unless such act or failure to act was justified.

4. **Bankruptcy crimes:** Discharge will be prevented by criminal behavior in connection with bankruptcy. Acts considered to be criminal include false oaths, false claims, bribery, and the withholding of information. Because issues under this provision arise under and are limited to the Bankruptcy Code, which has no direct prosecutorial effect, the standard of proof is a preponderance of the evidence, not proof beyond a reasonable doubt.

5. **Inadequate explanation of losses:** Discharge will be denied if the debtor has failed to explain satisfactorily any loss of assets or the reasons for its inability to meet liabilities.

6. **Refusal to cooperate:** The debtor may be denied a discharge for not assisting in the administration of the bankruptcy case. This provision in the statute lists a few examples of noncooperative behavior, including refusal to testify on the grounds of the privilege against self-incrimination after immunity from prosecution has been granted.

7. **Misbehavior in an insider's case:** If the debtor commits any of the acts described in **2.** through **6.** above, in connection with another bankruptcy case concerning an "insider," either during the year before the petition or during the administration of his case, the discharge will be denied. "Insider" is defined to include: relatives of the debtor or of a general partner of the debtor; directors, officers and controlling persons of a corporation; general partners of a partnership.

8. **Previous discharge in Chapter 7 or 11 case:** A discharge will be denied if the debtor has been granted a previous discharge under Chapter 7 or Chapter 11 in a case commenced within six years before the petition is filed.

9. **Previous discharge in Chapter 12 and 13 case:** With a few exceptions, discharge in a Chapter 7 case will be denied to debtors who received a discharge under Chapter 12 (family farmers) or Chapter 13 (individuals with regular income) in a case commenced within six years prior to the start of the Chapter 7 case.

    a. **Exceptions:** A discharge is available if: (1) the unsecured claims of the prior case were paid in full, or (2) 70 percent of the debts were paid and the previous plan was proposed in good faith and the payments represented the debtor's best effort.

10. **Waivers of discharge:** Discharge is prevented if the court approves a written waiver of discharge executed by the debtor after the order for relief in the case. A debtor may execute a waiver in order to take advantage of only some of the elements of bankruptcy relief (the automatic stay, avoidance of certain transfers, organization of claims, etc.) while remaining obligated to creditors.

C. **Debts discharged — § 727(b):** Subject to the exceptions to discharge in § 523, an individual is discharged from all debts that arose before the order for relief. Such debts are discharged regardless of whether a proof of claim was filed or allowed.

    1. **Money damages:** Claims must be for money or money's equivalent, although the amounts need not be established. Therefore, an order imposing future duties to act or refrain from acting cannot support a dischargeable claim until it gives rise to a money equivalent. If that does not occur until after the order for relief, it cannot be discharged.

    2. **Debts deemed to have arisen before order for relief:** Certain actions taken by the trustee after the order for relief, such as the rejection of a contract with a third person, or the avoidance of a fraudulent transfer to a third person, result in claims against the estate. These claims are dischargeable even though they may have arisen after the order for relief because they are deemed to have arisen before the order.

D. **Debts not discharged:** Liens (e.g., mortgages on real estate and security interests in personal property that secure payment or performance of an obligation) are protected by the Fifth Amendment and cannot be discharged in bankruptcy. If a creditor has a secured claim against the debtor, the claim itself (i.e., the right to payment) may be discharged, but the right to the property will not be.

CHAPTER 10
FILING UNDER CHAPTER 9 — MUNICIPAL BANKRUPTCY

I. NATURE AND STRUCTURE OF CHAPTER 9

A. Applicability of general provisions—§ 901: Chapter 9 is a little used chapter of the Code that deals with the bankruptcy of "municipalities," a term that includes any political subdivision, public agency, or instrumentality of the states. A Chapter 9 filing must be voluntary.

B. Reorganization approach: Chapter 9, entitled "Adjustments of Debts of a Municipality," is essentially a reorganization, much like a corporate reorganization under Chapter 11. For this reason, much of Chapter 11 is made applicable to Chapter 9.

C. Entities that may be Chapter 9 debtors: A municipality that may avail itself of Chapter 9 relief may not utilize any other form of bankruptcy. To be a debtor under Chapter 9, it is essential that the following five conditions be satisfied:

1. **Must be a municipality:** Under the definition of municipality, all of the following may file under Chapter 9: cities, towns, villages, counties, taxing districts, municipal utilities, school districts, and authorities established to operate highways, airports, bridges and similar facilities.

2. **Must have state authority:** The municipality must be specifically authorized by state law to be a Chapter 9 debtor. The authority may be given to municipalities in general or to specifically named municipalities. It may also be given by a government officer or organization that is empowered to make the authorization.

3. **Municipality must be insolvent:** The definition of municipal insolvency is the equitable test of not being able to pay debts as they become due.

4. **Demonstration of intent:** The municipal debtor must demonstrate to the court that it desires to effect a plan to adjust its debts.

5. **Satisfaction of one of the creditor-related tests:** The municipal debtor must demonstrate need and good faith through one or more of the following: (1) a majority of the creditors who will be impaired under a plan have agreed to the case; (2) the debtor has negotiated with its creditors in good faith and has failed to reach an agreement with them; (3) negotiation with creditors is impracticable, or (4) the debtor reasonably believes that a creditor may attempt to obtain a preferential payment.

II. ADMINISTRATIVE VARIATIONS FROM FILINGS UNDER OTHER CHAPTERS

A. Order for relief: A petition under Chapter 9 is not an automatic order for relief; the court must issue the order.

B. Automatic stay—§ 922: The general provisions for application of the automatic stay are made applicable to Chapter 9. In addition, the automatic stay is made available on two other grounds not available under the other Chapters:

1. **Application to officers or inhabitants of debtor:** The automatic stay applies to actions against a municipality's officers or inhabitants that seek to enforce claims against the debtor municipality. This ground applies to actions or proceedings that could be brought against persons or entities other than the municipality itself for debts owed by, or owing to, the municipality.

2. **Enforcement of certain liens:** The automatic stay applies to the enforcement of a lien related to taxes or assessments owed to the debtor municipality. This provision prevents actions, which may be permitted under the particular state law, that would enable a creditor to take the place of the municipality to enforce a lien for taxes or assessments.

C. **Debtor's duties:** For Chapter 9, there is a reduced set of duties that serve to give public notice of the bankruptcy and to supply a list of the municipality's creditors to the court.

D. **Effect of list of claims:** A proof of claim is deemed filed if the debt appears in the list of creditors filed by the municipality.

E. **Avoiding powers:**

1. **The "avoiding power" trustee:** The powers of the trustee are given to the debtor municipality. However, if a debtor municipality chooses not to use its avoiding power, the court has the power to appoint a trustee to exercise the unused avoiding power.

2. **Avoiding contracts:** The ability to avoid executory contracts is an important part of the municipality's protective arsenal. Burdensome contracts with municipal employees, labor unions, or the private sector can be a particularly serious element affecting a municipality's financial status.

3. **Preferential transfers to municipal bond or note holders:** Transfers of money or property to the holders of municipal bonds or notes are not subject to avoidance as preferential transfers.

F. **Dismissal:** The court has the authority to dismiss for cause. There is a non-exclusive list of causes, including want of prosecution of the case, unreasonable delay, failure to propose a plan, denial of confirmation of a plan and denial of additional time for filing another plan or modification of a plan.

III. THE REORGANIZATION PLAN

A. **Nature of plan:** The future of the debtor municipality, including the extent to which it will pay its debts, is embodied in a reorganization plan. The municipality drafts and submits the plan to its creditors for their approval, which is then confirmed by the bankruptcy court. The process by which a plan is written, voted upon, and confirmed largely duplicates the Chapter 11 process.

B. **Differences from Chapter 11 plans:** Unlike Chapter 11 plans, only the debtor may file a Chapter 9 plan. The plan is filed with the petition or at such later time as the court fixes.

C. **Confirmation of the plan:** Most of the provisions for court confirmation of a plan under Chapter 11 are made applicable to Chapter 9.

1. **Cram down:** The cram down tests of § 1129(b), under which creditors opposed to the plan may be forced to accept it, apply with some modifications to Chapter 9. For example, not all revenue of a municipality can be allocated to creditors; some revenue is required on a continuing basis to keep the community running.

2. **Lack of priority claims:** All administrative claims must be paid in cash when the plan becomes effective unless the claim holder agrees to a different treatment.

3. **Best interests of creditors test:** The "best interests of creditor" test requires that impaired claims either accept the plan or receive at least what they would get in a Chapter 7 liquidation.

IV. EFFECT OF PLAN CONFIRMATION—§ 944

A. **Debtor and creditors are bound:** The confirmed plan binds the municipality debtor and all creditors whether or not the creditor has filed a claim or accepted the plan. The plan apparently even binds creditors (except for discharge) that do not know of the plan.

B. **Discharge:** The plan discharges the debtor municipality of all debts when all of the following occurs:

1. **Confirmation:** The plan must be confirmed.

2. **Deposit with a disbursing agent:** The debtor must deposit with a disbursing agent appointed by the court any consideration to be distributed under the plan.

3. **Determination of binding obligation:** The court must determine that any security deposited with the disbursing agent is a valid obligation of the debtor and that any provision made to pay or to secure payment is also valid.

C. **Exceptions from discharge:** The following are excepted from the discharge under a confirmed plan:

1. **Exceptions in plan or order:** Any debts excepted from discharge by the plan itself or by the order confirming the plan are not discharged.

2. **Entities without knowledge:** A debt owing to any entity that had neither notice nor actual knowledge of the case is not discharged.

V. PLAN IMPLEMENTATION

A. **Role of court:** The court may retain jurisdiction over the case for as long as the court feels is necessary for the successful implementation of the plan.

B. **Role of municipal entity:** A legal duty is imposed on the debtor municipality to implement the plan.

CHAPTER 11

FILING UNDER CHAPTER 11 — REORGANIZATION

I. FILING UNDER CHAPTER 11

A. **Financial reorganization:** The usual Chapter 11 debtor is a business in financial difficulty. Through a Chapter 11 plan, it can pay a portion of its obligations and discharge the remainder; it can terminate burdensome contracts, including labor union agreements; it can recover assets transferred away in preferential or fraudulent transfers; and it can, in a reorganization plan that is accepted by its creditors, revamp its operations in order to return to a period of profitability.

B. **Individuals in Chapter 11:** The Supreme Court has held that ***individuals may use Chapter 11 without restraint***. The Court agreed that Chapter 11 was ***designed primarily for businesses***; however, this does not foreclose consumers from using it. *Toibb v. Radloff*, 501 U.S. 157 (1991).

C. **"Debtor in possession" — § 1101:** Chapter 11 provides for and creates a new entity in bankruptcy, the "debtor in possession," which allows the debtor the substantial benefit of being able to continue management of its business. In a minority of cases, a trustee is appointed.

D. **Comparison to Chapter 7:** Although Chapter 11 is designed primarily for the purpose of reorganization, a Chapter 11 debtor may adopt a liquidating plan. A Chapter 11 liquidating plan requires, as does a reorganization, the submission of a written plan, the vote of creditors, and the confirmation of the court. A liquidation under Chapter 11 is, therefore, a considerably more elaborate and structured form of liquidation than one under Chapter 7.

E. Comparison to Chapter 13: In comparison with Chapter 13 (the reorganization of individual debtors with regular income), a filing under Chapter 11: (1) has no limitation on the amount of debts (Chapter 13 is limited to unsecured debt of less than $250,000 and secured debt of less than $750,000); (2) does not require any particular commitment of income to the payment of debts as Chapter 13 does; and (3) gives a faster discharge than does Chapter 13.

II. CREDITOR COMMITTEES

A. Purpose: Since creditors in a Chapter 11 case can number into the hundreds of thousands, committees are necessary in order to create some sort of workable, representative instrument. However, with respect to small business debtors, a party in interest may request and the court may order, for cause, that a committee of creditors not be appointed. In order to qualify as a small business, the debtor's secured and unsecured debts cannot exceed $2,000,000.

B. Appointment — § 1102: The first committee, which must consist of unsecured creditors, is appointed by the United States Trustee; additional committees of creditors and of equity security holders may be ordered by the court and are established by the United States Trustee.

C. Number and function of committees: Since the goal of committees is to see that all creditors are appropriately represented, there is no particular number of committees and no particular number of members on a committee. The provisions of § 1102(b)(1) suggest, but do not require, that a creditors' committee be composed of the persons that hold the seven largest of the kinds of claims represented on the committee, and that an equity holders' committee be composed of the seven largest amounts of the kinds of equity securities represented on the committee.

D. Powers and duties — § 1103: A committee has a broad-ranging set of powers, including authority to: consult with the debtor in possession or the trustee concerning the administration of the estate; investigate the debtor's business and its operation; participate in the formulation of a plan; file acceptances or rejections of the plan with the court; employ lawyers, accountants, and other agents; and request the appointment of a trustee where it is deemed appropriate.

III. TRUSTEES AND EXAMINERS

A. Performance of the trustee's duties: In most Chapter 11 cases, the debtor in possession will operate its own business and perform the functions nominally assigned in some provision of Chapter 11 and in other chapters of the Code to the trustee.

B. Discretionary appointment of trustee — § 1104: The court may order the appointment of a trustee for cause, including fraud, dishonesty, incompetence, gross mismanagement, or in the interests of creditors.

    1. Power to appoint seldom used: The appointment of a trustee in Chapter 11 is considered an extraordinary event; the assumption is that an honest debtor in financial difficulties is the best one to manage the business. (That the debtor who jeopardized the business is given the authority to run it, has subjected Chapter 11 to major criticism by some commentators.) But, if necessary to protect creditors and equity holders, the debtor in possession may be removed and a trustee appointed.

    2. Right to elect: Within 30 days after the court orders the appointment of a trustee, a party in interest may request an election of that trustee. If a request is made, the United States trustee must convene a meeting of creditors for the purpose of electing one disinterested person to serve as trustee.

C. Trustee duties: As mentioned above, trustee duties are usually performed by the debtor in possession. It should be kept in mind that duties of the trustee, except where noted, apply also to debtors in possession. With some exceptions, the duties of the Chapter 11 trustee are the same as the Chapter 7 trustee. In addition, the Chapter 11 trustee has duties to: (1) file a list of creditors, a schedule of assets and liabilities, a schedule of current income and current expenditures, and a statement of the debtor's financial affairs; (2) investigate the acts, conduct, assets, liabilities, and financial condition of the business and the desirability of continuing it, and to report the findings to the court; (3) file a plan or recommend conversion to another bankruptcy chapter or a dismissal; (4) file whatever tax returns are required; and (5) after confirmation of a plan, file such reports as are required.

D. **Appointment of examiner:** If a trustee has not been appointed, either a party in interest or the United States Trustee may request the court to appoint an examiner. After notice and a hearing, the court may appoint an examiner if either: (1) the appointment is in the interest of creditors, equity stockholders, and other parties in interest, or (2) the debtor's unsecured debts, other than debts for goods, services, or taxes, or owing to an insider, exceed $5,000,000. Although an examiner is ordinarily appointed to make an investigation, there is considerable flexibility in the use of examiners.

    1. **Duties of examiner:** The basic duties of the examiner are to conduct an investigation of the affairs of the debtor, including any allegations of fraud, dishonesty, incompetence, misconduct, mismanagement, or irregularities in management. The examiner may also be asked to investigate any other matter relevant to the case or the plan, and submit a report. In addition, the court may give the examiner any other trustee duties that it wishes the debtor in possession not to perform.

IV. CONVERSION OR DISMISSAL — § 1112

A. **Conversion by debtor:** The ability to convert from Chapter 11 to Chapter 7 is important because Chapter 11 is only occasionally successful for rehabilitation of the debtor. Subject to three exceptions, the debtor has the right to convert a case to Chapter 7. The debtor may not convert to Chapter 7 where: (1) the court has ordered the appointment of a trustee, (2) the Chapter 11 case was begun through an involuntary petition, and (3) the case was converted to Chapter 11 by a party other than the debtor.

B. **Conversion by other parties for cause:** A Chapter 11 filing may be converted for cause to another chapter by parties other than the debtor. Parties in interest, the United States trustee, or the bankruptcy administrator (bankruptcy administrators serve in the few jurisdictions where United States trustees are not available) may generally ask the Court to convert a Chapter 11 case to Chapter 7 for cause. If the debtor is a farmer or a charitable corporation, the court may not convert a case to Chapter 7 unless the debtor requests the conversion.

C. **Dismissal:** Any party in interest and the United States trustee may request dismissal of a Chapter 11 case. The court may order dismissal for cause. "Cause" is broadly interpreted to include, but is not limited to, such events as: the likelihood of loss to the estate, inability to effectuate a plan, unreasonable delays by the debtor, and inability to effectuate substantial consummation of a confirmed plan.

    1. **Dismissal and good faith:** Although not specifically mentioned in the statute, if a petition is not filed in good faith, the court may dismiss the case. The good faith requirement frequently appears as the absence of good faith, i.e., bad faith.

        a. **Bad faith in operating the business:** If the initial capital was grossly insufficient, or the business plan was so unrealistic or impractical that the wasting of creditors' money and bankruptcy were essentially inevitable, there may be a finding of bad faith.

        b. **Bad faith and the filing:** Bad faith may be found where the filing was made to pervert rather than utilize the bankruptcy system. For example, the petition may have been filed principally for the § 362 automatic stay in order to slow down actions by legitimate creditors, or in order to attempt an evasion of an order properly made in a state court. Bad faith may also exist where there is simply no realistic likelihood of a successful reorganization.

    c. Conduct during bankruptcy: Bad faith may also relate to conduct in the bankruptcy proceeding itself.

  2. Later filings: If a case is dismissed, nothing in the Code prevents a subsequent filing, or even a series of subsequent filings, so long as they meet the tests of good faith.

V. OPERATING THE BUSINESS — NEEDS OF DEBTOR IN POSSESSION

  A. Use of property: Several Code provisions are designed to ensure that the debtor in possession has assets for its business purposes during the period of the bankruptcy.

    1. Use, sale, and lease by debtor: The debtor is able to use, sell, or lease property of the estate, either in the ordinary course of its business or, with court approval, other than in the ordinary course. This general rule is subject to certain limited rights by third parties with interests in the property.

      a. Encumbered property: The debtor in possession or trustee can continue to use property subject to liens. At the request of the creditor, the court can condition the use, sale, or lease of secured property on condition that adequate protection be provided by the debtor.

      b. After acquired property: If provided for in the security agreement, the creditor's liens can extend to proceeds, such as rents or profits, from the use of the property by the debtor.

    2. Creditor's relief from stay in order to recover secured interests: Creditors have the right to request relief from the automatic stay generally on two grounds: (1) *for cause*, including the lack of adequate protection, or (2) even where adequate protection is given, where the *debtor does not have any equity in the property* and the *property is not necessary to an effective reorganization*.

      a. Relief from stay for cause: Relief from a stay for cause is frequently given for failure of the debtor to give adequate protection. The ultimate test of adequate protection is whether the secured creditor receives "the indubitable equivalent of such entity's interest in such property."

      b. Relief from stay for lack of debtor equity and property not necessary to effective organization: Even if adequate protection is supplied, the secured creditor may recover its security if the debtor has no equity in the property and the property is not necessary to an effective reorganization.

      c. Relief from stay for single asset real estate: If substantially all of the gross income of a debtor is generated by the operation of a single piece or single project of real property, other than residential property of three or fewer units, and the total secured debt does not exceed $4,000,000, then the debtor is a "single asset real estate" debtor. With respect to such debtors, the court will grant relief from the stay at the request of a secured creditor of the real estate, if the debtor, within 90 days of the order for relief, has not filed a feasible plan of reorganization, or has not begun monthly interest payments to each creditor whose claim is secured by the real estate.

  B. Use of cash and its equivalents: There are various sources that the debtor in possession or trustee in Chapter 11 can look to for its money needs.

    1. Debtor's own money: Any unencumbered cash that the debtor has upon the filing, including, of course, money in the bank, becomes part of and may be used by the estate.

    2. Encumbered money — "cash collateral:" "Cash collateral" is the Code's term for *cash and its equivalents* (including negotiable instruments, securities, and documents of title) *that are subject to liens*. The term cash collateral includes *postpetition rents that fall within the perfected interest of the mortgagee under a mortgage*. Cash collateral also extends to postpetition proceeds, product, and profits of property that are perfectable under a security agreement or under state law. The debtor or trustee may not use, sell, or lease cash collateral unless each entity that has an interest in the collateral consents, or, after notice and a hearing, authorization is given by the court. Generally, the debtor and secured creditor agree on the terms of a cash collateral agreement which is then approved by the court.

3. **Accounts subject to setoff:** Where a debtor has money in the bank and, at the same time, owes money to the same bank, the bank is prohibited from making an immediate set off. However, the bank is able to put a brief and temporary administrative hold (freeze) on the deposit account to the extent of the unpaid debt, thus preventing the debtor's access to that portion of the account. *Citizens Bank of Maryland v. Strumpf*, No. 94-1340, 1995 U.S. LEXIS 7408 (1995).

C. **Access to credit:** In order to operate the business effectively, the debtor in possession or trustee must have access to new sources of cash and other credit. The special administrative expense priority, because of its ability to reach the assets in the debtor's estate before most other claims, gives creditors a major incentive to lend or otherwise advance credit to debtors in Chapter 11 with a reasonable assurance of repayment.

1. **Availability of super administrative expense priority —§ 364(c)(1):** If the debtor in possession or trustee is unable to obtain credit through use of the administrative expense priority, the court can raise the position of a creditor willing to extend credit to that of an administrative expense claimant ahead of all other administrative expense claimants and priorities.

2. **Money or credit secured by liens — § 364(c), (d):** If these administrative priorities are considered insufficient by a proposed creditor, the court may authorize that new credit be secured by liens on the property of the estate. The court may authorize a lien on property that is not encumbered by other liens. If that is not available, the court may authorize junior liens on encumbered property. In limited situations, the court may grant an equal, or even a senior, lien on property of the estate that is already fully encumbered with a prior lien. In creating an equal or superior property right on property that is already encumbered, the prior lienholder must be given "adequate protection."

D. **Rights with respect to collective bargaining agreements:** Before a debtor in possession or trustee may request the court to terminate a collective bargaining agreement, it must make a proposal to the employees for a new agreement that modifies the old only to the extent necessary to the reorganization. The employees may reject this offer only for good cause.

VI. CLASSES OF CLAIMS AND INTERESTS

A. **Purposes of classes:** The division of claims and interests into classes under a Chapter 11 plan serves two basic purposes. First, it *establishes voting groups*; a class must either accept or reject a plan as a class. Second, it *determines the priority of distributions made from the estate* to the creditors and interest holders.

1. **Importance of class selection:** Principally because of the way voting is conducted by classes, the creation of the classes (done by the drafter of the plan, which is usually the debtor in possession) is a subtle and complicated procedure that can have dramatic impact on creditors.

2. **Classification cannot be solely to influence voting:** An underlying policy of the classification process is that *classes may not be selected solely to influence voting results*.

B. **Similar and dissimilar claims**: All claims in a class must be similar to each other. Although the statute does not define "similar," the courts have considered the term to mean that secured claims must be kept separate from unsecured claims and that unsecured claims in the same class be of the same priority. However, similar claims need not be in the same class. ***Claims may be placed in different classes where there is a reasonable basis for the separation***. Also, each secured creditor will usually be in a class by itself because each item of security is different from all other items. For convenience, ***dissimilar claims up to a limited dollar amount set for each by the court can be placed in the same class***.

VII. UNDERSECURED CREDITORS — § 1111(b)

A. **Recourse rule for undersecured creditors:** In a Chapter 11 case, certain variations apply to the rights of an undersecured creditor — the secured creditor whose loan to the debtor exceeds the value of the collateral securing the loan. With a few exceptions, ***non-recourse claims*** (those claims in which the creditor has no recourse against the debtor other than against the property itself) ***are made into recourse claims*** (i.e., the creditor has a claim against the debtor for any deficiency that would result from foreclosure on the collateral). With two exceptions, a claim against a Chapter 11 debtor on a non-recourse loan will be considered a recourse claim, thereby ***establishing a deficiency claim for the undersecured portion of a loan***.

B. **Exceptions from the recourse rule:** There are two exceptions to which the rule for conversion of a secured loan from non-recourse to recourse status will not apply. The exceptions apply when (1) the ***property is sold*** or will be sold, or (2) an ***election*** is made by the secured creditors to ***treat the claims as fully secured loans*** (§ 1111(b)(2) election). If the class of undersecured creditors so elects, the secured claim and the unsecured deficiency claim of each member of the class are combined into one fully secured claim. To make this election, the affirmative vote of the class of claims must be two thirds of the amount of claims and more than half of the number of claims. Note that, although the claim is fully secured, the value of the collateral remains the same.

   a. **When election cannot be made:** The election under § 1111(b)(2) cannot be made if: (1) the holder's interest in the property subject to the claim is of inconsequential value, or (2) the holder of the claim has recourse against the debtor and the property either is sold or will be sold under a Chapter 11 plan.

   b. **Reasons for making election:** The § 1111(b)(2) election is based on the expectation that the secured property will continue to be held by the debtor as it operates under the plan and on the creditor's bet that it will rise in value during this period. Conceivably, the creditor might feel that the appraised value was too low. To whatever extent the property's value increases, the creditor will benefit because the property now secures more of the debt. The creditor may also be betting that the rise in value will be worth more than would its deficiency claim in the absence of the election.

   c. **Effect of making election:** The election under § 1111(b)(2) causes the creditor to lose its deficiency claim and whatever leverage it might have in the case by being unable to vote its unsecured claim. Without the election, a lienholder would lose any appreciation in the value of the property that might occur during the period of the plan.

VIII. THE PLAN

A. **General description:** The reorganization plan sets the debtor's future and establishes with particularity the financial relationship among the debtor, the creditors, and the other parties in interest. For the 120-day period after the order for relief, a plan may be filed only by the debtor. Also, a plan may be filed at any later time by the debtor.

   1. **Filing by others:** Any other party in interest may file a plan, if: (1) a ***trustee has been appointed***, or (2) the ***debtor has not filed a plan within 120 days after the order for relief***, or (3) if a ***plan filed by the debtor has not been accepted*** by all impaired classes ***within 180 days after the order for relief***. Parties in interest include the trustee, a creditor or creditors' committee, and an equity security holder or equity security holders' committee. The court, on request of a party in interest, may, for cause, reduce or increase the 120 and 180 day periods.

2. **Small business debtors:** If a debtor qualifies as a small business debtor and elects to be treated as such, shorter time periods apply. A "small business" is a business whose total secured and unsecured debts on the date of the petition do not exceed $2,000,000. The definition excludes businesses whose primary activity is related to owning or operating real estate. During the first 100 days after the order for relief, only the small business debtor may file a plan. All plans must be filed within 160 days after the date of the order for relief.

B. **Mandatory contents of a plan — § 1123(a):** The statute governing the contents of a Chapter 11 plan is essentially divided between mandatory and permissive contents. The Code does not attempt to limit the scope of a plan, but the plan must contain certain mandatory elements.

   1. **Classes of claims and interests:** The plan *must establish the classes* of holders of *claims and interests* (equity securities holders), which are the units into which votes for or against a plan are organized. For purposes of payment and inclusion in the plan, a claim is deemed filed if it is in the debtor's filed schedules. Because priority claims receive their entire claims in cash (unless they agree otherwise), they are not entitled to vote and, consequently, are not included in a class.

   2. **Unimpaired claims and interests:** *Claims that are not impaired* — those whose rights are not altered or "impaired" by the plan — *must be identified*. They will be deemed to have voted in favor of the plan.

   3. **Treatment of impaired claims and interests:** The *proposed treatment of impaired claims* — those whose rights are altered or "impaired" by the plan — *must be identified*. They will receive the right to vote on the plan.

      a. **Nature of impairment:** Impairment means that a claim or interest is being altered under a reorganization plan. If a loan was in default, curing the default does change the rights of the claimant, but not in such a way as to constitute impairment. Also, if an unpaid balance has been "accelerated" by the creditor pursuant to the terms of the contract (i.e., the remaining installments have been declared presently payable), a reinstatement of the original payment terms does not constitute impairment.

   4. **Equal treatment for each claim or interest in a class:** Each claim or interest in a class must receive the same treatment as all other claims or interests in the class, unless the holder of a particular claim agrees otherwise.

   5. **Adequate means for plan's implementation:** The Section includes a broad-ranging provision giving a series of examples of acts, not meant to be exclusive, that may be undertaken by the debtor in possession or the trustee in order to make the plan successful. Some of the provisions for implementation suggested by the statute include: retention or sale of the debtor's property, mergers or consolidations, satisfaction or modification of liens, and amendment of the debtor's charter. This provision preempts inconsistent areas of state law. For example, if a state law guaranteeing preemptive rights to stockholders (i.e., the rights of shareholders to retain proportionate share interests in a corporation) would interfere with a proposed stock distribution under a reorganization plan, the state law is preempted.

   6. **Amendment of corporate charter:** If new equity securities are to be issued, the plan may need to amend the debtor's charter to provide, for example, that the new securities have voting powers. Amendments may also be necessary to ensure that voting power for all securities is equitably distributed.

   7. **Provision for fair representation:** The plan must provide that officers, directors, and trustees under the plan be selected in a manner that is consistent with the interests of creditors, equity security holders, and public policy.

C. Permissive contents of a plan — § 1123(b): There are several additional provisions that the statute permits to be included in a plan. Plans can become quite lengthy and complex, particularly in the case of large, complicated businesses.

  1. Impair or not impair claims or interests: This provision allows the plan to impair or not impair claims and interests and is closely related to the mandatory provisions requiring that unimpaired classes be identified as such and that the treatment of impaired classes be specified.

  2. Executory contracts & leases: An executory contract or unexpired lease may be accepted or rejected at any time up to the confirmation of a Chapter 11 plan.

  3. Settlement or retention of specified claim or interest: The plan may provide for the settlement or adjustment of any claim or interest, or for the retention and enforcement of any claim or interest.

  4. Liquidation plans: The plan may provide for the sale of all or substantially all of the debtor's assets and the distribution of the proceeds among holders of claims or interests.

  5. Modification or retention of creditor claims: The rights of holders of secured claims, other than on debtor's principal residence, and of unsecured claims may be modified or retained.

  6. Other appropriate provisions in plan: The sixth permissive provision allows the inclusion of other appropriate plan provisions.

IX. DISCLOSURE AND SOLICITATION — § 1125

A. Importance of disclosure: Information concerning the plan must be disclosed to the holders of claims and interests who will vote on the plan. The disclosure documents, usually called a Disclosure Statement, must be approved by the court as containing adequate information.

B. The concept of "adequate information": What constitutes adequate information turns on the complexity of the particular plan and the relationship of the recipient to the debtor. In most cases, the recipients should be told such things as: (1) what payment or property they will receive under the plan, (2) how that payment or property will be obtained and from where, (3) how long the plan will take to be implemented, (4) what the business projections are and what they are based upon, (5) whether there are any major contingencies such as major lawsuits, (6) who will run the business, and (7) for purposes of the best interest of creditor test, what the liquidation value of the business is (i.e., a comparison between what the creditors would have received under a Chapter 7 liquidation and what they will receive under the plan).

C. Documentation required to be sent: The *plan, or a summary of the plan, and a written disclosure statement must be transmitted to the claims and interest holders*. This requirement must be fulfilled prior to solicitation of formal acceptances of a plan. However, communications just short of an actual solicitation of formal acceptance for a plan have been found permissible. All members of a class must receive the same disclosure documents. In actual practice, usually one set of documents goes to all parties eligible to vote.

D. Prepetition solicitation: A plan proponent is permitted to attempt to obtain approval for the plan before the bankruptcy begins. If prepetition solicitation is conducted, targeted voters must get either whatever disclosures may be required by the securities laws or, if no other laws are applicable, "*adequate information*" as required under § 1125.

E. Communications by other than plan proponents: Once adequate information has been supplied to the creditors with respect to a plan, there is almost no limit on communications among creditors for and against the plan. The *opponents of the plan may actively solicit votes against the plan*. The communications by opponents may include the draft of a different plan that has not received the approval of the court under the adequate information standard, but an actual solicitation for votes for an unapproved plan may not be made.

F. Good faith requirement: Although the Code affords great latitude to the creditors to communicate among themselves, there is a general good faith requirement with respect to voting and the solicitation of votes. One may solicit in good faith and in accordance with the provisions of § 1125 without concern for the application of statutes other than the Code.

G. Role of securities laws and the SEC: Prepetition solicitations must be prepared under the requirements of applicable laws other than the Code, usually federal securities laws. For postpetition solicitations, there are exemptions from federal and state securities laws for offers and sales of securities under a reorganization plan, depending on the nature of those offers and sales. Generally, sales for cash must be registered. Although the SEC is explicitly invited to appear and be heard on any issue in a Chapter 11 case, it does not have the right to appeal judgments, orders, or decrees of the court.

X. ACCEPTANCE BY CREDITORS AND EQUITY SHAREHOLDERS — § 1126

A. Acceptance by class of claims: A plan is accepted by a class if the plan is **approved** by creditors in the class holding at least **two-thirds in amount** and **more than one-half in number** of the allowed claims in that class.

B. Acceptance by class of interests: A **class of interests** (equity security holders) accepts a plan if interest holders that **hold at least two-thirds in amount of allowed interests approve**.

C. Non-impaired classes deemed to approve: If a class of claims or interests is **not impaired**, it is **conclusively presumed to have accepted the plan**.

D. Classes receiving nothing deemed to reject: If a **class receives nothing** under the plan, it is **deemed to reject** the plan. The Supreme Court has held that an equity interest in a business necessarily has value and thus one who receives such an interest under a plan receives more than nothing, because he gets an opportunity to share in future profits and in increases in the worth of the business. *Norwest Bank Worthington v. Ahlers*, 485 U.S. 197 (1988).

XI. CONFIRMATION BY THE COURT — §§ 1128 AND 1129

A. Confirmation: A plan becomes official and binding upon the parties when the court confirms it. The bankruptcy court must hold a hearing before a plan can be confirmed.

B. Requirements for confirmation — § 1129(a): There are 13 requirements that must be met for a plan to be confirmed. The only exception to these requirements is with respect to the eighth requirement, which need not be met if the plan and the vote satisfy the cramdown provisions, *infra*. Confirmation under § 1129 requires satisfaction of the following:

1. **Plan compliance:** The plan must comply with the requirements of the Code.

2. **Proponent of plan compliance:** The proponent of the plan must comply with the Code.

3. **Good faith proposal:** The plan must be proposed in good faith and not be in violation of any law. Good faith in proposing a plan usually means that there exists a reasonable likelihood that the plan will achieve a result consistent with the objectives and purposes of the Code.

4. **Fees in connection with case must be reasonable:** Payments made or to be made for costs in connection with the case or the plan are subject to the approval of the court as reasonable.

5. **Identities of proposed directors and officers and other major persons:** The identity of those who are proposed to be directors, officers, affiliates participating in the

plan, and successors under the terms of the plan must be disclosed. The identity of insiders who will be employed and the nature of their compensation must also be disclosed.

6. **Regulatory rate commission approvals:** If publicly regulated rates are to be changed by the plan, appropriate regulatory approval must be obtained or the rate changes must be conditioned on such approval.

7. **Impaired interests:** Assuming that a class is impaired, each member of that class must either have accepted the plan or receive sufficient property under the plan to satisfy the "best interests of creditor" test. The best interests of creditor test is a comparison between what creditors, both secured and unsecured, are to receive under the plan and what they would have received in a Chapter 7 liquidation. For undersecured creditors making the § 1111(b)(2) election, the creditor must receive at least the amount established under § 1111(b)(2) instead of what it would have received in Chapter 7.

8. **Acceptance by each unimpaired class:** The eighth requirement for confirmation is that each class must either accept the plan or not be impaired. The burden of this requirement that all impaired classes accept, is lessened by the provision in § 1129(b) (*infra*), which allows a plan to be crammed down on creditors who would otherwise reject and also provides protection to rejecting creditors.

9. **Priority claims:** The ninth requirement for confirmation deals with claims given priority under § 507, such as tax claims. Priority claims must be separated into groups: some receive 100% in cash as of the effective date, others must either receive cash or accept a plan providing for deferred payments valued in the amount of their claims at the effective date, and still others will receive payments over a period of not more than six years.

10. **Acceptance by one impaired class:** If any class of claims is impaired, which is the case in all but a very few bankruptcies, at least one class of impaired claims must accept the plan, i.e., at least one class whose rights are changed by the plan must decide affirmatively in its favor. The deemed acceptances of non-impaired classes are not counted for this purpose.

11. **Plan feasibility:** The eleventh requirement for confirmation is that the plan not be likely to result in liquidation or the need for further reorganization, unless liquidation or further reorganization is proposed in the plan itself.

12. **Payment of fees:** All fees must be paid or the plan must provide that they will be paid on the effective date of the plan.

13. **Retiree benefits:** The thirteenth requirement for confirmation is that the debtor's obligations for retiree benefits continue to be paid.

C. **Cram down — § 1129(b):** On its face, the eighth requirement for plan acceptance appears to require acceptance by 100% of the classes of claims and interests. However, under § 1129(b), there is relief from this requirement by allowing, as bankruptcy practitioners say, that the plan be "crammed down" on certain of those who have rejected it. The idea underlying the cram down provision is that creditors will receive no more but no less than is reasonably available under the circumstances of the bankruptcy. *A plan may be crammed down if the court finds, on the request of the proponents of the plan, that two basic tests are met:* first, that the plan *"does not discriminate unfairly"*; and, second, that it *"is fair and equitable"* with respect to each class of claims and interests that have not voted in favor of the plan.

1. **Unfair discrimination test:** The courts have frequently applied a four-part test to determine whether unfair discrimination exists: (1) whether the discrimination is supported by a reasonable basis, (2) whether the debtor can confirm and consummate a plan without the discrimination, (3) whether the discrimination is proposed in good faith, and (4) the nature of the treatment of the classes discriminated against.

2. **Fair and equitable test:** The heart of the test is the *"absolute priority rule,"* which decrees that one in a senior position must be paid in full before anyone in a junior position may receive anything. However, the rule is not the only test of "fair and equitable," as is made clear from the use of "includes" in the statute. Courts will also examine to see whether

the plan is fair and equitable to the impaired classes by looking at such basic factors as: (1) the feasibility of the plan, (2) the treatment of creditors, and (3) the rate of interest they are to receive and how it relates to market rates.

   a. **Secured creditors:** A plan may not be forced on a secured creditor unless it is fair and equitable, which includes but is not limited to the requirement that the secured creditor retain its security interest or the equivalent. A plan will be considered fair and equitable if it provides for the realization by the lienholder of the "indubitable equivalent" of its secured claim.

   b. **Unsecured creditors:** The plan may be crammed down in situations where classes of unsecured creditors fail to vote in its favor, provided that the "absolute priority rule" is observed. The rule dictates that classes of senior rank must be paid in full before classes of junior rank receive anything. *If all claim holders in a given class receive less than full payment, they may be crammed down if all claims that are junior to them receive nothing.*

      i. **Seniority of classes:** The seniority of classes is established by principles of law both inside and outside the Code. The most fundamental rule, and the one most often raised in cram down disputes, is the rule applicable to corporations, which provides that *creditors get paid before stockholders* (and are therefore senior in rank to stockholders).

      ii. **Definition of "nothing:"** A frequent question is what constitutes "nothing" for the stockholders, the only class lower in the pecking order than subordinated debt. *If the stockholders retain their stock* and their ownership interests, even in a corporation with a zero net worth and questionable prospects of paying dividends, *they are getting something*; therefore, a cram down of a class senior to the stockholders cannot be accomplished. There is an exception, however, for "new value" (discussed *infra*).

   c. **Classes of interests:** A plan will be found to be fair and equitable with respect to a class of interests (principally the equity interests of stockholders or partners) if either (1) each member of the class receives the greatest of the allowed amount of any liquidation preference, or the fixed redemption price to which it is entitled, or the value of the interest, or (2) as with unsecured claims, if any interest that is lower in the order of priorities receives nothing. For the typical stock corporation, all claims (which are necessarily senior to interests) must either be paid in full under the plan or accept the plan before the issue of whether the stock interests are subject to cram down arises.

3. **The new value exception:** Under the absolute priority rule, to cram down a claim on unsecured claimants, the holders of equity interests must be eliminated. However, the Supreme Court, well before adoption of the Code in 1978, had held that the *infusion of new capital by the holders of equity interests, gave these interests an exception from the absolute priority rule* and enabled them to remain as stockholders. *Case v. Los Angeles Lumber Co.*, 308 U.S. 106 (1939). Most of the courts considering the new value exception have held that it continues as good law under the Code. Typically, they have held that the infusion *must be of real value, in money or money's worth, and that it must be substantial*.

XII. EFFECT OF CONFIRMATION — § 1141

A. **The plan binds the parties in interest:** Upon confirmation, the plan binds the debtor, the creditors, and the holders of equity security interests.

B. Vests property in debtor: Except as otherwise provided in the plan, confirmation vests all of the property of the estate in the debtor. Thus, the debtor in possession disappears as a legal entity and the duties of a trustee end.

C. Effect upon liens: The property dealt with by the plan is free of all adverse claims, including liens, except as otherwise provided in the plan. No property interest can be taken if the result would violate the requirement for the payment of just compensation under the Fifth Amendment.

D. Discharge of debts: Confirmation of a plan discharges all of the debtor's debts that arose before the date of the confirmation.

   1. Contrast with Chapter 7: The discharge in Chapter 11 contrasts with a Chapter 7 discharge, which discharges only the debts that arose before the filing of the bankruptcy petition.

   2. Contrast with Chapter 13: In Chapter 13, debts of an individual are generally not discharged until payments under the plan are completed. The earlier date for discharge in a Chapter 11 plan is appropriate because, unlike Chapter 13, the creditors must approve the plan in order for it to be confirmed.

   3. Necessity of proof of claim: As with Chapter 7, debts are discharged whether or not a proof of claim is filed and whether or not the claim is "allowed."

   4. Liquidation plans: Because Chapter 11 also provides for liquidation plans, it includes a scheme compatible with Chapter 7 for such plans. A discharge will be denied for a liquidation plan under Chapter 11 if the debtor does not engage in business after its consummation and, if under Chapter 7, the debtor would be denied a discharge.

   5. Supplemental injunctions: In our discussion of §524, *supra*, C-12, we noted that a discharge operates as an injunction. The court may issue additional injunctions in support of the discharge. Such injunctions may, among other things, enjoin entities from taking legal action to collect or receive payment that would interfere with the effect of the discharge.

XIII. IMPLEMENTATION OF PLAN — § 1142

A. Debtor must carry out plan — § 1142: The plan becomes an order of the court and, as such, any effort to subvert it can be met with an action for contempt. The court retains jurisdiction over the case for this purpose until it is closed by an order.

CHAPTER 12

FILING UNDER CHAPTER 12 — FAMILY FARMER WITH REGULAR ANNUAL INCOME

I. UNIQUE NEEDS OF FARMERS

A. Creation of Chapter 12: Congress has always been sensitive to the unique needs of farmers, who have so much of their capital tied up in the land on which they live and work. The main impetus behind the creation of Chapter 12 in 1986 was the financial squeeze on farmers created by the rise in production costs and the accompanying reduction in commodity prices beginning in the early 1980s. Chapter 12 was adopted by Congress to fill the gap between Chapter 11 and Chapter 13 (individuals with consumer debts) and to deal with farmers' special problems.

II. WHO MAY BE A DEBTOR UNDER CHAPTER 12

A. **Definition of family farmer**: A debtor under Chapter 12 must be a "family farmer with regular annual income." "Regular annual income" is defined to mean income sufficient to make payments under a plan. A family farmer can be an individual, or individual and spouse, or a corporation or partnership more than half of which is owned by a family. There are also debt limitations — a top limit of $1,500,000 in aggregate debts, rather than Chapter 13's $1,000,000, and other restrictions related to earnings and debt designed to ensure that the farm is of a family nature.

III. ESTATE ADMINISTRATION

A. **Stay of acts against co-debtor — § 1201**: In addition to the § 362 targets, a stay is imposed against the collection of consumer debts from guarantors or co-signers of family farmer obligations.

B. **Trustee and debtor in possession — §§ 1202 and 1207**: A trustee is appointed for all Chapter 12 cases, but his duties are largely ministerial. The debtor remains in possession of the property of the estate; the trustee does not take over possession of the farm. The trustee's duties are as prescribed for a Chapter 7 trustee, except that he does not liquidate the estate, nor does he investigate the financial affairs of the debtor.

C. **Sale of farm property permitted — § 1206**: If a family farmer were trying to reduce farm operations, equipment can be sold. If there is a lien on the equipment, the restriction that either the sale price must cover the amount of the lien or the lienholder must consent, is liberalized. Subject to court supervision, a sale is permitted so long as the proceeds are held for the lienholder.

D. **Property acquired after petition — § 1207**: Property acquired after the petition is filed is property of the estate. In particular, earnings of the family farmer while in bankruptcy become property of the estate.

IV. THE PLAN — §§ 1221 AND 1222

A. **Who may file a plan and when — § 1221**: Only the debtor may file a plan. The plan must be filed within 90 days after the order for relief, except that the period may be extended for circumstances beyond the control of the debtor.

B. **Contents of plan — § 1222**: The Chapter 12 plan is very similar to the Chapter 13 plan (covering individuals with consumer debts). The following are the key differences between a Chapter 12 plan and a Chapter 13 plan.

1. **Modification by claim holders**: Claim holders are allowed to agree to less favorable treatment than others in the same class.

2. **Modification of all secured claims**: Chapter 12 permits the modification of all secured claims, including home mortgages.

3. **Extension of payments on secured claims**: Chapter 12 permits the modification of secured claims to allow payment to extend beyond the period for payments that is provided for in the plan; Chapter 13 does not give this latitude.

C. **Time of plans**: The time period over which a plan for payments may extend is normally three years, which is the same as for Chapter 13. The court may extend the period, but not to exceed a total of five years.

D. **Confirmation — § 1224 and § 1225**: The plan becomes effective upon confirmation by the court. Except for cause, the confirmation hearing must be concluded within 45 days after the filing of the plan.

E. Payments to creditors — § 1226: As with a Chapter 13 plan, the trustee usually makes payments to creditors; however, the plan may provide otherwise. Under appropriate circumstances, a court may order the debtor to start making the payments.

F. Effect of confirmation — § 1227: The confirmed plan binds the parties in interest. If the trustee had any title to property, the title is revested in the debtor.

V. DISCHARGE — § 1228

A. Nature of discharge: Discharge is available for debts included in the plan. A Chapter 12 discharge will not discharge debts whose payment period extends beyond the time of the plan or debts that are excluded from individual discharge under § 523. There are two kinds of Chapter 12 discharges, which have been called the payment discharge and the hardship discharge.

B. Payment discharge: As soon as practicable after payment of all debts under the plan, the court will grant the debtor a discharge of all allowed and disallowed debts provided for by the plan.

C. Hardship discharge: If the debtor fails to complete payments because of circumstances for which the debtor cannot justly be held accountable, a hardship discharge may be granted. This discharge may be granted only if: (1) a best-interests-of-creditor test is applied and it is established that each creditor has received property, valued as of the effective date of the plan, that was at least equal to what it would have received under a Chapter 7 liquidation, and (2) modification of the plan is not practicable.

CHAPTER 13
FILING UNDER CHAPTER 13 — INDIVIDUAL WITH REGULAR INCOME

I. WHO MAY ELECT CHAPTER 13 — § 109

A. Limitations on debt: Chapter 13, which is limited to an "individual with regular income," deals with smaller bankruptcies of individuals and their spouses. The ***amount of debt*** that may be owed is ***less than $250,000 in unsecured debt*** and ***less than $750,000 in secured debts***.

B. Scope of "individual" filings: In addition to its application to consumers and their spouses, "individual" within the meaning of Chapter 13 includes a business conducted as a sole proprietorship.

1. Sole proprietorships: Persons with businesses will qualify as "individuals" so long as they do not conduct the business as a separate entity, such as a partnership. An individual and spouse may be a "partnership by estoppel" (i.e., although they are not organized as a partnership, a third party is able to assert that they held themselves out to be partners with respect to a given transaction) and still be able to utilize Chapter 13 because they are, in fact, *not* a partnership.

C. "Individual with regular income" defined: The term "individual with regular income" is defined as an individual whose income is sufficiently stable and regular to enable him to make payments under a Chapter 13 plan. It is clear that the debtor need not be employed. Whether income will be considered "regular" will depend on the facts in each case, including the skills, opportunities, and motivation of the debtor.

II. CONVERSION OR DISMISSAL — § 1307

A. Rights of debtor to convert or dismiss: The Chapter 13 debtor may at any time convert to Chapter 7 or have the case dismissed. If a filing was initially made under another Chapter, a debtor may convert the case to Chapter 13.

B. Rights of other parties to convert or dismiss: Parties other than the debtor may request the court to either convert a Chapter 13 case to Chapter 7 or dismiss the case for cause, whichever is in the best interests of the creditors and the estate. Included in the list of ten grounds establishing cause are unreasonable delay, failure to file a timely plan, and failure to commence making timely payments. Any party in interest may, before confirmation of the Chapter 13 plan, request the court to convert a case to Chapter 11 or 12.

III. STAY OF ACTION AGAINST CO-DEBTOR — § 1301

A. Expanded stay: The automatic stay is expanded under Chapter 13 to protect accommodation parties of the debtor. The *expanded stay* applies to: (1) individuals who are liable on a debt with the debtor, such as *guarantors or co-signors of promissory notes*, and (2) *persons who secured the debtor's obligations*, such as one who gave a creditor a lien on his property to secure the debtor's obligation but did not assume personal responsibility. The expanded stay applies only to consumer debts, defined as debts for personal, family, or household purposes.

B. Exceptions from the expanded stay: The stay in behalf of an individual who shares liability with a Chapter 13 debtor does not apply if (1) the individual became liable or gave security in the ordinary course of his business, or (2) the case is closed, or dismissed, or removed from Chapter 13.

C. Expanded relief from stay: As the automatic stay is expanded, so the relief from the expanded stay is also expanded. Relief may be granted for a stay under Chapter 13: (1) against *accommodation parties where the property* that gave rise to the debt was *actually received by that party rather than the principal debtor*, (2) to the extent that the plan proposed by the debtor *does not propose to pay a claim in full*, and (3) if the creditor can demonstrate that it *will be irreparably harmed* by its continuation.

IV. TRUSTEE — § 1302

A. Appointment of trustees: Trustees are appointed by the United States Trustee in all Chapter 13 cases. A *"standing trustee"* is a trustee who is appointed to serve for all Chapter 12 and 13 cases filed in a given region.

B. Duties of trustee — § 1302(b): Although not specifically stated in Chapter 13, there is general agreement that the Chapter 13 trustee has the powers given in the Code to trustees generally. However, the duties of a Chapter 13 trustee are not as significant as those of a trustee in Chapter 7 or 11.

1. **Duties prescribed by Chapter 7:** The Chapter 13 trustee performs the duties assigned to a Chapter 7 trustee, *except* for the duties to liquidate the estate, file tax returns, and submit regular periodic reports for the operation of a business.

2. **Duty to distribute payments:** The receipt and distribution of funds to be paid to creditors is generally considered to be the most important Chapter 13 trustee duty. The debtor must begin payments under the plan within 30 days after the plan is filed. Payments by the debtor must be retained by the trustee until the plan is either confirmed or denied. Where business relationships dictate, the plan may provide that the debtor make payments directly to creditors.

3. **Other duties:** The trustee, consistent with its overseer duties, must appear and be heard at hearings that concern the value of property subject to a lien, the confirmation of

the plan, and, where applicable, the modification of the plan. If the Chapter 13 debtor is engaged in a business, the trustee also investigates the business and files reports that relate to the investigation. The trustee must ensure that the debtor make timely payments under the plan.

V.   RIGHTS AND POWERS OF DEBTOR — §§ 1303 and 1304

A.   General powers: The debtor is given most of the rights and powers of a trustee concerning the use, sale, or lease of estate property.

B.   Debtor operating business: The debtor may operate his own business, but is specifically subject to the limitations placed upon a trustee with regard to the use, sale or lease of property in order to obtain credit. The duty to file tax and other reports is assigned to the Chapter 13 debtor operating his own business.

VI.   POSTPETITION CLAIMS — § 1305

A.   Additional postpetition claims: In addition to postpetition claims that are generally available in bankruptcy cases, there are two additional types of postpetition claims available in Chapter 13 cases. *Taxes that become payable while a Chapter 13 case is pending are allowable. Also, a claim may be filed for consumer debt arising after the order for relief for property or services that are necessary for the debtor's performance under Chapter 13.*

B.   Allowance of postpetition claims: Unlike prepetition claims, a postpetition claim must first be allowed before it can be included in a Chapter 13 plan. If a postpetition claim has not been allowed, it cannot be included in the Chapter 13 plan and, if not provided for in the plan, it cannot be discharged.

VII.   PROPERTY OF THE ESTATE — § 1306

A.   Debtor retains possession: *Property of the estate* in Chapter 13 includes *all property acquired by the debtor after the petition is filed.* Most significantly, this includes income earned by the debtor while in bankruptcy. The debtor's income includes revenues from pension plans and Social Security benefits, unless the debtor elects to exempt such payments to the extent possible. Except as provided in a plan or in an order confirming a plan, the Chapter 13 debtor remains in possession of the estate.

VIII.   THE PLAN — §§ 1321 AND 1322

A.   Only the debtor may file a plan: Only the debtor may file a plan in Chapter 13. However, once a plan has been confirmed, it may be modified, if circumstances warrant, upon application by the debtor, the holder of an allowed claim, or the trustee.

B.   Term of plan: The normal period of a Chapter 13 plan is *three years*, but the bankruptcy court may, *for cause, approve plans that extend up to five years.* The courts will occasionally allow a period longer than three years where the debtor is trying to make relatively large payments to creditors, particularly when the debtor is faced with unusual problems, such as heavy medical expenses.

C.   Mandatory contents of plan: Again, in contrast to Chapter 11 but consistent with Chapter 12, the Chapter 13 plan gives the debtor maximum flexibility. The few elements that are required to be contained in a Chapter 13 plan are: (1) the *extent to which the debtor's future income will be subject to payments under the plan*, (2) provision for the *full payment of priority claims, unless the holder of such a claim agrees otherwise*, and (3) *if a plan classifies claims, that each claim within a class must receive the same treatment.*

D. Permissive contents of plan: There are ten items that are permitted to be included in a Chapter 13 plan.

1. **Designation of classes:** The debtor has the right to divide creditors into classes. Each class must contain similar claims. For administrative convenience, a plan may include a class of unrelated small claims. If classes are designated, the debtor cannot discriminate unfairly against any class.

2. **Modify the rights of secured or unsecured claimants:** The debtor has the right to change the rights of holders of secured and unsecured claims, *except as to the rights of the holder of a mortgage on real estate that (i) constitutes the debtor's principal residence, and (ii) whose final payment occurs after the period of the plan*. However, if a single mortgage document covers both the debtor's residence and other assets, the mortgage may be modified. Although Chapter 13 does not require that all claims be dealt with in the plan, a discharge will be granted only for claims dealt with by the plan, claims which are disallowed, and administrative claims.

3. **Curing or waiving of any default:** The plan may provide for curing of the debtor's default on an obligation and may also provide, in a proposal that will become firm when a plan is confirmed, for the waiver of a default by a creditor. By curing a default and resuming regular payments on a secured loan, the debtor is able to remain in possession of the collateral (e.g., a car or a home).

   a. **Curing of default on home mortgage:** The curing of a default on a mortgage of the debtor's principal residence is not considered to be a modification of a home mortgage. A default on the mortgage covering a debtor's principal residence may be cured at least until such time as the residence is sold at a foreclosure sale that is conducted in accordance with applicable nonbankruptcy law. If a particular state law provides a longer cure period, such as a redemption period after the foreclosure sale, the debtor may avail himself of that state law. Interest amounts owing because of the default, such as interest on mortgage arrearages or other late charges and fees, will be paid in accordance with the underlying agreement and applicable nonbankruptcy law.

4. **Arrange timing of payments:** The debtor has the right to arrange the timing of payments, which gives the debtor the flexibility to create the most feasible method of payment.

5. **Debts that extend beyond plan period:** The debtor has the right to cure existing defaults on debts that extend beyond the plan period, the right to maintain regular payments during the period the plan is in effect, and the right to continue under such obligations after the plan expires. Most commonly, this provision is applicable to home mortgages, which typically extend beyond the usual plan period of three years and even the maximum plan period of five years. This provision does not grant the power to modify obligations, only to cure them or to continue under them (*supra.*)

6. **Payment of postpetition claims:** This provision allows the debtor to provide for the payment of allowed postpetition claims.

7. **Assumption, rejection, or assignment of executory contracts:** This provision allows for the assumption, rejection, or assignment of executory contracts and unexpired leases.

8. **Sources of payment:** This provision allows the plan to provide for payment of a claim from property of the estate, or from property of the debtor that is outside the estate (for example, from exempted property). Most payments are made from the debtor's postpetition income, which is made a part of the estate.

9. **Vesting of estate upon confirmation:** This provision allows the plan, upon its confirmation or at a later point, to vest the property of the estate in the debtor or another entity. Where the debtor's future income is an expected source for plan payments, the

plan will normally provide that the income remains as part of the estate and will be paid to the trustee for distribution.

10. Other provisions: The tenth and final provision states that the plan may include other appropriate provisions.

IX. CONFIRMATION — §§ 1324, 1325

A. Confirmation hearing — § 1324: After notice, the court will hold a confirmation hearing on the Chapter 13 plan. At the hearing, the plan will be reviewed to establish whether it conforms to the prerequisites for confirmation. Parties in interest may make objections to the plan, which will be considered by the judge in the confirmation process.

B. Confirmation — § 1325: The bankruptcy court will confirm the Chapter 13 plan provided it complies with the following six factors.

   1. Compliance with the Code: The plan must comply with the dictates of Chapter 13 and the Code.

   2. Fees paid: Any charges required to be paid prior to confirmation must have been paid.

   3. Good faith and legality: The plan must be proposed in good faith and not by any means forbidden by law. At a minimum, good faith requires that the plan be based on accurate information.

   4. "Best interests of creditor" test: As was the case in Chapters 11 and 12, a plan will be confirmed only if it can be demonstrated that the creditors will receive at least as much as they would receive under a Chapter 7 liquidation.

   5. Protection of secured creditors: Since secured creditors do not vote on Chapter 13 plans, their property interests must be protected. The rights of secured creditors are protected by one of the following three alternatives: (1) the creditor may simply accept the plan, (2) the creditor may retain its lien and receive property under the plan with a present value as of the effective date at least equal to its allowed claim, or (3) the debtor may surrender the secured property to the creditor.

   6. Ability to pay: The sixth requirement is that the court be satisfied that the debtor will be able to make the payments scheduled under the plan.

C. Objections to confirmation: If an *unsecured creditor objects* to confirmation, the court cannot approve the plan unless one of the following two tests is met: (1) as of the date of the plan, *the value of the property to be distributed on account of the objecting claim is not less than the amount of the claim; or* (2) the plan provides that *all of the debtor's projected "disposable income" for three years will be applied to payments under the plan.* "Disposable income" is defined to mean whatever income is left over after personal and business requirements are met and up to 15 percent of the debtor's gross income is contributed to charity.

X. PLAN PAYMENTS — § 1326

A. When payments begin: If and when the plan is confirmed, the trustee begins making payment to creditors as soon as practicable; if confirmation is denied, payments are returned to the debtor after deduction for any allowed administrative claims.

B. Direct payment to trustee: After a plan is confirmed, the court has the power to order anyone owing income to the debtor to pay all or part of that income directly to the trustee.

C. Administrative claims and fees: "Before or at the time of each payment to creditors, administrative costs and fees must be paid and, if a standing trustee has been appointed (but not a trustee selected otherwise), the fees of such trustee. Thus, payments cannot be made to other creditors, even other priority creditors, until such expenses are paid.

D. Trustee makes payments: Unless the plan or the court order confirming the plan provides otherwise, the trustee receives payment funds from the debtor and then makes payments to creditors.

XI. EFFECT OF CONFIRMATION — § 1327

A. Plan binds debtor and creditors: The confirmed plan binds the debtor and all creditors, regardless of whether a creditor has objected to or rejected the plan, or has been provided for by the plan.

B. Estate reverts to debtor: Unless the plan or the order confirming the plan provides otherwise, the confirmation of the plan vests all of the property of the estate in the debtor.

C. Property vests free of claims: Unless the plan or the order confirming the plan provides otherwise, the property of the estate reverts to the debtor free and clear of any claim or interest. However, if property is not part of the plan, existing interests, such as liens, remain according to their original terms.

XII. DISCHARGE — § 1328

A. Scope of discharge: As an inducement for an individual to prefer filing under Chapter 13 rather than Chapter 7, the discharge under Chapter 13 is broader.

    1. Debts provided for by plan: If the debt is provided for in some manner by the plan, even though not paid, it is discharged. This general rule does not apply to postpetition claims that have not been allowed because a proof of claim has not been filed.

    2. Debts disallowed by § 502: Debts disallowed are discharged. To be disallowed, a proof of claim must be filed.

B. Exceptions from discharge:

    1. Debts extending beyond term of plan: *Debts whose payment terms are longer than the three to five-year period of a Chapter 13 plan are not discharged*; since they are not discharged, payments must be made as scheduled after the plan terminates.

    2. Exceptions under § 523: Family obligations, educational loans, and drunk driving obligations are excepted from a Chapter 13 discharge. By contrast, there are many additional exceptions from a Chapter 7 discharge.

    3. Restitution obligations: Restitution obligations included in a criminal sentence are not discharged.

C. Types of discharge: A Chapter 13 discharge occurs upon completion of payments under the plan. If payments have not been completed, a *hardship discharge* may be obtained provided (1) the *debtor cannot be blamed* for the failure, (2) the value of the *distributions actually made* to unsecured creditors as of the effective date (discounted back from time of payment) is *not less than what would have been received under a Chapter 7 liquidation*, and (3) *modification of the plan is not practicable*.

CHAPTER 14

JURISDICTION AND VENUE

I. JURISDICTION OF DISTRICT COURTS — 28 U.S.C. § 1334

A. Jurisdiction in the district courts: *Original jurisdiction with respect to bankruptcy matters resides in the district courts*, which are empowered to refer cases and proceedings to the bankruptcy judges. A *case is the adjudication of a bankruptcy filing* under Chapter 7, 9, 11, 12, 13, or § 304. A *proceeding is the adjudication of a specific dispute* that arises within a case. Although original and exclusive jurisdiction of all *bankruptcy cases* is given to the United States district courts, the district courts also have *original, but not exclusive*, jurisdiction over all *civil proceedings* arising under title 11, or arising in or related to cases under title 11. *State courts* may have concurrent jurisdiction over *proceedings*.

B. **Abstention:** The district court may abstain from *hearing a proceeding* arising under title 11, or arising in or related to a case under title 11. This provision is to *allow for abstention where, in the interests of justice, a matter is better handled in another court.* With respect to proceedings that are only related to cases under title 11 (as contrasted with proceedings arising under or arising in cases under title 11), conditions are set forth under which the court must abstain.

C. **State court jurisdiction over proceedings:** The *concurrent jurisdiction of a state court* to hear and determine a *bankruptcy proceeding* depends entirely upon the jurisdictional powers conferred on it by state law. As noted, the word "proceedings" is used to cover all disputes that may arise in a bankruptcy case.

II. JURISDICTION OF BANKRUPTCY COURTS — 28 U.S.C. § 151

A. **Status of bankruptcy courts:** Bankruptcy courts are established as units of the district courts. Bankruptcy judges, who serve as judicial officers of the district courts, are appointed by the circuit courts of appeals.

   1. **Referral of bankruptcy cases to bankruptcy courts:** The district courts, with their original and exclusive jurisdiction of bankruptcy cases, are empowered to provide that all Title 11 cases and all proceedings "arising under Title 11 or arising in or related to a case under Title 11" be referred to the bankruptcy judges. All district courts have adopted rules of referral.

   2. **Jury trials:** If the right to a *jury trial applies to a proceeding that a bankruptcy judge is empowered to hear*, whether by the Constitution or by statute, a jury trial may be conducted provided that the judge is empowered by the district court to do so and that express consent is given by the parties.

B. **Bankruptcy cases; "core" and "non-core" proceedings — 28 U.S.C. § 157:** A bankruptcy judge is empowered to hear and determine all title 11 cases and all proceedings defined as "core."

   1. **"Core" proceedings:** To be considered "core," an *issue* will generally deal, directly or indirectly, with the proper allocation of the bankruptcy estate or with the enforcement of a provision of the Code. In essence, most of the proceedings that will arise in a bankruptcy case are defined by Congress as core. These include such matters as the allowance of claims and the liquidation of property. Also considered core are issues which an adverse party has referred to the bankruptcy court's jurisdiction; e.g., the making of a claim gives the court jurisdiction over counterclaims.

   2. **"Non-core" proceedings:** *A bankruptcy judge may hear "non-core" proceedings but may not make a binding decision unless the parties consent.* If they do not consent, the judge may only refer his proposed findings of fact and conclusions of law to the district court.

III. VENUE — 28 U.S.C. § 1408

A. **Venue for cases:** The basic venue rule is that bankruptcy *cases must be brought in the district in which the domicile, residence, principal United States place of business, or principal United States assets were located for 180 days before the case was begun*. If there is a case pending concerning an affiliate, general partner, or partnership of the debtor, the case may be moved to the district court of the pending case.

B. **Venue for proceedings**: A ***proceeding*** may be brought in the district court where the case controlling the proceeding is pending. However, if the bankruptcy estate is attempting to recover a money judgment or property worth less than $1,000 or a consumer debt of less than $5,000, it must proceed in the district court where the defendant resides.

C. **Cases in the wrong district**: If a case is brought in the wrong district, it may be heard where brought if in the interests of justice and for the convenience of the parties.

D. **Cases in the right district**: Even if a case is brought in the right district, a court may transfer it to another district in the interests of justice or for the convenience of the parties.

C
A
P
S
U
L
E

S
U
M
M
A
R
Y

CHAPTER 1
SOURCES OF BANKRUPTCY LAW

I.   THE ORIGINS OF BANKRUPTCY LAW

A. Early social need: From the time that caveman Zog said to his friend Gub, "I'm sorry, but I'm out of shells. May I pay you when I'm able?" there was a need for a bankruptcy law. Society had to provide a structure for the possibility that Zog would remain in short supply. Bankruptcy laws, in one form or another, are among our earliest recorded statutes.

1. **Definition:** The word "bankruptcy" is derived from the Old Italian "banca" meaning bank or, more generally, place of business, and the Latin "ruptus" meaning broken. Thus, in its modern usage it means that one's place of business is broken.

2. **Debtor treated as scoundrel:** Early bankruptcy laws cast the debtor as a scoundrel. He had not paid his obligations and had to be punished. The Roman Twelve Tables (451-450 B.C.) required that a debtor who had not paid his creditors be brought before the court. The Tables continued:

   > when a defendant after thirty days have elapsed, is brought into court a second time by the plaintiff, and does not satisfy the judgment . . . the plaintiff, after the debtor has been delivered up to him, can take the latter with him and bind him or place him in fetters; provided his chains are not of more than fifteen pounds weight; he can, however, place him in others which are lighter if he desires to do so. . . . After he has been kept in chains for sixty days, . . . he shall be condemned to be reduced to slavery by him to whom he was delivered up; or, if the latter prefers, he can be sold beyond the Tiber. . . . Where a party is delivered up to several persons, on account of his debt . . . they shall be permitted to divide their debtor into different parts, if they desire to do so, and if any one of them should, by the division, obtain more or less than he is entitled to, he shall not be responsible.

3. **Evolution of less draconian measures:** This draconian approach to the defaulting debtor was considered extreme even by the Romans and evolved over the course of centuries into more "civilized" practices like debtor's prison, indentured servitude and ultimately liquidation of the debtor's assets for the benefit of creditors.

4. **Pro-creditor approach until recent times:** An extreme pro-creditor approach exemplified bankruptcy law well into the eighteenth century.

II. MODERN LAW OF BANKRUPTCY

A. Sympathy for debtor: The more modern bankruptcy laws are increasingly based upon the viewpoint that, while the creditors may indeed have been wronged, the bankrupt is deserving at least of sympathy and help.

    1. Balancing needs of creditor and debtor: Through the nineteenth and twentieth centuries, the industrialized world modified its bankruptcy laws so that those laws now typically balance the needs of the debtor against those of the creditor.

    2. Fresh start for debtor: *Rehabilitation, or a "fresh start"* as we typically express it, has become *a central part of the modern bankruptcy statute*. The United States has led the way among the major commercial nations in this evolution. A 1784 New York State statute enabled those imprisoned for debt to obtain their release upon turning their assets over to their creditors and allowed them to keep "the necessary wearing apparel and bedding of the said debtor and of his wife and children."

B. U.S. laws more debtor oriented: The United States bankruptcy laws today are more debtor-oriented than those in most of the rest of the world.

    1. Creditor as problem: It is not unfair to say that we now recognize the extension of credit by the creditor as part of the problem.

        a. "Debt" encouraged: Debt has become a product that is marketed and pushed as forcefully as soap. Credit cards, borrowings on home equity and other forms of consumer debt are major businesses and are widely advertised.

        b. Excess debt: In many instances, the debtor is influenced to contract more debt than he can handle.

    2. Debt as core social ingredient: Debt is, of course, also widely perceived as a core ingredient of a credit society.

        a. Sustaining industry: Consumer debt sustains major industries: automobiles and retailing, to name just two.

        b. No longer evil: A consumer is no longer considered evil for incurring debt that may be hard to repay. He is part of a larger commercial system.

III. BANKRUPTCY POWER UNDER THE CONSTITUTION

A. Bankruptcy law under federal power: The Constitutional Convention gave the federal government the power to write bankruptcy laws.

1. **Constitutional provision:** The bankruptcy power appears in Article I, Section 8 of the Constitution — "The Congress shall have Power...to establish... uniform Laws on the subject of Bankruptcies throughout the United States."

2. **Meaning of "bankruptcy":** This authorization did not, however, answer a fundamental question: what did the framers mean by "Bankruptcies," a word with at best a vague meaning, especially at the time of the Convention.

   a. **Reorganize debts?** Among the questions left unanswered was: Did Congress have the power to reorganize debts, or only to liquidate them?

   b. **Cover consumers?** Were consumers to be covered, or only businesses, as was the case in most bankruptcy laws before the Constitution?

   c. **Include voluntary bankruptcy?** Was voluntary bankruptcy included, or only the involuntary type known to earlier legal systems?

3. **Interpretation left to Congress:** Courts have generally left the process of definition to Congress and abided by Congress' judgment. Occasionally, as we shall see, the Supreme Court has restrained Congress where other Constitutional policies have seemed more important.

4. **Why federal preemption?:** It is difficult to establish why the convention gave authority over bankruptcy law to the federal government. After all, the obligations that cause the debtor's problems are generally incurred under state law. Some authorities even speculate that the financial problems of the delegates to the Convention had something to do with this.

   a. **Priority over state law:** It is clear, however, that the federal law of bankruptcy, with its support in the Constitution, preempts inconsistent state law.

   b. **Resolving Constitutional conflicts:** Because bankruptcy power in the Constitution exists alongside and sometimes conflicts with other Constitutional dictates, including the rights to property contained in the Fifth and Fourteenth Amendments and the Commerce Clause, the Supreme Court is forced from time to time to establish federal rules of priority when these provisions clash.

B. Legislative history: Bankruptcy law has seen a steady development from legislation offering temporary relief to the present sophisticated blanket of protection.

1. **Merchants covered first:** The first federal statute enacted under the bankruptcy power became law in 1800. It covered only merchants, and the only form of bankruptcy allowed was of the involuntary sort — i.e. his creditors could force a merchant into bankruptcy. The law was written to expire in 1805 and in fact was repealed in 1803.

2. **Voluntary filing introduced:** The next federal bankruptcy law was not enacted until 1841. It provided for voluntary as well as involuntary bankruptcies, covered nonmerchants as well as merchants and was repealed after only two years.

3. **Civil War prompts new legislation:** The third bankruptcy law was enacted in 1867 as a result of economic problems following the Civil War. It was a considerably more sophisticated statute, introducing a number of the ideas still retained today. It was repealed in 1878.

4. **First permanent statute—Chandler Act Amendment:** After 1878, the country went for twenty years without a federal bankruptcy law. Congress then enacted (in 1898) a statute which established bankruptcy law as a permanent part of our federal legal structure. The 1898 statute was amended by the Chandler Act in 1934. This was the last major bankruptcy enactment until the present Code. (For a history of federal bankruptcy law from 1898 to the present, see Jonathan C. Rose, *Shortsightedness Plagues Bankruptcy Courts' History,* Legal Times, Feb. 27, 1984, p. 13.)

C. The "Code" (Title 11 U.S.C.): In 1978, after years of study, Congress replaced the then-existing bankruptcy law with the law that exists today. Unchanged since in its essential conception and structure, the law is codified as Title 11 of the United States Code.

1. **Known as the "Code":** For convenience, we generally refer to the pre-1978 law as the "Act" and today's law as the "Code."

2. **Studies leading to the Code:** The studies leading to the Code stressed three major events that changed our views of bankruptcy law after the 1934 Chandler Act:

   a. **The Uniform Commercial Code:** The Uniform Commercial Code which fundamentally changed the law of secured transactions (in Article 9), occurred in the 1950s. The Bankruptcy Code which followed embodied a treatment of secured creditors that reflected the policies of the U.C.C.

    b. Consumer credit: The monumental growth in consumer credit after 1934 introduced a new body of debtors. Many of the provisions in the new Code were developed with these debtors in mind.

    c. Social acceptance of bankruptcy: Increasingly, the American public had grown to accept the debtor in bankruptcy as a sympathetic figure.

        i. Voluntary filings "invited": The essentially unlimited invitation to debtors to file in "voluntary" bankruptcies reflected the public's acceptance of bankruptcy as a social need.

        ii. Use of term "debtor": The use in the Code of the term "debtor" instead of the term "bankrupt" reflected this new attitude.

D. Amendments after 1978: The Code has been significantly amended four times since 1978:

    1. 1984 Amendments: The 1984 amendments were enacted to cure several problems.

        a. Jurisdictional problems: Before the 1984 amendments, it was not clear how jurisdiction over certain bankruptcy issues was divided between the district courts and the bankruptcy judges. (For a full discussion of this problem, see Chapter 14 dealing with Jurisdiction and Venue, *infra*, p. 249.) The 1984 amendments dealt in part with this problem.

        b. Collective bargaining issues: Until the 1984 Amendment, the bankruptcy courts exercised the power to reject existing collective bargaining agreements. The 1984 Amendment created a mini-collective bargaining procedure which enables a debtor-employer to renegotiate an existing agreement with his employees on the best possible terms for both parties, consistent with the bankruptcy reorganization. (See discussion of the *Bildisco* case, *infra*, p. 191.)

        c. Grain storage and fish processing: The 1984 Amendments dealt with specialized problems of grain storage and fish processing.

        d. Temper benefits to debtors: Creditor interests had argued that the 1978 Code leaned too heavily in favor of debtors. The

1984 Amendments attempted to readjust the balance between creditor and debtor.

2. **1986 Amendments – Family Farmers and United States Trustees:** The 1986 Amendments created a new Chapter 12 of the Code for filings by family farmers and also made permanent the role of the United States Trustee.

   a. **Relief for family farmer**: To provide for the special needs of the small family farmer, which were aggravated in the early 1980s by a rise in production costs and a reduction in commodity prices, Congress created a new chapter of the Code entitled Chapter 12. The chapter was originally meant to lapse in 1993, but has now been extended until 1998. (For a discussion of filing under Chapter 12 of the Code, see **Filing under Chapter 12,** *infra,* p. 221.)

   b. **Permanent office of United States Trustee:** Until 1986, the office of United States Trustee in bankruptcy cases had been an experiment designed to relieve bankruptcy judges of administrative duties in supervising bankruptcy cases. The 1986 Amendments made the office of United States Trustee a permanent fixture in bankruptcy administration. (For a discussion of the United States Trustee, see *infra,* pp. 7, 68.)

3. **1990 Amendments; savings and loan issues:** Largely as a result of the massive savings and loan failures throughout the 1980s, the Code was amended again in 1990. The changes reduced the benefits that persons involved in the S&L and bank frauds could obtain by using the Code.

4. **1994 Amendments; creditor benefits:** Reacting to an accumulating body of evidence that creditors' rights were unduly diminished by the 1978 Bankruptcy Code, Congress amended the Code in many respects in 1994, generally to enhance the collectability of consumer obligations.

5. **Potential Amendments:** As of August 2001, other amendments to the Code are being discussed in Congress. Should they be enacted, two major issues with which they will probably deal are:

   a. **International Insolvencies**: As commercial relationships that cross international borders become more common, the possibility becomes increasingly likely of a bankruptcy or equivalent insolvency proceeding affecting interests in more than one country. The problems can be perceived immediately by imagining a single corporation with assets in two countries that elects bankruptcy proceedings. The problems are largely insoluble as a matter of law; therefore such international situations have been resolved through agreements among the parties (usually called Concordats). The United Nations Commission on International Trade Law ("UNCITRAL") has accepted responsibility for approaching this problem, and, in May 1997, adopted a Model Law on Cross-Border Insolvency suggesting many approaches that can be taken. The Model Law has not been incorporated into the law of any country, but will undoubtedly serve as a reference as problems arise.

In the United States, Congress has generally looked favorably upon the Model Law and is considering some of its provisions as amendments to §304 of the Code. Among its provisions will probably be a formula for selection of the country that will supply the basic concepts in bankruptcy law and a guide for cooperation between the courts of different countries.

b. **Substantial abuse of Chapter 7:** Section 707(b) now provides that a court may "dismiss a case filed by an individual debtor under (Chapter 7) whose debts are primarily consumer debts if it finds that the granting of relief would be a substantial abuse of the provisions of (Chapter 7)." Problems in defining "substantial abuse" as well as the practical difficulties in applying the essentially discretionary test in some million-and-a-half cases have led Congress to consider a tighter test. A proposed amendment may invoke a dismissal in situations where a debtor's income exceeds necessary expenses by more than a specified percentage, a so-called "means test".

IV. OTHER STATUTES AFFECTING THE BANKRUPTCY CODE

A. **Procedural and administrative matters:** U.S.C., Title 28, deals with federal procedure generally. Some of its provisions cover bankruptcy cases.

1. **Jurisdiction and venue:** The jurisdiction and venue of the district and bankruptcy courts and of the bankruptcy judges are controlled by the provisions of Title 28. We discuss these provisions in detail in Chapter 14, "Jurisdiction and Venue," (*infra*, p. 249).

B. **The United States Trustee:** Title 28, Chapter 39, establishes a bankruptcy court officer called the United States Trustee.

1. **Office of Trustee made permanent:** The office of United States Trustee was created on an experimental basis in several federal districts in 1978. In 1986, the office of Trustee was established in all

districts except Alabama and North Carolina and was made permanent.

2. **Role of Trustee:**   Basically, the United States Trustee is assigned the job of supervising the administration of all cases under the Code.

   a. **Help for bankruptcy judges:**   The office of Trustee is designed to free the bankruptcy judges from ministerial duties and to leave them more time for judicial functions.

   b. **Supervision over trustees appointed in cases:**   In most bankruptcy cases, a trustee is appointed by the bankruptcy judge to help administer the estate (*infra*, p. 65). The United States Trustee is assigned general supervision over these case-by-case trustees.

   c. **Specific duties:**   Several sections of the Code assign specific duties to the United States Trustee. We will refer to these duties as they become relevant.

C. **Title 18— criminal sanctions:**   Title 18, Chapter 9 describes acts relating to bankruptcy cases that constitute federal crimes.

1. **Crimes of the debtor:**   Acts defined in Title 18 as constituting crimes of a debtor in bankruptcy are carried over in the Code as acts that will prevent or limit a discharge of obligations that would otherwise be granted. (Code § 726 and § 523). We will not discuss the bankruptcy crimes in this book except as they affect discharges.

V. THE BANKRUPTCY RULES AND OFFICIAL BANKRUPTCY FORMS

A. **Bankruptcy rules:**   Supplementing the Code are the Bankruptcy Rules.

1. **Authority in Supreme Court:**   The Supreme Court has the power to prescribe by general rules "the forms of process, writs, pleadings and motions, and the practice and procedure in cases" under the Code (28 U.S.C. § 2075).

2. **References to FRCP:**   The Court's Bankruptcy Rules provide supporting administrative details for the administration of the Code. In many cases dealing with procedure in the bankruptcy courts, the Bankruptcy Rules simply adopt and refer to the Federal Rules of Civil Procedure.

3. **Local district court rules:**   Rule 9029 authorizes each district court to provide its own local rules of bankruptcy. Thus, both the

Federal Bankruptcy Rules and local court rules operate to guide bankruptcy cases.

B. Steps for Rule adoption: The Bankruptcy Rules are written and proposed in the first instance by the Judicial Conference of the United States. The Supreme Court then reports the Rules to Congress. Under 28 U.S.C. § 2075, Congress has 90 days in which to make its comments. The most recent Rules were reported by the Supreme Court on April 30, 1991 and Congress made no comment.

C. Bankruptcy forms: The Bankruptcy Rules contain a set of forms for use in bankruptcy cases. The forms are created under Rule 9009 and may be modified as necessary for particular situations.

  1. Use of forms: The forms not only provide procedural guidance but are useful in interpreting statutory language. For example, they help us to understand what is meant by the term "statement of financial affairs," which must be produced by a debtor under Code § 521 (see *infra*, p. 34.)

VI. RELATIONSHIP OF FEDERAL AND STATE LAWS

A. State statutes—assignments for benefit of creditors: All states have some statutory scheme for dealing with insolvent entities. Often called "assignments for the benefit of creditors," these statutes may, in their simplest form, call for the sale of an insolvent debtor's assets, with the proceeds going to creditors.

  1. Sale followed by liquidation: Normally, in the case of a corporate or partnership debtor, the sale will be followed by liquidation.

   a. Individual debtor remains liable: However, an individual debtor cannot secure a discharge from debt in a state proceeding and will typically remain subject to whatever debts are left after sale of his assets.

   b. Limits on state authority: Under the Constitution, a state cannot enact a law to discharge a contract. Unless preempted by federal law, a state can enact laws that operate to discharge other types of obligations.

B. Federal bankruptcy supremacy: With its enactment of the first enduring bankruptcy law in 1898 (*supra*, p. 4), the federal government effectively preempted any state action on bankruptcy proceedings. This preemption has been continued and expanded under the various amendments to the bankruptcy laws.

1. **Related state laws:** Despite this federal preemption, the individual states have continued to enact laws dealing with *related* topics, such as assignments for the benefit of creditors.

2. **Encroachments on federal law:** As state laws encroach on provisions of the federal Code, they become subject to challenges as to their validity under principles of federal preemption. If Michigan, for example, were to pass a statute containing a section providing for discharge of the obligations of a debtor, it would stand a high risk of violating the Code and being declared void. Accordingly, no state today has attempted to give debtors a discharge from debt.

C. **Contrast with "dormant Commerce Clause":** It is useful to contrast the Bankruptcy Clause in Article I, Section 8, Clause 4 of the United States Constitution (*supra*, p. 3), with the Commerce Clause in Article I, Section 8, Clause 3.

1. **State power over commerce:** Under the law developed in interpreting the "dormant" Commerce Clause, a state may not enact *any* law unduly interfering with interstate commerce.

2. **State power over insolvency:** Under the Bankruptcy Clause, a state may enact laws affecting insolvency so long as the laws do not interfere with the Code.

VII. POLICIES OF BANKRUPTCY LAW

A. **Basic problems and policies:** As we approach our study of the Code, we need to review the basic policies and problems which had to be met in the development of bankruptcy law.

1. **Balance between creditors and debtors:** In the short run, and usually in the long run as well, everything kept by a debtor represents something taken from a creditor. Every protection accorded a debtor represents a reduction in protection to a creditor. How are the lines to be drawn and a proper balance created?

2. **Contrast between dissolution and reorganization:** We must strike a balance between providing for liquidation and dissolution on the one hand and encouraging reorganization and relief on the other.

   a. **Liquidation a short-term solution:** Liquidation and dissolution, the traditional bankruptcy approach, represent a short-term solution.

   b. **Reorganization as long-term promise:** Reorganization, accompanied by relief from, or reduction in or extension of debts, represents the promise of something in the future. It also helps to save an entity as a productive ingredient of the society. Should a bankruptcy law encourage reorganization? If so, how much? In what ways?

3. **Requirements of a credit-driven society — providing a fresh start:** Every effort to discharge a debtor from her obligations weakens the credit structure of a commercial society. Credit will not be extended unless there is a reasonable likelihood that it will be repaid, not escaped from through bankruptcy. When bankruptcy filings increase, credit decreases. Our sympathy for debtors and our inclination to give them a fresh start must be balanced with society's other needs, especially the need to maintain a viable credit structure.

4. **An ever-swinging pendulum:** Through the evolution of the Code in Congress, its interpretation in the courts and its development in the practice of bankruptcy law, we see an ever-moving pendulum swinging between choices, in constant search for the right balance between competing interests.

CHAPTER 2

THE BANKRUPTCY CODE: AN OVERVIEW

I. EQUITABLE BASE OF THE BANKRUPTCY CODE

A. Bankruptcy falls under equity jurisprudence: *"[C]ourts of bankruptcy are essentially courts of equity*, and their proceedings inherently proceedings in equity." *Local Loan Co. v. Hunt*, 292 U.S. 234, 240 (1934). The themes of equitable jurisprudence underlie the Bankruptcy Code.

B. Courts prevent abuses: In addition to the commitment to equity that attaches to the bankruptcy courts through their placement in the federal court system, the courts have an independent tradition that impels them to prevent abuse of the bankruptcy process.

C. Concern with good faith: A duty to act in good faith is imposed under certain provisions of the Code (as, for example, the duty to propose a Chapter 11 plan in good faith under Code § 1129(a)(3)). And the bankruptcy courts regard the exercise of good faith as a pervasive underlying requirement. This inherent discretionary attitude causes the courts to examine all transactions for their integrity, motives and general good faith as prerequisites for granting bankruptcy relief.

Example: Mortgaged property, part of a decedent's estate, had been before the state courts for ten years, and the mortgagee finally obtained a judgment of foreclosure. On March 10, title to the property was in an estate which was ineligible for bankruptcy. On that same day, a partnership was formed which took title to the property from the estate. Since a partnership is eligible for bankruptcy, it filed a petition on the next day in order to resume litigating about the property in the new court. The bankruptcy court refused to accept the case, applying its general equitable powers to find that the petition was not filed in good faith. *Matter of Jack Hemp Associates*, 20 B.R. 412 (Bkrtcy. S.D.N.Y. 1982).

II. STRUCTURE OF BANKRUPTCY CODE

A. Organized in odd-numbered Chapters: To work with the Code, one needs an understanding of its basic structure. With the one exception of Chapter 12 (deriving from the 1986 amendments), the Code is organized only in chapters with odd numbers. This structure retains references to bankruptcy cases that had already become familiar to the bankruptcy bar.

B. Chapters 1, 3, 5 — general application to other chapters: The first three chapters of the Code establish a series of general rules that apply to filings under the latter five chapters. The first three chapters are:

1. **Chapter 1 – definitions:** This chapter contains definitions and some basic rules of construction.

2. **Chapter 3 – administration of cases:**   This chapter deals with the administration of a bankruptcy case.

3. **Chapter 5 – defining the major "players":**   This chapter establishes rules relating to the major bankruptcy players — creditors, the debtor and the estate.

C. Chapters 7, 9, 11, 12 & 13 — cases which can be "filed":   There are five basic types of bankruptcy cases provided for by the Code. The cases are traditionally given the names of the chapters that describe them.

1. **Chapter 7 cases – liquidation cases:**   This chapter deals with liquidation of the debtor and the distribution of its assets among its creditors.

    a. **Dissolution:**   In the case of corporate or partnership debtors, liquidation under the code is followed by dissolution under state law.

    b. **Fresh start:**   In the case of individual debtors, liquidation is followed by discharge and a fresh start, free of most debts.

2. **Chapter 9 cases – municipalities:**   This chapter covers filings by municipalities which can no longer meet their debts.

3. **Chapter 11 – business reorganization:**   This chapter concentrates on business reorganizations. The debtor goes through a period of consolidation and emerges with a reduced debt load and a renewed existence.

4. **Chapter 12 – family farmers:**   This chapter deals with filings by family farmers.

5. **Chapter 13 – consumer reorganizations:**   This chapter offers a simpler form of reorganization than Chapter 11. It is used principally by individuals with fixed incomes.

6. **Foreign proceedings; § 304 cases:**   The five basic "filing" chapters identify all the bankruptcy cases — unless we add cases under

§ 304. This section deals with a special kind of "case," usually an extension of a foreign proceeding, (*infra*).

III. DEFINITION OF DEBTOR

A. Debtor essential element of case: A bankruptcy case necessarily involves a "debtor." The term "debtor" in the Code replaces the designation "bankrupt" that had been in the Act and was considered to have a pejorative connotation.

B. Broad definitions of "debtor" and "person": A debtor is defined in Code § 101(13) as being a "person" (or a municipality) concerning whom a case has been commenced. "Person" is in turn defined in the section on definitions (41) to "include" an individual, partnership or corporation. (See Code definition of "includes", *infra*, p 20.)

C. United States connection required: Any person that resides or has a domicile, a place of business, or property in the United States, or a municipality, may be a "debtor". Thus, bankruptcy relief is deliberately made broadly available.

IV. CASES ANCILLARY TO FOREIGN PROCEEDINGS — § 304

A. Cases involving U.S. assets of foreign debtors: If a French automobile manufacturer declares bankruptcy in France and owns an American distributorship, the creditors of the French company, both in France and in the United States, may attempt to go after the assets of the American distributorship. A conflict may develop as to whether distribution of the American assets should be governed according to the laws of the foreign jurisdiction or of the United States. To avoid inequitable distribution of the United States assets, the protection of the Code may be sought by the foreign representative to assist in this resolution.

B. Application of § 304: § 304 provides a device for dealing with these American assets. A case under § 304 is called a "case ancillary to a foreign proceeding."

1. **Broad relief:** While not one of the five basic cases in bankruptcy (Chapters 7, 9, 11, 12, and 13, *supra*, p. 14), the § 304 case is nevertheless a form of "case." It is, however, less formalized than the basic five cases and does not necessarily draw from the general provisions of the first three chapters of the Code (*supra*, p. 14). Essentially, the bankruptcy court is empowered to choose any or none of the rest of the Code as it may decide — it is authorized to order any appropriate relief to the foreign debtor.

    2. Available only to foreign representative: Only a "foreign representative" may start a § 304 case. A foreign representative is defined in Code § 101(24) as the representative of the bankrupt estate in the foreign proceeding; it is essentially the foreign equivalent of our trustee.

        a. Not available to creditors or debtors: The debtor and the creditors may not start a § 304 case.

        b. Court's volition: Where sticky problems relating to foreign bankruptcies arise, United States courts have been known to suggest the use of § 304 on their own volition.

C. Unfettered power: The Code gives the bankruptcy judge virtually unfettered power to handle the United States assets as it sees fit, in order to "best assure an economical and expeditious administration" of the estate. It may enjoin other proceedings, stay the enforcement of judgments, order the turnover of property or, as noted, "order other appropriate relief."

D. Law and procedure drawn from cases: The guidelines for the courts in administering § 304 cases, in the absence of clear statutory direction, are being crafted through a series of cases.

    1. Role of U.S. court clearly "ancillary": Essentially, the courts increasingly perceive their roles as "ancillary" to the foreign proceeding. They attempt to assist the foreign proceeding rather than enforce the specific rules of the Code.

    2. Sometimes resort to Code: To the extent that the foreign law resembles the Code, the Court's task is easy, and they are likely to abide by the tests of foreign law. However, where foreign law is radically different from the Code, they may resort to the remedies of the Code in order to justify the reasonable expectations of United States creditors in the United States assets.

E. Other Chapters of Code available: The existence of property in the United States will support a full bankruptcy case in the U.S. courts. Thus, if the debtor itself, a creditor or even the foreign representative is dissatisfied with the course of the § 304 case, it may elect to file for relief under one of the five basic Chapters.

V.   GENERAL DEFINITIONS — § 101

A. Definitions in § 101: Code § 101 provides us with some 60 definitions. We will refer to some of them as they occur in our text. For the moment we will consider some definitions that apply throughout the text.

B. "Claim" — § 101(5): "Claim" is very broadly defined in order to include the greatest possible kinds of economic obligations by a debtor in a bankruptcy case. It means a right to payment "whether or not such right is reduced to judgment, liquidated, unliquidated, fixed, contingent, matured, unmatured, disputed, undisputed, legal, equitable, secured, or unsecured." Each of these has a distinct meaning and function.

Example 1: Creditor C lends Debtor D $1,000 on January 1 to be repaid in 10 equal installments of $100 each plus interest. D makes payment of the first two installments, after which he files in bankruptcy. C's claim against D at the time of the filing is for $800, even though the final eight installments are not yet due. Those last eight payments are "unmatured."

Example 2: D has guaranteed the debt of X to C. D files in bankruptcy. X still owes C the debt; there has been no default. Nevertheless, C has a claim against D for the "contingent" debt.

1. **Must be capable of reduction to money damages:** Because the Code is concerned with economic obligations rather than behavior, the definition of "claim" goes on to provide that a right to an equitable remedy for breach of performance is not a "claim" unless it can be translated into money damages.

   Example 1: D is enjoined by the State of Ohio from spilling any waste on its premises. Because D's responsibility to the State is too uncertain to be translated into money damages, it is not a claim. *State of Ohio v. Kovacs*, 469 U.S. 274 (1985).

   Example 2: Assume that while D was subject to injunction in the foregoing example, toxic waste was discovered on its premises. The property was taken away from D and turned over to a receiver who started to clean up the land. Under the law, D was obligated to reimburse the receiver for its expenses. D's obligation to the receiver is a "claim" since it can be expressed in money. Because the precise amount due was unknown at the time of bankruptcy — the claim is "unliquidated." *State of Ohio v. Kovacs, supra.*

2. **Relationship of "claim" and "interest":** The Code frequently refers to "interests" along with its references to "claims." (For example, Code § 501 talks of the filing of proofs of "claims or of interests".)

   a. **"Interests" not defined:** The word "interests" is not defined in the Code, but it is used to mean that relationship between the holder of the interest and the debtor which entitles the holder to assert the right or opportunity to receive a payment, though he may not be owed a debt.

b. **Common examples:** The most common example of *"an interest"* is the ***relationship between a common stockholder and a corporation***. Other examples of "interests" include the interest of a general or a limited partner in a partnership, and the interest of a proprietor in a sole proprietorship. 124 Congr.Rec.H. 11,093.

c. **Environmental Claims:** The time a claim is deemed to come into existence is one of the most important decisions in a bankruptcy case. If it arises before the petition is filed, the bankruptcy assets will be applied against it and what is left will be discharged. If it arises after the petition, it will be unaffected by the bankruptcy assets and will remain in existence without discharge. Environmental claims present unique problems. For example, if a drum of toxic waste is dumped into the Love Canal, does this alone give rise to a claim? It might, if the Comprehensive Environmental Response, Compensation and Liability Act of 1980 ("CERCLA") makes this act a violation. For a claim to arise, is it necessary for it actually to have been observed? These questions, while significant, have not been fully answered by the cases, and environmental claims continue to present problems.

C. **"Debt" — § 101(12):** A "debt" is the liability on a claim. If D owes C $1,000, C has a claim against D for $1,000; D has a debt to C of $1,000.

D. **"Insolvent" — § 101(32):** A debtor is insolvent if her debts exceed her assets. This is the so-called "balance sheet" test of insolvency. It does not always test the debtor's economic health fairly.

1. **Ability to earn:** For example, a debtor may be earning enough money to cover the current cost of her debts even though her debts may exceed her assets.

2. **Illiquidity:** Similarly, assets may exceed debts, but if the assets are "illiquid" (such as large tracts of land), there may be financial troubles.

3. **Code test of insolvency:** The Code does not always employ the balance sheet insolvency test. For example § 303(h) uses the alternate "equitable" test of insolvency to establish whether an involuntary bankruptcy may be begun. This test looks at the ability to pay current debts.

VI. RULES OF CONSTRUCTION — § 102

A. Necessary to understand other provisions: Following the definitions in § 101, § 102 provides some rules of construction. Most of the rules require explanation. They are necessary to our understanding of the other provisions of the Code.

B. Term "notice and hearing" does not require a hearing: The term "after notice and a hearing" requires notice but not necessarily a hearing. It's important to understand this rule because the requirement that some act be done only "after notice and a hearing" appears frequently throughout the Code.

1. **Notice must be "appropriate":**   Wherever notice is required, it must be "appropriate in the particular circumstances."

2. **Notice not always required:**   Not everyone involved in a case need receive notice of a proposed action; it's sufficient if those who will be particularly affected by the action are informed.

3. **Other exceptions to "hearing":**   While § 102(1) requires that there be an *opportunity for a hearing*, the hearing need not actually be held if it is not requested by a "party in interest" or if the court authorizes action without a hearing when there is not sufficient time or need.

4. **When hearing required:**   A hearing is required in some instances specified by particular provisions of the Code.

5. **Expedient for saving time and cost:**   The concept of permitting the court to act in most instances without the impediment of a hearing was inserted by Congress to economize the procedures of the bankruptcy court and not take up its time on matters not in dispute.

C. "Party in interest":   This term, mentioned *supra*, is also used frequently throughout the Code. This term is also not defined. It clearly includes the major Code players: the debtor, the creditors and the trustee. It may include third parties, and the court may pick, choose, and include others.

Example: A public utility was in bankruptcy. Two states, their attorneys general, an office of the consumer advocate representing electric consumers in one of the states, a business and industry association, and three citizens interest groups, all sought to appear as parties in interest. The court refused to grant "party in interest" status to any of them except to the one state within which the debtor provided its principal utility service. *In re Public Service Company of New Hampshire*, 17 B.C.D. 1330 (Bkrtcy. D.N.H. 1988).

D. Meaning of "includes":   § 102(3) tells us that use of the word "includes" in a definition means that all items falling in the same class or category are included in the definition.

Example: A corporation is defined as "including" certain types of businesses. A land trust, not specifically listed in the definition, attempted to elect bankruptcy under the Code. To accomplish this it had to be classified as a corporation. The court evaluated the nature of a land trust and decided that, because of its inert nature, it should not be deemed a corporation and, consequently, it was denied Chapter 11 relief. *In re Treasure Island Land Trust*, (Bkrtcy. M.D. Fla. 1980).

VII. BACKUP POWER OF COURT — § 105

A. Backup power of court generally: The bankruptcy courts and the district courts have extremely broad power under § 105 to "issue any order, process, or judgment that is necessary or appropriate to carry out the provisions" of the Code. The courts may do this on their own motion or on the motion of a party in interest.

B. Orders must carry out Code: The orders issued by the courts must be in aid of the scheme outlined by the Code. They must support the objectives described in the Code sections and not contradict them.

C. Good faith required: However, § 105 has been used to deny rights that are asserted under the Code by a proponent who acts without good faith. *Taylor v. Freeland & Kronz*, 112 S.Ct. 1644 (1992).

Example 1: A debtor learns that his employer is planning to fire him because he has declared bankruptcy. This act of the employer is prohibited by § 525. The court may issue an injunction against the employer specifically prohibiting the firing.

Example 2: The court is asked under § 105 to approve a fund set up by a debtor in Chapter 11 to aid needy employees who were terminated because of the bankruptcy. The court may not do this under § 105, because Chapter 11 has its own procedures to establish how corporate funds may be used. *Official Comm. of Equity Sec. Holders v. Mabey*, 382 F.2d 299 (4th Cir.), cert denied, 108 S.Ct. (1988).

D. Contempt rules: Whether § 105 gives the bankruptcy court the authority to issue contempt decrees against persons who have violated the Code or other orders of the court is in dispute among the circuits.

E. Status conference: Under § 105, the court may also hold a status conference regarding any case, or proceeding within a case, and issue any order it deems appropriate to ensure that the case is handled expeditiously and economically. For example, the court may set a date for the assumption or rejection of contracts (see § 365, *infra,* p. 114) set a date for the filing of a plan in a Chapter 11 case (see § 1121, *infra,* p. 197) or set a date by which acceptances of the plan shall be solicited (see § 1125, *infra,* p. 203).

VIII. WAIVER OF GOVERNMENTAL IMMUNITY — § 106

A. **Sovereign immunity from suits:** A sovereign state, and its subdivisions, may not generally be sued without its consent. § 106 is designed to provide prescribed waivers of this general rule as to bankruptcy proceedings.

B. **Congressional power to waive:** Clearly, Congress can waive immunity as to the federal government. Congress may also have the right to waive immunity on behalf of the states when dealing with bankruptcy issues, because the bankruptcy power is contained in the Constitution and thereby applies to both nation and state (*supra,* p. 3).

C. **Waiver of immunity:** Congress provided in 1994 that sovereign immunity is waived as to claims made under most of the significant sections of the Code (which are individually listed). These include § 362 (automatic stay, *infra,* p. 36) and § 544–§ 548 (the avoidance of pre-petition transfers, *infra,* pp. 117-123). Courts may hear and determine all issues in such cases. They may also award money but not punitive damages against governmental units under these sections.

> However, in *Seminole Tribe of Florida v. Florida*, 116 S. Ct. 1114 (1996), a case interpreting the 11th Amendment to the Constitution, the Supreme Court decided that Congress may ***not*** deprive the states of their immunity from suit in federal court actions by private citizens. The *Seminole* case was a 5-4 decision which arose under the Commerce Clause, and presumably its effect extends to cases under the Bankruptcy Code. Waivers of immunity under the Code, may, however, still apply to the states in suits in state courts. (Remember that federal district court jurisdiction under 28 U.S.C. § 1334(b) for civil proceedings is not exclusive; suits in state court involving bankruptcy proceedings — but not full bankruptcy cases — are recognized.)

> Since the *Seminole* decision, most courts, including three United States Courts of Appeals, have found that §106 does not have the effect of waiving the states' sovereign immunity. *Sacred Heart Hosp. of Norristown v. Pennsylvania*, 133 F.3d 237 (3d Cir.1998); *Schlossberg v. Maryland*, 119 F.3d 1140 (4th Cir. 1997); *Louisiana Dep't of Trans. and Dev. v. PNL Asset Mgmt. Co.*, 123 F. 3d 241 (5th Cir.

1997)

Actions against both federal and state governments will also be permitted where they voluntarily subject themselves to Bankruptcy Court jurisdiction, as in the following two situations:

1. **Counterclaims:** § 106(b) provides that, where a government has filed a claim in the bankruptcy, it has waived its sovereign immunity on any claim against it that arose out of the same transaction or occurrence as its claim (i.e., a compulsory counterclaim), even if the claim does not arise under one of the listed Code sections. A compulsory counterclaim is unlimited in amount and is based on the idea that the government, by filing its claim, has submitted itself to the jurisdiction of the bankruptcy court.

2. **Offsets:** Under § 106(c), if the government files a claims as creditor against the bankrupt estate, immunity is also waived on all "offsets" (i.e., claims against the government based on other transactions), but only up to the amount of the government's allowed claim.

IX. JURY TRIALS IN BANKRUPTCY COURTS

A. **Seventh Amendment Guarantee:** The Seventh Amendment to the Constitution guarantees trial by jury in "suits at common law." The Supreme Court has held that the bankruptcy courts are essentially courts of equity, not of law. *Katchen v. Landy*, 382, U.S. 323, 327 (1966). Where actions are essentially "legal" rather than "equitable" in their qualities, a jury trial has been held to be required by the Seventh Amendment. *Granfinanciera, S.A. v. Nordberg*, 492 U.S. 33 (1989). But, because bankruptcy courts are courts of limited jurisdiction, there has been great uncertainty as to whether bankruptcy courts could conduct jury trials.

1. **Voluntary submission to jurisdiction of the court:** No   jury trial is required under the Constitution in a proceeding held in the bankruptcy court where a creditor submits a claim against the estate and the representative for the estate brings an action against the creditor. By making the claim against the estate, the creditor subjects itself to the equitable powers of the bankruptcy court; the subsequent action is an integral part of the claims and allowance process conducted under the bankruptcy court's equity jurisdiction. *Langenkamp v. Culp*, 111 S. Ct. 330 (1990).

B. **Core vs. non-core proceedings:** Bankruptcy courts are empowered to hear not only *cases under title 11*, but also *core proceedings arising under title 11* (i.e., specific disputes that, by their nature, can only arise under the provisions of the Bankruptcy Code.) There is no right to a jury trial in core proceedings. The bankruptcy court may hear non-core proceedings, but, in these proceedings, unless the parties consent to a final judgment, the judge can only submit proposed findings of fact and proposed conclusions of law to the district court. (See discussion of 28 U.S.C. § 157 in Chapter 14, "Jurisdiction and Venue," *infra* p. 249.)

C. **Power of bankruptcy courts to conduct jury trials:** In the 1994 amendments to the Code, Congress defined certain circumstances under which bankruptcy judges are authorized to hold jury trials. Where a bankruptcy judge is hearing a non-core proceeding for which a jury trial is constitutionally required, amended 28 U.S.C. §157 now authorizes the bankruptcy judge to hold a jury trial provided that the bankruptcy court is empowered by the district court to do so and the parties have given their express consent (*infra*, p. 76).

CHAPTER 3

COMMENCING A CASE — INITIAL STEPS

I.   THE VOLUNTARY CASE — § 301

A. Voluntary cases predominate: As we have seen, in the early days, bankruptcy was a creditors' remedy against debtors. The concept of voluntary bankruptcy was introduced to American law in 1841. Under the Code, voluntary bankruptcies now make up the bulk of all cases.

B. Filing a voluntary petition: Under § 301, a voluntary bankruptcy case begins when the debtor files a petition. The person preparing the petition will also need to consult Bankruptcy Rule 1002.

  1. Form of petition: The petition follows Official Form No. 1, which may be modified as needed.

  2. No specific showing required: The debtor need not satisfy any prescribed standard of insolvency in order to file a voluntary petition.

  3. Petition constitutes "order for relief":   The voluntary petition is itself an "order for relief." Without more, the operations of the Code begin when the petition is filed and the debtor is placed in bankruptcy.

C. The joint voluntary case: Under § 302, a joint case may be filed by an individual and the individual's spouse. The petition constitutes an order for joint relief.

  1. Separate assets: If the joint petitioners have separate assets, the court may *administer them separately* in the same case or may *"consolidate"* them under procedures contained in Rules 1015 and 2009. This decision will turn largely upon how the assets were used before bankruptcy.

   a. Consolidation: If the assets were used to satisfy the obligations of both spouses, the court is more likely to consolidate them.

   b. Joint administration: If the assets were used separately by each spouse, the two estates may be administered and disposed of in the same case, but consolidation is less likely.

D. Other documents: The voluntary debtor must submit a number of other documents to the court. These may be filed with the petition or within fixed periods after the petition.

1. **List of creditors:** A list of creditors is required, usually with the petition.

2. **Statement of financial affairs:** Within fifteen days after the petition, the debtor must file a statement of his financial affairs.

3. **Asset and liabilities:** Within fifteen days, the debtor must also file a schedule of assets and liabilities.

4. **Other schedules:** Various other schedules and forms may be required of the debtor in specific cases, depending upon his circumstances.

II.   THE INVOLUNTARY CASE — § 303

A. **Filing an involuntary petition:** An involuntary case begins when a creditor, or a group of creditors, files a petition against the debtor. Under § 303, *the petition has the effect of forcing the debtor into bankruptcy.* Involuntary cases represent less than one-half of one percent of all bankruptcy cases. Since an involuntary case obviously has serious business implications for the debtor, the debtor has an opportunity to answer the petition and creditors must show that they have acted in a responsible way. The court's determination of the merits of an involuntary case are resolved quickly, so as not to hold up an ongoing business.

B. **Requirements for an involuntary petition:** An involuntary petition must meet the following minimal criteria.

1. **Aggregate claims:** The claims by those joining in the petition must aggregate at least $10,000 more than the value of all liens held to secure those claims. No claim may be (1) contingent or (2) the subject of a bona-fide dispute.

2. **Case involving 12 or more claim holders:** The usual involuntary case will have 12 or more claim holders. If so, at least three of these claim holders must join in the § 303 petition.

3. **Cases involving fewer than 12 claim holders:** In the infrequent case involving fewer than 12 claim holders, one or more claimants may file the § 303 petition. In determining whether there are 12 claim holders, holders who are employees, insiders, and transferees of the debtor with voidable transfers are excluded.

4. **Other creditors join in petition:** After a petition is filed, other creditors may join in the petition. This may have the effect of correcting a defect in the original filing by adding to the number of creditors or by replacing a creditor who was not qualified to file.

C. Cases involving partnerships: In the case of a partnership, fewer than all of the general partners may file an involuntary petition against the partnership.

    1. May ignore agreement: The partners may file *even if they have signed an agreement prohibiting filing.*

    2. State law no impediment: Under the constitutional supremacy of bankruptcy law (*supra*, p. 3), the partners may file *even if the filing violates state law.*

D. Filings under Chapter 7 or Chapter 11 only: An involuntary case may be brought only against persons that qualify as debtors under either Chapter 7 (*infra,* p. 147) or Chapter 11 (*infra*, p.176).

    1. Parties excluded from involuntary petitions: An involuntary case may not be brought against a farmer, family farmer, or charitable corporation.

    2. Not available against consumers under Chapter 13: Creditors of consumers have tried to obtain the right to file involuntary petitions under Chapter 13. They want to force consumers with continuing sources of income to pay their obligations rather than secure discharges in Chapter 7. Congress has consistently resisted these proposals, in part because of a concern that a mandatory form of Chapter 13 might be construed as slavery in violation of the 13th Amendment.

E. Petitions by representatives of foreign proceedings: A foreign representative of an estate in a foreign proceeding (see discussion of § 304 *supra*, p. 15) may also file an involuntary petition in either Chapter 7 or 11, thereby forcing a domestic debtor into bankruptcy.

    1. Basis for filing: A domestic connection with the foreign proceeding may be the basis of the filing. Also, a limited case under § 304 may be changed to a full case under either Chapter.

F. Debtor may answer or contest petition: The debtor, or a general partner of a partnership debtor that did not join in the petition, may file an answer to a petition and contest it. Rule 1011 governs the procedure in such a contest.

    1. Proofs required of petitioner: If the involuntary petition is answered, the case has begun, but an order for relief does not issue until the petitioner satisfies one of two conditions.

        a. Nonpayment of debts when due: The petitioner may prove that the debtor "is generally not paying ... debts as such debts become due unless such debts are the subject of a bona-fide dispute." The phrase "generally not paying" is not defined. The court may examine such factors as: whether a large portion (not necessarily 50%) of the debtor's debts is unpaid; the periods of time over which the debts have been unpaid; and even the degree of care taken by the debtor in managing the payment of its debts. *In re All Media Properties, Inc.*, 5 B.R. 126 (Bkrtcy., S.D.Tex. 1980).

b. Appointment of custodian of assets: Alternatively, the petitioner may show that, within 120 days of the involuntary filing, a custodian of substantially all of the debtor's property was appointed.

Example: Creditor C has a security interest in Debtor D's inventory, which does not constitute substantially all of D's property. D defaults to C, and C has a trustee appointed to take possession of D's inventory and liquidate it. This act alone would not constitute the basis for an involuntary filing.

c. Rationale for requiring proofs: These tests are imposed on the petitioner to mitigate the severe remedy of bankruptcy. At the same time, the debtor is assured a speedy resolution of the issues of insolvency. Indeed, under 28 U.S.C. § 1411, the district court may order trial of those issues without a jury to speed up the determination.

G. Period between the petition and the order for relief — the gap: In involuntary proceedings, the period between the petition and the order for relief (i.e. the finding by the court that the petitioner has proved its case for bankruptcy), is called the "gap" period.

1. Debtor continues operations: Under § 303(f), the debtor may continue to operate its business during the gap as if the creditors' petition had not been filed.

2. Interim trustee: A party in interest in a Chapter 7 case who believes operation by the debtor will harm the estate may ask the court to appoint an interim trustee. The interim trustee will take possession of the business and operate it for the benefit of all.

a. Trustee in Chapter 11 cases: In addition to the general provisions of § 303 dealing with interim trustees,§ 1104 provides for the appointment of a trustee in Chapter 11 cases "after the commencement of the case ... for cause, including ... gross mismanagement of the affairs of the debtor."

3. Filing a bond: The debtor may file a bond to regain control of the estate from the trustee; the creditors may be required to file a bond indemnifying the debtor against damage to its business caused by the involuntary petition.

H. Dismissal and damages: If the debtor succeeds in its contest of the filing and the petition for involuntary bankruptcy is dismissed, the court may grant judgment against the petitioners for costs or attorney's fees. If the court finds the petition to have been brought in bad faith, it may award compensatory and punitive damages.

Example: Among Debtor D's creditors were its managers, Cs, who attempted to force D into involuntary bankruptcy. D purportedly owed money to Cs. However, as the managers of D, Cs were able to conceal D's other creditors from D; the only debts of D that were not paid as they became due were the debts that Cs had concealed. The petition was held to have been filed in bad faith and D was awarded its attorney fees, plus nominal damages. Actual damages could not be assessed because the extent of D's lost business during the gap period could not be determined. D was also awarded punitive damages of $1,000 as a warning to others. *In re Camelot*, 30 B.R. 409 (D.Ct. E.D. Tenn. 1983).

III. ABSTENTION; DISMISSAL; SUSPENSION

A. Court may dismiss or suspend case: Code § 305 is entitled "Abstention," but its text authorizes a bankruptcy or district court to "dismiss" a case or, in the alternative, to "suspend" all proceedings in a case. It may do either *if the interests of the creditors and the debtor would be better served* by the action.

1. **Used at beginning of case:** The application of § 305 comes into play most often at the beginning of a case, if the court is presented with facts that indicate there is a better way of resolving the issues.

2. **Reasons for abstention or suspension:** The court will dismiss the petition or suspend the proceedings under a number of circumstances.

   a. **Legal proceeding or settlement underway:** The court may resort to § 305 where the only real dispute among the parties is already under consideration in a state or foreign court and the bankruptcy would only complicate matters.

      i. **State proceeding in process:** If a state assignment for the benefit of creditors is in process, for example, with the potential of resolving all issues and distributing all available property, a bankruptcy proceeding might be inappropriate.

      ii. **Settlement discussions in progress:** Similarly, the court may abstain from acting if there are active settlement discussions in progress.

b. When the relief sought is not practical in bankruptcy: A court may refuse to act if it cannot enforce a practical remedy.

Example: Creditors, Cs, seek an involuntary Chapter 11 case against Debtor D, a rock singer. The goal is to force D to cut some records. The proceeds would defray D's obligations to Cs. The court refused to accept the Chapter 11 case because a court cannot realistically force someone to sing. *Matter of Noonan*, 17 B.R. 793 (Bkrtcy. S.D.N.Y. 1982).

3. **Full abstention distinguished from suspension:** Whether the court will abstain, dismiss or suspend will depend on the facts of each case.

   Example: In a case ancillary to a foreign proceeding under § 304, (*supra*, p. 15) the creditors ask for dismissal. They argue that the only real issue involving United States assets is being handled in an interpleader action in the district court. However, the foreign-representative petitioner believes that certain voidable transfers (subject to Code § 547) have occurred and should be dealt with in the bankruptcy case. The court suspended proceedings pending the disposition of the interpleader action, thus preserving whatever rights had existed to avoid preferential transfers and also advancing judicial economy. *In re Trakman*, 33 B.R. 780 (Bkrtcy. S.D.N.Y. 1983).

4. **Foreign representatives may invoke § 305:** A foreign representative who is acting in a foreign proceeding may also seek dismissal or suspension of a § 304 case or of a full case under Chapter 7 or 11 of the Code. Note also that Code § 304 gives the U.S. courts wide latitude to decide whether or not to accept cases ancillary to foreign proceedings.

   a. Just treatment of claim holders: Dismissal may be sought to protect the interests of claim holders in the foreign proceeding.

   b. Comity: The American court may also be asked to abstain in order to recognize or respect the superior interests of the foreign tribunal.

5. **Bankruptcy courts differ from common law courts:** In their ability to dismiss or suspend rather than hear and determine cases, bankruptcy courts (including district courts operating under bankruptcy jurisdiction) differ from common-law courts. More discretion is given to bankruptcy courts in this regard because they are courts of equity. A common-law court must hear and resolve cases properly brought before it and within its jurisdiction.

B. Dismissal under other Chapters: Each "filing" Chapter of the Code has its own provisions authorizing the court to dismiss a case.

1. **Sections listed:** The relevant "dismissal" sections are:

   - § 707 (Liquidation cases);

   - § 1112 (General reorganization cases);

   - § 1208 (Family Farmer cases); and

   - § 1307 (Consumer cases).

2. **Comparison to § 305:** The dismissal provisions of the four filing chapters are generally used to obtain dismissal after a case has gotten under way; § 305 is particularly suitable, as its title "Abstention" indicates, for a case at or near its inception.

3. **Tests under dismissal provisions differ:** The tests for dismissal provided under the different Chapters differ.

   a. **§ 1112 test:** Under § 1112, Chapter 11 cases may be dismissed "for cause," a sweeping rationale not included in § 305. For example, § 1112 was used to dismiss a Chapter 11 case that was alleged to have been brought in bad faith. *In re Northwest Recreational Activities*, 4 B.R. 43 (Bktrcy. N.D.Ga. 1980).

C. Appealing a decision to dismiss: Congress provided in the 1978 Code that a decision to dismiss or abstain by a bankruptcy judge was not reviewable on appeal. Appeals are not generally required under the American judicial system, but this particular legislation fared poorly in the courts. They looked askance at the notion that decisions by bankruptcy judges — who are, after all, only Article 1 judges — would not be subject to review, particularly where constitutional rights were at stake. As a result, § 305 was amended in 1990 to provide that ***dismissals are appealable to district courts only***, but not to Courts of Appeals or the Supreme Court. *In re Goerg*, 930 F.2d 1563 (11th Cir. 1991).

IV. CONSUMER ABUSES

A. Record bankruptcy filings after 1978 Code: Upon adoption of the Code in 1978, consumer bankruptcies skyrocketed. The increase could not be explained statistically by existing economic problems or increases in consumer debt. One possible explanation was the moderation in the burdens upon bankrupts — renamed debtors. Another was the wide-spread publicity given to the Code.

B. 1984 amendments curb increase: By 1984, Congress was convinced that the Code had given debtors too much leeway. As part of the 1984 amendments, therefore, Congress ***swung the pendulum back in favor of creditors***. Two provisions added in 1984 made it more difficult to start a case.

    1. Prior dismissals within 180 days: Under Code § 109(g), no individual or family farmer may be a debtor if he was a debtor in a case pending during the previous 180 days ***and*** either of two situations exists: (1) the prior case was dismissed by the court as a result of debtor's misconduct; or (2) the debtor obtained voluntary dismissal of the prior case after a request by a creditor for relief from the automatic stay under Code § 362. (See discussion of § 362(d), *infra*, p. 42.)

    2. Rationale: The rationale for the prohibition on filing where a previous case was dismissed for misconduct is obvious. The rationale for the alternative ground, i.e., that the debtor requested dismissal after a request by a creditor for relief from the automatic stay, is less obvious. In effect, the provision creates a presumption of misconduct. By way of illustration, assume that a creditor has asked the court for relief from the automatic stay under § 367. Assume also that the debtor, presumably knowing it had no right to the stay, thereupon requests that the case be dismissed. It's conceived as wrong for the debtor who seemingly acted improperly in obtaining the first stay, to come back within 180 days, start a new case, and obtain another stay.

C. Notice to consumer debtors of bankruptcy alternatives — § 342(b): To help individuals "whose debts are primarily consumer debts", the clerk of the bankruptcy court is required to give those debtors ***written notice of all Chapters of the Code under which they may proceed*** (§ 342(b), adopted in 1984). Notice to the debtor must be given "prior to the commencement of the case." The notice is presumably designed to inform an individual proposing to file under Chapter 7 of the Code (a liquidation proceeding; *infra*, p. 147) about the availability of relief under Chapter 13 (the consumer reorganization proceeding; *infra*, p. 227). The Code does not specify how a clerk is to learn, before a bankruptcy case has begun, what the debts or requirements of an individual are, or how the notice of alternatives can be given before the individual files his petition. However, in Official Bankruptcy Form No. 1 the debtor is asked to acknowledge that she has received complying material; presumably, this will encourage inquiry into the Chapter 13 alternative.

CHAPTER 4

THE DEBTOR — GENERAL RULES

Introductory note: This Chapter discusses the debtor's obligations in getting the case under way and his major obligations and benefits during the bankruptcy process. We study the automatic stay that protects the debtor and his assets against attack by his creditors and discuss such subjects as exemptions (i.e., assets that the debtor can retain). We also consider aspects of the discharge. This is usually perceived by the debtor as the major benefit of the bankruptcy case.

I. DEBTOR'S INITIAL DUTIES

A. **Initiate and maintain free flow of information:** When the bankruptcy case begins, the debtor faces a number of immediate duties. He learns very quickly that a lot of information must flow from him to the court, to the United States Trustee, and to the other parties in interest.

1. **Notice to creditors:** The creditors must be told at once that a bankruptcy has begun. Under the automatic stay imposed by § 362 (*infra*, p. 36), creditors must abstain from certain acts as soon as the bankruptcy begins. Obviously, they cannot comply unless they learn of the bankruptcy.

2. **Accounting for assets:** The debtor must identify his assets and disclose their location. The trustee, if serving in a case, must be helped to review recent transfers made by the debtor before the filing to see if they should be avoided by him.

3. **Information to court and United States Trustee:** The court and the United States Trustee must have information upon which to base an opinion as to whether the provisions of the Code are being substantially abused by the debtor or any party in interest.

B. **Schedules produced by debtor — § 521:** The debtor is required to file certain lists and forms with the court. These obligations are controlled by § 521 and Rules 1007 and 4002.

1. **List of creditors:** In a voluntary case, the debtor must file a list of its creditors with the petition (§ 521, Rule 1007). In an involuntary case, the list of creditors must be filed within fifteen days after entry of the order for relief (Rule 1007(a)(2)).

2. **Schedule of assets, liabilities, income and expenditures — Form 6:** The Rules provide a number of official forms which serve as models for supplying these schedules. Form 6 consists of several

schedules, each of which requires a list of information about the debtor and his estate.

3. **Statement of financial affairs — Form 7:** Under § 521, *a debtor must submit a statement of his financial affairs.* This requirement is covered by Form 7, which compels the debtor to disclose his financial history, including how his income was earned, all lawsuits against him, set offs, payments to creditors, recent transfers of property, prior addresses, and other information enabling a trustee to investigate, collect estate property, and challenge prefiling transfers that unfairly deplete estate property.

4. **Debtor's statement of intention as to secured consumer debts — Form 8:** As part of the creditor-oriented Code amendments of 1984, the debtor is now compelled to make decisions about any outstanding consumer debt. Under § 521(2), a debtor with consumer debts secured by property of the estate (for example, a home mortgage securing an equity loan or a lien on the family car in favor of a finance company) must disclose her intentions on Form 8 and act with respect to the property, within the specified times.

   a. **Options available:** *The debtor must disclose her intentions by selecting from among the following options: retaining the property and reaffirming the debt* (§ 524 *infra*, p. 60); *claiming the property as exempt and redeeming it* (§ 522 *infra*, p. 46); *or surrendering it to the secured creditor.* The debtor must then generally carry out her intentions by actually reaffirming the debt, or redeeming or surrendering the collateral.

   b. **Time limits:** Unless the court allows longer time periods, Form 8 must be filed within 30 days after the petition and the debtor must make good on her intentions within 45 days after the form is filed.

   c. **When debtor fails to reaffirm debt:** When a debtor fails to reaffirm a debt or redeem the collateral, but merely continues to make the payments scheduled under the underlying consumer contract, the courts are divided as to whether the debtor can retain the property with no further act.

      i. **Substantive right to recapture collateral:** Some courts will require the debtor to reaffirm the debt in order to retain it. *In re Edwards*, 901 F.2d 1383 (7th Cir. 1990). These courts see § 521(2) as affecting substantive rights between the debtor and her creditor.

      ii. **Contrary view:** Other courts see the provision as merely imposing a procedural requirement. They reason that the creditor should not obtain additional rights to the collateral so long as the correct payments continue (even if discharge ends the debtor's personal responsibility). *In re Boulanger*, 962 F.2d 345 (4th Cir. 1992).

C. **Other duties of the debtor:** Under § 521(3) and (4), *if a trustee has been appointed, the debtor must cooperate with the trustee and, in general, turn over all property of the estate and all records pertaining to the estate.* (In Chapter 12 and 13 cases, the debtor usually retains extensive management over estate property, *infra*, pp. 222 and 235.) This is true whether or not immunity from prosecution has been granted with respect to the records.

1. **Fifth Amendment right:** The Fifth Amendment right against self-incrimination may sometimes be in conflict with § 521, which purports to require that documents be turned over to the trustee even if incriminating and even where immunity has not been granted. The courts have generally found that the Code cannot require a debtor to turn over personal records in the face of valid claims under the Fifth Amendment. Rather, a claim against self-incrimination will generally require the court to conduct a two-part analysis to determine whether the right applies with respect to the contents of the records or with respect to the acts of producing the records (i.e., the acts compelling the testimony of the debtor). *Butcher v. Bailey*, 753 F. 2d 465 (6th Cir. 1985).

2. **Immunity under § 344:** Under § 344, the court may grant immunity against self-incrimination to persons providing information or testifying in the course of a case.

D. **Notice to creditors — § 342:** One of the debtor's basic duties involves getting sufficient information into the court so that creditors can be notified. Due process requires that creditors have notice that a proceeding affecting their rights has begun and is in progress.

1. **Statutory requirement:** Under § 342, appropriate notice of an order for relief must be given.

2. **Rule requirement:** Rule 2002(f) provides: "the clerk, or some other person as the court may direct, shall give the debtor, all creditors, and indenture trustees notice by mail of . . . the order for relief."

E. **Hearings, examinations, and other duties:** In his central role in the bankruptcy proceeding, the debtor is required to appear at various hearings and must perform various other duties.

1. **Purpose of hearings:** The purpose is to inform the court and the creditors of the debtor's financial condition, to assist in the other

proceedings that may arise throughout the case, and to receive information from the court concerning the case.

2. **The § 343 examination:** Under § 343, the debtor is required to appear and submit to examination under oath at the first meeting of creditors mandated under § 341 of the Code. The meeting must be held within a reasonable time after the order for relief and enables all interested parties to inquire into the affairs and assets of the debtor.

3. **The § 521(5) hearing:** Under § 521(5), the debtor is required to appear at the discharge hearing. (See § 524(d), which provides for the hearing, *infra*, p. 62.)

4. **Rule 4002 duties:** Rule 4002 imposes additional duties upon the debtor. Among these are the following:

    a. **Attendance at examination:** The debtor must attend and submit to any examination ordered by the court.

    b. **Hearing on objection to discharge:** If called, the debtor must attend and testify at any hearing held to resolve a complaint objecting to discharge.

II. THE AUTOMATIC STAY — § 362

A. **Automatic stay enjoins creditors:** Under § 362, ***the automatic stay is imposed to prevent creditors from enforcing their claims***. The automatic stay is one of the fundamental debtor protections provided by the bankruptcy laws. The stay casts a period of calm over the financial affairs of the debtor and enables the various parties to a case to work through its procedures in an orderly manner. Courts will apply the stay in a liberal way to achieve this policy of calm and methodical management. A court's readiness to apply the stay is encouraged by its ability under § 362(d) to grant relief from the stay when called for.

1. **Stay applies at once:** ***The stay begins when the petition is filed and the case begins***. In an involuntary case, this will normally precede the order for relief. This fact underscores the need for the court to resolve the appropriateness of involuntary relief as soon as possible.

2. **Applicable to all entities:** ***The stay is applicable to all "entities."*** Under the definitions in § 101(15), this term includes governmental units. The stay therefore extends to both the federal and state governments.

3. **Stay applies regardless of creditor's knowledge:** ***A creditor is subject to the stay whether or not it knows of the bank-***

ruptcy. Although contempt can be imposed for violation of the stay, this relief will normally be applied in a reasonable manner, if at all, where a creditor has not received notice.

B. Situations in which the stay applies: Under § 362(a), there are eight instances in which the automatic stay applies.

1. **Stay of actions, proceedings, and claims:** Under § 362(a)(1), *the stay applies to the commencement or continuation of any action or proceeding that (1) was or could have been begun against the debtor before the petition was filed, or (2) is to recover a claim that arose before the petition.*

   Example 1: Debtor D owes Creditor C $1,000. D files a petition in bankruptcy. C cannot sue D.

   Example 2: D is being sued in state court. The jury has been sworn, witnesses are ready, and the plaintiff's lawyer has risen to open her case. If a petition in bankruptcy involving D is filed, the case stops.

   a. **Broad impact of stay against actions:** By staying actions to recover all claims that arose before the case, the Code provides wide opportunities for use of the stay. For example, the bankruptcy court is given an opportunity to manage the thousands of demands made against a debtor in a mass tort situation.

   b. **Broad definition of "claims":** The definition of "claims" against the debtor as used in § 362, is based upon the broad definitions of § 101(5) (*supra*, p. 17).

   c. **Actions defined under federal law:** For purposes of § 362 and the breadth of the automatic stay, the courts apply federal law and are not limited to the concepts of causes of action under state law or by the periods of time within which a suit may be brought under state law.

   Example 1: Creditor C used a contraceptive device manufactured by Debtor D. The device resulted in C's injury. Debtor filed a petition in bankruptcy after C had used the device, but before C discovered any manifestation of the injury sufficient to establish a cause of action under the applicable state law. Under this state's tort law, C could not have brought an action against debtor before the bankruptcy began. C nevertheless had a claim recognizable under the Code and any action that C could bring against D was stayed under the automatic stay. The policies behind the bankruptcy stay — to enable a case to proceed in an organized manner and to afford maximum relief to the debtor — differ from the policies behind state tort law. Tort law is concerned with setting rules for the orderly conduct of litigation and answers such questions as: When may suits be brought? When does the Statute of Limitations begin to run? When does it expire? Bankruptcy law has to do with managing the economic affairs of the debtor. *Grady v. A.H. Robins Company*, 839 F.2d 198 (4th Cir. 1988).

Example 2: C was exposed to asbestos before D's bankruptcy but experienced no symptoms until after the bankruptcy. C's claim against D was deemed to arise before the bankruptcy under the federal concept of claim and was consequently stayed by the automatic stay. It was deemed "unmatured, unliquidated and contingent" under § 101(5). *In re Johns-Manville Corp.*, 57 B.R. 680 (Bkrtcy. S.D. N.Y. 1986).

2. **Stay of enforcement of judgments:** *A judgment obtained before the case cannot be enforced against either the debtor or property of the estate.* Property of the estate is very broadly defined in § 541 to include all "legal or equitable interests of the debtor" when the petition is filed. (See *infra*, p. 97.)

3. **Stay of acts against property of the estate:** *Any act to obtain possession of property of the estate, or to exercise control over property of the estate, is stayed.*

   Example: Debtor D leases property from Creditor C and defaults in its rental payments. C obtains a warrant of eviction. D then files a bankruptcy petition. C is stayed from evicting D even though, under the applicable state law, the warrant stripped D of any legal right to the premises. D still has an equitable right to possession. This was enough of a property right to make its tenancy a part of the estate. *In re Onio's Italian Restaurant Corp.*, 42 B.R. 319 (Bkrtcy. S.D.N.Y 1984).

4. **Stay of acts to effect liens against estate:** *The fourth application of the stay is to the creation, perfection, or enforcement of any lien against property of the estate after the petition is filed.*

   Example 1: Debtor D owns Blackacre when it files its petition. D owes Creditor C $50,000. C, concerned about its ability to collect from D, requests a mortgage (defined as a "lien" under § 101(37)) on Blackacre to secure C's claim. C cannot obtain the mortgage.

   Example 2: C already has a security interest (also defined as a "lien" under § 101(37)) in D's manufacturing equipment at the time of the petition. However, C has neglected to perfect its interest (perfection is an act which protects the interest of a secured party against other claims against the collateral) by filing with the Secretary of State. C may not perfect its interest after bankruptcy.

Example 3: The IRS levies against D's equipment for unpaid taxes before the petition, obtains possession, and is ready to liquidate the equipment at a public sale when D files its petition. The IRS is stayed from selling the equipment. Until the public sale actually occurs and ownership is transferred to the buyer, D has an equitable right to the equipment. The equipment becomes part of D's estate and D can pay its tax liability and get the equipment back. *U.S. v. Whiting Pools, Inc.*, 462 U.S. 198 (1983).

5. **Stay of liens affecting property of the debtor:** The fifth situation to which the stay applies exemplifies the scope of § 362 in protecting the debtor's peace of mind. *If a lien secures a claim against the debtor that arose before the petition, the lien may not be created, perfected, or enforced against the debtor's property after the petition.* Note that paragraphs (3) and (4) deal with property of the estate, whereas § 362(a)(5) deals with property of the debtor. This property is protected from actual or potential lienholders, just as property of the estate is protected under (a)(4).

   a. **Status of debtor's property on filing:** At the time of the bankruptcy, all of the debtor's property becomes property of the estate and is the main source of payments to creditors.

   b. **Some property remains with debtor:** However, under § 522, some property of the debtor may be exempt from the estate. This property becomes the debtor's own and is no longer property of the estate. Similarly, the debtor may receive property as a gift after the petition. Under § 541, this will usually remain as property of the debtor, not the estate's.

6. **Stay against acts to collect claims against debtor:** The sixth situation to which *the stay applies is any act to "collect, assess, or recover" a claim against the debtor that arose before the commencement of the case.*

   Example 1: Creditor C meets Debtor D on the street after D has filed a petition. C says, "Hello, D. How about that $50 you owe me?" C's question violates the automatic stay.

   Example 2: D graduated from the University of Illinois without paying his tuition. After filing a petition, D requested a transcript of his grades. The University refused, saying that it would not release them until D's tuition bill was paid. The University violated the stay; not releasing the transcript was an effort to collect its bill. *In re Heath*, 3 B.R. 351 (Bkrtcy. N.D.Ill. 1980).

7. Stay against asserting setoffs: As a matter of general legal principle, if A owes B $10 and B owes A $7, A need pay B only $3. A may "set off" the $7 that B owes A against A's larger debt. In bankruptcy, *if A owed B money before B's petition, A is stayed from setting off against that debt what B owes to A.* The debt from A to B is property of the estate, and A may not use it without court supervision.

Example: D owes its bank $50,000 for money D had borrowed. D has a checking account with a $40,000 balance when D files its petition. (In law, a bank account is a debt from the bank to the depositor.) The bank is stayed from applying the bank account against D's debt to the bank. However, the bank is able to put an administrative hold (freeze) on the bank account to the extent of the unpaid loan. This does not violate the automatic stay so long as the bank does not intend to reduce permanently the account balance by the amount of the defaulted loan. *Citizens Bank of Maryland v. Strumpf*, No. 94-1340, 1995 U.S. LEXIS 7408 (1995). (The administrative freeze is also discussed in conjunction with the setoff provisions of § 553, *infra*, p. 141 and again in the discussion of the term "cash collateral" under Chapter 11, *infra*, p. 188.)

8. Stay of proceedings in the Tax Court: *A special provision applies the automatic stay to proceedings before the Tax Court.* This may seem to be a redundant provision, but it does make the point that the Bankruptcy Code trumps the Internal Revenue Code.

C. Acts excepted from the automatic stay: Under § 362(b), there are a number of exceptions to the automatic stay. The most important of these are discussed here.

1. Criminal actions: Under § 362(b)(1), *the stay does not affect criminal actions or proceedings against the debtor.* This reflects the general tendency of the Code to deal with economic, not behavioral, problems.

Example: Before bankruptcy, Debtor D gives Creditor C a bad check. C has a friend in the DA's office and persuades him to prosecute D for the crime of knowingly passing bad checks. If D files for bankruptcy, the stay may well apply to the criminal proceeding if it can be demonstrated that the principal motivation of the criminal action was to collect the debt, even though criminal actions are generally excluded from the stay.

2. Alimony, maintenance and support: Under the second exception, *there is no stay (1) against an action or proceeding for paternity, nor (2) against the collection of alimony, mainte-*

nance and support "from property that is not property of the estate." The obligations under this exception are not discharged in bankruptcy and may be collected after the bankruptcy case. Therefore, there is no logical reason to prevent their earlier collection from assets that are not part of the estate and, thus, not dedicated to the claims of the creditors. (See our discussion of the term "estate," *infra*, p. 95.)

3. **Liens that relate back:**   Despite the prohibition in § 362(a)(4) against perfecting liens (*supra*, p. 38), *§ 362(b)(3) permits perfection under § 546(b)*. The latter section deals with *liens that are perfected after the lien is obtained and that "relate back" to the date of obtaining the lien*. Perfection is also allowed during the period provided for in § 547(e)(2)(A), which is based on the same "relation back" concept.

    Example: Uniform Commercial Code § 9-301(2) provides that, if a creditor with certain security interests files within 20 days after the interests are obtained, he is protected against adverse interests which may have arisen during those 20 days. This filing is not stayed under Code § 362.

4. **Police and regulatory powers:**   *The fourth exception to the stay applies to the commencement and continuation of an action or proceeding by a governmental unit under its police or regulatory powers*. For example, an action by the United States to enforce or to obtain reimbursement of costs under an environmental cleanup order is not stayed. *United States v. Nicolet, Inc.*, 857 F.2d 202 (3rd Cir. 1988) (*infra*).

    Example: The United States Postal Service hires D to paint its Stockbridge, Mass. building. D petitions in bankruptcy and defaults on its contract. The Postal Service was stayed from suing on its contract because it was acting as a private commercial party and not under its police power.

5. **Enforcement of governmental judgments:** *The fifth exception to the broad sweep of the automatic stay provides that the government, acting under its police or regulatory powers, may enforce a judgment for remedies such as specific performance, but is stayed from collecting a money judgment.* In the *Nicolet* case (*supra*), the United States was permitted to prosecute its case and to obtain a judgment for money damages, but it could not collect the judgment. Although collection was stayed, the suit did have more value to the government than mere nuisance value. The United States was able to establish the applicable law, to dem-

onstrate the seriousness of the violation, and to position itself to collect the money at such time as the stay was lifted.

6. **Tax deficiencies:** *The ninth exception to the automatic stay permits the IRS to conduct an audit to determine tax liability, issue notice of a tax deficiency* (but collection of the tax is stayed), *demand unfiled tax returns, assess a tax and issue a demand for its payment* (but any resulting tax lien does not take effect unless the tax will not be discharged in the bankruptcy and the affected property is transferred out of the estate).

7. **Lessors of real property:** Under the tenth exception to the automatic stay, *a lessor of real property may take action to dispossess a lessee under a nonresidential lease* (i.e., not a consumer lease), if the stated term of the lease expires before or during a case. A consumer lessee is protected against such action.

8. **Negotiable instrument notices:**   The eleventh exception to the automatic stay *permits the holder to present a negotiable instrument and to give notice of protest and dishonor under Article 3 of the Uniform Commercial Code*. These acts are necessary to keep promissory notes and checks alive and to preserve the remedies of parties to the instruments. They do not involve the payment of any money. The stay does prevent instruments such as checks from being collected against the debtor or its bank. (See § 542(c) and § 549(b) for special rules.)

D. **Duration of stay:** To determine the length of the stay, it becomes important to separate property of the estate from other property. As we have noted, § 362(a)(3) and (a)(4) deal with stays against property of the estate; § 362(a)(5) deals with stays against property other than property of the estate.

1. **Stays against estate property:** Under § 362(c), *the stay of an act against property of the estate continues until the property is no longer property of the estate.*

2. **Stays against non-estate property:** *All other stays* (including stays against property other than of the estate) *remain in effect until the earliest of the following events: (1) the case is closed; (2) the case is dismissed; or (3) a discharge is granted or denied.* The event of discharge occurs for all classes of debtor in cases under Chapters 9, 11, 12 and 13 of the Code but only to individuals under Chapter 7 (§ 727(a) *infra*, p. 160).

E. **Relief from stay:**   Of critical importance is the fact that, under § 362(d), the automatic stay *can* be terminated, annulled, or modified before it expires. Indeed, the broad reach of the stay can exist in the first place only because there is reasonable opportunity to have the stay lifted under proper circumstances. Notice is normally required under § 362(d) before relief from the stay can be granted. Notice is not required if a creditor can show "irreparable damage" (§ 362(f), Rule 4001(a)(2)).

1. **Termination for cause:**   Under § 362(d), ***the stay can be modified or terminated for "cause."*** Whether a stay will be terminated for cause is fact-sensitive and will be decided on a case-by-case basis.

   a. **Injury to collateral:**   Termination for cause generally applies when the protection the creditor would derive from its interest in collateral is being diminished. The prime example of diminished collateral is the normal depreciation suffered during the period that the collateral is held by the debtor and, because of the stay, the creditor is prevented from receiving payments on its obligation.

   b. **When creditor is undersecured:**   Cause for relief may be found in a Chapter 7 case where a secured creditor is undersecured (that is, the value of its security is less than the amount of its claim) and the debtor has no continuing interest in the property.

   c. **Other elements of cause:**   Cause may also consist of fraudulent behavior by the debtor; the passage of an undue period of time; failure of the debtor to care for or to insure the collateral; or failure of the debtor to live up to the terms of a reorganization plan (see discussion of Chapter 11 plans *infra*, p. 219).

2. **Payment of adequate protection:**   ***For a secured creditor, cause always includes a lack of "adequate protection."***

   a. **Definition of "adequate protection":**   Adequate protection basically means some form of benefit to the creditor (e.g., payments in money, as provided for in § 361) to ensure that the protection that the creditor gets from its collateral will not diminish while it is being held by the debtor and depreciating in value.

      Common examples of adequate protection are (i) the payment to a secured creditor of ***cash amounts*** equal to the depreciation of its collateral and (ii) a new security interest in other collateral given to protect the creditor's interest. As forms of adequate protection vary widely, § 361 includes a provision that whatever constitutes the "indubitable equivalent" of the creditor's interest will suffice. The term "indubitable equivalent" comes from a decision of Judge Learned Hand, *In re Murel Holding Corp.*, 75 F. 2d 941 (2d Cir. 1935).

b. Right to immediate possession by creditor: The doctrine is usually applied when the creditor has an immediate right to take possession of the collateral under the terms of the security arrangement with the debtor, but is prevented from reaching the collateral by the stay.

c. Time value of money: A question that plagued the courts for some years was whether adequate protection should include a factor for the time value of money.

i. Payment for delay in enforcement of rights: Since the secured creditor may have a right to its collateral today but will not receive it until tomorrow (in a Chapter 11 reorganization, this can take years), should the creditor be compensated for having to wait for its property in addition to receiving cash for its depreciation? Presumably, if it received the property today, it could use it or liquidate it and put the money to some profitable purpose.

ii. *Timbers of Inwood Forest*: Although money not paid over a period of time usually bears interest, ***the Supreme Court in*** United States v. Timbers of Inwood Forest, 484 U.S. 365 (1988), ***decided that the time value of money need not be included in compensation for adequate protection under § 361.*** Compensation will be measured only by the actual reduction in the value of the property.

3. Protection of creditors in reorganizations: In reorganizations, the debtor often remains in business for a prolonged period of time and may attempt to use the creditor's collateral for its operations. Under these circumstances, the creditor may need to be protected from the acts of the debtor.

a. Availability of relief: ***The creditor may obtain relief from the stay preventing his access to the collateral if (1) the debtor has no equity in the collateral*** (that is, it is worth less than the debt, so that it really belongs entirely to the creditor), ***and (2) the debtor does not need it for an effective reorganization*** under Chapters 9, 11, 12 or 13.

b. Relief in Chapter 11 cases: Relief from the stay is a key issue in Chapter 11 reorganizations and will be considered again in our discussion of Chapter 11 (*infra*, p. 186).

4. Single asset real estate cases: In 1994, the Code was amended to include special relief from the stay for creditors in "single asset real estate" cases. In these cases, the debtor frequently files for bankruptcy in order to prevent or delay foreclosure proceedings in state court and attempts to cram down a reorganization plan (see discussion of cramdown, *infra*, p. 212) despite the objections of the secured lender, to whom the vast majority of the debt in the case is usually owed.

    a. Definition: A "single asset real estate" case is a case in which the only asset is a single parcel of property or a project (other than residential real estate with fewer than four residential units) where the property or project generates substantially all the income of a debtor (or generates no income at all; *In re Oceanside Mission Associates*, 28 Bankr. Ct. Dec. 703 (S.D. Cal. 1996)), on which the debtor conducts no substantial business other than operating the property, and where the debtor has secured debts of no more than $4 million.

    b. Release from the stay: Single asset real estate may be released from the automatic stay unless, within 90 days after the order for relief (or such longer time as a court may order) either (1) the debtor has filed a plan of reorganization under Chapter 11 that has a reasonable possibility of being confirmed, or (2) the debtor has started making payments to the creditor equal to interest on the value of creditor's property in the real estate.

F. Penalty for violations: Under § 362(h), *actual and punitive damages are available for breach of the stay.* However, this provision is inartfully drafted; it awards damages only to an injured *individual*. Occasionally, the remedy of damages is therefore denied to others than individuals; there is no logical reason for this limitation. The courts generally ignore this limitation in practice and award damages to corporate and partnership debtors injured by violation of the stay.

    1. Contempt orders: Damages under § 362(h) are buttressed by the innate power of courts to punish for contempt. Although doubt has occasionally been expressed about the power of a bankruptcy (Article 1) judge to issue contempt orders, remedies have been fashioned which depend on the joint pressures of damages and contempt.

        a. Good faith violations: Where violation of the stay has been inadvertent or committed in good faith, contempt orders and civil damages have tended to be light or nonexistent.

        b. Intentional violations: In cases in which a creditor deliberately ignores the stay, as where a creditor with full knowledge of the bankruptcy demands payment of a debt in an appearance at the debtor's home after bedtime on Sunday night (*In re Carrigan*, 109 B.R. 167 (Bkrtcy. W.D.N.C. 1989)), or in an appearance at a party thrown by the debtor (*In re Neal*, 106 B.R. 90 (Bkrtcy.

E.D.N.C. 1989)), punitive damages are more likely to be awarded.

G. Court orders under § 105:   Under § 105, the bankruptcy court is empowered to issue supportive orders. Where a debtor is aware that a creditor is threatening to violate the § 362 stay, a court order issued under § 105 can have a chilling effect. It can also accomplish other useful objectives.

Example: In a mass tort litigation, the bankruptcy court may find that injured parties did not have "claims" before the bankruptcy and therefore cannot be stayed from bringing lawsuits under § 362(a)(1). But, the court may restrain them under § 105. The power to prevent a continuing series of lawsuits against a debtor in bankruptcy is supportive of the orderly disposition of a bankruptcy case and can be used so long as it does not violate any provision of the Code. *In re Johns-Manville Corp.*, 57 B.R. 680 (Bkrtcy. S.D.N.Y. 1986).

III.   EXEMPTIONS — § 522

A. Exemptions in general: The automatic stay has the effect of retaining property in the estate. In the absence of a system for exempting some property, the debtor would have nothing left to help her in rejoining society with the "fresh start" that she is supposed to reap from a bankruptcy case. However, under § 522, there is a method under which ***a debtor may designate a limited portion of her property when she files the petition, remove it from the bankruptcy proceedings, and use it for her own new life***. Under § 522(b), property that is thus "exempted" is removed from the property of the estate. Under § 522(c), exempt property is not liable for any debts of the debtor that arose, or that are determined to have arisen, before the petition. (Some claims, even though arising *after* the petition, are ***deemed to have arisen before*** the petition under special "as if" provisions of the Code. See discussion *infra*, p. 77).

1. **Exempt property reachable for certain debts:**   Exempt property remains liable for certain debts even after it has been returned to the debtor. As listed in § 522(c), these debts are:

   • Certain tax debts;

   • Certain alimony and child support debts;

   • Debts secured by liens on the exempt property;

   • Certain debts of individuals involved in bank fraud.

2. **Exemptions available only to individuals:** Under § 522(b), *exemptions under the Code are available only to individuals*, not to corporations, partnerships, or other entities.

3. **Approach of the Code:** Congress and the courts have searched continuously for the correct mix of exempted assets. The more property is exempted, the smaller the pot for creditors, but the more vigorous the fresh start for the debtor. In the deliberations leading up to the passage of the Code in 1978, Congress approached exemptions with a logical rationale. At the outset, all the property of the debtor would be included in the estate. This would bring all the debtor's assets within the purview of the court. Claims would be broadly defined in order to deal with all of the debtor's economic problems. Finally, exemptions would be specifically defined in the Code in order to give the debtor sufficient assets to make the fresh start meaningful. For political reasons, Congress made a hash of this logical and rational approach.

B. **Duties and rights of the debtor:** The debtor has the duty to file an exemption list and also has the right to act with respect to exemptions in situations where the trustee does not.

1. **Debtor's duty to file exemption list:** Under § 521(2), the debtor must file a list showing all secured property which he claims as exempt. In addition, under § 522(l), the debtor must file a list of *all* property claimed as exempt, whether or not it has been used as security. Rule 4003 indicates that the two lists may be filed together.

2. **Rights of debtor to recovered property from trustee:** A trustee has the right, under certain conditions, to recover property from transferees (including lienholders who are included as transferees under the § 101(54) definition of "transfer"). This right is confirmed in the avoiding powers under § 544, § 547 and § 548 (*infra*, pp. 117, 125, and 136). In certain cases, the debtor is given the right under § 522(g) to claim her exemptions in the property recovered by the trustee.

   a. **Not available if property previously transferred or if concealed:** The debtor may not claim an exemption with respect to property which she has previously transferred voluntarily or has concealed. The giving of a lien constitutes a transfer. It is deemed inequitable for a debtor to reclaim as exempt, property which she had freely conveyed previously simply because it has now come back into the possession of the trustee.

   b. **Involuntary transfers:** Some transfers are involuntary, in which case the debtor may claim exemptions if the property is returned. These include judicial liens designed to enforce unpaid judgments, and also property transferred to a creditor who has defrauded the debtor into making the transfer. *In re Gingery*, 12 C.B.C.2d 943 (Bkrtcy. D.Colo. 1985).

3. **Debtor's use of trustee's avoidance powers:**   The trustee may be unwilling to go to the trouble of reclaiming the property simply to enable the debtor to reclaim it as exempt. Under § 522(h) and (i), the debtor is essentially given all the powers to do the reclaiming himself if the trustee has the power and doesn't use it.

4. **Exchanging non-exempt assets for exempt assets:**   Some debtors facing bankruptcy will gather their non-exempt assets, sell them, and then buy exempt assets with the proceeds. Clearly, in these cases the creditors have been denied assets that now go to the debtor. Is this a kind of fraud or misconduct that should reduce the debtor's right to bankruptcy relief? The "fresh start," it is said, should be granted only to the unfortunate, not to the fraudulent.

   a. **Ability to convert to exempt assets:**   A lawyer who is consulted by the debtor prior to the petition may well have a duty to inform her client about the broad exemption provisions. The client has the right to act upon this advice. Is it a fraud to take advantage of the Code in accordance with this advice? Consider the case of a debtor who sold non-exempt stock in order to buy a 200-acre ranch exempt under state law. Should she be denied a discharge? (§ 727(a) dealing with discharge is discussed *infra*, p. 160.)

   b. **Factors in determining fraud:** The essential question for the courts is whether the assets claimed as exempt serve the function of the exemption design — to enable the debtor to make his fresh start — or, instead, whether they represent a device to defraud creditors out of what is rightfully due to them. The courts will examine the intentions of the debtor under all the circumstances. They will ask: did the debtor have a real need for the new assets; were the assets acquired openly or in secrecy: did they have any relationship to the debtor's normal life; did the debtor keep and use the nonexempt property after the conversion? *In re Johnson*, 124 B.R. 290 (Bkrtcy. D.Minn 1991).

C. **Choice of exemption scheme:** Under § 522(b), *the debtor is theoretically given a choice between the exemptions available (1) under § 522(d) of the Code, or (2) under state and federal (nonbankruptcy) laws.*

   1. **Exemptions under Code — § 522(d):** In   § 522(b)(1),   Congress further muddied the internal harmony of the Code by permitting a state to prohibit debtors in their states from selecting the option of

utilizing the exemptions listed in the Bankruptcy Code. ***Thirty-six states have passed opt-out legislation, leaving only 14 states in which the debtor may utilize the exemptions provided by the Code.*** Therefore, the exemption scheme under § 522(d) of the Code now has limited application and is not discussed here in depth. The Code exemptions are eleven in number, with some subdivisions under the eleven. The Code exemptions include such things as a $15,000 real property exemption, unlimited rights in a life insurance contract, and the right to one's pension, but only to the extent it is necessary for support.

2. **State and federal (nonbankruptcy) exemptions:** In states that have not opted out of the exemption scheme available under the Code, ***the debtor may still choose the exemptions allowed to him under the law of his state, plus all federal nonbankruptcy exemptions*** (i.e., exemptions under federal laws other those provided for in the Code scheme). Because a majority of states have opted out of the federal scheme, most debtors must choose this scheme. The Code defines as state law exemptions, all property which the state allows the debtor to keep free of attachment for the payment of debts. The applicable law is the law of the state in which the debtor was domiciled for 180 days before the bankruptcy.

   a. **Wide variance in state law exemptions:** State law exemptions vary widely throughout the country. For example, Texas permits the exemption of a homestead of one acre in a city, town or village, and of 200 acres for a family in the country. The New England states, due to the antiquity of their laws and their Puritan heritage, tend to restrict exemptions to such things as church pews and teams of oxen.

   b. **Legal problems raised by variations:** The Constitution requires that the law of bankruptcy be "uniform". Obviously, the state-by-state differences in the determination of exemptions undermine the concept of uniformity. However, the standard of uniformity is deemed met so long as the federal law under which the state variations exist is itself applied uniformly throughout the country. This is dubbed "geographic" rather than "true" uniformity.

   c. **Federal exemptions:** Federal (nonbankruptcy) exemptions are those exemptions provided in federal statutes other than the Code, such as under the Civil Service, Veterans, and Social Security laws.

3. **Single election for joint cases:** In joint cases (as by husband and wife), both debtors must agree on a single election. If they can-

not agree and they live in a state which has not nullified the option of selecting the exemptions under the Code, they are deemed to have elected the Code exemptions.

D. Power to avoid liens on exempted property — § 522(f):   Under § 522(f), *the debtor is granted limited rights to avoid certain types of liens on exempt property*. Liens are voidable if they are not "reliance liens," such as security interests or mortgages. A "reliance lien" is generally given to the creditor as a security interest at the inception of a transaction.

1. **Special status of liens generally:** The denial of exemption in the case of debts secured by "reliance" liens illustrates an important Code principle. These liens, which include security interests in personal property and mortgages on real estate, basically remain undiminished in a bankruptcy case because of their status as property protected by the Fifth Amendment.

   a. **Contracts distinguished from security interests:**   The Supreme Court has long allowed the courts to authorize the rejection of contracts in bankruptcy cases. Indeed, the whole idea of a discharge of a debtor's obligations, which is the basis of the "fresh start," is based upon the elimination of contract rights and causes of action. Although both contracts and security interests are economic interests, the Court does not consider contracts to be the kind of traditional property that was meant to be protected under the Fifth Amendment.

   b. **Security interests as property:** Because they are closer to traditional property rights, the Court has relied on the Fifth Amendment in not allowing the rejection of security-interest liens without the awarding of just compensation to the holders of the liens. *Louisville Joint Stock Land Bank v. Radford*, 295 U.S. 555 (1935).

2. **Application to two kinds of liens:** Under § 522(f), the debtor *is permitted* to avoid two kinds of liens against exempt property — judicial liens and nonpossessory, nonpurchase-money liens.

   a. **Judicial liens:** A judicial lien is defined by § 101(36) as *a lien established by a state procedure like attachment or execution that is used to enforce an unpaid judgment or to restrain assets of someone who may disappear with those assets*. The property must be owned prior to the time that the lien is imposed before the lien can be avoided under § 522(f).

   Example: A divorce decree provides that the husband will become the owner of a house previously owned by the married couple, but that the wife will have a lien upon it for amounts owed to her by the husband under the decree. The lien was held to be a "judicial lien" and the house was an exempt asset under state law. But the lien could not be avoided under § 522(f) because ownership of the house by the former husband and the lien of the former wife were established at the same time by the divorce decree; the lien was treated as a preexisting encumbrance. *Farrey v. Sanderfoot*, 111 S.Ct. 1825 (1991).

    i. **Exception for alimony and support liens:** *Judicial liens for alimony and child support as prescribed by the Code are not avoidable under this provision.* An example of the kind of lien that had been avoided before the 1994 Code amendments but is now protected is the alimony lien in *Farrey v. Sanderfoot.*

b. **Nonpossessory, nonpurchase-money liens:** *A nonpossessory* (i.e., the creditor has not perfected its security interest by taking possession of the collateral), *nonpurchase-money lien* (i.e., the loan was not made for the specific purpose of purchasing the asset) *upon exempt assets such as household furniture and health aids, is avoidable.* Such liens are commonly used by some creditors as arm-twisting devices to force repayment of a loan. They are not really intended as security devices. For example, used furniture does not have much value in a liquidation sale. The value of this type of lien to a creditor may lie mainly in the fear it creates in the debtor.

    i. **Liens avoidable:** Under § 522(f), nonpossessory, nonpurchase-money liens are avoidable for three types of exempt property of the debtor or a dependent of the debtor: (1) household furnishings and goods held primarily for personal, family, or household use, including animals and crops, (2) professional books or tools of the trade, or (3) professionally prescribed health aids. (These liens are now generally illegal in any case under the Federal Trade Commission Rule on Credit Practices, (16 C.F.R. Part 444 (1992)).

    ii. **Certain business liens retained:** Before 1994, liens on certain professional equipment otherwise exempt might similarly have been avoided in order to protect the debtor's exemptions. However, the addition of § 522(f)(3) in 1994 *protects creditors' lien interests in professional books, tools of the trade, farm animals, and crops if they resulted from consensual security interests given by the debtor before bankruptcy and exceed $5,000 in value.* This provision applies in cases in which the debtor is utilizing state exemptions (i.e., the debtor is in a state that has opted out of the exemption scheme under the Code or the debtor voluntarily choses the state rather than the Code system). If the state either allows an unlimited exemption of property (except as to consensual liens) or prohibits avoidance of a consensual lien on property that could otherwise be claimed as exempt, the debtor may no longer avoid a security interest on the specified types of property to the extent the value of the property is in excess of $5,000.

3. **Constitutional challenge:** The ability to avoid liens under § 522(f) has been attacked as a violation of the creditor's right to just compensation under the Fifth Amendment. However, the Supreme Court has held that, because the avoidance of liens under this provision applies only to liens written after § 522(f) was adopted, creditors who wrote these liens did so with the knowledge that they were subject to the avoidance provisions of the Code. The Court also held that no property right of the creditor is really "taken." *United States v. Security Industrial Bank*, 459 U.S. 70 (1982).

E. **Effect of § 522(f) on impaired exemptions:** Under   § 522(f),   ***a debtor may avoid the fixing of a lien on an interest in his property "to the extent that such lien impairs an exemption to which the debtor would have been entitled"*** under § 522(b). As will be seen, this language gave rise to several issues of interpretation.

1. **Judicial liens that affect exempt status:** One of the issues that frequently arose in the courts was whether judicial liens encumbering property can be eliminated where a state has defined a category of property as *exempt unless it is subject to judicial liens*, in which case the property is nonexempt. In other words, can the judicial lien be avoided under § 522(f) so that the nonexempt property is converted into exempt property? The Supreme Court held that, ***where a state limitation invalidates a state exemption, the lien may be avoided under § 522(f) and the exemption allowed***. As with laws affecting federal exemptions, the Court stated that the correct question in this situation is whether avoiding the lien would entitle the debtor to an exemption and, if it would, then § 522(f) can be applied to avoid the lien. *Owen v. Owen*, 111 S.Ct. 1833 (1991).

2. **Mathematical approach to determining extent of impairment:** Prior to the 1994 amendment to § 522(f), several questions arose in the courts as to whether a lien impaired an exemption within the meaning of the statute. The question arose in several contexts in addition to the judicial lien/ exempt status situation discussed above. The contexts included the ability to avoid a lien where

the debtor had no equity in property over and above a secured lien, where a judicial lien was partially secured, and where a state homestead exemption existed only with respect to execution sales. Under the 1994 amendment to § 522(f), all such liens are voidable if they meet the mathematical formula for what constitutes the impairment of an exemption. Under this formula, ***a lien is considered to impair an exemption to the extent that the sum of all liens on the property and the amount of the exemption that the debtor could claim if there were no liens on the property*** <u>***exceeds***</u> ***the value of the debtor's interest in the property in the absence of liens.*** If the result is zero or a negative number, there is no impairment of the exemption.

F. **Waiver of exemptions restricted:** Under § 522(e), ***the debtor's exemptions*** (under either the state or § 522(d) Code schemes) ***may not be waived in favor of an unsecured creditor.*** This has resulted in the virtual elimination of the "exemptions waived" language which had been included in so many consumer promissory notes. For all practical purposes, consumer borrowers never seemed to understand the broad impact of that contractual language.

   1. **Waiver permitted in secured transactions:** A waiver of exemptions may be included in a secured transaction. Thus, a waiver of exemptions in a mortgage on land or a security agreement on personal property will be valid in favor of the secured creditor.

   2. **Other waivers not valid:** Other waivers of exemption rights, such as the power to avoid a transfer under § 522(f), are not enforceable.

IV. EXCEPTIONS TO DISCHARGE — § 523

Introductory note: We will discuss discharge in each of the specific bankruptcy filing chapters (see *infra*, p. 160, 174, 218 and 246). In this section, we examine the exceptions to discharge under the provisions of § 523. These provisions are applicable to all the Chapters.

A. **General definition of discharge:** After exempting certain assets from the estate and committing the rest to creditors, the debtor looks for a discharge from remaining obligations.

   1. **Different from chapter to chapter:** Discharges are granted differently under each of the Code chapters. The time at which discharge occurs differs from chapter to chapter. The debts discharged also vary.

2. **Discharge a single event:** Discharge happens at a particular time in the bankruptcy and affects all outstanding debts at the same time; debts are *not* discharged one-by-one in a series of transactions.

3. **Exceptions from discharge:** § 523 lists a series of debts that are not dischargeable for various reasons, including public policy and the behavior of the debtor when he incurred the debts.

4. **Distinguished from § 727 bar to discharge:** § 523 must be distinguished from § 727(a) (*infra*, p. 160), which lists circumstances under which a Chapter 7 discharge may not be obtained at all.

B. **Exceptions from discharge apply only to individuals:** *Only the debts of an individual may be excepted from discharge under § 523.* Relief under Chapter 13 is limited to individuals, but Chapters 7, 11 and 12 are available to corporations and partnerships as well as individuals. Since Chapter 7 provides for liquidation of the debtor, there is no need to discharge a business entity that files under 7; the entity simply goes out of business.

C. **Exceptions that must be obtained from the court:** When a particular claim is not discharged, the creditor may pursue its legal remedies against the debtor after the general discharge as though the bankruptcy had never occurred. In general, exceptions from discharge occur automatically if the language prescribed by § 523(a) applies. Under § 523(c), however, *creditors for debts described in § 523(a)(2), (4), (6), and (15) must ask the court to determine that the debts are excepted from discharge*. Most of these categories of debts are for obligations colored by fraud or maliciousness. *In the absence of a request by the creditor, debts in these categories <u>are</u> discharged*.

D. **Eleven principal exceptions from discharge:** Only eleven of the sixteen enumerated exceptions from discharge under § 523(a) are sufficiently common to be discussed here.

1. **Certain tax claims:** Under § 523(a)(1), *tax and customs duty debts that are excluded from discharge* include (1) those arising in the ordinary course of the debtor's business during the "gap" period (see discussion of gap period in involuntary cases, *supra*, p. 28); (2) taxes for which returns were due (whether or not actually filed) for the three years before the petition; and (3) taxes due as to which a return was not filed or was fraudulent.

2. **Fraudulent representations:** *Upon application to the Court*, § 523(a)(2) can be used to *exclude discharge for debts for money, property, services or credit if obtained through fraud*.

Example: Debtor D obtains credit from Creditor C through fraud. Before the bankruptcy, C sues D and obtains a judgment under a stipulation between D and C that does not contain a description of the facts. D attempts to discharge the judgment debt in its bankruptcy, but C claims an exemption from the discharge under § 523(a)(2). D asserts that the fraud could no longer be asserted because the stipulation in state court was *res judicata* and could not be reopened. It was held, however, that the policies of § 523 not to allow discharge of a fraudulent debt overrode the policies behind *res judicata* and that the fraud could be examined in bankruptcy. *Brown v. Felsen*, 442 U.S. 127 (1979).

a. **Objective or subjective standard?:** Section 523(a)(2)(A), excepting from discharge debts incurred through fraud, involves two requirements. First, the debtor must have **committed fraud**; and second, the creditor who seeks the exception must have been **justified** in relying on the fraudulent act. Each requirement is subject to a subjective test or an objective test.

- *As to the creditor,* the Supreme Court has held that the **creditor must prove subjectively "justifiable" reliance** rather than objectively "reasonable" reliance. *Field v. Mans,* 116 S. Ct. 437 (1995).

- *As to the debtor,* the majority of courts have held that an **objective test applies** and the debtor has committed fraud only if he did n**ot have a reasonable basis for believing in the validity of his acts**. Based on *Field v. Mans*, however, the Eastern District of Louisiana Bankruptcy Court has joined a growing minority of courts in the position that the subjective test should apply. Under this test, there will be no fraud if the debtor honestly believed in the validity of his acts. *In re Totina*, 198 B.R. 673 (Bankr. E.D.La. 1996).

b. **Detailed set of requirements for fraudulent credit statements:** Under § 523(a)(2)(B), *in order for a fraudulent credit statement to be excepted from discharge, the credit statement must*:

- *be materially false* (not false in minor particulars),

- *deal with the debtor's or an insider's financial condition*,

- *have been reasonably relied upon* (the creditor must in fact have relied upon the false statement itself and not discovered it later in an effort to avoid the discharge), and

- *have been made by the debtor with intent to deceive* (e.g., the debtor did not make a reasonable and good faith attempt to disclose his financial condition).

c. **Rationale for special treatment of credit statements:**
The stricter standard for credit statements than for other instances of fraudulent behavior in § 523(a)(2) stems from the fact that financial statements are usually wrong in some particular or other, and creditors should not be able to use insubstantial or good faith errors as the basis for excepting a debt from discharge.

d. **Presumption of fraud:** In two cases, § 523(a)(2) *creates presumptions of fraudulent conduct that cause the underlying debts to be non-dischargeable*. The first case applies if a consumer aggregated debts of more than $1,000 to a single creditor for luxury goods or services within 60 days of the petition. The second applies if the consumer obtained cash advances under an "open end credit plan" (typically a credit card or overdraft checking plan) of more than $1,000 within 60 days of the order for relief. Both are presumed to be fraudulent and non-dischargeable. The debtor may, of course, rebut the presumption.

3. **Debts not listed, scheduled, or known:** Under § 523(a)(3), *an undisclosed or unlisted debt will be exempt from discharge*. The creditor who receives no knowledge of the bankruptcy will not receive payment. Under these circumstances, it is hardly right for the debt to be discharged. Lack of notice and of actual knowledge will prevent a creditor from participating in the case, but it will be able to pursue the individual debtor after the discharge. This can often be of greater value than participation in the bankruptcy. However, if either of the following exceptions applies, the debt will be discharged.

a. **Creditor is able to timely file claim:** *With respect to debts other than § 523(a)(2), (4), or (6) debts* (debts other than those incurred under fraudulent or malicious circumstances), *if the creditor has notice or actual knowledge of the bankruptcy in time to file a proof of claim, the debt is discharged — subject, of course, to a §523(a) exception.*

b. **Creditor is able to timely file claim or request exception from discharge:** *With respect to § 523(a)(2), (4) or (6) debts, if the creditor has notice or actual knowledge of the bankruptcy in time to timely file a proof of claim* (and to request that the debt be excepted from discharge), *the debt is discharged — subject to the court granting a §523 exception.*

4. **Fraud, defalcation, embezzlement, and larceny:** Upon application to the Court under § 523(a)(4), *a debt will be denied dis-*

charge if it was incurred though fraud or defalcation while the debtor was acting in a fiduciary capacity, or if it was incurred through embezzlement or larceny.

5. **Obligations for support or alimony:**   Under § 523(a)(5), *if a debt is for alimony, maintenance, or support stemming from a separation agreement, divorce decree, or court order, it will not be discharged*.

   a. **Effect of assignment:**   If the debt has been assigned by the individual designated to receive the payments under the agreement or decree, it will be discharged like any other debt. If the assignment is to a governmental agency (in which case it is assumed that the assignment grows out of a continuing need for alimony, maintenance or support), it will not be discharged.

   b. **Property agreements not excepted:**   The debt must truly be for alimony, maintenance, or support, not the result of a division of property between the parties. Bankruptcy courts will look to the intent of the parties and to such factors as (1) whether one of the parties needs the payments to continue a reasonable lifestyle, and (2) disparities in actual or anticipated income that would make alimony appropriate. The test is a federal one and, although the federal courts may be influenced by state law, they will not necessarily be bound by the labels the states have used. *In re Smith*, 114 B.R.457 (Bkrtcy. S.D.Miss. 1990).

   Example 1: In a divorce decree, one spouse agrees to make a contribution to the other spouse's college and labels it "alimony." Although it was in fact considered alimony under the applicable state law, the contribution will probably not be considered alimony under the Code.

   Example 2: A divorced spouse is compelled in a divorce decree to pay his ex-spouse's legal fees. The applicable state law holds such payments to be alimony. Under the Code, legal fees, usually an important part of the divorced spouse's needs, are also considered to be alimony and most courts have so held. *In re Song*, 661 F.2d 6 (2nd Cir. 1981).

   c. **Obligations other than alimony, maintenance, or support:** In 1994, Congress expanded this exception by adding § 523(a)(15). (See also *infra*, p. 59.) Henceforth, all obligations resulting from the court order, dealing with alimony, maintenance, and support, are also exempted. Congress had in mind debts arising from such obligations as property settlements, a duty to remit royalty payments, and the obligation of one spouse to hold the other harmless from tax deficiencies. However, for this new category of spousal obligations, the exemption applies only if the debtor is able to honor the obligations without undue economic hardship.

6. **Willful and malicious injuries:** Under § 523(a)(6), ***debts resulting from willful and malicious injuries to person or to property are, subject to the court's review under § 523(c), excepted from discharge.*** In this regard, note the different culpability standard under § 523(a)(9), dealing with the liability of the debtor in operating a motor vehicle while intoxicated (*infra*, p. 59).

7. **Fines, penalties or forfeitures:** Under § 523(a)(7), ***if owed to a governmental unit, a "fine, penalty, or forfeiture" that is "not compensation for actual pecuniary loss" is not dischargeable.*** Parking violations, criminal penalties, and fines for operating as a polluter are fines and are thus nondischargeable; but payment under a commercial contract with the government is not a fine or penalty, nor is restitution to the government for cleaning up a waste site. *Ohio v. Kovacs* (*supra*, p. 17). Under a special Code provision, fines owed on delinquent taxes are dischargeable unless the tax itself is of a sort that is nondischargeable.

   Example: Debtor Robinson defrauds the state Department of Income Maintenance, is tried, and pleads guilty. She is ordered to repay the unlawful welfare payments to the Probation Office. The repayment is found to be a fine that is not compensation for actual pecuniary loss and is therefore excepted from discharge. The system of restitution should be regarded not as compensation for loss but as part of the state criminal justice system, to which the Code generally defers. *Kelly v. Robinson*, 479 U.S. 36 (1986).

8. **Educational loans:** Many students who are tempted to discharge their educational loans in bankruptcy will probably be dissuaded by the Code. Under § 523(a)(8), ***debts for educational loans made, insured or guaranteed by a governmental unit, or under a program funded in whole or in part by a governmental unit or non-profit organization are not dischargeable*** unless the student debtor can show the debt imposes an ***undue hardship*** on her and her dependents. Courts typically take a careful look at a hardship claim to ensure that it is not being exaggerated.

   a. **Impact on cosigners:** Family members who cosign a student's promissory note may or may not be prevented from discharging the educational loan in the event of their bankruptcies. Although the Code language clearly exempts the debt from discharge, not all the courts are convinced that such an exemption honors the will of Congress. See *In re Hammarstrom*, 95 B.R. 160 (Bkrtcy. N.D.N.Cal.) for a review of the conflicting views.

9. **Drunk driving exception:** Under § 523(a)(9), *liability for death or personal injury caused by the debtor's operation of a motor vehicle while drunk or under the influence of drugs is nondischargeable.*

10. **Further limitations on divorce and maintenance obligations:** Under § 523(a)(15), *if the debtor has divorce or separation obligations incurred in connection with an agreement or court proceeding, they are discharged only if (1) the debtor is unable to make payments with funds above those necessary for his support* (in the case of a debtor who is in business, with funds above those necessary for its operation), *or (2) such a discharge results in a benefit to the debtor that outweighs the detrimental consequences to a spouse, former spouse, or child.*

11. **Condominium and cooperative fees:** Under § 523(a)(16), a fee that becomes due to a cooperative or condominium association after the order for relief is not discharged, even if the contract with the association was entered into before the order, if the debtor physically occupies the dwelling unit or leases it to a tenant during the applicable period.

V.   EFFECT OF A DISCHARGE — § 524

Introductory note: The discharges provided by Chapters 7, 9, 11, 12 and 13 of the Code differ from one to the other. In this section, we will discuss § 524, which relates generally to all of the Chapters (except where a Chapter has been specifically excluded from its impact) and spells out the effects of a discharge of a debtor's obligations.

A. **Discharge affects personal liability:** We have seen that the Code is more respectful of property rights (security interests) than of personal obligations (contracts). Although both clearly represent economic interests, the former are not generally dischargeable.

1. **Liens left intact:** *Discharge annuls unsecured obligations but leaves intact security interest liens against both real and personal property.* This principle is honored by § 524, which emphasizes that a discharge voids personal liabilities but not liens.

2. **Discharge voids judgments related to discharged debts:** *A judgment with respect to a debt that has been discharged is*

also discharged. On the other hand, a discharge does not void a judgment that affirms the validity of a lien.

B. Discharge enjoins future action: Under § 524(a)(2), *discharge will operate as an injunction against the "commencement or continuation of an action, the employment of process, or an act to collect, recover, or offset" any personal liability that was discharged.*

   1. Mirrors protection under automatic stay: The provisions of § 524(a)(2) mirror a similar set of protections given to the debtor under the § 362 automatic stay (*supra*, p. 36). As to personal liabilities dischargeable in bankruptcy, § 362 stays actions to collect them before discharge and § 524 enjoins collection after discharge. However, the § 362 automatic stay extends to actions against property interests (security interests and mortgages); the § 524 prohibitions do not.

      Example: Sam sees Moe on West 40th Street in New York City after Moe has been discharged in bankruptcy and says, "How about that five thousand you owe me?" Sam has committed a prohibited act and has violated the § 524 injunction.

   2. Notice to creditor required: As with the § 362 stay, the Code anticipates that creditors will be notified of the discharge if they are to be subjected to the § 524 injunction. Rule 4004(g) requires the court clerk to mail a copy of the discharge to the creditors.

C. Reaffirmation agreements — § 524(c): *Reaffirmation agreements are agreements between debtors and creditors that bind the debtors to the terms of obligations that are dischargeable in the bankruptcy.* For example, discharge may free a debtor from the terms of an agreement to pay the remaining installments on a loan; a reaffirmation agreement commits the debtor to make the payments nevertheless.

   1. Background: Originally the Code draftsmen had intended to prohibit reaffirmation agreements completely. They were viewed as the inevitable product of high-pressure tactics by creditors to take from debtors the benefits of their discharges. However, reaffirmation agreements offer some benefits to debtors. In particular, they enable debtors to retain collateral that they might otherwise lose to secured creditors. (As discussed above, although the discharge does eliminate personal obligations, it does not of itself eliminate liens that may have secured those obligations.)

   2. Restrictions on reaffirmation agreements: Under § 544(c), the terms of a reaffirmation agreement are circumscribed with enough consumer protections to insulate the debtor from possible creditor abuse.

a. **Debtor's intent to perform:** Obviously, it's not easy to get a debtor in bankruptcy to reaffirm a debt. A debtor who does enter into a reaffirmation agreement with the protections imposed by the Code may be assumed to have manifested his intent to perform its terms.

b. **Requirements of agreement:** *A reaffirmation agreement must (1) be made before the discharge; (2) contain a statement that the debtor can rescind it at anytime before the discharge or within 60 days after the agreement is filed with the court, whichever occurs later,* and that the agreement is not required under the Code, under nonbankruptcy law, or under any other agreement; *and (3) be filed with the court together with an affidavit of the debtor's lawyer that the agreement is voluntary and does not impose an undue hardship on the debtor or a dependent of the debtor,* that the debtor is fully informed, and that the lawyer has fully advised the debtor of the legal effects of the agreement and any default thereunder. *If the debtor is not represented by a lawyer, the agreement must be approved by the court,* unless it concerns a consumer debt secured by a lien on real property, e.g., an ordinary home mortgage.

c. **Suits for violations:** In 1998, in a highly publicized situation, Sears Roebuck & Co. publicly stated that it had used "flawed legal judgment" when it failed to file signed reaffirmation agreements. It concluded a class action against it by paying a large settlement. This was followed by a flurry of actions across the country in comparable situations: individual state and federal actions, class actions, and related actions such as claims in contempt. Some of these were allowed, others prohibited. As of this writing (August 2001) there is no consensus position on what may be done in the event of such violations. For example: the First Circuit has held that a district court wrongly dismissed a class action (*Bessette V. Avco Financial Services, Inc.*, 230 F.3d 439 (1st Cir. 2000)); the Ninth Circuit Bankruptcy Panel affirmed a Bankruptcy Court's dismissal of the class action (*Bassett v. American General Finance, Inc.*, 255 B.R. 747 (B.A.P. 9th Cir. 2000)); the Seventh Circuit also affirmed a Bankruptcy Court's dismissal of a class action (*Cox v. Zale Delaware, Inc.*, 239 F.3d 910 (7th Cir. 2001)). There is a general agreement that there is an individual remedy in contempt. We anticipate that litigation will continue at both the trial and appellate levels until the issue is resolved.

D. Hearing on discharge — § 524(d): In its determination whether or not to grant a discharge, the court need not conduct a hearing, but it has the option of holding a hearing for the purpose of informing the debtor of its disposition. *If a debtor was not represented by an attorney during the course of negotiating a reaffirmation agreement, the court must hold a hearing and ensure that the debtor is informed about the agreement and its effects.*

E. Voluntary payment of debts: Under § 524(f), it is clear that *a debtor who has been discharged may voluntarily repay any debt.*

1. Reasons for voluntary repayments: The debtor may wish to honor discharged commitments, despite the fact that they no longer carry the force of law, due to compelling family obligations, or obligations to persons for whom the debtor's reputation is important.

2. Difference between voluntary and reaffirmation payment: The difference between voluntary payments and payments under a reaffirmation agreement is that the debtor may simply discontinue voluntary payments at any time while a reaffirmation agreement is an enforceable contract. D

VI. PROTECTIVE MEASURES FOR THE DISCHARGED DEBTOR — § 525

A. Prohibitions on discriminatory and other acts: To reaffirm the positive effects of a discharge, certain acts are set forth in § 525 that may not be executed against a discharged debtor (no longer termed a "bankrupt") under the Code. Underlying the Code is the modern view that society should not demean the unfortunate individual who has resorted to bankruptcy and paid its price.

B. Prohibitions applicable to governmental units: Most of the prohibitions are with respect to acts of governmental units. In broad outline, *a government unit may not "deny, revoke, suspend, or refuse to renew a license" or a similar grant, discriminate with respect to such a grant, or deny or discriminate with respect to employment, "solely" because the individual has been a debtor under the Code*, was insolvent before a case was begun, or has not paid a debt that is dischargeable.

1. Importance of government functions to discharged debtor: The many prohibitions against government are in response to government's unique power. It is the only source for such essentials as a driver's license, an occupancy certificate, a building permit, a divorce decree, or a passport.

Example 1: Debtor D negligently injures Creditor C in an automobile accident. D does not pay his obligation to C and the debt is discharged in D's bankruptcy. Arizona refuses to renew D's driver's license. It relies on a state law that provides that a license can not be renewed for anyone under an unsatisfied judgment claim. The state's refusal violates the Code and interferes with the fresh start otherwise available to the debtor. *Perez v. Campbell*, 402 U.S. 637 (1971).

Example 2: D fails to satisfy its obligation to C for a motor vehicle accident and the obligation is discharged in D's bankruptcy. Ohio requires proof of adequate insurance from anyone with an unsatisfied judgment and refuses to renew D's license. This requirement does not violate § 525(a). A state is not discriminating against a debtor nor is it preventing his fresh start by requiring proof of future financial responsibility. The law applies equally to all persons who have not satisfied a judgment, whether or not they have been discharged in bankruptcy. Some burdens may be imposed by the state, even on debtors. *Duffey v. Dollison*, 734 F.2d 265 (6th Cir. 1984).

2. **"Solely" requirement:** *A government may not discriminate or deprive "solely" because of a bankruptcy or insolvency*, but it is not restricted from looking at the bankruptcy as a factor that bears upon an individual's qualifications.

Example 1: Debtor D fails to repay a government loan, has the loan discharged in bankruptcy and then applies for another loan which is refused. The government has the right to reject D for the second loan. The bankruptcy was not the sole cause of the rejection; it was simply one element in an evaluation of D's creditworthiness. *In re Rose*, 23 B.R. 662 (Bkrtcy. D. Conn. 1982).

Example 2: D is a debtor in a bankruptcy case when he applies for admission to the bar. The Committee on Character and Fitness establishes that the bankruptcy is one among many factors exhibiting that D did not have the requisite character to practice law. § 525 was not violated. *Matter of Anonymous*, 74 N.Y.2d 938, 549 N.E.2d 472 (1989).

C. **Prohibitions applicable to private employers:** Under § 525(b), there are restrictions on non-governmental parties, but in a much more limited way than on governments. *Restrictions on private employers are limited to discrimination in employment.* Again, factors other than the bankruptcy may justify the employer's actions, which will violate § 525(b) only if they are based "solely" on bankruptcy or insolvency.

Example: D goes through a bankruptcy case and is subsequently fired. The employer is found not to have violated § 525(b) because it was able to show that D had performed poorly in his work and that the employer had been considering releasing D even before the bankruptcy. *Stockhouse v. Hines*, 75 B.R. 83 (Bkrtcy. D.Wyo. 1987).

D. **Student loans:** *Neither a government entity that makes or guarantees student loans, nor a private business that makes loans guaranteed or insured under a governmental student loan program, may discriminate against an applicant solely because the applicant has been a debtor* under the Bankruptcy Code or because the debtor has failed to pay a debt dischargeable or discharged under the Code.

E. **Expansive application of § 525:** Congress has accompanied § 525 with its admonition that it be read broadly and that its list of examples of discrimination is not exhaustive. *The courts are encouraged to expand § 525 to prevent behavior that unduly interferes with the debtor's fresh start*.

Example: A private medical clinic denies treatment to an individual who had discharged a prior bill in bankruptcy. § 525 was violated even though the non-governmental party was engaged in other than employment discrimination. The court held that this constituted the type of discriminatory treatment that § 525 sought to eradicate. *In re Olson*, 10 C.B.C.2d 864 (Bkrtcy. N.D. Iowa 1984).

CHAPTER 5

THE TRUSTEE

Introductory note: A trustee — generally someone who manages assets for their true owner — is present in varying capacities throughout the Code. A trustee is always a part of any bankruptcy case under Chapters 7, 12 and 13 and, although not required, may be appointed under Chapters 9 and 11. The functions of the trustee differ from Chapter to Chapter. For example, the trustee's functions are much more important under Chapter 11 (where the trustee will need business skills in order to run the business during the period of the reorganization) than under Chapter 9. The specific duties of the trustee in each case are described separately in our discussion of the bankruptcy Chapters. In this chapter, concepts common to all trustees are discussed.

I. ROLE OF TRUSTEE — § 323

A. **The trustee represents the estate:** Under § 323(a), *the trustee "is the representative of the estate."* In this sense, he is like an officer of a corporation. Therefore, the trustee does not represent the creditors, although in the normal Chapter 7 case he will be elected by them; neither does he represent the debtor. Acting throughout the case on behalf of the estate, the trustee is a fiduciary who may take positions that favor creditors in one instance or the debtor in another. In specific instances, the trustee may:

- press the claim of a creditor for payment against an objection by the debtor;

- assert on behalf of the debtor that a claim should not be paid;

- try to have property taken away from a secured creditor and returned to the estate;

- claim that a debtor is abusing Chapter 7 and that the case should be dismissed.

B. **Trustee's right to sue and be sued:** As with corporate management, *the trustee may sue and be sued on behalf of the estate.* These rights are established by § 323(b) and confirmed by Rule 6009. *The trustee may also be sued personally for mismanagement of the estate.* Suits of this kind may be brought by the debtor or the creditors, since assets in the estate may ultimately benefit one or the other of them. Most courts hold that negligence by the trustee in the conduct of his fiduciary duties is enough to sustain his liability; others require an intentional or willful act. *In re Reich*, 13 C.B.C.2d 988 (Bkrtcy. E.D. Mich. 1985).

C. Relationship to Chapter 9 and 11 debtors: As noted, there is not always a trustee in Chapter 9 or Chapter 11 cases. A Chapter 11 reorganization enables the debtor to continue the operation of its business protected by the automatic stay. To enable it to carry on its business, the Chapter 11 debtor is given, under § 1107, the same powers as are ordinarily available to a trustee under the Code. Whenever we discuss the powers of the trustee, it should be noted that the debtor in a Chapter 11 case can exercise these same powers when no trustee has been appointed. Under § 902, there is a similar result in Chapter 9 cases involving municipal bankruptcies.

II.   ELIGIBILITY AND QUALIFICATION TO SERVE AS TRUSTEE

A. Individual as trustee: Under § 321(a)(1), *a trustee may be any individual who is competent to perform the duties of trustee.* Although a corporation may also act as trustee, most bankruptcy trustees are individuals. To qualify as trustee in a case under Chapter 7, 12, or 13, the individual must reside in or have an office in the judicial district where the case is pending or in an adjacent judicial district.

B. Corporate trustee: Under § 321(a)(2), *a trustee may be a corporation, so long as it is authorized by its charter or its by-laws to act as trustee.* In a case under Chapter 7, 12 or 13, it must have an office in the judicial district where the case is pending or in an adjacent judicial district.

C. Examiner ineligible: A person who has served as an examiner in a case is specifically excluded from eligibility to serve as trustee.

D. United States Trustee: If necessary, the United States Trustee for the judicial district in which the case is pending may serve as the trustee in the bankruptcy case. However, this is not customary. As we shall see (*infra*, p. 68), the United States Trustee is really designed to serve as an administrative officer of the court, not as the occasional trustee who acts for the estate. It's important not to confuse the two uses of the word "trustee."

E. Qualification and bond: To qualify, the trustee must normally file a bond under § 322(a) to secure faithful performance. Under Rule 2010(a), the United States Trustee may approve a blanket bond to cover a number of trustees serving in different cases. If a lawsuit is brought against the trustee, recovery may be had on the bond. The amount of the bond is determined by the United States Trustee, as is the sufficiency of the surety who has liability for payment of the bond.

III. FUNCTIONING AS TRUSTEE

A. **Employment of professionals:** Under § 327, the trustee is permitted to employ lawyers, accountants, appraisers, auctioneers, and other professional persons to assist him in carrying out his duties. ***The persons employed by the trustee must be disinterested and cannot represent an interest adverse to the estate.*** If the trustee is operating the debtor's business, the persons employed may be the debtor's former employees.

   1. **Trustee may assume professional roles:** With court approval, the trustee may also be counsel or accountant for the estate.

   2. **Advisers to creditors:** Professional persons are not disqualified from serving the trustee solely because they work for a creditor, although the court may review their employment if an objection is made.

B. **Compensation of professionals:** Under §330 the trustee is compensated and under § 329, the trustee may fix the compensation of professionals who are hired (*infra*, p. 182).

   1. **Subject to review by court:** The court may review this compensation and revise it if it proves "improvident" or if the professional person has an interest adverse to the estate.

   2. **Proof of service:** Rule 2016 requires that anyone seeking compensation from the bankruptcy estate file an application that sets forth the services rendered, the time spent, the expenses incurred and the amount of payment requested.

C. **Lawsuits against the trustee:** Lawsuits may be brought against trustees for various acts.

   1. **Acts within official authority:** In general, a trustee may be sued in state or federal court concerning an act in managing property subject to his control. If he violates the law while acting within his official capacity, it has been held (although there is not widespread authority on the point) that he may *not* be sued in a state court without leave of the bankruptcy court. *State v. Better Brite Plating, Inc.*, 483 N.W.2d 574 (Wis. 1992), interpreting 28 U.S.C. § 959. If the law violated is a state criminal law, the trustee can be prosecuted only in federal court because the crime becomes a federal crime and the penalty a federal penalty (18 U.S.C. § 1911).

   2. **Acts outside official authority:** When acting outside his official authority, a trustee may be sued in federal or state court. *Leonare v. Vrooman*, 383 F.2d 556 (9th Cir.), cert. den., 390 U.S. 925 (1968).

IV. THE UNITED STATES TRUSTEE

A. History and scope of office: In 1978, an experimental United States Trustee program was organized in order to take administrative duties off the shoulders of the bankruptcy judges. Not only was this program designed to give the judges more time to devote to their judicial functions, it was intended also to restore confidence in a system which was eroding. Among other things, participants were questioning the impartiality of judges' appointment of the very trustees who then appeared before the judges. The experimental U.S. Trustee program proved successful, and the 1986 Code amendments (28 U.S.C. § 581 *et seq.*) established the system as permanent and expanded it to all districts, except for the states of Alabama and North Carolina.

1. **Panel of trustees:** As one of her duties, the United States Trustee is instructed by 28 U.S.C. § 586(1) to ***maintain a panel of private trustees that are available to serve as trustees in cases under Chapters 7 and 11***. Under § 701, an interim Chapter 7 trustee is appointed by the United States Trustee from this panel (*infra*, p. 152).

2. **Supervision by Attorney General:** Continuing the concept in existence before the 1986 legislation that made the United States Trustee a permanent part of the bankruptcy process, the United States Trustee is under the supervision of the Attorney General of the United States (28 U.S.C. § 586(c)).

3. **Trustee as Administrative officer:** The United States Trustee is an administrative officer and, although ***he may often assist parties in mediating disputes among themselves***, he must not perform any judicial duties or intervene to resolve disputes.

   Example: In D's bankruptcy case, a trustee is appointed. Despite the trustee's objections, J.D. Lumber insists that he is a creditor and therefore entitled to certain information from the trustee. In order to sustain his position, J.D. Lumber writes a letter to the United States Trustee arguing the supporting law. The bankruptcy judge holds that the United States Trustee can not decide this dispute. He is not a judicial officer and the resolution of judicial disputes by him would violate the separation of powers; it would be the equivalent of allowing the Department of Justice, which has jurisdiction over the United States Trustee, to decide disputes. In addition, regular trustees are often appointed by United States Trustees and to a considerable degree, are dependent upon them for employment. Therefore, regular trustees should not be controlled by the views of the United States Trustee on how contested issues should be decided. *In re Johnson*, 23 C.B.C.2d 217 (Bkrtcy. N.C.Cal. 1990).

B. Duties of United States Trustees: Provisions relating to the United States Trustees' functions are scattered throughout the Code and the Rules. For example, the United States Trustee is permitted, under § 707(b), to move for dismissal where there is substantial abuse in a Chapter 7 consumer case (*infra*, p. 149). Also, Rule 2002(k) requires that the bankruptcy clerk send the United States Trustee copies of all notices sent to other parties in interest. Under 28 U.S.C. § 586, the United States Trustee is given the generalized duty to "supervise the administration of cases and trustees." The United States Trustee's basic duties are spelled out in detail. The functions include:

- scheduling and holding creditors' committee meetings;

- monitoring plans and disclosure statements in Chapter 11;

- reviewing applications for compensation and reimbursement;

- taking such action as may be appropriate to ensure that all reports are filed;

- monitoring Chapter 11 creditors committees;

- taking action to prevent undue delay; and

- reporting to the United States Attorney when necessary.

CHAPTER 6

THE CREDITOR — GENERAL RULES

Introductory note: The Code sets forth the entities that are permitted to make claims in a bankruptcy case. A creditor files a proof of claim; an indenture trustee (i.e., the trustee for a bond indenture) files a proof of claim on behalf of creditors (i.e., the bondholders); an equity security holder (i.e., a shareholder in a corporation or a limited partner in a limited partnership) files a proof of interest. "Proof" of claim or interest simply means that a formal submission of a claim has been made.

I. DEFINITION OF CREDITOR — § 101(10)

A. Creditors with claims arising at or before the order for relief:
Under § 101(10)(A), the term "creditor" is defined to mean "an entity that has a claim against the debtor that arose at the time of or before the order for relief concerning the debtor, . . . " As we have seen, the term "claim" is very broadly defined (§ 101(5), *supra*, p. 17). Because of this broad definition, most entities with any economic relationship to the debtor at the time of or before the order for relief will qualify as creditors, assuming that the debtor is obligated to them under the relationship.

B. Creditors with claims *deemed* to arise before the order for relief: Under § 101(10)(B), a creditor is defined to include entities with certain kinds of claims that are *deemed* by the Code to have arisen before the order for relief, even though they actually arise after it. The most important of these are listed as allowable claims in § 502(f)–(i). These claims arise after the order for relief from events inherent in the management of the bankruptcy, including such events as the termination of a contract under § 365, or the reclaiming of property under the avoiding powers of the trustee under § 544, § 547, or § 548 (see *infra*, pp. 106, 125 and 136).

Example: Prior to the bankruptcy, D and X enter into a contract. In the bankruptcy, D's trustee terminates the contract, using the power to reject executory contracts given to the trustee in § 365. X has a claim for breach of contract that obviously arose after the order for relief and, therefore, does not satisfy the definition of "creditor" in § 101(10)(A). But under § 502(g), X's claim is deemed to have arisen before the petition. X becomes a creditor as defined under § 101(10)(B).

II. FILING OF CLAIMS — § 501

A. Unsecured creditors must file proofs of claim in order to recover: The language of § 501 states that a claim may be filed by a creditor. However, with certain exceptions in Chapter 9 and 11 cases that will be discussed, ***creditors must file "proofs" of claims if they wish to participate in the bankruptcy and share in the distribution.*** Because the language is permissive, a secured creditor who will be able to take its property and run, need not file a proof of claim; bankruptcy will not affect the consensual, properly perfected liens of secured creditors.

1. **Meaning of "proof":** As noted, a "proof" of claim is not really a proof; the term is a remnant from pre-Code procedures. It is merely a statement of the creditor's claim.

2. **Filing necessary for participation:** If a creditor wants to share in the distribution and receive his pro-rata share along with similar claims and interests, he must file a timely proof under the requirements of Rules 3002 and 3003. For example, Section 726 (a), (b), and (c), which govern distributions to ordinary creditors in Chapter 7 cases, all refer to "allowed" claims.

    These Rules do not apply to cases in Chapter 9 (§ 925) or Chapter 11 (§ 1111), where claims that are "listed" will be recognized without the filing of proofs. Where all the requirements for a proof of claim have not been adhered to, a proof of claim may be considered to be timely filed if the documents filed fairly reflect the existence of a claim against the estate.

    Example: Debtor D adopts a plan in its Chapter 13 case under which D agrees to pay all of its creditors 71 percent of their claims. C is included among the creditors. C files an objection to the confirmation of a plan and attaches its proof of claim, but does not actually file its proof of claim until several months after the deadline for a timely filing. In *In re Joiner*, 19 C.B.C.2d 1446 (Bkrtcy. N.D.Ohio), it was held that C had timely filed a sufficient, informal proof of claim with its objection, even though the proof was neither date-stamped nor made a part of the Court's file of proofs of claims.

3. **No asset cases:** If the bankruptcy has no assets left for distribution to the unsecured creditors, or the assets are so small that a distributive share in them is not worth the effort, creditors are not likely to file at all.

B. Debtor may file proof for creditor: There may be circumstances in which a creditor does not wish to file a proof, but the debtor wishes to force the creditor's participation in the bankruptcy. Under § 502(c), ***the debtor is permitted to file a proof of claim for the creditor***.

Example: Creditor C has a claim for alimony against Debtor D that will not be discharged because of § 523(a)(5) (which prevents a discharge of debts for alimony or child support) (See *supra*, p. 57). C may choose to skip the bankruptcy and collect from D later on. If C is forced to file a proof of claim and thus to collect a share of the bankruptcy, the debt from D to C (the amount of unpaid alimony that is due as of the time of the petition) may be paid in a reduced amount under the distribution in bankruptcy without other consequence to D. Under § 502(c), D is allowed to file on C's behalf to force C's participation. Because alimony is not a dischargeable debt, the debtor is not relieved from paying amounts due after the date of the petition.

C. Trustee may file claim for creditor: Under § 501(c), ***the trustee is allowed to file a proof for a creditor***. This power is important where a creditor has not filed a proof of claim and the creditor's interest, such as the lien of a secured creditor, may be voided.

Example: Secured Creditor C does not file because all he wants is to remove his collateral. If Trustee T suspects that C's secured claim is invalid and can be challenged under § 502(b) (*infra*, p. 77), he may file a proof in C's behalf. He may then be able to invalidate C's lien under § 506(d) (*infra*, p. 84).

III. CONTRIBUTION AND SURETYSHIP — §§ 502, 509

A. Situations to which applicable: There are several situations where a third party is entitled to step into the shoes of a creditor to assert a claim in bankruptcy. In these situations, the creditor may have no incentive to file a proof of claim against the debtor in bankruptcy because he has been made whole by the third party, usually called a guarantor or surety. ***The guarantor who has an interest in recovering from the debtor is allowed to file a proof of claim***. These situations are best illustrated by the following examples, in all three of which G (guarantor) is a surety.

1. **Joint tortfeasors:** D and G are joint tortfeasors who injure C. G pays C and looks for some contribution from D in D's bankruptcy.

2. **Guarantors:** G guarantees D's debt to C, pays C upon D's default, and looks to some reimbursement from D in D's bankruptcy.

3. **Providing security for another's obligation:** G secures D's debt to C with G's assets. Upon D's default to C, C takes possession

of those assets. G looks to some reimbursement from D in D's bankruptcy.

B. Contribution or subrogation — § 502 or § 509:   A surety has the option of filing a contribution claim (arising from the right to recover from a co-debtor for payment of a debt) in its own right under § 502(c), or as a subrogee of the prime creditor (C in the foregoing examples) under § 509. The election of either § 502 or § 509 is exclusive; if a co-obligor or surety takes one route, it cannot also take the other. Whether a surety will use one or the other section depends upon the particular situation. Typically, if the debtor has given security to the surety for the latter's protection, contribution under § 502 is preferable. If, however, the debtor has given security to the prime creditor, subrogation may turn out to be more beneficial.

1. **Prime claim must be allowed:** Under   both   § 502(e)(1)   and § 509(b), the claim of the surety (G's claim against D) will not be allowed if the prime claim (C's claim against D) is not allowed.

2. **Surety must have paid creditor:**   Under both § 502(e) and § 509(a), the surety must actually have made payment to the prime creditor in order to assert its rights in bankruptcy against the debtor.

3. **Timing of claim:** Under certain circumstances, the guaranty will be honored (that is, payment will be made by the surety), or the security will be turned over to the creditor after the petition. Under § 502(e)(2), the claim will be deemed to have come into existence before the petition, which enables the claim to be allowed in its proper amount under § 502. (This also enables the debt to be discharged under § 727(b), *infra*, p. 164.) No special relation back is necessary under § 509. *In subrogation, the surety steps into the shoes of the prime creditor of the co-obligor and its claim dates as of the creditor's claim.* Presumably, this is before the date of the petition.

IV. DEFENSES TO CLAIMS AVAILABLE TO THE ESTATE — § 558

A. Debtor's defenses available to estate: Under § 558, *a defense available to the debtor before bankruptcy is available to the estate in bankruptcy.* This is particularly significant since the estate is a separate legal entity from the debtor. Except for § 558, the personal defenses available to the debtor would not be available to the estate.

Example: Creditor C misrepresents a material fact to Debtor D and thereafter claims money due from D in D's bankruptcy. The trustee may defend against C's claim by proving the misrepresentation.

B. **Debtor's ability to waive a defense:** *A waiver of a defense made by the debtor after bankruptcy is ineffective*. However, a waiver made before bankruptcy is part of the relationship between debtor and creditor that is brought into the case and will be given effect.

V. ALLOWANCE OF CLAIMS OR INTERESTS — § 502

A. **Allowance of claims generally:** *If a proof of claim or interest is properly filed under § 501, it is deemed allowed under § 502(a) unless a party in interest objects.* Parties in interest include the trustee, the debtor, and other creditors. Claims can be disallowed under the provisions of §§ 502(b), (d), and (e). Once a claim has been allowed or disallowed, it may be reconsidered for cause under § 502(j). "Cause" includes new evidence that would justify a hearing on the merits of allowability.

1. **Meaning of "allowed":** The terms "allowed" and "allowable" are used in various sections of the code to mean that a claim has been accepted as a debt of the estate. Each time the concept is used, it means that a proof of claim has been filed and has satisfied the language of § 502.

2. **Time of petition controls:** *The amount of a claim is its amount at the time of the petition.* This is a benchmark time for all claims. If the trustee believes a claim arose at a later time (except with regard to legitimate post-petition claims), he will usually contest the claim. If the court determines that the claim arose after the petition, its amount at the time of the petition was obviously zero, so the claim will be disallowed.

3. **Court may modify or reject proof:** Under § 502(b), if an interested party objects to a proof of claim, the court will determine whether to allow the claim in full, modify the amount of the claim, or disallow it entirely. The bankruptcy courts are virtually unrestricted in their ability to utilize any procedure which will help to resolve a dispute over claims. "[T]he court is bound by the legal rules which may govern the ultimate value of the claim . . . . However, there are no other limitations on the court's authority to evaluate the claim save those general principles which should inform all decisions made pursuant to the Code." *In re Lane*, 68 B.R.609 (Bkrtcy. D.Haw. 1986).

a. Notice and hearing: The Court will proceed after notice to all interested parties. It need not conduct a hearing in the traditional formal sense. (See discussion of "hearing" under § 102(1) rules of construction, *supra*, p. 19).

b. Jury trials: Jury trials have been utilized in those extreme situations in which difficult issues of fact needed to be resolved. *Bittner v Borne Chemical Co.*, 691 F.2d 134 (3d Cir. 1982). (See discussion of jury trials, *supra*, p. 23.)

4. **Estimation of unliquidated claims:** A particularly troublesome situation arises whenever an unliquidated claim of great complexity has been asserted against the bankrupt estate. One example is a claim for damages for violation by the debtor of the antitrust or securities laws. More common is a tort claim which is moving slowly through the state courts. Lawsuits in a case such as these typically take years and it would be a perversion of the bankruptcy laws to delay relief for all while the case winds its way through the state courts. In these cases, *the court is required under § 502(c) to estimate the ultimate amount of the claim if waiting to fix it exactly would "unduly delay the administration of the case."* While this language seems imperative, the courts normally exercise discretion in deciding whether the estimation method is appropriate in a particular case.

Example 1: Claims against an airline in Chapter 11 are filed by employees, unions, and pension funds. The claims amount to almost $4 billion. The bankruptcy court is asked to lift the automatic stay which prevented trial of the claims in state court. The bankruptcy court held that to try the claims in state court would hamper efficient administration of the estate and decided to estimate them in the bankruptcy on a "case-by-case" basis. *In re Continental Airlines, Inc.*, 57 B.R. 842 (Bkrtcy. S.D. Tex. 1985).

Example 2: Before bankruptcy, Debtor D sues Creditor C in state court for pirating trade secrets. C counterclaims that D has tortiously interfered with a proposed merger. After the bankruptcy begins, the bankruptcy court lifts the automatic stay on this complicated state lawsuit and permits it to proceed. Rather than attempt an estimation of the dollar value of the lawsuit under § 502(c), the court used its discretion and assigned the claim a temporary value of zero pending resolution of the state action. It also ensured that D would retain sufficient assets in its Chapter 11 reorganization to make the appropriate payment to C at the end of the state action. (This would seem to have required at least a rough estimate of the potential damages, but the court did not go into detail as to how that was accomplished.) *Bittner v. Borne Chemical Co., Inc.*, 691 F.2d 134 (3rd Cir. 1982).

    5. **Claims may be barred by defenses of debtor:** Under § 558, *the trustee may assert any defenses available to the debtor, including statutes of limitations, the statute of frauds, and usury.*

    Example: A claim is made for interest that may be usurious and illegal. Whether the claim is allowed will depend on the definition of usury in the relevant state.

B. Claims arising after the petition: There are several instances where claims will arise after the petition and will be allowed. Claims listed in § 502(e)(2), (f), (g), (h), and (i) by their nature can only arise after the petition and are allowable as if they had arisen before the petition (*supra*, p. 46).

    1. **"Gap" claims in involuntary cases:** In involuntary cases, a "gap" in time occurs after the filing of a petition but before the order for relief or the appointment of a trustee. This is called the "gap" period. In this period, claims can arise against the estate in the ordinary course of the debtor's business or financial affairs. Because they arise after the petition, these claims are not be allowed under the preamble to § 502(b), but, under § 502(f), *gap claims are permitted to relate back to a period before the petition and thereby become allowable.*

    2. **Claims arising from the rejection of executory contracts:** *A party against whom an executory contract has been rejected under § 365 or in a Chapter 11 plan has a claim* (resulting from the breach of its contract) that arises after the petition. As in the case of "gap" claims, this claim is moved back before the petition and will be allowed under § 502(g).

    3. **Claims arising from the avoidance of pre-petition transactions:** Various sections in the Code enable the trustee to undo transfers made by the debtor before the bankruptcy and to recover the assets transferred. The transferees are required to return the property to the estate. *After the assets are returned, the transferee has a claim against the estate based upon the assets taken from him.* These claims also arise after the petition but they are deemed to have been moved back before the petition in the same manner as "gap" claims. Under § 502(d), no claim may be made until the return of assets is completed.

C. Grounds for disallowance of claims: The court may deny a claim entirely in the following instances:

1. **Claims unenforceable under agreement or applicable law:**
   Under § 502(b)(1), *a claim will be denied if it is unenforceable either due to an agreement between the creditor and the debtor or due to applicable law* but *not because the claim is contingent or unmatured.* Under § 502(b)(1), the fact that a claim is contingent or unmatured at the time of the petition does not prevent its being entered for its full amount.

   Example 1: Before bankruptcy, Debtor D and Creditor C settled a claim for half the full amount. The claim will be disallowed because of the prior settlement.

   Example 2: C loans D $5,000 on June 1, 1996, repayable on November 1, 1996. D files in bankruptcy on September 1, 1996. At the time of the bankruptcy, the obligation was not yet due and the claim was therefore unenforceable under state law. But the unmatured claim will be allowed in the bankruptcy for its full amount. This is consistent with the broad definition of "claim" in § 101(5) (*supra*, p. 17).

2. **Claims for unmatured interest:** Under § 502(b)(2), *claims will not be allowed for unmatured interest.* Unmatured interest is interest which accrues after the date of the petition. Although the unmatured portion of principle is allowable as a claim, only interest that has matured will be allowed.

   Example 1: Creditor C loans Debtor D $5,000 on May 1, 1992 repayable with interest at eight percent on December 1, 1992. D files a petition in bankruptcy on August 1, 1992. D may file a claim for principal of $5,000 and interest at eight percent but only up to August 1, 1992.

   Example 2: On May 1, 1992, D receives $4,672 from C and signs a note to C for $5,000 payable on December 1, 1992. (This is called a discounted loan. The interest is built into the face amount of the note.) D files a petition in bankruptcy on August 1, 1992. The difference between the amount received and the note (i.e., $328) is deemed to be interest. Because the rate of interest was calculated over the entire term ending December 1, 1992, it is recalculated and C is allowed interest at that rate up to August 1, 1992, plus the principal amount of $4,672.

   a. **Unmatured principle:** Any part of the principal that is due under the original obligation after the date of the petition is deemed to be "unmatured." But, since the principal amount of an obligation is established as of the date of the petition (*supra*, p. 75), unmatured principal is allowable.

    b. Exception for unmatured interest in Chapter 7 cases: In a Chapter 7 case the creditor may recover interest accruing after the petition if there are sufficient funds available in the bankruptcy estate. (See discussion *infra*, p. 159.)

3. **Taxes against property in excess of value:** Under § 502(b)(3), *taxes in excess of the value of the estate's interest in the property will not be allowed.*

4. **Charges by an insider or attorney in excess of reasonable value:** Under § 502(b)(4), *charges for services by an insider or an attorney which exceed the reasonable value of those services, will be disallowed.* (See definition of "insider" under § 101 (31).)

5. **Unmatured family debts:** Under § 502(b)(5), *a claim for an unmatured alimony, maintenance, or support obligation that is excepted from discharge under § 523(a)(5)* (*supra*, p. 57) *will be disallowed*. The rationale is that these debts will continue as obligations of the debtor after the bankruptcy. To the extent they are unmatured at the filing, they are difficult to measure and may stretch far into the future. If allowed as claims they may sop up the estate. It is therefore better policy to exclude these claims from the bankruptcy and continue the debtor's obligation after the case is closed. As we have seen (*supra*, p. 72), a debtor may file a claim on behalf of his uncooperative spouse in order to reduce the total amount that he will be forced to pay to the spouse. However, the claim will be limited to the amount of alimony which has matured at the time of the petition.

6. **Limitations on claims for rent under leases:** Because lease terms, particularly for commercial leases, may stretch many years into the future, under § 502(b)(6), *the amount of unmatured rent that may be claimed in a bankruptcy is limited.* If the claim is for damages resulting from the debtor's termination of a lease on real estate, the claim may not exceed the future lease rent for the greater of either: (1) one year's rent, or (2) the amount represented by 15 percent of the total future rent over not to exceed three years, following the earlier of (a) the date the petition was filed, and (b) the date that the lessor repossessed the property or the tenant surrendered it, *plus* any unpaid rent that was already due under the lease on the earlier of these two dates.

7. **Limitations on claims arising from employment contracts:** Under § 502(b)(7), *a claim for breach of an employment contract may not exceed the wages due for one year following the earlier of (1) the date of the petition or (2) the date the*

employment ended, plus any unpaid compensation due under the contract on the earlier of these two dates.

8. **Claims resulting from reduction in federal tax credit:**
   Under § 502(b)(8), the court will not allow a claim to the extent that it results from a reduction, due to late payment, of an otherwise applicable credit taken by the debtor in connection with an employment tax on wages, salaries, or commissions earned from the debtor. This provision was designed to *disallow claims for a reduction in the federal tax credit for late payment of state unemployment insurance taxes.*

9. **Claims not timely filed:** Under § 502(b)(9), *if a claim is not timely filed, it is generally not allowable.* In Chapter 7, there are exceptions for claims that are tardily filed but within the time permitted (*infra*, pp. 158, 149) and for claims by governmental units that are filed within 180 days after the order for relief. The time period under the latter exception can be extended under the bankruptcy rules.

VI. TREATMENT OF SECURED CLAIMS — § 506

A. **Secured claims generally:** Bankruptcy recognizes two types of secured claims: those secured by a lien under state law and those with a right of setoff against property of the estate under § 553 (*infra*, pp. 82 and 141). The usual state lien is a mortgage on real estate of the debtor or a security interest under Article 9 of the Uniform Commercial Code in the debtor's personal property. There may also be judicial liens established by state law. The lien is designed to support the debtor's obligation to the creditor. If the debtor fails to pay, the creditor can reach the security (the collateral) to satisfy the obligation. *Almost all properly perfected liens remain in effect in bankruptcy*; minor exceptions exist as to judicial liens and to nonpossessory, nonpurchase-money liens on exempt property, which are voidable under § 522(f) (*supra*, p. 51). There are several provisions under the Code that acknowledge the special status of secured claims, most of which relate to valuation of the security interest and the respective treatment of oversecured and undersecured claims.

1. **Valuation varies according to its purpose:** The value given to property is not necessarily fixed at one amount for all purposes. Under § 506(a), "[S]uch value shall be determined in light of the purpose of the valuation." Also, at various stages in the proceeding, both creditor and debtor may have varying interests in applying lower or higher values to the collateral.

Example 1: *Creditor wants low valuation.* Property of the estate is subject to the automatic stay (*supra*, p. 38). If the estate has no equity in the property and it is not necessary for an effective reorganization, the property may be released from the automatic stay under § 362(d) (*supra*, p. 44). A creditor seeking a release of property from the stay will want the asset to have a low value. The lower the value of the asset, the less likely that the debtor will have any equity in the asset.

Example 2: *Creditor wants high valuation.* Under § 506(b), if a creditor is oversecured (the security is worth more than the debt), he is entitled to interest on his claim, plus any reasonable fees, costs, or charges provided for under the agreement between debtor and creditor. In this case, a creditor will naturally want the collateral valued as high as possible.

2. **Consequences of valuation:** Valuation of the security, in addition to determining whether the creditor is fully secured, will have several consequences in the bankruptcy.

   - **Automatic stay** — Under § 362(d)(2)(A), the value will affect the amount of the debtor's equity and thus the ability of the debtor to keep property subject to the automatic stay (*supra*, p. 44).

   - **"Adequate protection"** — Under § 361, the value will affect the amount of "adequate protection" to be paid to the creditor (*supra*, p. 43; see Subject Matter Index).

   - **Payments** — Under § 1129(a)(7), the value will affect the amount to be paid to a creditor under a Chapter 11 plan.

   - **Interest** — Under § 506(b), the value will also determine whether the creditor is oversecured and thus whether interest must be paid.

3. **Times of valuation:** The Code strongly suggests that valuation, depending on its purpose, may be needed and made at different times during a single bankruptcy. It is not precise on this point, however, and cases have differed. In one situation, a secured creditor had no measurable financial interest in an item of collateral at the time of bankruptcy because the collateral was subject to two tax liens that far exceeded its worth. When the debtor's mother paid off the tax claims, however, the secured creditor found itself in a potential windfall. The court, however, did not permit the later valuation and insisted that the secured creditor value the collateral as of the time of the bankruptcy filing — when the property was under water. *In re Whalley*, 202 B.R. 58 (Bankr. W.D. Pa. 1996). The case is

unusual and *should not be taken as a definitive statement of the law*.

B. Valuation of security interest under § 506: The basis for the resolution of issues concerning the valuation of the creditor's security interest is found in § 506. Note that, before the security can be valued under § 506, the creditor's claim must be allowed under § 502 (*supra*, p. 75).

1. **Division into secured and unsecured portions:** The fundamental rule of § 506 is that *a claim is secured only to the extent of the value of the collateral*. If the security is worth less than the amount of the claim, there is a secured claim equal to the amount of the security and an unsecured claim to the extent by which the debt exceeds the value of the security. The unsecured portion of the debt is often called the "deficiency."

2. **Setoffs as secured claims:** Some creditors may owe money to the debtor. They will have claims against the estate if the amount each such creditor owes is less than what is owed to them by the debtor. The amount that such a creditor owes the debtor may be set off against the amount that the debtor owes the creditor, which reduces the claim. Under § 506, *a setoff is deemed a secured claim to the extent of the amount subject to setoff, i.e, the amount that the creditor owes the debtor*.

   Example: A bank loans $50,000 to the debtor, who has $100,000 on deposit. The bank is secured under § 506, to the extent of its set-off of $50,000.

3. **Valuation by court:** The wording of § 506 requires that *the court fix the value of the security*. The valuation is made with the help of whatever expert witnesses or other evidence the court can obtain. The value is not necessarily the price that the collateral may have brought at a sale. The price may not have reflected the true value of the property.

   Example: Debtor D buys a house for $200 thousand. She borrows $150 thousand from Creditor C bank, which secures the loan with a mortgage on the house. At the time of the loan, the house is worth $150 thousand. At D's bankruptcy, the market value of the house has diminished to $125 thousand. The value is established by appraisal in the bankruptcy. Under § 506(a), assuming that no payments have been made by D to C, C's secured claim is valued at $125 thousand and its unsecured claim at $25 thousand. If D has few assets beyond the house, the unsecured claim is of little value.

4. **Calculating interest on oversecured claims:** If a creditor is oversecured, he is likely to be paid in full. For this reason, § 506(b)

of the Code allows interest, fees, costs and charges until the oversecured claim is paid. The interest is on the entire claim, so long as the value of the security continues to exceed the amount of the claim. The interest paid to the creditor is deemed applied to the secured interest. As it is paid, therefore, it reduces the amount of the security until it reaches the amount of the claim, at which time the payment of interest will stop.

a. **Rate not specified:** The Code does not say what the rate of interest should be. Most of the cases accept the interest specified in the agreement under which the claim arose. *In re Hamilton Associates, Inc.*, 66 B.R. 674 (Bkrtcy.D,Nev. 1986). Some, however, do not consider themselves bound by the agreement and fix a "reasonable rate" on a case-by-case basis. *In re Laya*, 69 B.R. 669 (Bkrtcy. E.D.N.Y. 1987).

b. **Nonconsensual oversecured liens:** Some courts have held that interest would be paid only to those oversecured creditors who held security under agreements and not to those who had nonconsensual liens, such as judgment liens. However, the Supreme Court has held that the language of § 506(b), "[T]here shall be allowed to the holder of such claim, interest on such claim, and any reasonable fees, costs, or charges provided for under the agreement . . ." provides for *interest on all oversecured liens*. The "under the agreement" language does not apply to the allowance of interest but *only limits the granting of fees, costs, and charges to these situations in which these items have been provided for in the agreement that gives rise to the claim. United States v. Ron Pair Enterprises, Inc.*, 489 U.S. 235 (1989).

5. **Expenses can affect value of collateral:** Under § 506(c), if a trustee (or a debtor in possession under Chapter 11) incurs expenses in caring for or disposing of collateral that is in his possession and those *expenses benefit the holder of the claim that is secured by the collateral, the trustee (or debtor in possession) may charge the expenses against the value of the collateral.*

Example 1: Creditor C makes a loan to Debtor D secured in favor of C by D's cattle and farm machinery. In D's bankruptcy, D's trustee feeds the cattle and oils the machinery. C is benefitted by those acts because they keep the collateral alive and in good condition. The trustee may deduct those expenses from the collateral, or, if it is sold, from the proceeds. The courts are divided about how directly the trustee's acts must relate to the collateral itself.

Example 2: Creditor C makes a loan to Debtor D secured by D's equipment. The trustee, in the management of D's business, pays D's withholding taxes to the I.R.S. The trustee attempted to charge the collateral with the amount of those taxes, claiming that the payments permitted the trustee to preserve the entire business and, indirectly, the value of the collateral. Some courts have deemed such expenses to be too remote from the collateral to permit a charge against it under § 506(c). *In re Flagstaff Foodservice Corp.*, 762 F.2d 10 (2nd Cir. 1985). Others take a more liberal view and permit the charge. *In re North County Place, Ltd.*, 20 C.B.C.2d 158 (Bkrtcy. C.D.Cal. 1988).

C. **Voidability of liens generally:** *If a secured claim is disallowed, the lien is generally void because there is no longer a debt to which the lien can attach.* But under § 506(d), liens will not be void on disallowed secured claims in the following two situations.

   1. **Failure to file proof of claim:** *A lien will not be voided merely because the creditor did not file a proof of claim under § 501.* A proof of claim is required for a claim to be "allowed," but the proof of claim is not mandatory (*supra*, p. 72). It is often not filed where the secured creditor merely wants to remove his property from the proceeding. Thus, it would hardly make sense to void the lien under this circumstance.

   2. **Disallowed unmatured family and reimbursement claims:** Liens with respect to claims that are disallowed under § 502(b)(5) as *unmatured family claims, or under § 502(e) as claims for reimbursement or contribution are not voided.*

D. **Voidability of liens on undersecured claims:** If a debt is undersecured (the value of the property subject to the lien is less than the debt owed), the unsecured portion of the debt, or the deficiency, is handled like any other unsecured claim. The creditor may file a proof of claim as to the deficiency if it wishes to share in the distribution and typically will receive only a modest recovery. (Note that, under § 1111(b)(2), *infra*, p. 196, there is an option for the undersecured creditor in Chapter 11 cases to elect to have the entire debt treated as one secured claim.) When the secured portion of the claim is allowed, the question has arisen whether the lien that applies to the unsecured portion of the claim is void under § 506. Under § 506(a), "An allowed claim of a creditor secured by a lien on property . . . is a secured claim to the extent of the value of such creditor's interest . . . in such property, . . ." Under § 506(d), "To the extent that a lien secures a claim against the debtor that is not an allowed secured claim, such lien is void, ..." In other words, *under the operation of these two subsections, the question*

*is whether the lien on undersecured property is "stripped down"
to the value of the collateral.*

1. ***Dewsnup:*** In 1992, the Supreme Court held in a Chapter 7 case
   that, despite the division of a claim under § 506(a) between secured
   and unsecured portions and the language of § 506(d), ***the entire
   lien was valid.*** The Court preferred an interpretation of § 506(d)
   such that it would operate to void a lien only when a secured claim
   has been disallowed. The Court was apparently persuaded by the
   argument that the Code's fresh start policy is limited to a discharge
   of personal liability and cannot justify an impairment of a lienholder's property rights. The Court said that the Code must be read
   in the light of the traditions of bankruptcy law to leave liens
   untouched. While its decision seemed to contradict the language of
   § 506(d), the Court said that it was honoring the traditional view
   that a secured creditor should get whatever the collateral is worth
   whenever it is liquidated. Thus, any appreciation in the collateral's
   value over the amount established under § 506(a) and before foreclosure would go to the secured party. *Dewsnup v. Timm,* 112 S.Ct.
   773, 116 L.Ed.2d 903 (1992).

2. **Application of *Dewsnup* to other Chapters:** The *Dewsnup*
   decision was in a Chapter 7 case. Whether it governs Chapter 11
   and 13 bankruptcies is an open question. ***The court in Dewsnup
   carefully limited its holding to the facts, raising speculations
   about its general application.*** Since *Dewsnup,* the Second Circuit has held in a Chapter 13 case that a lien should be void under
   § 506(d) to the extent it exceeds the property value established
   under § 506(a). *Bellamy v. Federal Home Loan Mortgage Corp.,*
   962F.2d 176 (2nd Cir. 1992). The court stressed the different needs
   of a reorganization proceeding and of a Chapter 7 liquidation of the
   kind dealt with in *Dewsnup.*

3. **Increase in value before foreclosure:** As pointed out in *Dewsnup,* where property increases in value after the division under
   § 506(a) but before the creditor forecloses on the property, the
   increase belongs to the secured party if the entire lien remains
   valid; it does not if the lien is void under § 506(d).

VII. PRIORITY OF CLAIMS — § 507

A. **Priorities:** Because the money available for payment to creditors in a
   bankruptcy is typically less than the total of their allowed claims, a system for payments is essential to bankruptcy administration. The distribution of proceeds is not pro rata; the Code has adopted a system of
   priorities under which some obligations are deemed of greater social

significance than others and will be paid ahead of others. For example, payments for the support of one's child may precede payments to one's grocer. There are some 14 levels of priority in the Code, most of which are described in § 507. Others are dealt with under the provisions in § 364 for obtaining new credit during the period of the bankruptcy (*infra*, p. 189). How the priorities, as established under § 507 and elsewhere, are honored varies according to the specific bankruptcy filing Chapter and will be discussed under each specific Chapter. See Chapter 7 cases (*infra*, p. 157); Chapter 11 cases (*infra*, p. 199), and Chapter 13 cases (*infra*, p. 236).

1. **Priorities vs. liens:** Although it's not always easy to distinguish a lien from a priority, the difference is important to understanding the payment of claims under bankruptcy law. Priorities are matters of federal law as prescribed by the Code. Liens, on the other hand, are almost always (except when some special federal law applies) matters of state law, determined principally under laws relevant to real estate mortgages or under the Uniform Commercial Code (*supra* p. 74). As will be discussed, a variation on this underlying principle exists in connection with subordination agreements (*infra*, p. 91). When a lien is dealt with in bankruptcy, its validity as a lien is generally measured by state law. But the states are not permitted to set up a priority system dealing with the order of payments in bankruptcy, which is reserved for federal law under the Bankruptcy Code.

   Example: An Alaska statute governing the sale of liquor licenses requires that creditors of the seller whose obligations derived from its liquor business be paid from the proceeds of sale before other creditors are paid. Against a claim that the distribution scheme was an invalid state priority, the Court of Appeals held that it was in reality a valid lien under state law. The liquor-related creditors were lienholders. *In re Anchorage Int'l. Inn, Inc.*, 718 F.2d 1146 (9th Cir. 1983).

B. **Order of priorities:**   Under § 507(a), the following order of priorities is established in a bankruptcy proceeding:

1. **Administrative expenses:**   The first priority is for administrative expenses that are allowed under § 503. This generally means that administrative expenses will be paid before all other claims. However, through the operation of § 507(b) (superpriority given to secured claims where adequate protection has not been supplied, *infra*, p. 89) and § 364(c)(1) (superpriority given to those who extend new credit to the estate, *infra*, p. 190), this priority can drop into third place in the course of the bankruptcy. Before an administrative expense will be allowed, the court must approve it after

"notice and a hearing" (§ 102(1), *supra*, p. 19.) Under § 503, a non-exclusive list of administrative expenses includes:

- Most taxes levied or incurred after the bankruptcy;

- Administration fees and expenses due to the trustee, and to examiners, professional advisors, and the debtor's attorney;

- Costs associated with administering and preserving estate property; and

- Certain actual and necessary expenses incurred by creditors. These include the expenses of filing an involuntary petition under § 303; the expenses of a creditor who recovers property transferred or concealed by the debtor; and the expenses of a creditor, equity security holder, or creditors' committee that makes a substantial contribution to the case in a Chapter 9 or Chapter 11 proceeding.

a. **Preservation of estate:** The most significant administrative expenses are the expenses incurred in preserving the estate after the bankruptcy has begun. The term *"expenses" covers a broad range of items, including the wages of employees who work for a business in bankruptcy, the rent it pays, its debts for money borrowed, and its debts for goods bought*. Even a state's costs of cleaning land on which toxic waste has been dumped can be an administrative expense when the obligation to clean is imposed upon the trustee by statute. *In re Wall Tube & Metal Products Co.*, 831 F. 2d 118 (6th Cir. 1987).

b. **Generally limited to post-filing expenses:** Subject to the exception described in **d.** below, *only expenses incurred by, and which benefit, the debtor or the debtor's business after the commencement of the case* are considered administrative. This limit can create difficult problems of allocation. The following two examples are not clearly distinguishable. *In re Amarex* more closely represents the tenor of current decisions.

Example 1: A bonus was earned by a bankrupt firm's general counsel for a year's service performed partly before and partly after bankruptcy. Administrative priority was given only to the portion of the bonus attributable to the service after bankruptcy. *In re Amarex*, 853 F.2d 1526 (10th Cir. 1988).

Example 2: A debtor in bankruptcy is party to a labor contract that obligates the debtor to give vacation pay to those employees who have worked at least 110 days. Some of those days are worked before and some after the petition. The court found that all of the vacation pay should be considered an administrative expense. The court reasoned that the right to the vacation pay did not actually accrue until the vacation time arrived, which was after the bankruptcy, even though the pre-filing days of work were counted towards the requirement of 110 days of service. *In re Valley Concrete Corp.*, 118 B.R. 174 (Bkrtcy. 174 D.R.I. 1990). Other courts, particularly when dealing with severance pay, divide the payment between days worked before and days worked after the date of petition. *In re Russell Cave Co.*, 248 B.R. 301 (Bkrtcy. E.D. Ky. 2000).

c. **Expenses must benefit estate:** To be allowed as an administrative claim, ***the expense must be shown to have benefitted the estate during the bankruptcy.*** The expenses cited above (wages, vacation pay, rent, etc.) will generally satisfy this standard.

Example 1: After its bankruptcy began, Debtor D negligently causes a fire that damages the property of Creditor C. C's claim against D constitutes an administrative expense even though it could hardly be said to have preserved the estate. It was, however, seen as part of the overall costs of running D's business. *Reading v. Brown*, 391 U.S. 471 (1968).

Example 2: D and C enter into a contract before D's bankruptcy and observe its terms. After bankruptcy, D operates for a time under the contract and then rejects it under the provisions that preceeded the Code and § 365 (*infra*, p. 108). The court found that the contract did not benefit D in the bankruptcy and that C's claims under it were not entitled to administrative priority. (Because C had been a party to the contract before the petition, however, the court permitted C to enter a standard proof of claim for its damages.) *American A.& B. Coal Corp. v. Leonardo Arrivabene, S.A.*, 280 F.2d 119 (2nd Cir. 1960).

d. **Expenses rendered before petition may benefit estate:** Occasionally a court is asked to consider whether services rendered entirely before the bankruptcy may have benefitted the estate after the petition. In that case, they may be given administrative priority despite the § 503(b) language requiring the services to have been performed after the petition.

Example: A lawyer's advice given before the petition may benefit the estate after the petition. *In re Russell-Taylor, Inc.*, 59 B.R. 871 (Bkrtcy. W.D. Va. 1986). More often, however, the court will require that the services be performed in whole, or at least in part, after the petition. *In re Consolidated Oil & Gas, Inc.*, 110 B.R. 535 (Bkrtcy. D.Colo. 1990).

e. **New credit priority:** The fact that credit is regularly extended during an administration shows that a bankrupt debtor is not necessarily a bad credit risk. Under § 364(c)(1), the creditor who extends credit after the petition may join in the first priority position and the debtor's assets may be more than sufficient to cover the credit. Departments of large banks have been built on this concept.

f. **Claims for adequate protection:** Under certain circumstances cited in § 361, a creditor is entitled to ask for adequate protection of an interest in property, as in the case of an application for relief from the § 362 automatic stay. However, the creditor may not actually receive adequate protection for the use, sale, or lease of the creditor's property. This may happen because insufficient protection is agreed upon in the first instance or because the agreed protection is not paid. Under § 507(b), *if the secured party has a claim for the loss that qualifies as an administrative claim under the first priority, the secured party is bumped up to an administrative priority ahead of any other § 507(a)(1) administrative priority.* The following exemplify certain situations where the absence of adequate protection may result in this "super" priority.

   i. **Payment of compensation — § 362:** Under § 362, in order to retain possession of assets that are subject to a security interest and are depreciating in value, the trustee must generally commit that it will keep the lienholder's property interest undiminished by compensating the creditor. By receiving compensation, often measured by the amount of depreciation, the lienholder is not prejudiced financially in not obtaining actual possession of its collateral.

   ii. **Other requirements for adequate protection:** Other sections of the Code provide for adequate protection of a creditor's interest. These sections also require the debtor or trustee to commit to compensate a lienholder under § 361 to keep the lienholder's interest in the property from being diminished. For example, under § 363, the debtor has the right to use property subject to a lien (*infra*, p. 104). Under § 364, the debtor has the right to obtain new credit by the use of property subject to a lien.

   iii. **Commitment not necessarily adequate:** The trustee's commitment to pay may not necessarily compensate the lienholder adequately. The payments may not actually be made, or the losses suffered as events transpire may exceed the original expectations under which protection was established (§ 362, § 363 or § 364).

2. **"Gap" claims:** Under § 507(a)(2), *the second priority in order goes to "gap" claims made in the ordinary course of the debtor's business.* These are claims incurred after a § 303 involuntary petition and before the earlier of the order for relief or the appointment of a trustee (*supra*, p. 28).

3. **Priority for wage claims:** Claims under an employment contract are limited by § 502(b)(7) (*supra*, p. 79). However, under § 507(a)(3), *a third priority status is given to certain wages and commissions, including vacation, severance, and sick leave pay.* These are limited to the amount earned by an employee within 90 days before the petition or the cessation of the debtor's business, whichever occurs first, but *not exceeding $4,000 per employee*.

   a. **Rationale for priority:** The wage claim (third) priority was established for the assistance of those who are dependent for their survival upon their wages. With this goal in mind, wages may be assigned to a non-employee third party and still not lose their priority status. The goal of the priority is to assist the wage earner and it's considered a valid exercise of the bankruptcy concept to permit her to cash in on her wage claim by assigning it.

   Example: Employee E has a five year employment contract beginning on January 1, 1996 at $120,000 per year. The employer, Debtor D, pays the contract in full for the first year, but defaults after the first four months of the second year. On July 1, 1997, D goes out of business and makes no further payments under the contract. On January 1, 1998, D petitions in bankruptcy. E's proof of claim in the bankruptcy is for $20,000, the amount with respect to which D was in default when it went out of business, plus $120,000, the wages for one year in advance. E's priority claim is limited to $4,000; her wages for the 90 days before the petition exceeded this sum, but § 507(a)(3) limits the priority to $4,000.

   b. **Sales commissions by sole independent contractors:** Sales commissions earned by an individual or a corporation with one employee during the period ending 90 days before the petition are similarly given a third priority to the extent of $4,000 if, during the 12 months preceding the end of the 90 days, at least 75 percent of the commissions earned by the creditor was earned from the debtor.

4. **Claims for contributions to employee benefit plan:** Under § 507(a)(4), *the fourth priority is for contributions to an employee benefit plan*, arising from services rendered within 180 days before the petition or before the date of cessation of the debtor's business, whichever occurred first. This priority is *limited to $4,000 per covered employee*, less the priority wage claims paid to the employees under the wage claim (third) priority and less also whatever amount the estate may have paid to another employee benefit plan for the benefit of the employee.

5. **Grain storage and fishermen claims:** Under § 507(a)(5), *the fifth priority is for claims by grain farmers against grain storage facilities and claims by fishermen against fish processors, in the maximum amount of $4,000*.

6. **Claim resulting from consumer deposits:** Under § 507(a)(6), the sixth priority is designed to protect *consumers who made deposits before the bankruptcy case in connection with the purchase or hire of goods or services for personal, family, or household purposes, in those instances when the goods or services were not delivered*. These claims are *limited to $1800 per person.*

7. **Alimony and support claims:** Under § 507(a)(7), *the seventh priority is for alimony and support claims for spouse or child*, but only to the extent embodied in a property settlement agreement, separation agreement, divorce decree, or other order by the court or a governmental unit. The claim must not be assigned to a third party.

8. **Certain tax claims:** Under § 507(a)(8), *the eighth priority gives governmental units, both state and federal, a priority tax claim for a designated list of taxes.* The most significant among the dozen items listed are income taxes due within three years of the petition.

9. **Bank and savings and loan claims:** Under § 507(a)(9), the ninth and last priority was added by the 1990 amendments to the Code to cure certain problems experienced by banks and savings and loan associations. *If a debtor has made a commitment to a bank regulatory agency to sustain the capital of a bank or an S&L, the regulator has a priority claim*.

VIII. SUBORDINATION OF CLAIMS — § 510

A. **Definition of "subordination":** Subordination in bankruptcy is a legal concept meaning that one creditor will stand behind another creditor; that is, he will not be paid until the other creditor is paid. The concept of subordination clearly varies the order of priority of creditors imposed by the Code and runs counter to the general principle that only the Code may establish priorities. However, it has been established that **creditors may take the order of distribution into their own hands by the device of subordination**. *In re Aktiebolaget Kreuger & Toll*, 96 F.2d 768 (2nd Cir. 1938).

1. **Reasons for subordination:**   Why will one creditor agree to accept a position inferior to another's? In the financial marketplace, a subordinated creditor will usually earn a higher interest rate than a more senior creditor. The prospect of a higher return may motivate a creditor to subordinate. "Subordinated notes," are a conventional device for lending money under an agreement to take a subordinated position. A new investor may agree to make funds available to a business only if its other creditors agree to subordinate themselves to his new money. The existing creditors may be willing to accept the risk of a subordinated position in order to encourage the new investment.

2. **Subordination by agreement:** Cases upholding subordination all involve parties who created their relative priorities in payment by agreements among themselves. Under § 510(a), these agreements will be honored in bankruptcy in the same way as under non-bankruptcy law.

3. **Code defers to subordination:** In accepting subordination, the Code defers to the agreement of parties to the bankruptcy and permits them to set their own priorities outside the Code. Subordination, in effect, forces the bankruptcy Court to look to state law, which it otherwise rarely does. This is because most subordination agreements are entered into under the law of a particular state and are interpreted under that law.

B. **Equitable subordination:**   Under certain circumstances, the bankruptcy court will apply the concept of equitable subordination to create a priority of one creditor over another.

Example 1: Entrepreneur E starts a corporation with one million dollars in contributed capital and issues all the common stock to herself. Creditor C lends the corporation one million dollars. The corporation goes into a Chapter 7 bankruptcy with $1,500,000 in assets to distribute. Under standard principles of corporate law, honored in bankruptcy, C will be paid in full for his debt claim and E will receive only $500,000 for her equity interest.

Example 2: E starts up a corporation with one million dollars. She contributes only ten dollars to capital and issues all the stock to herself.

She lends the corporation the remaining $999,990. The corporation files in Chapter 7. Under the same principles as in Example 1, she should share (to the extent of $999,990) along with other general creditors. But if E's scheme has resulted in an "undercapitalized" corporation, she may be deemed a stockholder and not a creditor to the extent fixed by the Court, which will apply the concepts of equity. By applying her investment as she did, E may have acted against the interest of other creditors and be "equitably subordinated" to them by the bankruptcy court, with part or all of her original investment treated as capital. This means that in the distribution of the corporation's assets, other creditors will receive money before E does. This concept is often called the "deep rock" doctrine memorialized by the Supreme Court in *Taylor v. Standard Gas & Electric Co.*, 306 U.S. 307 (1939).

1. **Application of doctrine:** *Equitable subordination* is often applied under the following criteria, taken from the decision in *In re Mobile Steel Co.*, 563 F.2d 692 (5th Cir. 1977):

   "1. The claimant must have engaged in *some type of inequitable conduct.*

   2. The misconduct must have resulted in *injury to the creditors of the bankrupt* or *conferred an unfair advantage* on the claimant.

   3. Equitable subordination must *not be inconsistent* with the provisions of the Bankruptcy Act."

2. **Examples of inequitable conduct:** In Example 2 above, the inequitable conduct was E's misallocation of funds; the injury to the creditors resulted from dilution of the assets which would otherwise have been available to them. Collusion and other acts can also constitute inequitable conduct.

   Example: C1, who has a close relationship to D corporation (debtor), causes D to enter into a consent judgment in C1's favor for an obligation allegedly due from D to C1. C1 executes on the judgment and thereby obtains a lien on D's assets. C1 does not intend to enforce the lien; but when D files in bankruptcy and another creditor, C2, asserts a claim in the bankruptcy, C1 tries to enforce his lien on D's assets to the detriment of C2. The court found that C1 and D were essentially the same entity and that the debt was not an honest debt. C1 was deemed subordinated to C2 in D's bankruptcy. *Pepper v. Litton*, 308 U.S. 295 (1939).

C. **Liens on subordinated claims:** If a claim is secured by a lien on property of the debtor, the lien confers preferred rights for payment. But suppose the underlying claim is subordinated to another. This will create a problem for the Court. If C1 has a secured lien but is subordinated to C2, under § 510(c)(2), this Gordian Knot is cut by simply allowing the court to annul C1's lien. As the Code puts it, the Court orders that the lien "be transferred to the estate." This is another example of a device the Code uses in limited circumstances to undo a valid lien. (See discussion of § 522(f), *supra*, p. 50.)

CHAPTER 7

THE BANKRUPTCY ESTATE

Introductory note: The "estate" consists of those assets of the debtor that are available for distribution to creditors and, in the case of reorganizations, form the basis for the reorganized entity. The nature of the estate will vary somewhat according to the particular bankruptcy Chapter. (See § 902(1), *infra*, p. 168; § 1207, *infra*, pp. 222 and 223; and § 1306, *infra*, p. 235.) This chapter examines how the estate is created and managed during the bankruptcy.

I. NATURE OF THE ESTATE — § 541

A. Background: The concept underlying the Code was originally that essentially all of the assets of the debtor would be gathered together in the "estate." A modern system of exemptions would then permit the debtor to extract from the estate those assets that the debtor needed for a "fresh start." The debtor's financial problems would be reviewed and dealt with and, under a liberal definition of "claims," the remaining assets would be applied for the benefit of creditors. When Congress, for political reasons, divided exemptions between federal and state law, the logic of this concept was undermined (*supra*, pp. 44-45).

B. Creation and formation of the estate: Under § 541(a), *the estate is created upon the filing of the petition*. This occurs both as to the filing of a voluntary petition under § 301 and § 302 and an involuntary petition under § 303. The estate is a new legal entity distinct from the debtor. Upon its creation, the debtor's assets are transferred from the debtor to the estate. The estate exists principally for the benefit of the creditors.

1. **Importance of state law:** *Bankruptcy law determines whether or not an interest is property. State law determines the nature and extent of the debtor's ownership interest in an item of property*, for example, a tenancy or a future interest. Other federal laws may also determine the nature and extent of the debtor's ownership interest.

Example 1: The IRS imposes a tax lien on the property of Debtor D. It then takes possession of the property, prepares to sell it and apply the proceeds to the tax. Before the sale, D's bankruptcy occurs. The property is part of the estate because D still had an equitable interest in it, i.e., the ability to pay the tax and recover the property. The equitable interest would not be lost until sale to a third party. *U.S. v. Whiting Pools*, 462 U.S. 198 (1983).

Example 2: Debtor D is required by the Internal Revenue Code (IRC) to pay withholding taxes to the IRS. The IRC provides that moneys not paid are automatically held in trust for the IRS by the debtor. D does not pay its withholding taxes. Funds held by D that should have been paid were being held in trust for the IRS and were not part of the bankruptcy estate. *Begier v. IRS*, 496 U.S. 53 (1990).

Example 3: Debtor D writes a check, but goes bankrupt before the check can be honored by the bank on which it is drawn. Under the rules governing commercial transactions, the funds still belong to D at the time of bankruptcy. When the bank, without notice of the bankruptcy, honors the check, the funds are technically already in the estate and the check should not have been paid. Nevertheless, the Supreme Court did not require the bank to reimburse the estate. Bankruptcy is an equitable remedy and a contrary decision would run counter to the "grain of our decisions requiring notice before a person is deprived of property." *Bank of Marin v. England*, 385 U.S. 99, 102 (1966). The thrust of the holding was later incorporated in the Bankruptcy Code as § 542(c). However, under § 549, the recipient of the funds may be required to account to the estate for them.

2. **Relation of exemptions to determination of estate:**   Under § 541, the scheme devised by the framers of the Bankruptcy Code throws the debtor's assets into the estate on the filing of the petition and then permits the debtor to regain some of the assets through a system of exemptions under § 522 (*supra*, p. 46). Because Congress allowed states to opt out of the federal exemption scheme in preference for their own scheme, exemptions vary greatly according to the state in which the debtor resides. This lack of uniformity sometimes creates situations that are less than equitable and the courts, therefore, are sometimes inclined to define the estate narrowly to permit the debtor to retain more benefits.

Example: A retired sailor has a pension. He transfers to the Naval Reserves, which imposes certain minor duties upon him as a precondition to his receipt of the pension. He is, for example, required to report for active duty for up to two months every four years if ordered to do so by the Secretary of the Navy. He files in bankruptcy and is unable to exempt the pension under state law. It was held that, because the pension was contingent upon his performing continuing duties, it was not part of the estate. Furthermore, no part of it was allocated to the period before the petition. *In re Haynes*, 679 F.2d 718 (7th Cir.) cert den., 459 U.S. 970 (1982).

3. **Treatment depends upon which bankruptcy Chapter:** How the assets will be handled depends upon the bankruptcy Chapter under which the petition is filed. In Chapter 7, the estate will be liquidated and the funds paid to the creditors. In Chapter 11, the estate will be operated by the trustee in an effort to yield funds for the creditors (and also benefit the debtor by winding up with a healthy on-going business).

C. **Property in the estate:** Subject to special modifications established in the particular bankruptcy Chapters, the estate generally consists of the following property.

1. **All property interests of the debtor:** Under § 541(a)(1), *the estate consists of "all legal or equitable interests of the debtor in property as of the commencement of the case."* As will be discussed, this all-inclusive statement is modified somewhat by exclusions contained in § 541(b) and (c)(2). Included under § 541(a)(1) are such assets as:

   • legal ownership of the family car and Blackacre;

   • rights in tangibles such as machinery and equipment;

   • rights in intangibles like contracts and movie scripts;

   • rights in property leased to others;

   • rights of lessees under leases;

   • rights in lawsuits;

   • equitable rights to redeem collateral from lienholders or to receive income from trusts; and

   • contingent interests and future interests, whether or not transferable by the debtor.

2. **Some community property included:** Under § 541(a)(2), *certain property that a debtor owns communally with a spouse is includable in the estate.* The property included is defined as all interests of the debtor and his spouse in community property that is (1) under the sole, equal, or joint management and control of the debtor and (2) liable for claims against the debtor, or for claims against the debtor and his spouse, to the extent it is so liable.

3. **Recovered property:** A number of provisions throughout the Code provide for the return to the estate of property that has been transferred by the debtor before the filing. These provisions are generally to undo transfers made in ways that violate the letter or the spirit of the Code. Although the return occurs after the petition, the property becomes property of the estate. Examples of recovered property that are included in the estate under § 541(a)(3) are:

- excessive payments made by the debtor to lawyers (§ 329(b));

- sales of estate property in which the bidders at the sale controlled the price by agreement among themselves (§ 363(n));

- turnovers to the estate by a custodian to whom the property had previously been transferred (§ 543(b));

- the return of property recovered by the trustee under one of his avoiding powers (§ 550);

- the return of an improper setoff of an obligation to the debtor against a debt owed by the debtor (§ 553);

- the return to a partnership of assets held by a partner, when the assets are needed by the partnership to pay its debts in the partnership's Chapter 7 bankruptcy (§ 723).

4. **Subordinated liens:** Liens on property in favor of lienholders whose positions have been subordinated under § 510 may be transferred to the estate under § 510(c)(2) (*supra*, p. 93). Although these transfers come after the petition, the property freed from these liens as a result of the transfers is made part of the estate under § 541(a)(4).

5. **Interests debtor acquires after filing:** Under § 541(a)(5), *certain interests that the debtor acquires, or becomes entitled to acquire, within 180 days after the petition are made part of the estate.* These after-acquired interests include interests acquired (1) by bequest, devise, or inheritance, (2) in a settlement with the debtor's spouse or in a divorce decree, and (3) as a beneficiary of a life insurance policy or death benefit plan.

6. **Interests flowing from assets of the estate:** *Interests that flow from assets already in the estate become property of the estate.* Under § 541(a)(6), the Code uses the all-inclusive language, "proceeds, products, offspring, rents or profits" to indicate its intent to include all interests flowing from assets.

   a. **Similarity to Uniform Commercial Code:** The broad language is similar to Article 9 of the Uniform Commercial Code. However, the Bankruptcy Code is intended to be more inclusive than the more technical use of these terms in the U.C.C.; the Code takes in everything included in the U.C.C. and more.

   b. **Earnings not included:** However, under § 541(a)(6), *"earnings from services performed by an individual debtor after the commencement of the case" are not proceeds.* Except for filings under Chapters 12 and 13, earnings belong to the debtor, not to the estate. This is a fundamental ingredient in the debtor's fresh start. The Code gives the individual debtor the opportunity to earn a living once a case has been begun and to retain what is earned.

Example 1: The estate consists of a shoe business that continues to sell shoes after the filing. The income from the shoe sales becomes part of the estate.

Example 2: The estate consists of cows. Their calves will also be part of the estate.

Example 3: Debtor owns a law firm that he operates as a single proprietorship. He hires several other lawyers and a clerical staff, all of whom work for him. In his bankruptcy, the firm was part of the estate and all firm income that was attributable to the firm's invested capital, good will, and employment of the firm's staff, was part of the estate. However, income that was attributable to the debtor's personal services was free of the estate and part of his personal assets. A salary of $3,500 a month that the firm paid the debtor had to be divided between income attributable to the efforts of others in the firm (income to the estate) and income attributable to the debtor's efforts. *In re Fitzsimmons*, 725 F.2d 1208 (9th Cir. 1984).

Example 4: A doctor divorces his wife before he files in bankruptcy. His medical degree is given a value in the divorce proceeding under state law. The value is divided between husband and wife. However, in bankruptcy, the degree was found to be indispensable to the doctor's future earnings and was therefore outside the estate. *In re Lynn*, 18 B.R. 501 (Bkrtcy. D.Conn. 1982).

7. **Interests estate acquires after filing:** Under § 541(a)(7), any interest in property that the estate acquires after the commencement of the case is property of the estate. This should be distinguished from the provision under § 541(a)(5) (see *supra*, p. 98), which includes in the estate certain interests of the debtor that are obtained within 180 days after the filing.

D. **Items not included in estate:** Under § 541(b), several assets are specifically excluded from the estate even though they would seem to fall under the broad language of § 541(a). *The most significant exclusion is any power that the debtor may exercise solely for the benefit of an entity other than himself.* For example, the debtor may be appointed a trustee of a trust for the benefit of X. The debtor's trust interest, although a "legal" interest, will not be part of the estate.

E. *Ipso facto* **clauses invalid:** In bankruptcy, an *ipso facto* clause is a restrictive clause relating to an interest in property that provides within its own terms (*ipso facto*) that the interest may not be included in the bankruptcy estate. Under § 541(c)(1), ***any provision in an agreement or law that restricts or conditions the transfer of a debtor's assets in the event of a bankruptcy, or that is conditioned on the insolvency or financial condition of the debtor, is invalid.*** With the exception of "spendthrift trusts" (see *infra*), property that is part of an estate is unaffected by such provisions.

1. **Clauses arise by agreement or statute:** The restriction may appear in an agreement or in a state or federal statute. Usually, an *ipso facto* clause in an agreement will provide that upon bankruptcy the property will return to the original transferor rather than become part of the transferee's estate.

2. **Rationale for doctrine:** The framers of the Code reasoned that the Bankruptcy Code, not the agreement of the parties or even the law outside the Code, must prescribe and control what happens to assets in bankruptcy. For example, a restriction by a transferor to the debtor that the property transferred shall continue to be owned or rented by the debtor, or shall revert to the transferor, and not be included in his bankruptcy estate, would be an impermissible interference with the bankruptcy laws.

   Example 1: Secured Creditor C sells a car to Debtor D. The purchase price is payable in installments. One provision of the installment sale agreement is that, in the event of D's bankruptcy, C can repossess the car. Throughout D's bankruptcy and after discharge, D continues to pay the installments under the agreement, but C claims a default under the *ipso facto* clause and attempts repossession. It was held that the clause was invalid and, so long as D made the payments, she could keep the car. The discharge in bankruptcy ended her obligation under the agreement and she could not be held personally liable on default; but, in the event of default, C would have a right to the car. *In re Brock*, 23 B.R. 998 (Bkrtcy. DDD. 1982).

   Example 2: D buys a car on time from secured Creditor C. The agreement contains an *ipso facto* clause giving C the right to repossess the car upon D's bankruptcy. D exempts the car from the bankruptcy estate under § 522. When C files a claim for the car, the court awards it to C. It was held that the purpose of § 541(c) was to see that property becomes part of the estate. When D exempted the car from the estate, § 541(c) was no longer applicable. *In re Schweitzer*, 19 B.R. 860 (Bkrtcy. E.D.N.Y. 1982).

F. **Restrictions on transfers of trusts exception:** Under § 541(c)(2), ***a trust interest whose transfer is restricted under nonbankruptcy law, is excluded from the estate.*** This provision has traditionally been held applicable to *"spendthrift trusts,"* a device by which a parent or other benefactor may preserve the interest of a minor, a spouse, or another beneficiary who may need financial protection. The benefactor wants to be assured that the trust will continue to perform its intended function.

1. **Trusts under ERISA:** Problems have been created by trusts protected by the Employee Retirement Income Security Act (ERISA), which contain restrictions on transfer of trust interests. At the outset, the courts disagreed on the question whether these trusts came under the language of § 541(c)(2). Most courts held that ERISA trusts are excluded from the bankrupt estate only if they qualify as the equivalent of a "spendthrift trust" under the applicable state law. The Supreme Court settled the issue in *Patterson v. Shumate,* 112 S.Ct. 2242 (1992). It held that *qualified pension plans are not included in the bankruptcy estate because the restrictions on transfer applicable to such plans satisfy the plain language of § 541(c)(2).*

II. ABANDONMENT OF ASSETS

A. **Right of trustee to abandon property:** Under § 554, the trustee may abandon any property of the estate that is burdensome or of inconsequential value.

1. **Property subject to abandonment:** Some property can have a negative value to the trustee. One example is property that is completely burdened with a lien and is of no use to the debtor. Another is property that requires cleanup under pollution regulations or other circumstances when the value of the property is less than the cost of cleanup. In these cases, the only prudent action for the trustee to take is to abandon the property. The Code wisely permits him to do this.

2. **Notice and "hearing" required:** Under § 544, abandonment must be preceded by "notice and a hearing." As we have seen, this language is interpreted to mean that an actual hearing may not be necessary (§ 102, *supra,* p. 19). *The court has considerable discretion to establish whether abandonment is in the best interest of the estate and in accordance with the Code and other applicable laws, such as environmental laws.*

3. **Abandonment typically to lien holder:** Where property is burdened with a lien, abandonment will typically be to the lien holder. If the property is not subject to a lien and the burden is an environ-

mental obligation, abandonment may be to the appropriate regulatory agency or to the debtor.

B. Conflicts with other laws: A proposed abandonment can sometimes result in a violation of laws governing the management of the property. Although § 554 appears to give the trustee an unqualified right of abandonment, a statute outside the Code, dealing with trustees and receivers generally (28 U.S.C. § 959(b)), requires a bankruptcy trustee to "manage and operate" property in compliance with state law. In 1986, the Supreme Court in *Midlantic Nat'l v. New Jersey*, 474 U.S. 494 (1986), stated that ***the right of abandonment may be restricted by other laws where necessary to protect the public health or safety from imminent and identifiable harm.***

1. **Application of *Midlantic* decision:** The courts have tried to apply *Midlantic* in a reasonable manner. Where the estate is dry of funds and the trustee has attempted to do what it can to clean up the site and has cooperated reasonably with the environmental authorities, abandonment has usually been permitted, especially if an immediate public health hazard cannot be shown. *In re Franklin Signal Corp.*, 65 B.R. 268 (Bkrtcy. D.Minn. 1986).

III. USE, SALE, OR LEASE OF ESTATE PROPERTY

A. Management of estate property generally: The estate consists of the assets of the debtor at the time the petition is filed, with some additions (for example, property returned to the estate by use of the avoiding powers) and some deletions (for example, property returned to the debtor under the exemption provisions). The assets in the estate are protected by the automatic stay of § 362 and are retained by the debtor or trustee free from the claims of adverse interests, including lienholders who wish to take possession of them to cover their debts. The trustee, or the debtor in cases where a trustee has not been appointed, needs additional authority to be able to control and manage the property of the estate during the period of the bankruptcy. In cases where the trustee or debtor in possession must continue to operate a business, the control and management of estate property is particularly critical to maintaining an effective operation. The basic authority under which the debtor or trustee will use or deal with the assets is contained in § 363 (which, significantly, immediately follows § 362, the automatic stay). In addition to the discussion here, there is a separate discussion of the management of estate property in Chapter 11 cases (*infra*, p. 185).

B. Operating a business: In some cases, the debtor or trustee will need to operate a business whose assets are part of the estate. In Chapter 7 cases, the need may be over a relatively short time because the goal is liquidation; in Chapter 11 reorganization cases, the need is more difficult to predict. For the operation of a business during bankruptcy, the Code makes a critical distinction between two classes of action by the trustee or debtor: (1) those in the ordinary course of business, and (2) those *other* than in the ordinary course of business.

1. **Actions in the ordinary course of business:** Under § 363(c)(1), *if the debtor's business is authorized to be operated during the bankruptcy* (unless the court orders otherwise), *actions in the ordinary course of business may be taken without notice or a hearing, or other intervention by the Court.*

2. **Actions other than in the ordinary course:** Under § 363(b), *the debtor or trustee may take actions other than in the ordinary course of business only after notice and hearing.*

3. **Distinguishing between two types of actions:** To determine whether an action is or is not in the ordinary course of business, two tests have been used. The first test, know as the "vertical test," looks at the action in relation to the business dealings of the debtor with its creditors. The basis of the inquiry is whether a creditor would characterize an act as in the ordinary course or *not* in the ordinary course of the debtor's business. The second test, known as the "horizontal test," looks at how the act would be regarded by businesses that are similar to the debtor's.

   Example 1: A department store files a petition in bankruptcy. It has inventory on its shelves which it owns free and clear. Under either test, the store may continue to sell that inventory without judicial clearance.

   Example 2: A department store is remodeling a department and plans to sell its old chandeliers. Notice and a hearing are required. The ordinary business of a department store is to sell its inventory, not its chandeliers.

   Example 3: A department store operates in part through departments licensed to others. Granting such licenses is in the ordinary course of business for department stores. *In re Glosser Bros., Inc.,* 124 B.R. 664 (Bkrtcy. W.D.Pa. 1991).

   Example 4: The leasing of premises to others by a business that normally conducts a dinner theatre on the premises is not in the ordinary course of the dinner theatre business. *In re Franklin Signal Corp.,* 65 B.R. 268 (Bkrtcy. D. Minn. 1986).

C. **Effect of automatic stay:** In general, the provisions for the use of property under § 363 are subject to the automatic stay and release from the automatic stay provisions of § 362. Thus, if the court has ordered collateral to be released to a lienholder under § 362(d), the collateral may not be used by the trustee or debtor under § 363.

D. Adequate protection to creditor: Under § 363(e), *the court can require a debtor or trustee who uses, sells or leases an asset to give adequate protection to anyone, usually a secured creditor, who has an interest in that asset.* The concept of adequate protection is that the value of an interest should be maintained during bankruptcy. Adequate protection is defined in § 361 and occurs again in § 362(a) (*supra*, p. 43; See also Subject Matter Index).

1. **Purpose of protection:** The purpose of adequate protection is to insure that the lienholder will not lose the value of his security in the hands of the debtor, during a time when the lienholder has a legal right to the property (*supra*, p. 43). Protection is extended to lessors of personal property for unexpired leases of the debtor, pending a decision to assume or reject the lease.

2. **Treated as administrative expense:** *Adequate protection payments are an administrative expense under § 503.* If protection is granted under § 363(e) and it proves to be inadequate, the obligation is bumped up under § 507(b) so that it has a priority ahead of all other administrative expenses (*supra*, p. 89).

E. Sale of asset free of lien: The property rights of a lienholder are generally protected in bankruptcy. Thus, when estate property is sold under § 363, it must be done in a way that protects the interests of others in the property, particularly the interests of lienholders. Under § 363(f), property in which others have interests may not be sold free and clear of those interests unless their rights are protected. However, five situations are described in § 363(f) in which sales free of third party interests are permitted. The provisions are stated in the alternative; if any one applies, the sale may be made.

1. **Sale permitted by law outside Code:** *The court will respect an applicable nonbankruptcy law that permits the sale of property free and clear of a lien.*

   Example 1: Secured Creditor C has a mortgage on Blackacre, owned by Debtor D. C fails to record its mortgage. Under applicable real estate law, D may sell Blackacre to a good faith purchaser free of C's interest. The court may approve the sale in D's bankruptcy.

   Example 2: Secured Creditor C has a blanket security interest under the Uniform Commercial Code in all of the inventory of Debtor D. U.C.C. § 9-307 permits D to sell its inventory in the ordinary course to good faith purchasers free of C's security interest.

The sales may be made in D's bankruptcy under § 363(c) (without court approval) free of C's interest (§ 363(f)(1)).

2. **The creditor consents:** The creditor may voluntarily join in the arrangement made by the debtor, the trustee, and/or the court for the sale of the property free and clear of its interest.

3. **Sale for price greater than all liens:** *If all liens on the property are covered by the sale price, the court will normally permit the sale, provided* (although the Code does not specifically address this issue) *the sale proceeds are held by the debtor or trustee to cover the liens.* This result is consistent with the operation of U.C.C. § 9-306 and its treatment of proceeds from the sale of collateral. These sales will normally be for cash, but the same principle can govern exchanges, in whole or in part, for other forms of property.

   a. **Inadequate proceeds:** *If the proceeds of a sale do not cover the liens, the property generally cannot be sold.* In this situation, the other alternatives under § 363(f) will not ordinarily apply.

   b. **Family farmer exception:** Because family farmers were adversely affected by the dilemma of trying to simplify their operations and get rid of farm equipment that was subject to a lien, a special procedure was introduced in § 1206 to solve the problem (*infra*, p. 222).

4. **Bona fide dispute:** *If there is a genuine dispute as to whether a third party really has an interest in the property, sales free of that interest may be made.*

5. **Release in exchange for cash:** *This alternative enables the debtor to sell property free and clear of a third party's interest if it pays the third party the price required by law for a release of the interest.* One example arises under U.C.C. § 9-506, which gives the debtor the right to redeem collateral from a secured party upon satisfying the underlying obligation.

F. **Sales of property subject to dower and curtesy:** Under § 363(g), *the trustee may sell estate property free of the interests of any party who has the rights of dower or curtesy in that property.* Under § 363(j), the owner of dower or curtesy rights will be paid the value of his or her interest from the proceeds. Any balance will revert to the estate.

G. **Sales of co-ownership interests:** Under § 363(h), *property that the estate owns in co-ownership as defined by state law, such as a tenancy in common, joint tenancy, or tenancy by the entirety,* *may also be sold free of the co-owner's interest.* Before a sale will proceed, the debtor or trustee must show: (1) partition would be impracticable; (2) sale of the estate's interest alone would realize significantly less for the estate than sale of the entire undivided property; (3) the benefit to the estate would outweigh any adverse consequences to the co-owners; and (4) the property is not used for electrical energy, natural or synthetic gas, heat, light or power. Under § 363(j), the co-owner will be paid the value of her interest after the sale.

H. ***Ipso facto* clauses invalid:**   In the same way that *ipso facto* clauses imposed by creditor instruments are invalid to prevent the debtor's estate from using or assuming control over assets (§ 541(c) *supra*, p. 99), under § 363(*l*), ***any contract or statute that by its terms attempts to tie the return of assets to an event of insolvency or bankruptcy is invalid to prevent a sale of assets by the debtor or trustee.*** The overriding principle under which *ipso facto* clauses are invalidated is that it is not the province of transferors of property to the debtor to control what happens when bankruptcy occurs or is imminent. Nor can any statute supersede the intent of the Code. The future of a debtor's property is established by the Code, particularly by § 541 (property of the estate) and § 363 (sale or use of estate property).

IV. EXECUTORY CONTRACTS AND UNEXPIRED LEASES — § 365

A. **Overview of debtor's executory contracts:**   Almost every debtor will bring into bankruptcy a variety of continuing contracts and agreements. Some of these may be prudent commitments that the trustee will wish to honor. Others will represent burdens or imprudence that the trustee will wish to disallow. ***The trustee has a statutory right under § 365 to assume or reject the class of contracts called "executory" contracts.*** The trustee can, of course, simply fail to perform an improvident contract and leave the other contracting party with a cause of action for breach. Since the trustee's failure to perform will typically occur after the bankruptcy has begun, the other party will not have a claim allowable under § 502 (*supra*, p. 75). However, under § 365, the other party has a claim against the estate that dates back to immediately before the petition was filed and gives that party a right to file a proof of claim for damages in the bankruptcy.

B. **Leases as executory contracts:**   With some modifications of the basic rules, ***unexpired leases are considered the equivalent of executory contracts.*** The rules are applicable to leases both of personal property and real estate and to debtors in their capacities both as lessors and lessees. In deliberations about the Code, one view was that, once the lessor delivered the property to the lessee, performance was complete and the lessee could not reject it and avoid performance. But Congress simply provided that unexpired leases are to be included within the framework of classic executory contracts.

C. Definition of executory contract: Legal classicists would argue that all outstanding contracts are executory. If a contract has been fully executed, they say, it is no longer a contract. The definition of an executory contract under the Code would satisfy the classicists to a degree, but it has its own twist.

1. **Both sides must perform:**   *The usual requirement for an executory contract under the Code is that there be meaningful performance due on both sides.* The rationale is as follows: if performance is due only from the debtor, it will not be fair to the other party to permit the debtor to reject; on the other hand, if performance is due only from the other party, the debtor will not want to reject.

2. **Full performance by other party:**   *If at the time of the petition, performance is due only from the debtor and that performance is the payment of money (rather than a physical act), it is usually held that the contract is not executory and the debtor does not have the right to assume or reject under § 365.* In re Cornwall Hill Realty, Inc., 128 B.R. 378 (Bkrtcy. S.D.N.Y. 1991).

3. **Three views on definition of executory contract:**   Three views have evolved on the definition of an executory contract:

    a. **Some performance required by both sides:** The Supreme Court has indicated that a contract that involves performance by both sides, however minor the performance, will be considered executory. *NLRB v. Bildisco & Bildisco*, 465 U.S. 513 (1984). However, the executory nature of the contract in that case was not disputed by the parties and the issue was not essential to the Court's decision.

    b. **Performance whose breach excuses counter-performance:** The view adopted by most courts is that espoused in a seminal article: *Executory Contracts in Bankruptcy, Part I*, 57 Minn. L.R. 439 (1973) by Vern Countryman. Professor Countryman concluded that an executory contract exists where "the obligations of both the bankrupt and the other party to the contract are so far unperformed that the failure of either to complete the performance would constitute a material breach excusing the performance of the other." 57 Minn. L.R. at 460.

Example 1: C contracts to build a house for D. Payment is to be made by D in four installments against periodic construction. After three payments, D files a petition in bankruptcy. Both the duty of C to finish the house and the duty of D to make the final payment make the contract executory.

Example 2: Assume in this contractual arrangement between C and D that, when D files its petition, C has completed the house except for the brass number plate on the front door. The contract is no longer considered executory in bankruptcy. C's failure to complete performance would not entitle D to refrain from paying the final installment under the laws of most states.

c. **Burdensome to debtor:** A third position, called the "functional approach," is that any contract that puts a substantial burden upon the debtor may be rejected by the debtor. The consequences of rejection will be dealt with in the bankruptcy. *In re Arrow, Inc.*, 60 B.R. 117 (Bkrtcy. S.D.Fla.). This position is not widely accepted.

d. **Collective bargaining agreements:** The collective bargaining agreement, executory in nature, which is entered into between an employer and its unionized employees is dealt with in § 1113 of the Code. This provision creates a special process for dealing with collective bargaining agreements in Chapter 11 reorganizations (see *infra*, p. 191).

D. **How contracts are rejected:** *Permission to assume or reject a contract under § 365(a) must be obtained from the court.* The standard for decision is the "good business judgment" of the trustee.

1. **Trustee's test:** The trustee is not required to show that the business will fail or suffer cataclysmic consequences if it does not reject the contract; it need only show that the contract is a bad deal. *The court must only find that the trustee has exercised sound judgment and that its decision was not the result of bad faith, whim, or caprice.*

Example 1: D, a hotel owner, employed a management company to run the hotel. D filed in bankruptcy. The management was poor, but not disastrous. The debtor believed that better results could be achieved if a different management style were tried and rejected the management contract, which was found to be executory. The court affirmed the business judgment of the debtor. *In re Prime Motor Inns*, 124 B.R. 378 (Bkrtcy. S.D.Fla. 1991).

Example 2: Debtor D licensed a metal coating process to licensee, Creditor C. D then entered into bankruptcy. D believed that it would benefit from rejecting the executory license agreement. Its decision was contested by C, whose business would be hurt if it lost the license. D's rejection was allowed. C's argument had little weight against D's good judgment about what was good for it and for C. *Lubrizol Enterprises v. Richmond Metal Finishers*, 756 F.2d 1043 (4th Cir.), cert den., 475 U.S. 1057 (1986). (See, however, § 365(n) (*infra*, p. 116) dealing with intellectual property license agreements, adopted as a consequence of the *Lubrizoil* decision.)

2. **Interplay of state and federal law:**   The applicable state and non-bankruptcy federal laws define the rights of the parties under an underlying contract or lease. Federal bankruptcy law establishes whether a contract or lease may be assumed or rejected.

   Example: The Atlantic Richfield Company (ARCO) leased a gas station to Debtor D. In financial difficulty, D failed to pay rent to ARCO and filed in bankruptcy. ARCO terminated the lease under the provisions of the federal Petroleum Marketing Practices Act (PMPA). Under the terms of PMPA, ARCO had no further obligations to D. The court found that the lease had expired under PMPA; there was nothing left for D to assume or reject under the Code. *In re Herbert*, 806 F.2d 889 (9th Cir. 1986).

E. **Rejection constitutes breach:** Under § 364(g), *the rejection of an executory contract or an unexpired lease annuls the contract or lease.* It also constitutes a breach of the contract or lease and gives the non-debtor party a cause of action in damages.

   1. **Claim relates back:** The effect of using § 365 is that the creditor is enabled to relate its claim back before the time of the petition in order to assert a claim that will be honored in the bankruptcy (*supra*, p. 77). *Upon rejection of an executory contract, the creditor is given an opportunity to file a proof of claim in the bankruptcy as if the claim had arisen immediately before the petition.* Of course, a debtor can simply default under any contract without the niceties of a rejection under § 365 and leave the creditor with the same action for damages. In this case, the creditor's cause of action would, but for § 365, arise too late to permit the assertion of an allowable claim under § 502. The bankruptcy court can give full relief, i.e., termination of the contract or lease under § 365(g) together with a claim for damages under § 502(g) (which specifically pertains to a claim arising from nonassumption of an executory contract).

   2. **Measuring effect on creditor:**   Whether the right to file a claim ultimately helps or harms the creditor cannot be answered categorically. True, the right to share in bankruptcy assets after filing a

valid claim will benefit the creditor. On the other hand, in a Chapter 7 case it will also probably result in a discharge of the claim. If the creditor could not assert its claim and could not share in the bankruptcy assets, it would then have a non-discharged claim that continues after the bankruptcy. However, this may not be as desirable as it seems. If the bankrupt is a corporation that simply dissolves after Chapter 7, the post-bankruptcy claim will be worthless.

a. **Measuring damages for breach:** The measure of damages is usually whatever is allowed under the state law dealing with breach of contract. Until a contract is rejected, the usual rule is that the estate is liable for the value it received from the other party's performance, rather than for strict performance of the contract. *In re Midland Capital Corp.*, 82 B.R. 233 (Bkrtcy. S.D.N.Y. 1988).

b. **Rights of creditors under commercial real estate leases:** Until the lease is assumed or rejected, the trustee is required under § 365(d)(3) to perform the obligations specified in any lease of nonresidential real estate. The court may for cause extend the time for performance of any such obligation that arises within 60 days after the order for relief; but the time for performance may not extend beyond the 60-day period. (For example, if the obligation arises 30 days after the order for relief, the court may extend the time for performance for up to 30 additional days.) *In re Cardian Mortg. Corp.*, 127 B.R. 14 (Bkrtcy. E.D.Va. 1991).

c. **Rights of creditors under equipment leases in Chapter 11 cases:** Under § 365(d)(10), which was added in 1994, the trustee in a Chapter 11 case must pay all obligations under non-consumer leases of personal property (i.e., equipment leases) arising 60 days or more after the order for relief until the lease is assumed or rejected. If equities warrant, the court may modify this obligation. This provision allows the trustee 60 days to make a decision as to the lease; if a decision isn't made within the 60-day period, payments must begin unless the court orders otherwise.

3. **Effect of rejection:** *The rejection by the trustee or the debtor of an executory contract releases both parties to the contract from all its provisions.*

Example: Creditor C, a franchisor of fast food operations, franchised an operation to Debtor D. Included in the franchise agreement was a clause providing that D could not compete with C for 18 months after the franchise was terminated. Upon D's bankruptcy, the issue was raised whether the franchise agreement was executory. C claimed that it had completed its duties upon delivery of the franchised operations. The court held that C had continuing duties; the franchise was an executory contract and it could be terminated by D. D was thereby freed from the non-compete restriction. *In re Rovine Corp.*, 6 B.R. 661 (Bkrtcy. W.D. Tenn. 1980). In *Rovine*, C was prevented from obtaining an injunction against D to enforce the non-compete agreement. Rejection did not, however, relieve D of the responsibility to pay the damages resulting from its default. C was permitted to claim the damages it suffered as a result of D's competition.

F. **Defaults occurring before bankruptcy:** Frequently there will have been a default by the debtor under an executory contract or an unexpired lease before the bankruptcy begins.

1. **Three conditions to assuming contracts in default:** *In the event of default of an executory contract, the trustee may not assume the contract or lease unless it satisfies the three conditions under § 365(b)(1).*

   a. **Must cure default or give adequate assurance:** The trustee must cure the default or give adequate assurance that it will be promptly cured.

   b. **Must provide compensation for damages:** The trustee must compensate any other party to the contract or lease for losses resulting from the breach or provide adequate assurance that losses will be compensated.

   c. **Must provide assurance of future performance:** The trustee must give adequate assurance that there will be future performance under the contract or lease.

2. **Not applicable to *ipso facto* breaches:** An executory contract or lease may contain an *ipso facto* clause. If so, a party who declares bankruptcy, becomes insolvent, or manifests a severe decline in its financial condition, would be in default solely as a result of any of these events. Under § 365(b)(2), clauses containing these or similar provisions are not enforceable; there is no responsibility to cure the default and/or give adequate security under the requirements of § 365(b)(1).

3. **Meaning of "adequate assurance":** "Adequate assurance" under § 365(b)(1)(A) is not to be confused with "adequate protection" under § 361 (dealing with the automatic stay). *"Adequate assurance" here implies a satisfaction with, or confidence in, the situation of an affected party, so that the obligations due to it appear likely to be performed by the debtor.* Except in relation

to a shopping center, adequate assurance is not specifically defined under § 365(b).

Example: A debtor, the lessee of a store, defaults in its rental payments before bankruptcy. It may "assume" the lease in bankruptcy if it brings its payments current and satisfies the court that its volume of sales gives adequate assurance that future rents will be paid. *In re R.H.Neil, Inc.*, 58 B.R. 969 (Bkrtcy. S.D.N.Y. 1986). Similarly, an assurance of continuing supplies of merchandise, the payment of rents in advance, and even the general desirability of the lease itself, help to prove that adequate assurance of future rental payments has been provided. *In re The Hub of Military Circle, Inc.*, 19 B.R. 460 (Bkrtcy. E.D.Va. 1982).

4. **Scope of "adequate assurance" for shopping centers:** The Code has special requirements that apply only to "shopping centers." The overall objective is not only to assure future rental payments by a debtor-tenant but also to help retain the nature of the shopping center. Under § 365(b)(3), *"adequate assurance" in a shopping center lease must apply not only to the tenant assuming the lease but also to any new tenant to whom the bankrupt tenant assigns the lease.* It's not always clear that a contiguous group of stores actually is a shopping center as intended by § 365(b)(3). A shopping center means a group of independent stores that are contractually interrelated, contiguous to a common area, and planned as a single unit. Where the lease of a store permits unlimited assignment without control of either the inventory to be sold, store hours, advertising or operations, the store is not part of a shopping center. The fact that the location may look like a shopping center is not determinative. *In re Ames Dept. Stores, Inc.*, 121 B.R. 160 (Bkrtcy. S.D.N.Y. 1990). Adequate assurance in connection with shopping centers has the following requirements.

    a. **Source of rent:** In order for there to be adequate assurance, *the source of the rent must be assured.* If the lease is assigned, the financial condition of the assignee and its guarantors, if any, must be similar to that of the debtor and its guarantors, if any.

    b. **Rentals geared to sales:** Adequate assurance requires that *any percentage rentals under the lease, i.e., rentals geared to sales in the leased premises, must not decline substantially.*

    c. **Lease restrictions:** Adequate assurance requires that the *restrictions in the lease dealing with factors like "radius, location, use, or exclusivity" continue to apply to the* *assuming debtor and to any assignee*; they must also agree not to breach any other lease or agreement concerning the shopping center.

   d. Tenant mix and balance: *Assumption and assignment must not disrupt the tenant mix or balance in the shopping center.*

G. Assumption followed by assignment: If an executory contract or an unexpired lease has substantial economic value, the debtor or trustee may wish to sell the contract or lease to a third party. The Code requires first that an assumption of the contract or lease under § 365 be made before an assignment to the third party. As with shopping center leases, these steps are regulated in various ways throughout § 365.

   1. Unassumable and unassignable executory contracts: Under § 365(c), *there are three types of executory contracts and leases that may neither be assumed nor assigned:*

      a. Personal service contracts: The estate is a different legal entity from the debtor. Consequently, a third party is confronted with the need to accept performance from an entity he did not contract with. Applicable state law usually defines certain situations, particularly in the area of personal service contracts, where the third party may be excused from accepting performance by the estate. (See discussion of property of the estate under § 541, *supra*, p. 97.)

      Example: Creditor C contracts with a painter, Debtor D, to paint C's portrait. Upon D's bankruptcy, the contract may not be assumed by the bankruptcy estate, nor may it be assigned by the estate to a third party. However, C may voluntarily agree to accept performance from the new party, in which event the contract may be assumed and assigned.

      b. Underwriting and credit accommodation contracts: Contracts to lend money, to extend other forms of debt financing, or to issue a security (underwrite a stock or a bond) for the debtor may not be assumed or assigned. Contracts of this type are personal to the individual debtor and are typically based upon its financial standing.

      c. Nonresidential leases: If a lease of nonresidential real estate has expired before the order for relief, it may neither be assumed nor assigned. (See also § 362(b)(10) relating to the automatic stay and expired leases of nonresidential real estate.)

   2. Procedures for assumption and assignment: A trustee will seek to derive economic benefit from an executory contract or an unexpired lease. In a Chapter 7 bankruptcy, his goal will be the most profitable liquidation of the estate. In a Chapter 11 reorganization, he may wish to profit from a contract or lease that was entered into by a debtor-tenant at an earlier time when rents were lower, especially if the trustee has no need for the premises in the reorganization. In these cases, the trustee may sell his rights to some willing third-party buyer under § 365(f).

a. **Assumption must precede assignment:** *The trustee must first assume the contract or lease.*

b. **Adequate assurance by the assignee:** *Before the contract or lease may be assigned, the assignee must give adequate assurance of future performance.* This is separate from the adequate assurance that must be given by the trustee who wishes to assume where there has been a default previous to the filing (*supra*, p. 111). Adequate assurance here is required whether or not there has been any default.

c. **Prohibitions against assignment invalid:** *A contract or lease may not by its terms, nor may any law outside the Code, prohibit or restrict assignment to a trustee in bankruptcy* (except in the three situations described *supra*, p. 113). Essentially, this is another application of the *ipso facto* doctrine.

d. **Release of the assignor:** Under § 365(k), *upon assignment of contract or lease, the trustee and the estate are relieved of any liability for breach of the contract or lease that may occur subsequent to the assignment.*

3. **Timing of assumptions and rejections:** Under § 365(k), the Code sets forth rules controlling the timing of the assumption and rejection of executory contracts and leases. The court has discretion to shorten or extend these time periods and will usually act to retain the status quo for a reasonable time in order to enable the trustee to make a reasoned decision whether to assume or reject. *In re Sweetwater*, 40 B.R. 733 (Bkrtcy. D. Utah), aff'd, 57 B.R. 743 (D. Utah 1985).

a. **Chapter 7:** *In a Chapter 7 case, if the trustee does not assume or reject within 60 days after the order for relief, the contract or lease is deemed rejected.* This is consistent with the goal of liquidation.

b. **Cases under other Chapters:** In cases under Chapters 9, 11, 12, or 13, assumption or rejection of an executory contract or unexpired lease of residential real estate or of personal property must come before confirmation of a bankruptcy plan.

c. **Unexpired lease of nonresidential real estate:**   *If an unexpired lease of nonresidential real estate is neither accepted nor rejected within 60 days after the order for relief, it is deemed rejected.*

d. **Status of contract before assumption or rejection:**   During the time before an executory contract or lease is either assumed or rejected, it remains in doubt. A party receiving benefits under it must pay reasonable value for these benefits. The price set by the agreement or lease will not necessarily control. However, note that there are special rules requiring the trustee to perform the obligations incurred under commercial real estate and equipment leases during the period in which they have neither been accepted nor rejected (*supra*, p. 110).

4. **Assumption followed by breach:**   A contract which is assumed by the trustee or debtor is no more sacred than any other contract; it may or may not be performed. However, *if a contract is assumed after the case has begun and then is breached during the course of the case, the chances are high that damages will give rise to an administrative claim subject to § 503* (*supra*, p. 86) and a first priority under § 507 (*supra*, p. 86). *American A. & B. Coal Corp. v. Leonardo Arrivabene, S.A.*, 280 F.2d 119 (2d Cir. 1960) (*supra*, p. 86). A request then can be made for payment in the case under § 503(a) (*supra*, p. 86). As an administrative claim, the claim will be allowed even though it did not arise before the bankruptcy.

H. **Leases and sales of real property and timeshare interests:**   In our complicated society, people regularly enter into leases and sales of real property and into a variety of timeshare arrangements. The Code had to recognize the need of a debtor in bankruptcy to escape from the pressure of these commitments.

1. **Termination of leases of real estate and time-share interests:**   Under § 365(h), *if a bankrupt lessor terminates a real property lease or timeshare interest, the lessee has the option either to treat the lease or interest as terminated or to remain in possession.* If the lessor's termination causes any damage to the lessee, he may offset the damages against future rent, but he does not have an affirmative claim against the lessor.

2. **Termination of executory sales contract where buyer is in possession:** Under § 365(i), *if a bankrupt seller of real estate or timeshare interests rejects an executory sales contract, a buyer in possession of the premises has the option either to treat the contract as terminated or to remain in possession.* If the buyer remains in possession, she must make all payments when

due, but may offset the amount of damages she suffers as a result of the rejection. She does not have an affirmative cause of action.

3. **Delivery of title:**   *If a creditor-purchaser is in possession under a sales contract or a timeshare arrangement, the trustee must deliver title, but has no other obligations to perform.* A claim against the trustee will probably not be meaningful since the buyer's damages may be asserted only as offsets against payment of the purchase price. If a buyer treats an executory contract as terminated, he has a lien on the real estate for the recovery of any portion of the purchase price he has previously paid.

I. **Rights to intellectual property:**   Until 1988, as a result of the *Lubrizoil* decision (*supra*, p. 108), a licensor under an executory contract could terminate the contract under a standard that was not difficult to meet and thus deprive the licensee of what might have been a vital source of income. Concerned with the harshness of this rule, Congress added § 365(n) to protect licensees of rights to intellectual property. The principle underlying § 365(n) is that *protecting licenses of intellectual property is the best way to assure the financing, marketing and development of advancements in technology.* The inventor or artist can be rewarded by the benefits of his creativity and the user can profit from its development and sale.

1. **Definition of "intellectual property":**   Intellectual property is defined in § 101(56) as *trade secrets, inventions, processes, or designs protected by the patent laws, patent applications, plant varieties, works of authorship and certain materials relating to semi-conductors.* They are the types of products and ideas whose manufacture and distribution would normally be the subject of licenses by the creator to a producer.

2. **Options upon rejection:**   If the executory contract at issue is an intellectual property license, the licensor may still affirm or reject the contract upon its bankruptcy (*supra*, p. 106). Upon rejection, however, the licensee has an option similar to the option that § 365(h) gives to a lessee of real property. The licensee may treat the license as terminated or may continue to enforce its rights.

CHAPTER 8
THE TRUSTEE'S AVOIDING POWERS

Introductory note: This section examines the trustee's avoiding powers, limitations on those powers, and the provisions pertaining to enforcement of the powers. The avoiding powers allow the trustee to set aside certain transactions that were entered into before the bankruptcy petition, in order to bring property back into the estate and to provide, therefore, a more equitable distribution to creditors. Thus, the debtor's effort to favor certain creditors at the expense of others (preferential transfers), or to transfer property without receiving full value for it (fraudulent transfers), or the vagaries of state law as applied to lien creditors (which is based largely upon the concept of first in time, first in right), will not prevail.

I. POWERS TO AVOID PREPETITION TRANSFERS AND OBLIGATIONS — § 544

A. **Scope of the power:** The trustee is given several powers under § 544 to avoid certain transfers made and obligations incurred by the debtor prior to the filing of the bankruptcy petition. The trustee exercises these powers in two ways: (1) as a hypothetical creditor under § 544(a), and (2) in the place of actual creditors or purchasers under § 544(b). The powers are most often exercised to avoid unperfected security interests in the debtor's property, which are generally unknown to creditors and have been called "secret liens." The powers of hypothetical creditors under § 544(a) are derived from rights available outside of bankruptcy law (such as the right of a lien creditor to enforce its lien). When combined with the special status of the trustee (such as the disregard of actual knowledge on the part of the trustee or a creditor), these give the trustee greater powers than those of lien creditors under nonbankruptcy law. For this reason, the statutory provision conferring the powers of hypothetical entities — § 544(a) — is one of the most potent of the trustee's powers and has become known as the "strong arm clause."

B. **Transfers before bankruptcy:** The trustee is given the power under § 544 to avoid any "transfer" or "obligation incurred" that is voidable by specified entities. The word "transfer" is very broadly defined in § 101(54) to mean every mode of parting with an interest in property and includes both voluntary and involuntary transfers. Among transactions falling within the definition of transfer are: giving a security interest or mortgage, allowing a judicial lien to help collect a judgment, and giving a repairman's lien in enforcement of a price.

C. The "strong arm clause" — § 544(a): The so-called "strong arm clause," § 544(a), is one of the most potent and most used of the trustee's avoiding powers. The clause allows the trustee to avoid a prior transfer by, or obligation incurred by, the debtor by giving the trustee powers to ***affect transactions in the same way that a creditor could if it had obtained a lien on the property and, with respect to real estate, in the same way that a good faith purchaser of the property could.*** Therefore, the power is said to be that of hypothetical entities — hypothetical lien creditors or hypothetical good faith purchasers. Under § 544(a), the trustee does not succeed to any powers or rights already existing prior to the bankruptcy, but attains the powers solely by operation of the clause. In order to make the clause operate effectively, the trustee exercises the powers under § 544(a) without regard to actual knowledge by the trustee herself or by any creditor (see *infra*, p. 122).

1. **Three powers — three hypothetical entities:** The strong arm clause provides the trustee with powers that would be available to ***three hypothetical entities: a judicial lien creditor, an execution lien creditor, and a good faith purchaser of real estate.***

   a. **Hypothetical judicial lien creditor — § 544(a)(1):** Under § 544(a)(1), the trustee is given the same ability to avoid a prior transfer or an obligation that would be possessed by:

   > a creditor that extends credit to the debtor at the time of the commencement of the case, and that obtains, at such time and with respect to such credit, a judicial lien on all property on which a creditor on a simple contract could have obtained such a judicial lien, whether or not such a creditor exists.

   In other words, ***if a transfer of personal property or an obligation made before the bankruptcy petition (for example, an unperfected security interest) could be upset by the hypothetical unsatisfied judicial lien creditor, it can be upset by the trustee acting for the estate.*** The trustee is given the power of a hypothetical creditor who at the same time — at the commencement of the case — both (1) extends credit to the debtor, and (2) obtains a judicial lien on property of the debtor with respect to the credit. Since normally a judicial lien first requires that a judgment be sought, won, and not satisfied by the debtor, it is a legal fiction that all of this can happen at the same moment. And, that is precisely the point; the creditor whose rights are given to the trustee is hypothetical — that creditor does not actually exist. Since the hypothetical creditor is also unaffected by any actual knowledge of a prior transfer or obligation (see *infra*, p. 122), he is sometimes called the "best possible lien creditor." The strong arm clause establishes the rights of a best possible lien creditor at the moment that the petition is filed, not at any prior point in time. *Lewis v. Manufacturers Nat'l Bank of Detroit*, 364 U.S. 603 (1961).

b. Hypothetical execution lien creditor — § 544(a)(2): Under § 544(a)(2), which supplements (a)(1), ***the trustee is given the rights of a creditor who, under exactly the same conditions as a hypothetical lien creditor, gives credit and obtains an unsatisfied judgment execution against the debtor***. The rights of such a creditor are very similar to those of an unsatisfied lien creditor and vary in modest ways depending upon the laws of particular states.

c. Hypothetical good faith purchaser of real estate — § 544(a)(3): With respect to ***transfers of real estate, the trustee is given the power of a hypothetical good faith purchaser***, in addition to the powers of a lien creditor and an execution creditor. As with the first two hypothetical powers, the hypothetical good faith purchaser's powers are exercised without regard to actual notice; however, the language of this part of the statute, "against whom applicable law permits such transfer to be perfected" means that, if the hypothetical purchaser has constructive notice, he cannot be a good faith purchaser. Actual notice depends on what is actually known by the purchaser; constructive notice depends on what could be known based on a reasonable inquiry. The following examples contrast the respective rights of a secured creditor, as against a judicial lien creditor and a good faith purchaser. As will be seen, a good faith purchaser generally has greater rights than a lien creditor.

Example 1: A department store, Debtor D, borrows money and gives the lender, Secured Creditor C1, a lien on all of the inventory of the store. Creditor C2 also lends money to D, is unpaid, sues D, is still unpaid and gets a judicial lien on D's assets. C1's interest, assuming that C1 has perfected the interest, will be superior to C2's judicial lien.

Example 2: The same facts as Example 1, but Good Faith Purchaser P goes into the store, buys something from the inventory and takes it home. P's interest will be superior to those of both C1 and C2.

2. Applicability of state law: When establishing the rights of each of the three hypothetical entities, the Code defines the entity, but does not tell us its rights. Those are established by looking to state law. Similarly, the property rights established in the prior transfer or obligation that the trustee is looking to upset are also established by state law. To give answers in the previous two examples, the rules of the Uniform Commercial Code were applied, which are uniform throughout the country on the issues presented. However, there are variations in state law that will in some cases put the property interests of parties in a different order. The order prescribed by the particular state law will be observed in bankruptcy.

3. **Unperfected security interests in personal property:** *The most common use of the strong arm clause is in voiding prior liens that are not perfected.* For example, assume that Secured Creditor C1 lends money to D before the bankruptcy and takes a security interest in D's inventory. If C1 obeys "the legal niceties" of perfection, C1 will prevail over a contesting unsatisfied judgment lien creditor and, therefore, C1's security interest will be valid despite D's bankruptcy. Where all the legal formalities have not been followed, however, either deliberately or through a mistake, C1 may find itself in a position where it will lose that security interest to a subsequent lien creditor and, therefore, to the trustee. Security interests that are unperfected are often referred to as "secret liens." As a result of not conforming with the perfection procedures, they are not legally "known" to future creditors who extend credit to the debtor. Even if there is actual knowledge of unperfected security interests, (actual knowledge is discussed, *infra*, p. 122), they may be upset by other creditors who achieve the status of judicial lien creditors.

   a. **Formalities for establishing and perfecting security interests:** The following is a brief review of how security interests are established and perfected, which is important to understanding the use of the strong arm clause to void unperfected security interests.

      i. **Establishing a security interest:** In establishing a security interest, there are carefully defined steps that must be taken by a creditor. For example, U.C.C. § 9-203 prescribes that the security agreement must be in writing and signed by the debtor.

      ii. **Perfecting a security interest:** To achieve validity against future competing interests, like that of a subsequent lien creditor, a creditor's interest must also be "perfected." Perfection is usually by means of some action that is deemed to give general public notice of the existence of a lien. How it is accomplished will be provided in whatever law governs the transaction. For a security interest in inventory, perfection under the U.C.C. consists of filing a particular form in a designated place. For other types of collateral and other situations, perfection may involve a transfer of possession of the collateral to the secured party. For a motor vehicle, it may involve notation on a certificate of title. In some situations, it may occur automatically by operation of law.

b. **Consequences of unperfected security interests:** Under U.C.C. § 9-301, *an unperfected security interest loses to a subsequent judicial lien creditor*. Through use of the strong arm clause, the trustee in a bankruptcy can similarly avoid the unperfected security interest. The careful trustee will be sure to look at all security interests in existence as of the time of the bankruptcy to see if they are perfected. If they are not, the secured parties will lose to the trustee, who will acquire the property and bring it into the estate. There are many reasons why a security interest may not be perfected. A mistake in handling the papers is the most typical reason. A misunderstanding of the legal requirements for perfection may also exist. Occasionally, a creditor may make a deliberate decision not to perfect because of confidence in the debtor. Under the U.C.C., all these instances will result in the collateral being lost by the secured creditor to a subsequent judicial lien creditor; it will also be lost to trustee for the bankruptcy estate.

4. **Real estate mortgages and the strong arm clause:** If a mortgage on real estate is unrecorded, it will generally still be valid under state real estate laws against a subsequent judicial lienor. However, *the trustee has the status of a good faith purchaser of real estate. In most jurisdictions the good faith purchaser will win over the unrecorded position.*

5. **Other interests and the strong arm clause:** While an unperfected security interest is the most common object of a strong-arm clause attack, it is not the only one. Under U.C.C. § 2-402(2), a sale of goods where delivery is not made to the buyer may under the applicable state law be deemed to be fraudulent as to creditors of the seller. In a seller's bankruptcy, this doctrine may enable the trustee of the seller's estate to claim goods previously sold but not delivered. Another example subject to strong-arm attack relates to a contractor who, having done repairs on land, typically has a "mechanic's lien," (a statutory lien) on the land to secure his price. The lien may have to be filed to be effective against other creditors, including a judicial lien creditor. *In re APC Const., Inc.*, 112 B.R. 89 (Bkrtcy D.Vt.), aff'd, 132 B.R. 690 (D.Vt. 1991).

6. **Actual knowledge of adverse interests:**   Where an interest in property is not perfected and a creditor acquires a later interest in the same property with actual knowledge of the prior interest, state law is not uniform as to the relative rights of the two secured creditors'. Under the U.C.C., actual knowledge is given a relatively lower status when compared to the more objectively ascertainable event of filing; but, even in the U.C.C., actual knowledge has its place as the equivalent of a subordinate perfection. The Bankruptcy Code has practically eliminated knowledge as a factor. *Under the strong arm clause, the trustee is given the enumerated rights "without regard to any knowledge of the trustee or of any creditor."* What the trustee actually knows, and what any creditor in the bankruptcy actually knows, is largely irrelevant in measuring avoiding powers. The one exception is that the hypothetical good faith purchaser of real estate is charged with constructive notice, i.e., notice that is imputed to the purchaser due to the existence of a recording or other circumstance with respect to the property. Thus, unlike actual notice, if the hypothetical good faith purchaser of real estate can be said to have constructive knowledge under the law of the relevant jurisdiction, he will not have good faith purchaser status.

Example: Real estate owner O creates a lien in favor of secured creditor C prior to bankruptcy. The lien is invalidly recorded, but of course O knows about it because he created it. Chapter 11 follows and, as in most Chapter 11 cases, the estate is managed by O, who becomes a new entity called a "debtor in possession." (See Chapter 11 discussion, *infra*, p. 176.) The Code in § 1107 gives the debtor in possession the same rights as a trustee, including the trustee's avoiding powers under § 544. O, as debtor in possession, attempts to avoid C's lien. It was held that actual notice did not prevent it from asserting the rights of a good faith purchaser under § 544(a)(3), but that constructive notice *would* prevent it from asserting those rights, depending on whether the recording of the lien, even though improper, constituted constructive knowledge under the relevant state law. *In re Sandy Ridge Oil Co., Inc.*, 807 F.2d 1332 (7th Cir. 1986).

D. **Rights of actual unsecured creditors — § 544(b):** In addition to the powers of hypothetical entities under § 544(a), the trustee is invested with the rights of actual creditors under § 544(b). Thus, *the trustee has the right to avoid a prior transfer of property or a debt that could be voided by an actual unsecured creditor with an allowed claim* (or whose claim has been disallowed only because of a technicality dealing with reimbursement or contribution under § 502(e)).

1. **Typical § 544(b) situations:**

   a. **State fraudulent transfer laws:** Where a debtor transfers her house to her spouse before the bankruptcy in order to protect it from her creditors, the applicable state Fraudulent Conveyance Law may provide that such transfers may be voided by creditors, whether they existed before or after the transfer. The trustee acquires the rights of these creditors and may void the transfer. (Compare this example with the workings of § 548, *infra*, p. 136, which gives a trustee the right to void fraudulent transfers under bankruptcy law.)

   b. **State Bulk Sales Acts:** Where a debtor sells all of its inventory without giving notice to its creditors as prescribed by a state Bulk Sales Act, the law generally provides that any unpaid creditor of the seller who does not receive such notice may void the sale. Where such a creditor exists in a bankruptcy, the trustee acquires its rights and may void the sale.

2. **Charitable exception:** Rights given to creditors as a result of charitable gifts that would be exempt from fraudulent transfer restrictions under §544(b). Any claim for a recovery under federal or state law as a result of such a gift is preempted by the Bankruptcy Code upon the commencement of a case.

E. **Doctrine of *Moore v. Bay*:** Under the doctrine of *Moore v. Bay*, **when a trustee acquires rights to avoid a mortgage, it may for the benefit of the estate avoid the entire mortgage without reference to the amount owed to the creditor.**

   Example: A trustee avoids a mortgage in the amount of $10,000 on the debtor's property through powers acquired from a creditor who is in existence in the bankruptcy and who is owed only $2,000. The trustee is able to avoid the entire mortgage, not just $2,000 of it. *Moore v. Bay*, 284 U.S. 4 (1931).

II.   POWER TO AVOID STATUTORY LIENS — § 545

A. **Scope of power:** Statutory liens (liens that arise by virtue of a statute for the benefit of otherwise unsecured creditors) are generally valid. Under § 545, the trustee has the power to avoid a statutory lien if it is either: (1) created under a statute that operates "in contemplation of bankruptcy," (2) not perfected or enforceable against a hypothetical good faith purchaser of property (who is considered to have made the purchase at the commencement of the case); or (3) for rent or of distress for rent.

B. Definition of statutory lien — § 101(53): Not every lien provided for by statute is a statutory lien within the meaning of the Code. Statutory liens are defined in § 101(53) as: (1) ***liens arising solely by force of statute on specified circumstances and conditions*** and (2) ***liens of distress for rent*** (power in a landlord to take a defaulting tenant's property) ***whether by statute or common law***. The definition of statutory lien excludes, regardless of whether provided for or only made fully effective by statute: (1) judicial liens, which are those liens typically obtained to enforce an unpaid judgment and which are also available in unusual situations to attach a debtor's property even before judgment, and (2) security interests.

Statutory liens under § 101(53) include:

- artisan liens, which give one who repairs or works on property a lien on the property to secure his unpaid bill;

- repairman liens, which give one who repairs an object a lien upon it to secure his unpaid price;

- storageman liens, which give one who stores property a lien upon it for payment of the storage cost;

- lawyers' liens, which give an unpaid lawyer a lien upon the work product; and

- liens imposed for unpaid taxes.

C. In contemplation of bankruptcy — § 545(1): Statutory liens are avoidable under § 545(1) if a statute provides that a lien becomes effective upon the commencement of a bankruptcy case, or upon some similar event such as the debtor's insolvency or reduced financial condition. In such an event, the statutory lien becomes functionally similar to an "ipso facto" clause in a contract (see *supra*, p. 99), in that it tries to control what will occur upon bankruptcy and, if given effect, would interfere with the federal bankruptcy power.

Example 1: Creditor C repairs Debtor D's barn before D's bankruptcy and is not paid by D. State S, in which the repairs are done, has a statute stating that one who makes a repair upon real property and is not paid will have a lien upon the property if as the property owner goes into bankruptcy (or starts a state insolvency proceeding, or has his income drop by more than 25 percent). Any lien claimed by the repairman under this statute may be voided by the trustee in D's bankruptcy because the statute is in contemplation of bankruptcy.

Example 2: Creditor C makes repairs under the same conditions as just described, except that State S's statute says that one who makes a repair upon real property and is not paid for 60 days after payment becomes due will have a lien upon the property. Such a lien will be valid in D's bankruptcy because the statute operates irrespective of D's financial condition or the occurrence of an event in bankruptcy.

D. Unperfected or unenforceable against a hypothetical good faith purchaser — § 545(2): The trustee may also avoid a statutory lien, as defined above, that is not perfected or is not enforceable at the time of the commencement of the case against a hypothetical bona fide purchaser, who is considered to have purchased the property on the date of the commencement of the case. In other words, ***in order to be valid, a statutory lien, as defined, must be good against a hypothetical good faith purchaser of property***. Thus, the trustee as the hypothetical good faith purchaser is given the same right that a good faith purchaser for value has in nonbankruptcy law. The good faith purchaser is hypothetical because, for purposes of this section, he is considered to have bought it at the time that the petition is filed. Although the state statute will ordinarily require that a filing procedure be complied with, it is possible that the statute creating the lien will by its own terms provide that the lien, upon its creation and even without filing, is valid against good faith purchasers of the property subject to the lien. Note that under such a clause, the trustee will have the strongest of the rights described under the § 544(a) strong-arm clause — the rights of a good faith purchaser (see *supra*, p. 121).

E. Rent or distress of rent — § 545(3), (4): The trustee also has the power to avoid statutes that give landlords liens for unpaid rent or for "distress" (derived from the term "distraint", which means the seizure or detention of property by a landlord) of rent from defaulting tenants. Note that, under the definition of statutory lien in § 101(53), liens for distress of rent may arise either by statute or by common law (see *supra*, p. 124). This provision reflects a congressional decision that landlords should be treated together with other unsecured creditors. Only landlord statutory liens are avoided under this provision; security agreements, which are often included in leases with the consent of the tenant, are not affected.

III. POWER TO AVOID PREFERENCES — § 547

A. Scope of power: The trustee is also given the power to avoid "preferential" transfers made by the debtor during the 90-day period prior to the filing of the bankruptcy petition. The rules on preferential transfers apply objectively to transactions that are considered to give some creditors advantages (i.e., preferences) over other creditors; the intent of the parties is largely irrelevant. The categories of avoidable preferences are covered in § 547(b); some preferences, although they fall under (b), will nevertheless be permitted to stand; they are covered in § 547(c). (*infra*, p. 125).

1. **Comparison to state law:** Transfers that are considered preferential under § 547 would otherwise be valid under nonbankruptcy law.

   Example: Under traditional state debtor-creditor law, if D is indebted to C1, C2, and C3 and decides to pay C2, state law will generally not interfere with this decision. D may prefer C2 to the other creditors because D intends to do additional business with C2, because D may fear that C2 will otherwise cancel D's credit card, or because D and C2 have a special relationship. C2 also may get paid because C2 was the first to win a suit against D and, under state law, first-in-time, first-in-right prevails. In these examples, C2 may be said to have been "preferred" by D over the other creditors. Under § 547, the trustee is given the power to protect C1 and C3 and enable them to participate in the distribution. C2 is also thus discouraged from racing C1 and C3 to the courthouse.

2. **Importance of transfer date:** Critical to the operation of the power to avoid preferences is ascertaining the date of transfer, which is subject to specific rules. If the debtor gives a creditor a security interest (i.e., makes a transfer) in order to obtain property, the date of perfection of the security interest is not necessarily the date of transfer. The statute sets forth specific rules defining how the date of perfection affects the date of transfer.

B. **A preference involves a "transfer" of a debtor's "property" — 547(b):** The trustee is given the power to avoid "any transfer of an interest of the debtor in property" that has certain preferential qualities.

1. **A "transfer":** We have noted the breadth of the definition of "transfer" contained in § 101(54),(*supra*, p. 117). A transfer includes selling goods, making a money payment, and giving a security interest in goods to stand behind an obligation. ***A transfer can be involuntary as well as voluntary.*** Thus, if a creditor executes on a judgment obtained against the debtor and takes the debtor's property, the debtor has made a transfer.

2. **"Property" of the debtor:** The transfer, in order to be considered preferential, must, of course, be a transfer of the debtor's property. This requirement is generally straightforward, but has been strictly applied.

Example 1: Debtor D owes money to Creditor C before bankruptcy. C feels that the debt is shaky and asks D to give C a lien on some of D's property to stand behind the debt. D complies. The lien is clearly a transfer of D's property.

Example 2: D claims that, when money went to the IRS by virtue of a provision of the Internal Revenue Code providing for a trust for unpaid withholding taxes, the transfer was preferential in nature because it caused the IRS to be preferred to other creditors. It was held that there was no preference because the money was required to be withheld from employee wages and held in trust and was therefore not the property of the employer debtor. *Begier v. IRS,* 496 U.S. 53 (1990).

3. **Rights in property must be acquired:** Under § 547(e)(3), a transfer for § 547 purposes is not made until the debtor acquires rights in the property transferred.

   Example: On June 1 Debtor D gives C a security interest in a drill press that D is planning to buy. The security interest is properly perfected by filing under the U.C.C. The drill press is bought and received on June 10. The transfer occurs for § 547 purposes on June 10 because perfection actually occurred when D acquired rights in the drill press. Prior to that time, D does not have an interest that it can transfer to C.

C. **Relationship of perfection of a security interest to date of transfer — § 547(e):** Where a transfer involves the perfection of a security interest, § 547(e) sets forth specific rules to determine the date on which a transfer will be considered to have been made.

   1. **When perfection occurs — general rule:**

      a. **Real property:** With respect to a transfer of real property, perfection occurs when (i) the transfer is valid under state law and (ii) it will stand up against a subsequent good faith purchaser.

      b. **Personal property:** For a transfer of personal property, perfection occurs when it is valid against a subsequent judicial lien creditor. (As discussed in connection with § 544, this is a less demanding requirement than that for the good faith purchaser, *supra,* p. 119.)

   2. **Date of perfection fixes date of transfer:** Subject to the special rule that a transfer is not made until the debtor acquires rights in the property transferred (*supra*), there are three basic rules under § 547(e) under which the *date of perfection* of a security interest affects the *date of transfer* of the security interest. Note that a

special time period of 20 days is allowed for the perfection of purchase money security interests.

a. **Perfection within 10 days:** If perfection occurs at or within 10 days after the actual transfer (20 days for a purchase money security interest), the transfer occurs for § 547 purposes at the time of the actual transfer.

b. **Perfection after 10 days:** If perfection occurs after the 10 days (20 days for a purchase money security interest) but before the case begins, the transfer occurs for § 547 purposes at the perfection date.

c. **Perfection after filing of bankruptcy petition:** If perfection occurs after the case begins, the transfer for § 547 purposes is deemed to occur immediately before the filing of the petition. An exception from this rule is that, if perfection occurs after the case begins but within the ten (or 20) days permitted above, the transfer occurs at the time of the actual transfer.

d. **No perfection:** If perfection does not occur at all, the transfer is deemed to occur at the beginning of the case. The effect of this is that the transfer will be for an antecedent debt. (As will be seen shortly, *infra*, one of the requirements for an avoidable preference is that the transfer be for an antecedent debt.) Note that liens that are not perfected, or are legally "secret," can be avoided under the strong arm clause (§ 544(a) *supra*, p. 120), which exists as an alternative remedy to § 547.

Examples: On June 1, Creditor C makes a loan to Debtor D. Simultaneously with the loan, D gives C a security interest in property of D. To perfect C's interest against subsequent lien creditors of D, the property interest must be filed with the Secretary of State.

i. **Perfection within 10 days:** If filing is made with the Secretary of State on June 10 and the bankruptcy petition is filed on June 15, the transfer occurs for § 547 purposes on June 1, the date of the loan.

ii. **Perfection after 10 days:** If the state filing is made on June 25 and the bankruptcy petition is filed on June 30, the transfer occurs for § 547 purposes on June 25, the date of filing the security interest.

iii. **Perfection after filing of bankruptcy petition:** If the state filing is made on June 30 and the bankruptcy petition is filed on June 25, the transfer occurs for § 547 purposes on June 25 (just prior to the filing of the petition).

iv. **No perfection:** If the state filing is not made at all and a bankruptcy petition is filed on June 30, the transfer occurs for § 547 purposes immediately before the filing of the bankruptcy petition and the transfer is for an antecedent debt.

Example: Debtor D borrows money from Creditor C and gives C a security interest in D's car. Delays in perfecting the lien on the certificate of title consume 33 days. C asserts that the perfection was "substantially" contemporaneous and, therefore, an exception to the rules on preferential transfers (see *infra* p. 132). However, the trustee contends that § 547(e) creates a specific method of evaluating liens and that, since perfection occurred after the time specified, it should be fixed as the 33rd day. The Court of Appeals agreed with the trustee and most courts have followed suit. *In re Arnett*, 731 F.2d 358 (6th Cir. 1984). An opinion in disagreement, holding that the particular facts should be looked to in order to determine whether a transaction reflects a substantially contemporaneous exchange, is *In re Telecash Industries, Inc.*, 104 B.R. 401 (Bkrtcy D.Utah 1989).

D. The five requirements of an avoidable preference: Under § 547(b), for the trustee to be able to avoid a prior transfer as a preference, the transfer must satisfy all five of the following requirements:

1. **Transfer must benefit the creditor:** Under some circumstances, a transfer to a third party can benefit a creditor without there being an actual transfer to that creditor. This is illustrated in the following example.

   Example: G guarantees the debt of D to C. If D pays C, the payment, by letting G off the hook, was to the detriment of D's other creditors. See *Smith v. Tostevin*, 247 F. 102 (2nd Cir. 1917).

2. **Transfer must be for an antecedent debt:** The requirement that the transfer be on account of an antecedent debt, as opposed to a contemporaneous debt, is essential to support the concept of one existing creditor being preferred over another.

   Example 1: Debtor D buys five juice oranges and gives the seller one dollar. The transfer of the dollar is for present, not for antecedent, value. D has received something in exchange for the dollar in a contemporaneous exchange.

   Example 2: D borrows $10,000 from C, repayable in ten equal installments of $1,000 each. D pays each installment when due. Payment of the installments are for an antecedent debt despite the fact that they were not due until specified dates in the future. When

D borrowed $10,000 from C, the "debt" to C was established at that time, defined in § 101(12) as "liability on a claim." (Claim is defined in § 101(5).) The fact that installment payments were due in the future made the debt "unmatured," but did not change its quality as an existing debt. D's payments, when made, applied to that antecedent debt.

3. **Transfer must be made while the debtor is insolvent:** This requirement is to separate permissible from impermissible payments on antecedent debts. At the time a debtor is healthy and flourishing, the Code permits payments to creditors as the debtor chooses. It is only when there is financial difficulty that the selection of one creditor over another becomes an issue. "Insolvent" is defined in § 101(32) in terms of the balance sheet approach: an excess of liabilities over assets. *§ 547(f) creates a rebuttable presumption that the debtor is insolvent for 90 days before a petition is filed.* (As a general rule, transfers must occur during the 90-day period to be treated as a preference. See the fourth (**4.**) requirement in the next paragraph.) Thus, the trustee does not have to introduce proof of insolvency in order to sustain the third requirement for a voidable preference if the transfer was made within 90 days. The transferee of the assets who wants to retain them must prove the debtor's solvency at the time of the transfer.

4. **Transfer must be on or within 90 days before petition:** To be considered an avoidable preference, *a transfer must have occurred on or within 90 days before the date that the petition is filed.* If the creditor to whom the assets were transferred or who entered into an obligation with the debtor was an *"insider," the period is extended to a year*. (§ 101(31) defines the relationships that will cause an entity to be considered an insider. Generally, the definition includes relatives, partners and affiliates, and, in the case of corporations, officers, directors and stockholders.) Within these periods, the statute presumes that a transfer was made in contemplation of bankruptcy. In addition, the property transferred must, under the preamble to § 547(b), be property in which the debtor has an interest. An income execution on a debtor's income obtained before the 90-day period will be considered a valid transfer as of the time it is obtained. If payments are made by the debtor's employer to the creditor during the 90 day period because of the income execution, they are not preferential because, even though earned by the debtor, they are no longer property of the debtor.

Example: Creditor C wins a suit against Debtor D and collects an income execution against D and D's employer. This execution requires the employer to pay C ten percent of D's wages each pay period. The income execution is obtained before the 90-day period; payments under it are made during the 90-day period. It was held that none of the payments were preferential because D had no right to them. The transfer occurred at the time of the income execution, before the start of the 90 day period. *In re Riddervold*, 647 F.2d 342 (2nd Cir. 1981).

a. **Transfers to an insider and a non-insider:** Where a transfer benefits both an insider and one who is not, the question arises as to how the two different time periods should apply to the transaction. A typical example is an obligation to a creditor that is guaranteed by a stockholder. Payment to the creditor will, of course, benefit the creditor; it will also benefit the stockholder because his guaranty obligation is eliminated. Since the stockholder is an insider under § 101(31), the time period during which a preference may occur is one year before the bankruptcy rather than 90 days. The time period within which to avoid the preference is likewise one year. A dominant line of cases exemplified by the *Deprizio* case, whose formal title is *Levit v. Ingersoll Rand Financial Corp.*, 874 F.2d 1186 (7th Cir. 1989), held that the proper time period to examine back for preferences in this type of transaction is one year and also that any preference within that time period may be recovered from both the insider (the stockholder) and the non-insider (the creditor). Obviously, that imposed a considerable risk upon the ordinary creditor when it obtained a guaranty from an insider, and the doctrine was subject to considerable criticism. It was changed by amendment to § 550 in 1994. This now provides that, if the preference occurs during the time between the usual 90 days and one year, the trustee may recover from only the insider and not from the ordinary creditor.

5. **Transfer must allow creditor to receive more than it otherwise would:** A transfer is not an avoidable preference if it does not improve the position of the transferee creditor. ***The position of the creditor is improved if it receives more than it would have received if the transfer had not been made and the creditor had been paid through an ordinary Chapter 7 liquidation.*** A transfer that may appear preferential does not necessarily result in a creditor's receiving more than it otherwise would. The clearest example is where a creditor is fully secured before the 90 days starts to run. If the debtor makes a payment to the creditor within the 90 days, the fifth requirement for an avoidable preference is not satisfied because the creditor was fully secured and would have received full payment in any case.

Example 1: Creditor C, a lawyer, has a lawyer's lien on property of Debtor D, his client, that is established before the 90 day period. When D makes a recovery in the case for which C represented D, payment is made to C. It was held, against a dissent, that the preferential payment was not voidable because C was already fully secured. (The dissent was based on the fact that under the court's reading of § 547(e)(3), *supra*, p. 127, C's lawyer's-lien could not apply until D had rights in the recovery. This occurred during the 90 day period and, when related to the debt to C, was for an antecedent debt and, therefore, preferential. *In re Hagen*, 922 F.2d 742 (11th Cir. 1991).

Example 2: C holds security worth $50,000, but its claim against D is $75,000. Thus, C is undersecured.Within the 90 days, D pays C $10,000. C would have recovered the equivalent of two-thirds of the payment in a Chapter 7 liquidation. Thus, C's condition has been improved by one-third of the total amount of the payment. One-third of the amount of the payment is a voidable preference under § 547. *Barash v. Public Finance Corp.*, 658 F.2d 504 (7th Cir. 1981).

E. **Exceptions from the voidable preference rule — § 547(c):** Some transfers satisfy the five conditions, described above, but for policy reasons they are specifically made not avoidable (*supra*, p. 120). To prove these exceptions, § 547(g) prescribes that the trustee has the burden first of proving the existence of a preference under subsection (b); the creditor then has the burden of proving nonavoidability under subsection (c). The eight exceptions are as follows:

1. **Substantially contemporaneous exchanges for new value:** If, before bankruptcy, a debtor received new value (§ 547(a) defines "new value," in part, as "money or money's worth in goods, services or new credit.") in a contemporaneous exchange, he has exchanged his cash for new goods. Such exchanges are not for an antecedent debt (see *supra*, p. 129); the debtor has not preferred one creditor over another in this type of transaction. Many transfers are intended to be contemporaneous exchanges for new value but payment may lag the obligation to pay. This first exception from the voidable preference under § 547(c)(1), applies to a transfer that: (1) was *intended by the parties to be a contemporaneous exchange for new value* — a subjective test, and (2) *was in fact a substantially contemporaneous exchange* — an objective test.

    Example 1: A vendor hands the buyer five juice oranges, following which the buyer gives the vendor one dollar. This is considered a contemporaneous exchange; the one-dollar payment will not be deemed to be for an antecedent debt that was created when the oranges were transferred.

Example 2: Seller sells goods to a buyer who gives the seller a check. The check is not paid by buyer's bank for two days, when the buyer's funds are actually transferred to seller. The transfer will most likely be considered a contemporaneous exchange.

Obviously, where there is a dispute as to whether a transfer is "substantially contemporaneous", an evaluation of the facts by the court is required. Where the debtor transfers a security interest that is perfected after the transfer, the specific rules of § 547(e) are now generally held to determine the date of transfer (*supra*, p. 127), rather than § 547(c)(1).

2. **Ordinary and regular transactions:** Many payments ordinarily made on a regular basis meet the definition for preferential transfers. A debt to the telephone company accrues, for example, when a call is made; but it is paid after the bill is sent. In order not to upset ordinary payments of this type, the § 547(c)(2) *exception denies voidability to a transfer that was: (1) in payment of a debt incurred in the ordinary course of business or financial affairs between debtor and transferee, (2) made in the ordinary course of business or financial affairs between debtor and transferee, and (3) made according to ordinary business terms.* The terms are not defined and courts have interpreted them differently. The first two tests are often said to be "subjective" tests — whether the debt and its payment are normal business for the debtor and the transferee. Issues may also include whether late payments are or are not normal. Most courts will conclude their investigation if the first two tests are satisfied. Others will go on to the third, which is said to be an "objective" test — what is standard in the industry? *In re Fred Hawes Organization, Inc.*, 957 F.2d 239 (6th Cir. 1992). Consumer payments for rent, heat and light exemplify the sort of transaction covered. Note that the words "ordinary course of...financial affairs" are used to cover payments by a nonbusiness debtor. Payments may be deemed not in the ordinary course if they are made in the following ways: by cashier's check or money order rather than an ordinary check, in a pressured situation or in unusually large amounts compared to other payments, or in haste after a business downturn.

3. **Enabling loans:** The term "enabling loans", also known as a "purchase money loans," has come into general use to designate the third exception. The concept is that a creditor lends money to a borrower to enable the borrower to buy specific property. The technical-

ities of the subsection track closely the provisions of U.C.C. § 9-301(2), which give protection to a purchase money lender in the collateral it receives. ***The loan must be: (1) made at the time of or after a security agreement describing the property as collateral is signed; (2) made by the secured party to enable the debtor to acquire the collateral under that agreement; and (3) actually used to acquire the property.*** Equally important, ***the security interest in such loans ("purchase money security interest") must be perfected within 20 days after the buyer receives possession of the goods bought.*** As was discussed (*supra*, p. 127), § 547(e) defines perfection as occuring at the point that a security interest is valid against a judicial lien for personal property and against a good faith purchaser for real estate (much like the tests employed in § 544, *supra*, p. 119). The variations in the following fact patterns illustrate how the requirements of this third exception are or are not met:

Example 1: Bank Creditor C lends Debtor D $20,000 to buy a new car. At the time of the loan, D signs a security agreement giving C a security interest in the car effective at such time as D buys it. After a month of shopping, D uses the money to buy a car. Within five days after D buys the car, C perfects its interest on the certificate of title so that one who obtains a judicial lien on the car would not prevail over C. D's transfer of the security interest in the car to C is not preferential.

Example 2: C makes an unsecured loan to D of $20,000 to use as D sees fit. After a month, D uses the $20,000 to buy a car and, upon D's purchase, pressured by C, gives C a security interest in the car. Within five days, C perfects its interest upon the certificate of title so that it is good against a subsequent lien creditor. The transfer of the security interest in the car from D to C is preferential because the security agreement was not made prior to or at the time of the loan.

4. **The "net result" rule:** The fourth exception defining transfers which are not avoidable is a modification of the "net result" rule which was contained in the prior Bankruptcy Act. Under that rule, payments out and payments in were netted against each other for the 90-day preference period. If preferential transfers were made out of the estate but were compensated for to some extent by transfers back into the estate, the estate was a loser or winner by the amount of the difference. ***Under the fourth exception, an otherwise preferential transfer may be reduced only by amounts coming back to the estate after the transfer out; a complete offset is not permitted.*** Computations can be complex and the

courts are not in full agreement. For example, *In re Meredith Manor, Inc.* 902 F.2d 257 (4th Cir. 1990) states that transfers back to the estate can be netted only against transfers out that occurred previously, noting its disagreement with other courts that subtract transfers back only up to the next preferential transfer out.

5. **Floating liens on inventory and receivables**: The U.C.C. enables a secured creditor to establish a so-called floating lien on a debtor's inventory or accounts receivable and have that lien apply to every item of inventory and every individual account receivable as they flow in and out of the debtor's possession or ownership. Before the Bankruptcy Code, it had been difficult to relate these assets to the preference rules. For example, should every pair of shoes in a debtor's inventory be tested under the preference rules as it is transferred to the creditor for security purposes? Or should all the shoes be deemed one mass that was all transferred to the creditor at one time? This problem is resolved by the fifth exception in the following manner: Two dates are selected, the first 90 days before the petition is filed, the second the date of filing. (Note that the resulting 90-day period accords with the time period established for preferential transfers under § 547(b)(4), *supra*, p. 130.) As of both dates, the amount by which the debt exceeds the inventory (or receivables) collateral is computed. To the extent that the excess is reduced from the first date to the second, there is a voidable preference. (The creditor is deemed to have improved its position by that amount at the expense of the other creditors.) ***If the transactions are with an insider (see definition at § 101(31)*** *(supra*, p. 123)***, the 90 days is extended to a year.*** If transactions between debtor and creditor had not begun within 90 days before the petition was filed, the first date for the comparison is the date on which they did begin.

Example 1: Ninety days before the petition, Debtor D owes Creditor C $100,000 secured by inventory worth $80,000. At the date of the petition, D owes C $140,000 secured by inventory worth $130,000. The extent to which the debt exceeds the inventory collateral has been reduced from $20,000 to $10,000. Therefore, there is a voidable preference of $10,000 which can be recovered from C by the trustee of D's estate.

Example 2: The same facts in the example above, but at the date of the petition the inventory is worth $150,000 and the debtor is thus fully secured. Therefore, the extent to which the debt exceeds the inventory collateral has been reduced from $20,000 to $0. Therefore, the preference is $20,000. D also has a right to the surplus of collateral in the amount of $10,000.

Example 3: The same facts as to the debt as in the first example above, but at both dates the inventory collateral exceeds the debt. There is no preference. C was always fully covered at both relevant dates and was not preferred to other creditors during the 90 day time period. D has a right to the surplus as of the date of the petition.

6. **The fixing of a statutory lien under § 545:**   A statutory lien under § 545 will normally be for an antecedent debt, which is one of the requirements of an avoidable preference under § 547(b) (*supra*, p. 122). A debt will occur, it will be unpaid, and, if available in the jurisdiction, a statutory lien will follow. The sixth exception therefore provides that, *if a statutory lien is not avoidable under the tests of § 545, it is also not preferential*.

7. **Bona fide payment of debt to spouse or child:** Under the seventh exception, *a transfer that is a bona fide payment of a debt to a child, spouse, or former spouse for alimony, maintenance, or support is not avoidable.* The debt for the payment must have arisen from either a court order, a determination by a state agency, or a property settlement agreement. However, the debt is avoidable to the extent that it is assigned, voluntarily or otherwise, to another entity (*supra*, p. 91).

8. **Certain consumer transfers:**   For an individual debtor whose debts are primarily consumer debts, the eighth exception provides that *the aggregate value of a transfer totalling less than $600 is not avoidable.*

F. **Debtor's ability to avoid a preferential transfer:** The estate will not be increased if the assets are voided and returned as preferential transfers and are then claimed as exempt by the debtor under § 522 and removed from the estate, (*supra*, p. 47). It is for this reason that § 522(h) permits a debtor acting for himself to avoid a preferential transfer under § 547 (and under the other avoiding sections) if the transfer is avoidable by the trustee and the trustee chooses not to do so.

IV.   POWER TO AVOID FRAUDULENT TRANSFERS OR OBLIGATIONS — § 548

A. **Scope of power:** A trustee has the power to avoid fraudulent conveyances occurring within one year before bankruptcy under § 548, which bears many similarities to the Uniform Fraudulent Conveyance Act. The fraudulent act may consist of a transfer (note again the broad definition of transfer under § 101(54), which includes the creation of a security interest as well as an outright conveyance, *supra*, p. 117), or the incurring of an obligation. There are two alternative tests for fraud under this section. Transfers of interest may be avoided by the trustee under this section where the debtor made a transfer or incurred an obligation either: (1) with actual intent to hinder, delay, or defraud, or (2) that meets the criteria for constructive fraud. § 548 applies to voluntary and involuntary transactions. The transfer of an interest in property is voidable without reference to its value. Thus, if the property increases in value while in the hands of the transferee, the increase is to the benefit of the estate.

B. Charitable gift exception: Gifts made by natural persons to charities by cash, check, or equivalent instrument that do not exceed 15 percent of the debtor's gross annual income for the year in which the gift is made or, if more than that amount, are consistent with the practice of the debtor in making charitable contributions, will not be considered fraudulent transfers even if the other tests are satisfied.

C. Intent to hinder, delay, or defraud test of § 548(a)(1)(A): Voidability under § 548(a)(1) is premised on the debtor's intentional act to hinder, delay, or defraud some or all of the creditors. It is sufficient that the intent be merely to hinder or delay in order to constitute a fraudulent transfer. For example, shifting assets among affiliated corporations may leave those assets at the disposal of creditors only if they can find them. Intent, which is frequently difficult to prove, is sometimes proven through necessary inferences derived from other acts. Through the centuries, acts by debtors from which intent can be inferred have become known as "badges of fraud".

Example 1: Debtor D borrows money from his brother-in- law and gives him a real estate mortgage on D's property (this is the transfer claimed to be fraudulent). D uses the money to pay a bank on an antecedent debt so that he can avoid a criminal prosecution. The mortgage was held to be void because the debtor and the mortgagee were aware of the insolvency and the court inferred that they must have anticipated the impending bankruptcy. Knowledge by the brother-in-law prevented him from being a good faith purchaser for value. (See *infra*, p. 140.) *Dean v. Davis*, 242 U.S. 438 (1917).

Example 2: A new corporation is set up to take over D's assets and assume D's obligations. The objective is to save the assets from irresponsible acts of D's manager. However, by intentionally removing the assets from the reach of D's creditors, a fraudulent transfer was made. *Perkins v. Becker's Conservatories*, 61 N.E.2d 833 (Mass. 1945).

Example 3: D sets up two bank accounts, one in the name of D and the other in someone else's name. The creditors do not know of the second account, which is used exclusively for the benefit of D's business. Transfers into the second bank account were fraudulent. *Matter of Beechwood Medicenter of Flint, Inc.*, 23 B.R. 939 (Bkrtcy. E.D. Mich. 1982).

D. Constructive fraud test: In view of the difficulties inherent in proving that an act was intentional, a second test for a fraudulent transfer was added in § 548(a)(1)(B). Under this provision, it must be proven that: (1) the transfer was made in exchange for less than a reasonably equivalent value, **and** (2) one of the following three situations also applies: (a) the debtor was insolvent on the date that the transfer was made or became insolvent as a result of the transfer; or (b) the debtor was engaged, or was about to engage, in business or in a transaction for which it was left after the transfer with unreasonably small capital; or (c) the debtor intended to incur, or believed that it would incur, debts beyond the debtor's ability to pay as they matured.

1. **Rule for determining "reasonably equivalent value" of foreclosed real estate:** The Supreme Court resolved the issue of determining reasonably equivalent value with respect to mortgage foreclosures of real estate in *BFP v. Resolution Trust Corporation*, 114 S. Ct. 1757 (1994). The Court held that "so long as all the requirements of the State's foreclosure law have been complied with," the property will be deemed to have been sold for "a fair and proper price, or a 'reasonably equivalent value.'" The Court emphasized: (1) the conclusive presumption of the fair and proper price can be rebutted if the State's prescribed procedures are not followed; (2) no intent to hinder, delay or defraud creditors need be shown if an improper price is ultimately proven, since the proceeding comes under § 548(a)(2) rather than (a)(1); and (3) the decision is applicable only to mortgage foreclosures of real estate; on all other transfers, including foreclosures on security interests in personal property, the issue of value must still be tested in the courts.

2. **Application of constructive fraud provision to leveraged buyouts:** An examination of how the constructive fraud provision applies to leveraged buyouts illustrates the potentially broad reach of § 548(a)(2).

   a. **Typical LBO situation:** A leveraged buyout typically involves both transfers made and obligations incurred by a debtor that can be attacked later as fraudulent transfers under § 548. Assume that Takeover Specialists A and B want to acquire Debtor Corporation D but have little cash. D may be able to get cash from a bank by giving the bank a lien on D's assets. If D does borrow, there is a transfer (the lien in the bank's favor) and an obligation (the debt to the bank). D may also be able to borrow without security (the incurring of an obligation). Once D has the cash, it can buy out its stockholders by making them an offer they can't refuse. Along the way, A and B have, through corporate manipulation, acquired a stock interest in D, which D does not buy out, and they ultimately find themselves in control of D. D has a new and possibly heavy debt load to the bank or to its other lenders, or a combination of both, and perhaps also a lien on its assets. If D finds that it can't pay the debt, it may find itself in bankruptcy.

b. **Potential application of § 548:** The trustee will look at the various transfers and obligations to see whether they can be upset under § 548 as fraudulent transfers. For this purpose, we look back to § 548(a) in order to see whether the elements of a fraudulent transfer are present. It is difficult to apply the subsection (a) standards to the transaction. It would seem that the requirement under § 548(a)(1) (see *supra* p. 137) that there be intent to "hinder, delay, or defraud creditors", is not met. The intent of the leveraged buyout was to enable A and B to take over D with a minimal investment. As to the constructive fraud standard of § 547(a)(2) (*supra*, p. 138), it has often been asserted that in this situation D incurred obligations and pledged its assets and received nothing of tangible value in return. *Moody v. Security Pacific Business Credit, Inc.*, 127 B.R. 958 (W.D. Pa.), aff'd, 971 F.2d 1056 (3rd Cir. 1992). On the other hand, in measuring whether the transfer was for "reasonably equivalent value," it may be shown that A and B are particularly astute managers who bring expertise previously lacking to D. Their association with D may have stimulated new bank connections of potential future value. The issues are at least debatable. Furthermore, was D necessarily rendered insolvent? Was it left with an unreasonably small capital? Will it be unable to pay its debts as they mature? The difficulty in proving these points, a combination of which is essential to a fraudulent transfer, has left the leveraged buyout essentially untouched by the courts under § 548. *Mellon Bank, N.A. v. Metro Communications, Inc.*, 945 F.2d 635 (3rd Cir.), cert.den., 112 S.Ct. 1476 (1992).

E. **Applicable to transfers made within one year — § 548(d):** *By its terms, the application of § 548 is limited to transfers made within one year of the filing of the bankruptcy petition.* For purposes of establishing when a transfer was made, § 548(d) dictates that the transfer will be deemed to occur when it is perfected, so that the interest of the transferee will stand up against a good faith purchaser. Note that the "good faith purchaser" test is harder for a transferee to satisfy than the lien creditor test (see discussion under § 544, *supra*, p. 118). If the interest is not perfected at all before the bankruptcy, the transfer is deemed to occur immediately before the date of the filing of the petition, clearly within the one-year period.

F. Rights of one to whom property is fraudulently transferred — § 548(c): *Assuming that the transferee took in good faith, it may keep what was transferred to the extent that it gave value.* If the transferred assets cannot be divided, they must be returned, but the transferee has a lien on them to the extent of the value given. Knowledge by the transferee that the transfer was fraudulent or circumstances placing a duty of further inquiry upon the transferee, will negate good faith.

Example: Debtor D borrows money from a bank and gives the bank a lien on D's assets (the transfer claimed to be fraudulent). The bank is aware that D is insolvent when it makes the loan. The bank did not receive the lien in good faith. *In re Heath Gourmet, Inc.*, 29 B.R. 673 (Brktcy. D. Mass. 1983).

G. Transfers occur upon creation of lien and *again* upon enforcement of lien: In *Durrett v. Washington Nat'l, Ins. Co.*, 621 F.2d 201 (5th Cir. 1980), the Court of Appeals held that, even though a transfer had certainly been made when the lien was originally created, a second transfer occurred upon foreclosure because the debtor's equity of redemption (including its rights to pay off the loan and get the property back, and to receive a surplus if the property were sold for more than the debt) was transferred. In 1984, the definition of transfer in § 101(54) was amended to add the words "foreclosure of the debtor's equity of redemption". § 548(a) was also amended to provide that a voluntary or involuntary transfer could be a fraudulent transfer. Congress thus seems to have confirmed that *Durrett* represents correct law and the Supreme Court confirmed the *Durrett* position in *BFP v. Resolution Trust Corporation* (*supra*, p. 138), without discussion.

H. Comparison of § 548 with other Code provisions affecting fraudulent conveyances: If a state fraudulent conveyance law has been violated, a remedy may exist under provisions of the Code other than § 548. If state law says that a transfer may be avoided by a judgment lien creditor, or, in the case of real estate, by a good faith purchaser, the strong arm clause under § 544(a) may be used (*supra*, p. 119). If the fraudulent transfer was preferential in nature, § 547 may be utilized (*supra*, p. 126). Most commonly, where an actual creditor exists to whom state law gives the right to void the transfer, 544(b) will be used. In some cases, all the above grounds may be asserted. On the other hand, § 548 operates exclusively under its own provisions, although some of the concepts employed are similar to those under state law.

V.   POWER TO AVOID SETOFFS — § 553

A. **Setoffs generally valid:** Setoffs are generally valid in bankruptcy; but they are invalid in specific situations that would give one creditor an unfair advantage over other creditors. Section 553 determines whether setoffs for mutual debts occurring before bankruptcy will be allowed or can be avoided. Under § 362(a)(7), the automatic stay prevents actual setoffs after the petition is filed (*supra*, p. 40). Although setoffs are generally valid in bankruptcy, the automatic stay must be lifted under § 362(d) before a setoff can be asserted. Until the stay is lifted, adequate protection must be supplied under § 361 (*supra*, p. 43). However, financial institutions are able to place an administrative hold on the portion of depository accounts represented by the amount of a defaulted loan, thus temporarily preventing a debtor or the debtor's estate access to those funds (*infra*, p. 178). *Citizens Bank of Maryland v. Strumpf*, No. 94-1340, 1995 U.S. LEXIS 7408 (1995).

Example: If Debtor D owes Creditor C $5,000 and C owes D $4,000, C may apply D's debt against its own, pay nothing to the estate, and put in a claim for $1,000. However, the setoff will not be effective until the automatic stay is lifted in behalf of C.

B. **Setoff must be on directly mutual obligations:**   The obligations of affiliated entities, such as a parent and a subsidiary, cannot be combined in a setoff with a debtor or creditor. Likewise, a consolidated tax return will not unify the entities for setoff purposes. Also, if one is acting in a dual capacity (for example, both individually and as a fiduciary), debts incurred in one capacity cannot be combined with the other for setoff purposes. Courts apply this doctrine strictly except in very few situations. For example, a landlord holding a security deposit in trust is often allowed to set off the amount in trust against rent owed by the tenant. *In re Alchar Hardware Co.*, 759 F.2d 867 (11th Cir. 1985).

C. **Presumption of insolvency — § 553(c):** For purposes of § 553, there is a presumption that the debtor was insolvent during the 90-day period before the petition is filed (the same period provided for in § 547(f) for avoidable preferences, *supra* p. 130). Note that the presumption of insolvency is rebuttable and shifts the burden to an opposing party to prove solvency.

D. **Avoidable setoffs:**   The trustee may avoid a setoff by a creditor in the following situations:

1. **Disallowed claims — § 553(a)(1):**   Disallowed claims cannot be set off.

2. **Claims transferred within 90 days — § 553(a)(2):** The   trustee may avoid a debt if it was transferred by a prior claimant to the

creditor either (1) after the case has begun or (2) after 90 days before the petition was filed and while the debtor was insolvent. This rule is to prevent an unfair collusion that would give some creditors an advantage over other creditors.

Example: Debtor D owes Creditor C $5,000 and Entity E owes D $4,000. Upon D's bankruptcy, C will be able to get only a pittance from D and E will have to pay the full $4,000 to the estate. If C sells its claim to E for $1,500, C may be much better off than it would otherwise be. In addition, E can set the full $5,000 debt owed by D off against its $4,000 obligation to D and, therefore, pay D nothing. The trustee can avoid the setoff that E would otherwise assert.

3. **Debt incurred to obtain setoff — § 553(a)(3):** The debtor may avoid a debt if it was incurred by the creditor within 90 days of the petition while the debtor was insolvent and for the purpose of getting a right of setoff. This is to prevent a favored creditor from acquiring an illusory "debt" that would be set off against D's preexisting debt to C.

Example: D, who is insolvent 85 days prior to filing, owes C $1,000. D is planning a Chapter 7 case and is friendly with C. D says to C: I have $1,000; why don't you just borrow it; and you won't have to pay it back because you can offset your new debt against the debt I owe you. The loan to C may be voided.

4. **Insufficiencies — § 553(b):** An "insufficiency" is the amount by which a claim by a creditor against the debtor exceeds a claim by the debtor against the same creditor. If D diminishes the insufficiency by making a payment to the creditor, the creditor has benefitted at the expense of D's other creditors. If a creditor offsets an obligation within 90 days before the petition, then the trustee may recover from the creditor the amount offset to the extent that any insufficiency is less than the insufficiency that existed either 90 days before the petition, or the first time that an insufficiency existed within the 90 days before the petition, whichever is later. This is best illustrated by the following example.

Example: 90 days before the petition, D owes C $150 and C owes D $100. 20 days before the petition, D pays C $25 and then owes C only $125. At that time, C sets off the $100 it owes D against the $125 C now owes D. D has really not improved its position between the two dates, but the insufficiency has diminished and the estate has been deprived of $25. The trustee may recover $25 from C.

VI. LIMITATIONS ON AVOIDING POWERS — § 546

A. Statute of limitations: Under § 546(a), actions under the avoiding powers must be brought before a case is dismissed or closed and not later than: (1) two years after the order for relief, or (2) one year after the appointment or election of the first trustee if such appointment or election is made within two years of the commencement of the case.

B. Relation back of perfection affecting rights of trustee: The rights of a trustee under § 544 (avoidance powers derived from state law), § 545 (avoidance of statutory liens), and § 549 (avoidance of unauthorized postpetition transfers), all of which generally accrue at the time of the bankruptcy, may be cut off by a "generally applicable law" that causes an act of perfection to relate back to an earlier point in time. Under such a law, perfection occurring after bankruptcy can relate back to a time before the bankruptcy and thereby destroy an avoidance right of the trustee. § 362(b)(3) provides an exception to the automatic stay for this form of perfection. The most obvious example of this device is that of a purchase money security interest under U.C.C. § 9-301(2), which can relate back for 20 days after the debtor has acquired the goods and oust another creditor who acquired his rights during that time. (Note that, in determining whether an avoidable preference exists, there is a 10-day relation back for perfecting transfers generally and a 20-day relation back for purchase money security interests; § 547(e)(2), *supra*, p. 133.) Also, some state laws dealing with real estate mortgages permit relation-back perfections when dealing with the assignment to the lienholder of rents produced by the mortgaged land. *Matter of C.G. Chartier Const. Inc.*, 126 B.R. 956 (E.D.La. 1991).

C. Seller's reclamation rights: U.C.C. § 2-702 grants those who sell goods to an insolvent buyer the right to reclaim the goods. The prior Bankruptcy Act created questions about whether the trustee could upset the seller's right as voidable under the strong arm clause of § 544, (*supra*, p. 118), as a preference under § 547, (*supra*, p. 117), or otherwise as an ineffective claim. § 546(c) attempts to settle the dispute and put the Bankruptcy Code into harmony with the U.C.C. (One of the reasons for the 1978 Bankruptcy Code was to establish harmony between the U.C.C. and the Code (*supra*, p. 4.) Under § 546(c), the reclaiming seller who satisfies the tests (a sale in the ordinary course of business, written demand within 10 days after the debtor receives possession or, if the 10-day period expires after the case is filed, within 20 days after the debtor receives possession) is given a position superior to the trustee. The prescriptions of § 546(c) are similar to, but not identical with, those of the U.C.C. The court has the right under § 546(c) to deny reclamation to the seller (if, for example, the goods sold would be significant to a debtor's reorganization), but only if it gives the seller an administrative priority under § 503(b) and a lien on the goods.

VII. ENFORCEMENT OF AVOIDING POWERS — § 550

A. **Enforcement powers overlap:** The avoiding powers in § 544, § 545, § 547, § 548 and § 553 contain authority for the trustee to avoid certain transfers, all of which could be construed as self-executing. However, for various reasons (including the enumeration of rights of subsequent transferees), there are provisions in § 550 for the enforcement of avoidances.

B. **Initial and subsequent transferees — § 550(a):** The trustee has the right under § 550(a) to recover property from the initial transferee (or the entity for whose benefit the transfer was made) and from subsequent transferees of the initial transferee. Note that the particular voiding sections themselves provide certain protective rights to the initial transferees, including the ability to assert causes of action in the bankruptcy, *infra*, and the rights of a good faith transferee of a fraudulent transfer in § 548 (*supra*, p. 140).

C. **Limits on recovery from good faith subsequent transferees — § 550(b):** While the trustee may recover from the initial transferee under § 550(a), the trustee may not recover property from a subsequent transferee that takes for value and without knowledge of the voidable transfer. This second transferee is generally known as a "good faith purchaser." The trustee is also prevented under § 550(b) from recovering from subsequent transferees of the good faith purchaser who take simply in good faith (irrespective of whether they also took for value). Thus, if a subsequent transferee acquires property for value and without knowledge, it acquires the ability to transfer good title to any subsequent transferee who takes in good faith. Good faith is not defined, but is generally taken to mean "whether the grantee knew or should have known that he was not trading normally." *In re Coleman*, 21 B.R. 832 (Bkrtcy. S.D. Texas 1982). Of course, as the *Coleman* case indicates, although value is not part of the test, the adequacy of the price paid is regularly considered as a factor in determining good faith.

D. **Rights of transferee to recover for improvement costs — § 550(e):** If a transferee, immediate or subsequent, has improved the property taken from him, he has a lien on it for the lesser of the costs incurred to make the improvement or the increase in value of the property as a result of the improvement. Improvements include not only physical changes but the payment of taxes and the satisfaction of superior liens.

E. **Statute of limitations — § 550(f):** A separate statute of limitations in § 550 provides that a § 550 enforcement action must be commenced within one year after the avoidance, or before the case is closed or dismissed, whichever occurs first. This period, when added to the three years to effect an avoidance under § 546(a) (*supra*, p. 143), could allow the trustee (unless the case were closed) up to four years to avoid a transfer and recover property.

VIII. VOIDED TRANSFERS BENEFIT THE ESTATE — § 551

A. **Voided transfers benefit estate:** When a trustee avoids a lien under one of the avoiding statutes, § 551 provides that the transfer "is preserved for the benefit of the estate." This provision prevents any benefit from accruing to other lienholders who might otherwise advance in their status as lienholders. The meaning of this provision is best illustrated by the following:

Example: Debtor D gives Creditor 1 a lien on D's property and subsequently gives Creditor 2 a second lien on the same property. After D's bankruptcy, the trustee finds that C1's lien is voidable and voids the transfer to C1 under § 550. C2 does not, as it would under the operation of the typical state lien statute, advance to a number one position. Rather, the "transfer is preserved for the benefit of the estate" and the estate acquires C1's position. In the foregoing example, if C1's lien is for $5,000, then the estate would obtain an interest of $5,000 ahead of C2, just as C1 had been ahead of C2. *In re Barry*, 31 B.R. 683 (Bkrtcy. S.D.Ohio 1983).

CHAPTER 9

FILING UNDER CHAPTER 7 — LIQUIDATION

Introductory note: Chapter 7 of the Bankruptcy Code provides for the *total liquidation of a debtor's estate* and *distribution of the proceeds to creditor*s. In the case of an individual, the debtor achieves a "fresh start." If the case involves a business entity, such as a partnership or corporation, the entity generally dissolves under the law of the state under which it was organized. Chapter 7 is by far the most widely used of the five chapters in the Code providing for bankruptcy filings. The materials covered thus far, from Chapters 1, 3 and 5 of the Code, generally apply to all bankruptcy cases. Thus, provisions dealing with — *the debtor*, (such as the automatic stay and the ability to exempt assets from the estate), *the creditor* (such as the filing of claims), *the trustee* (such as the trustee's ability to sue and be sued), and *the estate* (such as the definition of estate property) — all apply to Chapter 7. What follows here are those Code provisions that (except where specifically noted otherwise) deal only with the relief available in Chapter 7 cases.

I. WHO MAY BE A DEBTOR IN CHAPTER 7 — § 109(b)

A. **Debtor must be a "person":** Subject to certain limited exceptions, any "person" may be a debtor in Chapter 7. "Person" is, in turn, defined by § 101(41) to include individuals, partnerships, and corporations. "Person" specifically excludes governmental units (except under very limited circumstances), which must file under Chapter 9, *infra*, p. 168.

   1. **Stockbrokers and commodity brokers included:** Chapter 7 contains provisions specifically applicable to stockbrokers and commodity brokers, who are prohibited from filing under Chapter 11.

B. **Entities excluded:** The following entities are *excluded from Chapter 7 relief*:

   1. **Railroads:** Railroads must file under special provisions contained in Chapter 11 of the Code.

   2. **Domestic insurance companies and banks:** Insurance companies are primarily state regulated and have their own forms of relief under state law. Domestic banks and related insured institutions have their own forms of relief under both federal (particularly as administered by the Federal Deposit Insurance Corporation and the Credit Union Share Insurance Fund) and state banking laws. Entities falling under this category, and therefore also excluded from

utilizing Chapter 7, include savings and loan and building and loan associations, and small business investment companies.

3. **Foreign insurance companies and banks:**   Essentially, these entities are excluded from filing under Chapter 7 if they are regularly engaged in business in the United States to the extent that they become subject to federal or state regulation. Mere ownership of some domestic assets will not subject them to regulation by United States authorities or to the special liquidation procedures established for regulated institutions. They may therefore avail themselves of Chapter 7 so long as they limit the filing to those domestic assets.

Example: A foreign bank borrows from American banks and maintains bank accounts in the United States. The foreign bank is not excluded from Chapter 7 with respect to these activities or those assets. The accounts provide a sufficient jurisdictional basis for Code relief; the bank's presence and activities are not of the type that would subject the bank to domestic regulatory supervision sufficient to exclude it from Chapter 7. *Israel-British Bank (London) Ltd. v. Fed. Dep. Ins. Corp.*, 536 F.2d 509 (2d Cir. 1976).

II. CONVERSION FROM CHAPTER 7 TO ANOTHER CHAPTER — § 706

A. **Debtor conversion:**   The debtor has the ability at any time to convert from a Chapter 7 case to a case under Chapter 11, 12 or 13, provided that the debtor is eligible for the relief under the other chapter and that the case was not previously transferred to Chapter 7 from one of those chapters.

B. **Interested party conversion:**   A party in interest other than the debtor may transfer a Chapter 7 case to Chapter 11 but not to the other Chapters. Court approval is required if the debtor is not the moving party. § 706(b).

Note: The right to transfer from Chapter 7 to Chapter 11 is broader than the right to move from 11 to 7. (See § 1112, *infra*, p. 183.) Congress has often said that it prefers the reorganization relief of Chapter 11 to the liquidation relief of Chapter 7.

III. DISMISSAL BY THE COURT — § 707

A. **Dismissal generally:** Chapter 7 cases may be dismissed *for cause*. Included as justifications for dismissal are unreasonable delay, nonpayment of required fees, and failure of the debtor to honor its responsibilities to give information as required by the Code. The statute requires "notice and a hearing" before a dismissal and, although the general rules of construction (applicable to all cases) state that a hearing is not required under certain circumstances, (*supra*, p. 19), Rule 1017(a) does stipulate a hearing for most Chapter 7 dismissals.

Example: Debtor D in a Chapter 7 case does business on land that is highly contaminated. D's assets cannot be liquidated because of the condition of the land. The expenses of cleanup probably exceed D's assets and there would be little if anything left for creditors. The environmental-protection authorities are pressing D for action and the Chapter 7 trustee has little experience with environmental issues and should not be burdened with dealing with state and federal authorities who had already started remedial actions in other courts. "Cause" existed for a § 707(a) dismissal. *In re Commercial Air Service*, 58 B.R. 311, *aff'd*. 88 B.R. 126 (Bankr. N.D. Ohio 1987).

B. **Dismissal of consumer cases — § 707(b):** Congress added a provision to Chapter 7 in 1984 in response to the increase in consumer bankruptcies that occurred after passage of the Bankruptcy Reform Act of 1978. The provision states that there is a ***presumption of non-abuse*** by the debtor, but gives the bankruptcy court the ability to dismiss a Chapter 7 case filed by an individual whose debts are ***"primarily" consumer debts if the court finds that the granting of relief would be a substantial abuse of the provisions of Chapter 7.***

1. **Who may move for dismissal:** The court may dismiss a consumer debt case on its own motion or on a motion by the U. S. trustee, ***but not at the request or suggestion of any party in interest***. There must be notice and a hearing prior to dismissal. The prohibition against parties in interest is for the purpose of preventing harassment of debtors by creditors. This does not prevent a creditor from submitting information to the U.S. trustee, who can make an independent judgment about the appropriateness of filing a motion to dismiss. *In re Clark*, 927 F.2d 793 (4th Cir. 1991).

2. **"Primarily" consumer debts:** Consumer debts are defined as debts incurred by an individual ***primarily for personal, family, or household purposes***. Congress deliberately did not define the types of cases that would be considered "primarily" consumer debt cases, preferring to leave this to judicial interpretation. In applying the standard, the courts have looked at such factors as the extent to which the debts are business related, the reasons for the bankruptcy, the debtor's attitude towards the process, and the debtor's underlying honesty and ability to pay. In one interpretation of the term, having 46% of a debtor's total debts in consumer debts was

considered to constitute "primarily for consumer debts." *In re Bryant*, 11 C.B.C.2d 987 (Bkrtcy. W.D. N.C. 1984). However, in another case, having 53% in consumer debts was considered insufficient to be characterized as primarily for consumer debt. *In re Restea*, 17 C.B.C.2d 132 (Bkrtcy. D.S.D. 1987).

3. **"Substantial abuse":** Chapter 7 can be abused by a consumer in many ways. There may be fraudulent statements in the papers submitted to the court; the debts may have been incurred through living beyond one's means; the case may have stemmed from anger with one's creditors. Courts may also consider the debtor's future income and ability to file under other Chapters, particularly Chapter 13 (reorganizations by individuals with regular income, *infra*, p. 214). Generally, a court will look at what is called the "totality of the circumstances" to measure whether Chapter 7 is being abused. *In re Green*, 934 F.2d 568 (4th Cir. 1991).

   a. **Future income factor:** The most controversial measure of possible abuse is the extent to which the debtor's future income would be sufficient to pay all or a large portion of his debts. ***The prevailing view is that the debtor's ability to pay debts in the future is the best single measure whether Chapter 7 is being appropriately used***. A minority of courts say that the debtor's future income is not relevant to the issue of abuse, because Chapter 7 is designed to give a fresh start, and income after the fresh start should not be considered as available to creditors.

      Example: A consumer's monthly income greatly exceeds his monthly expenses and the surplus would repay all of his outstanding unsecured debt in five years. These facts *rebutted the statutory presumption* in favor of granting the Chapter 7 relief requested by the debtor. *In re Walton*, 866 F.2d 981 (8th Cir. 1989).

   b. **Availability of other Chapters:** The Court may consider whether a debtor would be able to file under the bankruptcy reorganization chapters if there were a dismissal of the Chapter 7 filing. For example, if a debtor cannot qualify for a filing under Chapter 13 because his debts exceed the prescribed limits of the Chapter, some courts will refrain from a finding of substantial abuse. Some courts will also look to the possibility of a Chapter 11 case where Chapter 13 is unavailable. However, other courts do not consider this issue at all, since there is no guaranty that a debtor foreclosed from Chapter 7 will necessarily elect either Chapter 11 or Chapter 13. *In re Wegner*, 19 C.B.C.2d 997 (Bkrtcy. D. Minn. 1988).

C. **Effect of dismissal — § 707:** The dismissal of a Chapter 7 case is *without prejudice*. Therefore, unless the court mandates otherwise, a dismissal does not prevent a debtor from refiling in bankruptcy and discharging its debts in a subsequent case. There are a few exceptions to this rule.

1. **Exceptions:** There is a 180-day prohibition on refilings by individuals and family farmers in certain circumstances (*supra*, p. 32). Furthermore, if a discharge is obtained in a case before dismissal, a most unusual event, there are limitations on a subsequent discharge.

2. **Effect on trustee actions:** Upon dismissal, the following occur under § 349 in all bankruptcy cases, including Chapter 7: transfers avoided by the trustee return to their pre-petition conditions; liens voided under § 506(c) return into being; and the estate again becomes the property of the debtor.

D. **Comparison between § 707 and § 305:** As already noted, § 707 overlaps with § 305 (a general provision authorizing dismissal, which is applicable to all bankruptcy cases; *supra*, p. 29). § 305 is generally used more at the start of a case; § 707 is generally used at a more mature stage. Under § 305(a), a court may dismiss a bankruptcy case *if dismissal is in the interests of both the creditors and the debtor.* As we have just seen, under § 707, which only applies to Chapter 7 cases, there are two grounds for dismissal. The court may dismiss: (1) *for cause*, and (2) *for substantial abuse in consumer cases*.

Example: Debtor D has income well in excess of his expenses and Creditor C moved for dismissal under both § 305 and § 707. § 305 did not apply because it requires a finding that dismissal will benefit both creditors and debtors, and there was no finding that dismissal would benefit D. § 707(a) was inapplicable because of the Congressional history indicating that an excess of income over expenses was not sufficient to warrant dismissal. § 707(b) was also inapplicable because D's debts were not primarily consumer in nature. § 105 (a general provision, *supra*, p. 20, empowering the court to issue any order, process, or judgment necessary or appropriate to carry out the provisions of the Code) was unsuccessfully asserted as a basis for dismissal, because the legislative history was interpreted as restricting its potentially limitless application. *In re Goulding*, 79 B.R. 874 (Bkrtcy. W.D. Mo. 1987).

IV. SELECTION OF THE TRUSTEE

A. **Interim trustee — § 701:** Promptly after the order for relief, the United States Trustee appoints a disinterested person to serve as the ***interim trustee*** in the Chapter 7 case.

1. **Involuntary cases:** Because an involuntary case is commenced before the order for relief, a creditor may request under § 303(g) that an interim trustee be appointed to preserve the property of the estate during the period between the filing of the involuntary petition and the order for relief. There must be notice to the debtor and a hearing prior to the court's order to the United States trustee to appoint the interim trustee.

2. **United States Trustee's panel:** Normally, the interim trustee will be selected from a panel of private trustees that the United States Trustee maintains (*supra*, p.00).

3. **Eligibility:** The interim trustee may become the permanent trustee. The United States Trustee may serve as interim trustee if none of the members of the panel is willing to serve.

4. **Powers:** The interim trustee has all the powers of a permanent trustee and serves unless and until the permanent trustee is chosen under § 702.

B. **The permanent trustee — § 702:** Unsecured creditors may elect a permanent trustee if, at the § 341 meeting (first meeting of creditors and equity security holders; see *supra*, p. 36), ***eligible creditors holding at least 20 percent of the amount of the claims request an election.*** A candidate is elected trustee if ***eligible creditors holding at least 20 percent of the amount of the claims actually vote and the candidate receives a majority of those votes.*** If no permanent trustee is elected, the interim trustee becomes the permanent trustee.

1. **Eligible creditors:** The ***eligible creditors are those that hold allowable*** (as defined under § 502, *supra*, p. 75), ***undisputed, fixed, liquidated and unsecured claims;*** as such, they are entitled to participate in the distribution of the bankruptcy estate. Note that eligible creditors under § 702 are those having claims that are more established than the broad definition of claims in § 101 (*supra*, p. 17.)

    a. **No adverse interest:** To be eligible to vote, creditors cannot have interests materially adverse to that of the debtor and cannot be insiders (see definition of "insider" under § 101(31) (*supra*, p. 123).)

2. Secured creditors not eligible: Secured creditors cannot vote for trustee; typically, they will be looking only or principally to their security for satisfaction of their claims against the debtor. They are less likely to be involved in the elaborate disputes that usually concern unsecured creditors, who battle over such issues as the size of the estate that will be divided among them and their relative priorities.

C. Loyalty of trustee: Although elected by the unsecured creditors, the loyalty of the trustee is to the entire estate, not to those making the election. Among other duties, the trustee is required, for the protection of the estate, to contest claims that should be disallowed.

V. DUTIES OF TRUSTEE

Note: Most of the duties of a Chapter 7 trustee are summarized in § 704. As will be seen in greater detail, *infra*, some of the duties enumerated in § 704 are made applicable to trustees in cases brought under other Chapters — Chapter 11 (§ 1106) *infra*, p. 180; Chapter 12 (§ 1202) *infra*, p. 222; and Chapter 13 (§ 1302) *infra*, p. 232.

A. Duty to liquidate and close estate: The trustee's primary duty under Chapter 7 is summarized in § 704: to *"collect and reduce to money the property of the estate. . . and close such estate as expeditiously as is compatible with the best interests of parties in interest."* This duty to liquidate is considered to be the most significant contained in § 704.

1. Powers to perform duties: The Code gives the trustee considerable discretion in carrying out his responsibilities. To enable him to liquidate the estate, Chapter 5 of the Code gives the trustee various powers to accept or reject contracts and to avoid various pre-petition transfers. (See discussion of trustee's powers, *supra*, pp. 106-145.)

2. Significance of duty to liquidate: In some situations, the duty to liquidate and close the estate has been considered superior to other duties.

Example: In a Chapter 7 case, one claim of little significance is contested by the trustee. Since the estate is solvent, the claim is not contested by any of the creditors, who will be paid in full. Nevertheless, the trustee contests the claim for 18 months under his authority in § 704(5) to examine proofs of claims. It was held that an examination of a less than vital proof of claim should not hold up closing the estate. *In re Riverside-Linden Inv. Co.*, 85 B.R. 107, (Bkrtcy. S.D. Ca.), aff'd, 99 B.R. 439 (9th Cir. B.A.P.), aff'd 925 F.2d 320 (9th Cir. 1991).

3. **Must act "expeditiously":** The trustee is required to act with diligence but not precipitantly in order to get the best price for liquidated assets. A reasonable time may pass while the trustee carries out this duty. This latitude is consistent with § 721, which allows the court to authorize the trustee to operate the business of the debtor for a limited period of time if it is in the best interest of the estate and consistent with the orderly liquidation of the estate. In this regard, liquidation under Chapter 7 is similar to "liquidating plans" under Chapter 11, which are discussed *infra*, p. 202.

4. **Sales not in the ordinary course:** If the trustee wishes to make sales of assets of an estate other than in the ordinary course of business, the approval of the court is required under § 363 (*supra*, p. 103).

B. **Trustee's other duties:** In addition to the duty to liquidate and close the estate, there are several other duties of the trustee enumerated in § 704.

1. **Property received:** The trustee is accountable for all property received.

2. **Debtor's intentions:** In the case of an individual with some consumer debts, the trustee must ensure that the debtor performs his intention with respect to the retention or surrender of consumer property (see discussion of § 521(2)(B) *supra*, p. 34).

3. **Debtor's financial affairs:** The trustee must investigate the debtor's financial affairs. This duty can be particularly significant because it can serve as a review of the estate and its assets (§ 541, *supra*, p. 97). It can also help account for missing assets under § 727(a)(5), *infra*, p. 162. In consumer cases, it can help in determining whether the debtor is abusing Chapter 7 (*supra*, p. 90, pp. 149-142).

4. **Claims:** If a good purpose would be served, the trustee must examine proofs of claims and object to allowances that are improper (see § 502, *supra*, p. 75).

5. **Discharge:** If advisable, the trustee must object to the debtor's discharge (see § 727(a), *infra*, p. 160).

6. **Information:** Unless the court orders otherwise, the trustee must furnish information requested by parties in interest.

7. **Taxes and reports:** If the business of the debtor continues in operation, the trustee must deal with taxes and file reports concerning the debtor's business.

8. **Final report and accounting:** The trustee must make a final report and accounting of the administration of the estate.

C. **Duty to examine debtor — § 341:** Prior to the conclusion of the § 341 meeting of creditors or equity security holders, the trustee is required to examine the Chapter 7 debtor orally to ensure that the debtor is aware of: the potential consequences of seeking a discharge in bankruptcy, including the effects on credit history; the effect of receiving a discharge of debts; the ability to file a petition under a different Chapter; and the effect of reaffirming a debt.

VI. REDEMPTION OF ASSETS BY DEBTOR — § 722

A. **Nature of redemption:** "Redemption" is the right of an individual debtor to procure the *release from lien and return of property that is intended primarily for personal, family, or household use*. Such assets — for example, household furniture or the family car — may be worth a good deal more to the debtor than to the creditors in a foreclosure sale. The property must be *either exempt or abandoned by the trustee*. In order to effect the redemption, the debtor must file a statement of intention under § 521(2) stating whether or not the property will be redeemed. The debtor then has 45 days in which to make the redemption.

1. **Property belongs to the estate:** Because the right to redeem collateral from a secured obligation is considered to be an equitable right of the debtor, it causes the property that is subject to the right of redemption to become part of the bankruptcy estate. (See *supra*, p. 97, for definition of property of the estate.)

2. **Personal or household use:** Property subject to redemption must be "tangible personal property intended primarily for personal, family, or household use."

3. **Property must be secured:** Property subject to redemption must be subject to a lien.

4. **Property must be exempt or abandoned:** Property subject to redemption must be either exempt (§ 522 *supra*, p. 46), or abandoned by the trustee as either burdensome or of inconsequential value to the estate (§ 554 *supra*, p. 101).

B. **Making a redemption:** Property is redeemed by the debtor's payment to the creditor of "the amount of the allowed secured claim." In other words, certain consumer property is returned to the debtor if the debtor pays the creditor what the creditor expected to get for it. Essentially, assuming that the asset has been accurately valued, the debtor is given a right of first refusal to buy the exempt assets. Presumably, the debtor could also buy the assets at the foreclosure sale, but he might not know about the sale, might find it difficult to attend, or might conceivably be outbid by someone for whom the asset has special value. The "amount of the allowed secured claim" is determined as follows:

1. **Fair exchange:** In a fair exchange (i.e., the value of the security is equal to the amount of the debt), the amount of the allowed secured claim is the same as the debt. The debtor pays that amount and redeems the property.

2. **Oversecured claims:** If the debt is oversecured (i. e., the security is worth more than the dollar amount of the debt), the amount of the allowed secured claim is also the same as the amount of the debt.

3. **Undersecured claims:** *If the debt is undersecured* (i. e., the value of the security is worth less than the amount of the debt), *the amount of the allowed secured claim is equal to the value of the security.* The debtor will pay the dollar value of the security.

   Example: A creditor has a debt of $1,000 and the security is worth $600. The debtor can make a redemption by paying $600, which is the amount of the allowed secured claim (§ 506 supra, p. 82).

C. **Right to entire property:** The right to redeem extends to the entire property, not just the debtor's exempt interest in it.

   Example: Assume that a debtor has a car worth $2,000, which is subject to a lien for a $1,200 debt, resulting in an equity interest by the debtor of $800. Assume also that the debtor is entitled to a $1,500 exemption under the applicable scheme of exemptions. Under § 722, the debtor is permitted to pay the lien creditor his claim of $1,200 and redeem the entire car, regardless of the fact that its value exceeds the amount subject to exemption.

D. **Comparison with the U.C.C.:** A debtor subject to a secured obligation will generally have the right to pay off the obligation and recover his property. Under U.C.C. § 9-506, the amount the debtor must pay to the creditor is the full amount of the obligation ($1,000 in the example of the undersecured claim, See **B.3.**, *supra.*), not the value of the security ($600 in the same example). The Bankruptcy Code thus gives the individual debtor a benefit not obtainable under the U.C.C. The secured creditor gets only the value of its security.

VII. DISTRIBUTIONS — § 726

A. Review of steps prior to distribution: We have already studied in detail the steps prior to distribution. The property of the estate was identified; the debtor's exemptions were removed; assets were applied to deal with the secured creditors as needed; assets available to the claims of the unsecured creditors were assembled; allowed unsecured claims were established; and creditor priorities were determined. The next step in a Chapter 7 case is to divide the remaining assets among the unsecured creditors.

B. Division among creditors: The basic distribution system is that the assets, which by the time of distribution have usually been reduced to money, are allocated in the order specified by § 726(a). Assets go first to the first in line; to the extent there are any left over, they go to the second in line; then to the third; and so on until the assets are exhausted. Generally there is more than one entity at each place in line; the distribution among those of equal rank is handled pro rata. (See discussion of § 726(b) *infra*, p. 159.)

1. **Priority claims:** *First in line for distribution under § 726(a) are priority claims, which must be paid in the order specified in § 507.*

    a. **Order of priority under § 507:** § 507 *(supra*, p. 85) establishes an order of priority claims, but that order may be altered by other events. For example, the failure to pay adequate protection will bump the affected claim to an administrative priority ahead of other administrative priorities (§ 362 and § 363, *supra*, pp. 89 and 104). A like event can occur in connection with money or credit under Chapter 11 (§ 364 *infra*, p. 190).

    b. **Filing of Proof:** The proof of claim must be either: (1) *timely filed* (under Rule 3002(c), generally within 90 days after the first date set for the meeting of creditors) *or*, (2) *under a special provision that is applicable only to priority claims under Chapter 7, filed before the date on which the trustee commences distribution.* Note that, under this latter provision, a creditor may make a late filing of a priority claim without regard to the reason for the lateness.

2. **Ordinary claims:** Most of the claims in a bankruptcy will fall into the second priority category — ordinary claims. With one set of exceptions (claims for fines, penalties or forfeitures or for multiple, exemplary, or punitive damages, which are subordinated to fourth position), this is the general category of unsecured claims.

a. **Allowance and filing of claims:** The allowance of ordinary claims is covered by § 502, (*supra*, p. 75). Filing is covered by § 501, (*supra*, p. 72.)

b. **Time for filing:** The time for filing is covered by Rule 3002(c), which generally provides that claims must be filed within 90 days after the first § 341 meeting of creditors.

c. **Excusable tardy claims:** Tardy claims may also be paid within the second category if the creditor originally did not have knowledge of the case but then learned of it and managed to file the claim *before all payments were concluded*.

3. **Late-filed claims:** The third priority position is given to non-priority claims that are filed late when the creditor knew of the bankruptcy and, therefore, presumably was itself at fault in filing late. These claims must, however, be filed within the time required for allowance).

4. **Fines, penalties and forfeitures:** Claims filed for fines, penalties or forfeitures, or for multiple, exemplary or punitive damages — *if they are not compensation for actual pecuniary losses* — are reduced to a fourth position. In general, it is unlikely that fourth position claims will be paid in the usual Chapter 7 case, because payment depends upon the existence of a surplus of estate assets after the general creditors have been paid in full under the prior categories.

a. **Governmental claims for restitution:** Even though they compensate for and are measured by actual loss, governmental claims for restitution payments as part of a criminal sentencing will be deemed in the category of fines or penalties.

Example: A debtor, convicted of fraudulently obtaining welfare payments under a state criminal code and ordered to make restitution, seeks to have the amount of the restitution discharged in bankruptcy. The Supreme Court held that any condition imposed by a state criminal court as part of a criminal sentence is not dischargeable (see exceptions to discharge under § 523 *supra,* p. 54). In other words, even though the restitution payments may appear to be compensation for actual pecuniary losses, they are considered to be a fine or penalty and therefore not dischargeable. *Kelly v. Robinson*, 479 U.S. 36 (1986).

i. **Measure of claim:** The Supreme Court has stated in *dicta* that the measure of a governmental fine, penalty, or forfeiture is the same under § 726 as it is under § 523. *Pennsylvania Public Welfare Dept. v. Davenport*, 495 U.S. 552 (1990).

ii. **Distribution under § 726 broader than discharge under § 523:** Note that the fourth category of distribution is broader than the exception from discharge under § 523, because under § 726 all civil fines, penalties and forfeitures are covered, whereas in § 523 such obligations are covered only when they are owed to the government.

5. **Post-petition interest:** Interest earned after the petition on any claim owing under the previous four orders of distribution ranks fifth in the order of distribution. The interest accrues at the "legal rate" from the date of the filing of the petition.

   a. **Legal rate defined:** The term "legal rate" has been given several meanings by the courts. It can mean: the rate in the original agreement evidencing the debt, the highest legal rate of the applicable jurisdiction, or a rate to be applied by the court based upon market factors. In one case, the "legal rate" was held to be the federal judgment rate. *In re Laymon*, 117 B.R. 856 (Bkrtcy. W.D. Tex. 1990).

   b. **Unmatured claims:** Interest on a claim that is unmatured as of the filing of the petition is in the first instance disallowed (§ 502(b)(2) *supra*, p. 78). However, to the extent that the estate has funds after payment of prior claims, it may pay interest that matures after the petition.

6. **Remainder, if any, to the debtor:** If the estate still has assets after paying off the five levels of distribution discussed above, any remainder will be returned to the debtor.

C. **Pro rata payments:** If, at any level in the order of distribution, the available assets are insufficient to pay claimants at that level in full, distribution is made to those claimants on a pro rata basis. § 726(b).

   1. **Exception for subordination:** The doctrine of subordination (covered by § 510 and discussed *supra*, p. 91) applies to distributions in all bankruptcy cases, including Chapter 7, and can affect pro rata payments. In some cases, subordination will not affect payment priorities, but will affect the relative standing of the subordinated creditor.

D. **Impact on other Chapters:** While § 726 prescribes the order of distribution only for purposes of Chapter 7, it has an indirect effect upon Chapters 11, 12 and 13. In testing plans under the other Chapters, one standard that must be met for the protection of creditors, known as the best-interest-of-creditor test, is that creditors must receive at least as much as they would have received under a Chapter 7 liquidation. In applying those standards, it is § 726 that establishes how the creditors would have been treated in Chapter 7.

VIII. DISCHARGE — § 727

A. **Importance of discharge:** The discharge from debt is the pot of gold at the end of the debtor's rainbow and the basis of the "fresh start." It comes as one of the earlier events in a Chapter 7 case.

   1. **Concept of discharge:** A discharge means that the ***debtor has no further personal responsibility to the creditor***. It does ***not*** mean that the creditor will receive no payment on account of its debt. Payments to creditors, however, will be from the bankruptcy estate, will be made as part of the bankruptcy process and will be made until the estate is depleted. The debtor is not responsible for what is left unpaid when a debt is discharged.

   2. **May precede settlement of disputes:** Disputes over such issues as the validity of claims and rights to property may extend over years. But, if a debtor has exhibited the right to a discharge, it is granted and the debtor is given his opportunity for a fresh start free of his obligations, even before these disputes are resolved.

B. **Right to a discharge — § 727(a):** A debtor has a right to a discharge unless any one of 10 reasons for denial is proven. Presence of any one of the reasons will cause a discharge to be denied in full. § 727(a) should be distinguished from § 523, which denies discharge for particular debts.

   1. **Only individuals:** In Chapter 7 cases, discharge ***is restricted to individuals***. This is because corporations, partnerships, and other business entities do not need discharges from their debts; they simply dissolve.

      a. **Comparison with other bankruptcy Chapters:**   As we shall see, entities other than individuals can receive discharges in Chapter 9, 11 and 12 reorganizations, (*infra*, pp. 174, 218 and 224). This is because reorganization is designed to continue the existence of the entities, usually with a reduced debt burden, and a discharge is required to free them from the debts they have incurred.

      b. **Denial of discharge to individuals:** If discharge is denied, the debtor's obligations to creditors remain intact except to the extent that the creditors receive distributions from the estate.

   2. **Fraudulent transfers by debtor:** A discharge will be denied if either the debtor with intent to hinder, delay, or defraud creditors, or an officer of the estate charged with custody of property, has transferred, removed, destroyed, mutilated or concealed property, or has permitted any of those events to occur. This provision applies

both to transfers of the debtor's property made within one year before the filing and to transfers of estate property after the filing.

a. **Intent:** The intent to hinder, delay or defraud is an essential ingredient of the act preventing discharge. There is no constructive fraud provision corresponding to the power to avoid fraudulent transfers (§ 548(a)(2) *supra*, p. 138). It is usually impossible to prove fraudulent intent other than by proving the facts to the court and demonstrating that no other motivation can explain the debtor's actions. The courts have differed as to what specific acts will support a finding of fraudulent intent. However, ***acts done openly will tend to mitigate a finding of fraudulent intent***. In consumer cases, even if there are insufficient grounds to deny discharge for fraudulent transfer, the court can dismiss a case that it finds to be a substantial abuse of the provisions of Chapter 7. (§ 707(b) *supra*, p. 149.)

Example 1: Debtor conveys title to the non-exempt family homestead to his spouse without consideration six months before bankruptcy and both continue to live in it as before. A discharge may be denied.

Example 2: Debtor conveys title to the family homestead to his spouse for its fair market value six months before bankruptcy and both continue to live in it as before. The debtor proves that he was in need of funds to capitalize a new business and that his spouse was independently wealthy. The facts may negate an intent to defraud creditors.

Example 3: Five years before bankruptcy, the debtor transfers a bank account in New York to a Swiss numbered account and keeps it secret from his creditors. A discharge may well be denied because the Swiss account was "concealed" during the entire five-year period, which included the one-year period prior to bankruptcy. (Recall the discussion of this problem when dealing with the question whether a debtor has legitimately converted non-exempt assets into exempt assets under § 522, *supra*, p. 48.)

Example 4: An individual does careful prepetition bankruptcy planning with the advice of counsel and is able to move $180,000 of her assets out of the reach of her creditors before filing. Nevertheless, discharge was granted because all transfers were fully disclosed in the debtor's statement of affairs and there was no direct evidence of concealment or fraud. On the other hand, the debtor was found to have come perilously close to failing the "smell test;" that is, another court might have inferred fraud from the totality of the circumstances. *In re Carey,* 96 B.R. 336, *aff'd,* 112 B.R. 401 (Bankr. W.D, Okl.), *aff'd,* 938 F.2d 1073 (10th Cir. 1991).

b. Recovery of transferred assets — § 727 and § 548 distinguished: The trustee of the debtor's estate has the right to avoid fraudulent transfers under § 548, but that right proceeds from a different purpose than § 727. § 727 prevents discharge; § 548 enables a trustee to recover property (*supra,* p. 136).

Section 548(d)(1) dates a transfer at the ***time it is perfected*** against a bona fide purchaser from the debtor. There is no such definition in § 727 and the Ninth Circuit has held that, since § 548 and § 727 serve different purposes, the definition in § 548 should not be imported into § 727. Therefore, it held that a transfer under § 727 is made at the time it is valid between the parties to the transfer, whether or not it is valid against bona fide purchasers. *In re Roosevelt,* 87 F. 3d 311 (9th Cir. 1996). This will tend to date the transfer at an earlier time than if the bona fide purchaser test applied and consequently tend to take it out of the one-year fraudulent-transfer period.

3. Inadequate records: Discharge may be denied if the debtor "has concealed, destroyed, mutilated, falsified, or failed to keep or preserve any recorded information...from which the debtor's financial condition or business transactions may be ascertained, unless such act or failure to act was justified..."

Example 1: A business systematically destroys its payroll records every year. A discharge may be denied.

Example 2: A consumer throws away his credit card and his telephone bills when they are paid. This may be justified as normal consumer behavior.

4. Bankruptcy crimes: Discharge will be denied for criminal behavior in connection with the bankruptcy. Acts considered to be criminal include false oaths, false claims, bribery, and the withholding of information. Because the purpose and effect of this provision is nonprosecutorial in nature, the standard of proof is a preponderance of the evidence. A criminal proceeding would require proof beyond a reasonable doubt.

5. Inadequate explanation of losses: Discharge will be denied if the debtor has failed to explain satisfactorily any loss of assets or the reasons for her inability to meet liabilities. This limitation on discharge turns on the veracity of the debtor and the completeness of her explanation.

Example: Over the course of three years, a debtor loses $500,000. He explains to the court that he was dependent upon narcotics and was a compulsive gambler. The court did not consider the explanation sufficient to justify a discharge. *In re Dolin*, 799 F.2d 251 (6th Cir. 1986).

6. **Refusal to cooperate:** As the most important player, the debtor is obliged to assist in the administration of the bankruptcy case. The debtor may be denied a discharge for noncompliance with this obligation. The provision in the statute lists a few examples of non-cooperative behavior, including: refusal to obey a lawful court order, refusal to testify on the grounds of the privilege against self-incrimination after immunity from prosecution has been granted, or refusal to testify on grounds other than the privilege against self incrimination.

7. **Misbehavior in an insider's case:** If the debtor commits any of the acts described in sub-paragraphs **2-6** of this section (§ 727(a)(2)–(6) (*supra*, p. 160) in connection with another bankruptcy case concerning an "insider," either during the year before the petition or during the administration of his case, the discharge will be denied. "Insider" is defined at § 101(31) to include: relatives of the debtor or of a general partner of the debtor; directors, officers and controlling persons of a corporation; and general partners of a partnership (*supra*, p. 130).

8. **Previous discharge in Chapter 7 or 11 case:** A discharge will be denied if the debtor has been granted a previous *discharge under Chapter 7 or 11 in a case commenced within six years before the petition is filed*.

Example 1: Case 1 is commenced on January 2, 1980. A discharge is granted on January 2, 1982. A petition for Case 2 is filed on January 3, 1986. It is unaffected by the six year rule; the determining dates are the dates on which the cases are commenced.

Example 2: Case 1 was commenced on January 2, 1980 and a discharge was granted on January 2, 1982. A petition for Case 2 is filed on January 2, 1985. Case 2 may proceed, but no discharge may be granted.

a. **Rationale for commencing a second case within six years:** Debtors may have reasons for requesting bankruptcy relief other than to obtain a discharge. For example, they may be seeking a device to manage voluminous claims, as in the notorious asbestos and Dalkon Shield bankruptcies. *See In re Johns-Manville Corp.*, 36 B.R. 743 (Bankr. S.D.N.Y. 1984), *aff'd*, 52 B.R. 940 (S.D.N.Y. 1985) (asbestos case); *In re A. H. Robbins, Inc.*, 88 Bankr. 742 (E.D. Va.), *aff'd*, 880 F.2d 694 (4th Cir. 1988), *cert. denied*, 493 U.S. 959 (1989) (Dalkon Shield case).

9. **Previous discharge in Chapter 12 and 13 case:** With a few exceptions, discharge in a Chapter 7 case will be denied to debtors who received a discharge under Chapter 12 (family farmers) or Chapter 13 (individuals with regular income) in a case commenced within six years prior to the start of the Chapter 7 case. The exceptions are designed to encourage debtors in Chapters 12 and 13 to pay their debts in full.

   a. **Exceptions:** A discharge is available if: (1) the unsecured claims of the prior case were paid in full, or (2) 70 percent of the debts were paid **and** the previous plan was proposed in good faith **and** the payments represented the debtor's best effort.

10. **Waivers of discharge:** Discharge is prevented if the court approves a written waiver of discharge executed by the debtor after the order for relief in the case. Waivers of discharge, while rare, are not unknown. A debtor may execute a waiver in order to take advantage of some of the elements of bankruptcy relief (the automatic stay, avoidance of certain transfers, organization of claims, etc.) while remaining obligated to creditors. A waiver of discharge should be distinguished from:

    - A *reaffirmation by the debtor* of a specific debt under the protections of § 524(c), (*supra*, p. 60);

    - A *debtor's decision to pay voluntarily* any or all of his debts, as provided in § 524(f), (*supra*, p. 62); and

    - A *dismissal of the case* under § 707.

C. **Debts discharged — § 727(b):** Subject to the exceptions to discharge in § 523 (*supra*, p. 53), an individual is discharged from all debts that ***arose before the order for relief***. If a debt meets this definition, the debt is discharged regardless of whether a proof of claim was filed or allowed.

1. **Order for relief date:** The determinative date is the date of the order for relief, not the date of the filing of the petition. In an involuntary case, the order for relief will normally follow the petition and the two will be separated by the "gap" period, (*supra*, p. 28).

2. **Debts defined:** Debts, it should be recalled, are liabilities on claims under § 101(12) (*supra*, p. 18). Claims are very broadly defined under § 101(5), (*supra*, p. 17).

    a. Federal Law applies: Whether debts or claims arose before the order for relief are questions of federal rather than state law and are determined in light of the purposes of the Bankruptcy Code.

    b. Money damages: Claims must be for money (as demonstrated in *Ohio v. Kovacs*, (*supra*, p. 17), although the amounts need not be established (as when the claims are "unliquidated" under the definition in § 101, *supra*, p. 17). Therefore, an injunction imposing future duties to act or refrain from acting cannot support a claim until it gives rise to a money equivalent. If that does not occur until after the order for relief, the obligation cannot be discharged.

  3. Debts deemed to have arisen before order for relief: Certain actions taken by the trustee after the order for relief, such as the rejection of a contract with a third person (§ 365, *supra*, p. 106), or the avoidance of a fraudulent transfer to a third person (§ 548, *supra* p. 136), result in claims against the estate. These claims by their nature arise after the petition, but they are considered under § 502 to have arisen before the petition. They are therefore dischargeable.

D. Debts not discharged: Liens (mortgages on real estate and security interests in personal property that secure payment or performance of an obligation) are protected by the Fifth Amendment and cannot be discharged in bankruptcy.

  1. Non-recourse claims: The discharge of debts in bankruptcy does not undo property rights. A secured creditor has a right after discharge to take possession of property under its lien; it does not, however, have the right to sue the debtor on the discharged debt. A secured claim that is discharged is usually a "non-recourse claim," under which the creditor has its rights to the security but does not have recourse against the debtor.

E. Difficulty of construction: It is important in understanding discharge — as it is in understanding other aspects of bankruptcy — to be certain of the implications of the relationship between various sections of the Code. For example, the Fourth Circuit Court of Appeals has held that certain claims against an estate were subject to the automatic stay in § 362, because the claims were in existence before the petition. Although the implications of the case, and the implications of similar cases dealing with mass claims for asbestos injuries, suggest that the claims should also be discharged under § 727, the court specifically abstained from ruling on the issue of discharge at the same time as it ruled on the § 362 automatic stay. (*A.H. Robins*, *supra*, p. 37.)

CHAPTER 10

FILING UNDER CHAPTER 9 — MUNICIPAL BANKRUPTCY

Introductory note: Chapter 9 is a seldom used chapter of the Code that deals with the bankruptcy of "municipalities," a term that includes any political subdivision, public agency, or instrumentality of the states. Between 1980 and 1990, Chapter 9 was invoked only 69 times. Only seven of those cases involving cities, villages or counties; the rest dealt with special tax districts and municipal utilities.

I. CONSTITUTIONAL BACKGROUND

A. Constitutional history: The first Municipal Bankruptcy Act was passed in 1934. The Act was held to be unconstitutional because, in its system of avoiding the obligations due under state-based bonds, it gave the federal government too much power to interfere with the ability of states to manage their own fiscal affairs. *Ashton v. Cameron County Water Improvement Dist.*, 298 U.S. 513 (1936). Quickly amended in 1937, the amendments were found to be constitutional largely because of the emphasis they put on the voluntary nature of the Chapter. Other factors supporting constitutionality included the necessity that a Chapter 9 case be approved by at least 51 percent of the creditors and the holders of at least 66 2/3 percent of the debt of the municipality; the requirement of good faith; and an expanded provision for notice to creditors. *United States v. Bekins*, 304 U.S. 27 (1938). Whatever the soundness of the Court's distinction of *Ashton*, the finding of constitutionality of Chapter 9 under *Bekins* has remained firm.

B. Balancing of powers: Underlying the administration of Chapter 9 is the constitutional requirement that the federal bankruptcy power must give way to the separation between federal and state governments which is fundamental to the Constitution. Chapter 9 carefully separates bankruptcy powers in the federal government from political powers that rest with the states. Much of the variance between Chapter 9 and the remainder of the Code is based upon the principle that Congress may not cause the federal government to interfere with the governing processes adopted by the states. For example, §903 makes clear that "the power of a State to control, by legislation or otherwise, a municipality of or in such State in the exercise of the political or governmental powers of such municipality" is undiminished by the Code. This theme is continued by §904, which provides that the jurisdiction of the bankruptcy and district courts does not extend to political or governmental powers of the debtor. On the other hand, under the Constitution's bankruptcy power, state law may not compel a creditor to accept a modification of its claim. That kind of creditor management is a bankruptcy function and within the power of Congress and the Code.

II. NATURE AND STRUCTURE OF CHAPTER 9

A. Applicability of general provisions—§901: Chapters 1, 3 and 5 of the Code establish the basic rules for bankruptcy cases (*supra*, p. 14). However, in order for Chapter 9 to maintain the proper federal-state relationship, not all of Chapters 1, 3 and 5 of the Code apply to Chapter 9 cases.

1. Provisions that apply: General provisions peculiar to Chapter 9 are listed in §901. Among the provisions included are all those of Chapter 1; also, §362—the automatic stay; §365—the ability to reject executory contracts and leases (but the duty to bargain a new agreement under §1113 is not included); §501—filing claims; and the sections that provide avoiding powers.

2. Provisions that do not apply: Provisions that do not apply include the sections dealing with the trustee; §303—involuntary bankruptcies; §523—claims that are not discharged; and §541—the property of the estate. In place of §541 is §902(1), which simply makes the property of the debtor the property of the estate for purposes of a municipal bankruptcy. Since the municipality has no separate existence apart from the entity in bankruptcy and simply owns and controls all of its property, none of the subtleties of §541 are necessary.

B. Reorganization approach: Chapter 9, entitled "Adjustments of Debts of a Municipality," provides essentially for reorganization, much like a corporate reorganization under Chapter 11. For this reason, much of Chapter 11 is made applicable to Chapter 9 by means of §901. While we have not yet reached our discussion of Chapter 11 (*infra*, p. 175), note that the Chapter 11 sections made applicable, in whole or in part, to Chapter 9 include: §1122—the division of claims into classes (*infra*, p. 193); §1123—the plan (*infra* p. 197); §1125—disclosure of the plan (*infra*, p. 203); §1126—voting on the plan (*infra*, p. 208); and §1129—confirmation of the plan, including the "cram down" provision (*infra*, pp. 209 and 212).

III. ABILITY TO FILE IN CHAPTER 9 — §109(c)

A. Entities that may be Chapter 9 debtors: To be a debtor under Chapter 9, it is essential that all five conditions of §109(c) be satisfied:

1. **Must be a municipality:** "Municipality" is defined under §101(40) as a "political subdivision or public agency or instrumentality of a State." A state itself may not obtain Chapter 9 relief. Under the definition, all of the following may file under Chapter 9: cities, towns, villages, counties, taxing districts, municipal utilities, school districts, and authorities established to operate highways, airports, bridges and similar facilities.

2. **Must have state authority:** The municipality must be specifically authorized by state law to be a Chapter 9 debtor. The specific authority may be given to municipalities in general or to specifically named municipalities. The specific authority may also be granted by a government officer or organization that is empowered by statute to make the authorization.

3. **Municipality must be insolvent:** We have previously referred to the definition of insolvency at §101(32) and categorized it as a "balance sheet" rather than an "equitable" standard (*supra*, p. 130). However, ***with respect to municipalities, the definition of insolvency that applies is the equitable test of not being able to pay debts as they become due.*** This is an appropriate variation from the balance sheet test, since a Chapter 9 bankruptcy does not attempt to liquidate the assets of the debtor municipality and their value is consequently largely irrelevant. ***The definition also provides that the non-payment of debts as they become due is not necessarily proof of insolvency, if the debts are the subject of a bona fide dispute.*** The equitable concept was confirmed in the bankruptcy of the City of Bridgeport, in which the bankruptcy court dismissed the petition because the city did not show that it was unable to meet its obligations as they became due. *In re City of Bridgeport*, 129 B.R. 332 (Bkrtcy. D.Conn. 1991).

4. **Demonstration of intent:** The municipal debtor must demonstrate to the court that it desires to effect a plan to adjust its debts.

5. **Satisfaction of one of the creditor-related tests:** To prove that it is suitable for a Chapter 9 case free of undue interference by the federal government in its affairs, ***the municipal debtor must demonstrate need and good faith by showing one or more of the following: (1) a majority of the creditors who will be impaired under a plan have agreed to the case; (2) the debtor has negotiated with its creditors in good faith and failed to reach an agreement; (3) negotiation with creditors is impracticable, or (4) the debtor reasonably believes that a creditor may attempt to obtain a §547 voidable preference*** (*supra*, p. 125).

B. Voluntary filings only: A Chapter 9 filing must be voluntary. Involuntary filings are prohibited at least in part for Constitutional reasons, i.e., to prevent interference by creditors and the federal courts with the administration of state government.

C. Suitability of other chapters: A municipality that may avail itself of Chapter 9 relief may not utilize any other form of bankruptcy. Note that §109 makes Chapters 7 and 11 relief available to "persons" and that the definition of a person under §101 does not include a governmental unit.

IV. ADMINISTRATIVE VARIATIONS FROM FILINGS UNDER OTHER CHAPTERS

A. Order for relief: Chapter 9 petitions are filed under §301. However, a petition is not an automatic order for relief. Under §921(d), the court issues the order only if the case does not warrant dismissal.

B. Automatic stay — § 922: The automatic stay under §362 (*supra*, p. 36) is made applicable to Chapter 9 cases through §901. In addition, the automatic stay is made available under §922 on two grounds not covered by §362. The two grounds are as follows:

    1. Stay applies to officers or inhabitants of debtor: The *automatic stay applies to actions against a municipality's officers or inhabitants, the real object of which is to enforce claims against the debtor municipality.* This ground applies to actions or proceedings against persons or entities other than the municipality itself for debts owed by, or owing to, the municipality. Creditors are thus prevented from bringing a mandamus action against an official of the municipality for debts owed by the municipality. Likewise, creditors are prevented from bringing an action against inhabitants of the municipality (i.e., property owners) to compel payment of taxes that may be owed to the municipality.

    2. Enforcement of certain liens: The *automatic stay applies to the enforcement by a creditor of a lien related to taxes or assessments owed to the debtor municipality.* This provision prevents actions, which may be permitted under the particular state law, that would allow a creditor to take the place of the municipality to enforce a lien for taxes or assessments.

C. Debtor's duties: The Code section generally prescribing the debtor's duties (§521 *supra*, p. 33) is not applicable to Chapter 9. For Chapter 9, there is a reduced set of duties. Their purpose is to give public notice of the bankruptcy (§923) and to supply a list of the municipality's creditors to the court (§924).

D. Effect of list of claims: Under §925, a proof of claim is deemed filed if it appears in the list of creditors filed by the municipality. This is also the approach under Chapter 11 (§1111(a) *infra*, p. 198). Under Chapter 7, a claim that is listed by the debtor is not deemed "filed" to the extent that the creditor listed can participate in the bankruptcy distributions. The creditor must actually file a proof of claim under §501 (*supra*, p. 72).

E. Avoiding powers:

1. **The "avoiding powers" of the trustee:** A trustee is normally not appointed in Chapter 9. Under §902(5), the powers of the trustee are given to the debtor municipality. However, if a debtor municipality chooses not to use its avoiding power (for example, against a preference under §547, *supra*, p. 125; or against a fraudulent transfer under §548, *supra*, p. 136), the court has the power under §926 to appoint a trustee upon the request of a creditor. The powers of this type of trustee are limited to pursuing the specific unused avoiding power.

2. **Avoiding contracts:** The ability to avoid executory contracts under §365 (*supra*, p. 108), is given to the debtor under §901 and is an important part of the municipality's protective arsenal. Burdensome contracts with municipal employees, labor unions, or the private sector can be a particularly serious element affecting a municipality's financial status, and the courts have been encouraged by Congress to take a liberal view on decisions to terminate these commitments. Because a decision to abort an executory contract is less well defined than is the use of other avoiding powers, and is also considered to be subject to the discretion of the municipality, a trustee is not substituted for the debtor in making decisions about its contracts.

3. **Preferential transfers to municipal bond or note holders:** Transfers of money or property to the holders of municipal bonds or notes are not subject to avoidance as preferential transfers under §547 (*supra*, p. 125). The Congressional history treats such transfers as not generally within the purpose of the preference provisions. If the transfers are indeed inappropriate, they may be subject to attack under the §548 fraudulent transfer provisions (*supra*, p. 136).

F. Dismissal: Chapter 9 dismissals are governed by §930. Dismissal, or abstention, under the general power contained in §305 (*supra*, p. 29), is inapplicable to Chapter 9 because §901 does not include §305 as a provision applicable to it. Although Rule 1017 (which deals generally with dismissals) makes no specific mention of §930, the Rule would appear to cover Chapter 9 dismissals along with dismissals under other Chapters.

1. **Discretionary dismissals:** The court has the authority under §930(a) to dismiss "for cause." There is a non-exclusive list of causes, including want of prosecution of the case, unreasonable delay, failure to propose a plan, denial of confirmation of a plan under §943(b) (which requires that the court confirm a plan if certain criteria are met), and denial of additional time for filing another plan or modification of a plan.

2. **Mandatory dismissal:** Under §930(b), the court is required to dismiss "if confirmation of a plan is refused." This latter provision appears to overlap with the discretionary ground for dismissal for "denial of confirmation of a plan" under §930(a) and may be a legislative oversight. The legislative intent of the discretionary provision in § 930(a) is to give the court the opportunity to allow a debtor to propose a new amended plan if the first plan is not confirmed, without having to commence the case all over again. In order to make sense out of these two provisions, the mandatory provision should probably be read to apply only where the filing of another plan is not feasible.

V.   CHAPTER 9 – THE REORGANIZATION PLAN

A. **Nature of plan:** The future of the debtor municipality, including the extent to which it will pay its debts, is embodied in a "plan." The municipality drafts and submits the plan to its creditors for their approval. The plan is then confirmed by the bankruptcy court. Because of the constitutional limitations upon how much the bankruptcy court can interfere with state government, a Chapter 9 plan is not as all-encompassing as a Chapter 11 plan. However, the process by which a plan is written, voted upon, and confirmed largely duplicates the Chapter 11 process, which is discussed in detail (*infra*, p. 197). It is important, however, to note some of the main distinctions between Chapter 9 and Chapter 11 plans.

B. **Contents of plan:** The portions of §1123 (contents of a Chapter 11 plan) that are appropriate to a municipal bankruptcy are made applicable to Chapter 9 plans by §901.

C. **Differences from Chapter 11 plans:** Unlike Chapter 11 plans, under §941 only the debtor may file a plan. The plan is filed with the petition or at such later time as the court fixes.

D. Disclosure and voting: To the extent appropriate to a municipal bankruptcy, §1125 (disclosure of the plan to creditors) and §1126 (voting on the plan) are made applicable to Chapter 9 by §901.

E. Confirmation of the plan: Most of §1129 (court confirmation of a plan under Chapter 11) is made applicable to Chapter 9 through §901.

   1. Cram down: The cram down tests of §1129(b), under which creditors opposed to the plan may be forced to accept it, apply to Chapter 9, but some modifications are necessary for application to a municipality rather than a business. For example, while the two basic tests—that the plan be fair and equitable and that it not discriminate—apply in Chapter 9 as well as Chapter 11, it is clear that a fair and equitable situation can exist even when not all revenue of a municipality is allocated to creditors, because some revenue is required on a continuing basis to keep the community running.

   2. Priority claims: Under §943, all §507(a)(1) administrative claims (*supra*, p. 86) must be paid in cash when the plan becomes effective unless the claim holder agrees to a different treatment. The elaborate system of priority claims in Chapter 11 cases (§1129(a)(9) *infra*, p. 212) is not carried over into Chapter 9.

   3. Best interests of creditors test: The "best interests of creditors" test under §1129(a)(7) requires that impaired claims either accept the plan or receive at least what they would get in a Chapter 7 liquidation. The difference between the Chapter 11 and Chapter 9 approach is largely based upon the fact that liquidation under Chapter 7—the basis for the Chapter 11 test—is simply not relevant to Chapter 9. There is no possibility that a municipality will be liquidated and its assets shared among its creditors. Aside from the obvious impracticality of such a procedure, the Constitution forbids, as we have already noted, such an interference by the federal government in state affairs. At bottom, what the best interest of creditor test means in Chapter 9 is that, upon court review of the municipality's entire financial situation, the creditors will receive what is appropriate. The plan must neither milk the municipality on the one hand nor interfere with its functions on the other. *Feno v. Newport Heights Irr. Dist.*, 114 F.2d 563 (9th Cir. 1940).

VI. EFFECT OF PLAN CONFIRMATION – § 944

A. Debtor and creditors are bound: The effect of confirmation of a Chapter 11 plan (§ 1141 *infra*, p. 198) is not carried over by § 901 to Chapter 9. The effect of a confirmed plan in Chapter 9 is governed by §944. Under §944(a), the confirmed plan binds the municipal debtor and all its creditors whether or not a creditor's claim is filed or deemed filed under §501 or accepted under §502, and whether or not a creditor has accepted the plan. The plan apparently even binds creditors (except with respect to discharge, *infra*) that never heard of the plan.

B. Discharge: The plan discharges the debtor municipality of all debts if all of the following occurs:

1. **Confirmation:** The plan must be confirmed.

2. **Deposit with a disbursing agent:** The debtor must deposit with a disbursing agent appointed by the court any consideration to be distributed under the plan.

3. **Determination of binding obligation:** The court must determine that any consideration deposited with the disbursing agent is a valid obligation of the debtor and that any provision made to pay or to secure payment is also valid.

C. Exceptions from discharge: The following are excepted from the discharge under a confirmed plan:

1. **Exceptions in plan or order:** Any debts excepted from discharge by the plan itself or by the order confirming the plan are not discharged.

2. **Entities without knowledge:** A debt owing to any entity that had neither notice nor actual knowledge of the case prior to the confirmation is not discharged.

VII. PLAN IMPLEMENTATION

A. Role of court: Under §945, the court may retain jurisdiction over the case for as long as the court feels is necessary for the successful implementation of the plan. When administration of the case has been completed, the court closes the case.

B. Role of municipal entity: A legal duty is imposed on the debtor municipality to implement the plan under §1142(b), which is made applicable to Chapter 9 through §901.

FILING UNDER CHAPTER 11 — REORGANIZATION

Introductory note: Chapter 11 of the Code is designed principally for the reorganization, rather than liquidation, of business debtors; Chapter 13 is generally more suitable for the reorganization of consumer debtors. Chapter 11 is based on the social concept that it is preferable to retain a business entity in existence, producing goods and services, creating employment, helping to keep the community where the business is located economically sound. Despite this laudable objective, Chapter 11 has been subject to heavy criticism. Although reliable statistics have not been kept, estimates are that, of those entities that select Chapter 11, somewhere between 70 and 95 percent are liquidated before the case is closed; Chapter 11 has been dubbed a slow Chapter 7. We do not enter this debate; rather, we present a straightforward description of the Chapter 11 process. Again, we start our analysis with a reminder that Chapters 1, 3 and 5 of the Code apply generally to Chapter 11.

I. REASONS FOR FILING UNDER CHAPTER 11

A. Financial reorganization: The normal Chapter 11 debtor is a business in financial difficulty. Through a confirmed Chapter 11 plan, it can pay a portion of its obligations and discharge the remainder; it can terminate burdensome contracts, including labor union agreements; it can recover assets transferred away in preferential or fraudulent transfers; and it can, in the plan which it offers and which must be acceptable to its creditors, revamp its operations in order to return to profitability.

B. Other reasons: As occasions demand, Chapter 11 may be used for other purposes. Significantly, it has been used by businesses without financial difficulties in the usual sense. For example, Texaco used Chapter 11 as a means of adjusting a claim against it by Pennzoil for some $13 billion. *See In re Texaco, Inc.,* 84 Bankr. 893 (Bankr. S.D.N.Y. 1988). Manufacturers of asbestos and defective contraceptive devices have used Chapter 11 as a method of dealing in an organized manner with tens of thousands of lawsuits. *See In re Johns-Manville Corp.,* 36 B.R. 743 (Bankr. S.D.N.Y. 1984), *aff'd,* 52 B.R. 940 (S.D.N.Y. 1985) (asbestos case); *In re A. H. Robbins, Inc.,* 88 Bankr. 742 (E.D. Va.), *aff'd,* 880 F.2d 694 (4th Cir. 1988), *cert. denied,* 493 U.S. 959 (1989) (Dalkon Shield case).

II.   ADVANTAGES OF CHAPTER 11

A. "Debtor in possession" — § 1101:   Chapter 11 provides for a new entity in bankruptcy, the ***"debtor in possession,"*** which allows the debtor the substantial benefit of being able to continue management of its business. However, if a trustee is appointed and takes over operation of the business or management of the assets of the estate, the debtor in possession ceases to exist.

B. Comparison to Chapter 7:   Although Chapter 11 is designed primarily for the purpose of reorganization, a Chapter 11 debtor may adopt a liquidating plan under § 1123(b)(4) at the beginning of the case, or may convert to a liquidating plan if the reorganization plan has not been substantially consummated. The primary advantage of a Chapter 11 filing over a Chapter 7 liquidation is that the debtor has more power to negotiate with the creditors and can retain more control over the administration of the estate. Under § 704(1), a trustee is required to liquidate a Chapter 7 debtor "as expeditiously as is compatible with the best interests of parties in interest" (*supra*, p. 153). A Chapter 11 liquidating plan requires, as does a reorganization, the submission of a written plan, the vote of creditors, and the confirmation of the court. A liquidation under Chapter 11 is, therefore, a considerably more elaborate and structured form of liquidation than one under Chapter 7.

C. Comparison to Chapter 13:   The following are advantages of a filing under Chapter 11 over Chapter 13 (the reorganization of individual debtors with regular income, *infra*, p. 227).

- Chapter 11 has no limitation on the amount of debts. (Chapter 13 is limited to unsecured debt of less than $250,000 and secured debt of less than $750,000, *infra*, p. 228).

- Chapter 11 does not require any particular commitment of income to the payment of debts as Chapter 13 does (§ 1325(b)(1) *infra*, p. 244).

- Chapter 11 gives a faster discharge than does Chapter 13.

III.   WHO MAY BE A DEBTOR IN CHAPTER 11 — § 109(d)

A. Eligibility: Under § 109(d), anyone who is eligible to be a Chapter 7 debtor can, with certain exceptions, be a Chapter 11 debtor.

1. Eligibility under Chapter 7:   In order to file under Chapter 7, a debtor must be a "person." "Person" is defined to include, but is not limited to, individuals, partnerships, and corporations (*supra*, p. 147); the term excludes governmental units, which must file under

Chapter 9 (*supra*, p. 167). Insurance companies and banks are also excluded because they have specific forms of relief available under separate federal and state laws (*supra*, p. 147).

2. **Railroads included:** Railroads, which are excluded from Chapter 7, are eligible for Chapter 11 under specific provisions.

3. **Stockbrokers and commodity brokers excluded:** Stockbrokers and commodity brokers are ineligible for relief under Chapter 11; they must file under specific provisions of Chapter 7.

B. **Individuals in Chapter 11:** Until 1991, it was unclear whether Chapter 11 could be used by individuals who were not in business. Some courts had held that individuals who were not in business were limited to Chapters 7 or 13; other courts had held that, since there are limitations on a Chapter 13 filing, the debtor must first show that Chapter 13 was unavailable. The Supreme Court, in *Toibb v. Radloff*, 501 U.S. 157 (1991), held that the clear language of § 109(d) should control and that any entity coming under the definition of *individuals may use Chapter 11 without restraint*.

1. **Rationale:** The Court agreed that Chapter 11 was designed primarily for businesses; however, this did not foreclose consumers from using it. The Court considered Chapter 11 sufficiently complex that it would naturally discourage consumers from its provisions and a natural division between Chapter 11 and Chapter 13 would therefore be maintained.

C. **Voluntary and involuntary:** Chapter 11 may be entered voluntarily with a petition under § 301 or involuntarily with a petition under § 303 (*supra*, pp. 25 to 26).

IV. CREDITOR COMMITTEES

A. **Purpose:** Assuming that the Chapter 11 case has gotten under way, either voluntarily or involuntarily, and assuming that the debtor (who by now is probably the debtor in possession) has begun the satisfaction of its Chapter 5 duties (*supra*, p. 33), the creditors are ready to participate in the case. Since creditors can number into the hundreds of thousands, committees are necessary in order to create some sort of workable, representative group.

1. **Small business debtors:** In order to make Chapter 11 more flexible for small business debtors, a party in interest may request and the court may order, for cause, that a committee of creditors not be appointed. In order to qualify as a small business, the debtor's secured and unsecured debts cannot exceed $2,000,000. (Other

small business debtor provisions provide for reduced time periods for filing a reorganization plan.)

B. Appointment — § 1102: The first committee, which must consist of unsecured creditors, is appointed by the United States Trustee; additional committees of creditors and of equity security holders may be established by the United States Trustee or may be ordered by the court.

C. Number and function of committees: Since the goal of committees is to see that all creditors are appropriately represented, there is no particular number of committees and no particular number of members on a committee. The provisions of § 1102(b)(1) *suggest, but do not require, that a creditors' committee be composed of the persons that hold the seven largest of the kinds of claims represented on the committee,* and that *an equity holders' committee be composed of the seven largest amounts of the kinds of equity securities represented by the committee.* In a large case, a creditor may serve on two committees. The objectives are the same, i.e., the committees must represent the interests of the creditors and they must be able to function effectively.

D. Powers and duties — § 1103:

1. **Powers of committees:** A committee has a broad-ranging set of powers. Under § 1103(c), they include authority to:

   - consult with the debtor in possession or the trustee concerning the administration of the estate;

   - investigate the debtor's business and its operation;

   - participate in the formulation of a plan;

   - file acceptances or rejections of the plan with the court;

   - request the appointment of a trustee where it is deemed appropriate; and

   - perform such other services as are in the interest of those represented.

   The final item makes clear that the list is not exclusive but rather only indicative of the powers and duties of a committee.

2. **Specific authority to employ lawyers and accountants:**
   Under § 1103(a), a committee may employ lawyers, accountants, and other agents.

V. TRUSTEE'S DUTIES — EXERCISED BY DEBTOR IN POSSESSION, TRUSTEE, OR EXAMINER

A. **Performance of the trustee's duties:** As we have seen, every Chapter 7 case has a trustee to liquidate and distribute the estate (*supra*, p. 153). Chapter 13 also provides for a trustee in all cases although his functions are more limited (*infra*, p. 232). In *most Chapter 11 cases, the debtor in possession will operate its own business and perform the functions of the trustee.* An order appointing a trustee or examiner is issued in a limited number of cases. *In re Cumberland Investment Company*, 118 B.R. 3 (Bkrtcy. D.R.I. 1990), aff'd, 133 B.R. 275 (1991).

B. **Discretionary appointment of trustee — § 1104:** Under § 1104, the court is given certain grounds under which to order the appointment of a trustee after the start of any Chapter 11 case and before the confirmation of a Chapter 11 plan. These grounds apply to involuntary as well as voluntary cases.

1. **Criteria for appointment:** *The court may order the appointment of a trustee for such reasons as "cause, including fraud, dishonesty, incompetence, or gross mismanagement" and "the interests of creditors."* The court is not limited to the events specified in § 1104 and need not even find "cause" as it is generally understood. The court may examine such other factors as it deems informative about the debtor's business competence, including the debtor's general trustworthiness, the confidence the marketplace has in it, its track record in anticipating successes and problems, and the like. *In re Ionosphere Clubs, Inc.*, 113 B.R. 164 (Bkrtcy. S.D. N.Y. 1990).

2. **Power to appoint seldom used:** The appointment of a trustee in Chapter 11 is considered an extraordinary event; the assumption is that an honest debtor in financial difficulties is the best one to manage its business. But, *if necessary to protect creditors and equity holders, the debtor in possession must be removed and a trustee appointed.* The court must decide whether the events brought before it are within the realm of reasonable business reverses that may be accepted as "part of the game" or whether they have tilted over into the area of mismanagement or fraud. However, even the most egregious errors in the operation of the business — errors which would justify actions for contempt of the Code against the debtor — may not require the appointment of a trustee. *In re Hester*, 899 F.2d 361 (5th Cir. 1990).

3. **Right to elect:** Within 30 days after the court orders the appointment of a trustee, a party in interest may make a request for an election of that trustee. If a request is made, the United States Trustee must convene a meeting of creditors for the purpose of electing one disinterested person to serve as trustee.

4. **Qualifications of the Chapter 11 Trustee:** The trustee in Chapter 11 requires very different abilities from trustees in Chapter 7 and the other chapters. The Chapter 11 trustee is authorized to operate the debtor's business under § 1108, which is in furtherance of the goal of Chapter 11 to continue the business during the reorganization. In Chapter 7, the trustee's duties are largely financial and ministerial in nature. Principally, the Chapter 7 trustee liquidates the estate and makes payment to creditors. Along the way, the trustee must conduct or supervise such tasks as the claiming of the debtor's exemptions, the determination of the validity of claims, and the return of property improperly transferred. The Chapter 7 trustee may operate the debtor's business, but only for such limited time as is required to carry out the liquidation. The Chapter 11 trustee, on the other hand, is usually (except in a liquidation plan case) responsible for the conduct of a business that is looking for rejuvenation. The duties are obviously more complex and longer lasting.

C. **Trustee duties:** As we have seen, ***trustee duties are usually performed by the debtor in possession***; the appointment of a trustee is seldom ordered in a Chapter 11 case. Although the statute and our discussion generally refer to the trustee, it should be kept in mind that the duties of the trustee, except where noted, are required also of debtors in possession. The Chapter 11 trustee's duties are based in part on the duties of a Chapter 7 trustee, which are described in § 1106 largely by reference to the specific provisions of § 704, and in part on provisions in Chapter 11. (Recall also that there is a general power in the trustee to employ professional persons under § 327, *supra*, p. 67).

1. **Duties derived from Chapter 7:** ***With some exceptions, the duties of the Chapter 11 trustee are the same as the Chapter 7 trustee*** (§ 704, *supra*, p. 153). However, the first and most important duty of the Chapter 7 trustee, that of liquidating and closing the estate, is excluded, since that is contrary to the purpose of a Chapter 11 reorganization. The Chapter 11 trustee is also not required to perform the § 704(3) duty, relating to consumer obligations because it is generally not appropriate to Chapter 11 (*supra*, p. 154). (But see *Toibb v. Radloff* with respect to the fact that consumer debtors are not foreclosed from Chapter 11 (*supra*, p. 177)). The § 704(4) duty to investigate the financial affairs of the debtor is

also excluded because it is covered separately in § 1106 (*infra*, p. 181).

2. **Chapter 11 duties:** The trustee has duties under § 1106 in addition to the § 704 duties. They include duties to:

- file the following documents: a list of creditors, a schedule of assets and liabilities, a schedule of current income and current expenditures, and a statement of the debtor's financial affairs, as required by § 521(1) (*supra*, p. 34);

- investigate the acts, conduct, assets, liabilities, and financial condition of the business, the desirability of its continuance, and the allegations that led to the trustee's appointment, and to report the findings to the court (this duty does not apply to the debtor in possession);

- file a plan or to recommend conversion to another bankruptcy chapter or a dismissal;

- file whatever tax returns are required; and

- after confirmation of a plan, file such reports as are required.

D. **Appointment of examiner:** If the court is asked to order the appointment of a trustee, it has the option of ordering the appointment of an examiner instead. Although an examiner is ordinarily appointed to make an investigation, there is considerable flexibility in the use of examiners. Thus, where the appointment of a trustee would seem excessive, the court, with the possible assistance of creditors, may give the examiner some of the trustee's duties — and simultaneously remove those duties from the debtor in possession — as the court may feel is appropriate. *In re Boileau*, 736 F.2d 503 (9th Cir. 1984).

1. **Criteria for appointment — § 1104(c):** If a trustee has not been appointed, a party in interest or the United States Trustee may request the court to appoint an examiner. After notice and a hearing, ***the court may appoint an examiner if either: (1) the appointment is in the interest of creditors, equity stockholders, and other parties in interest, or (2) the debtor's unsecured debts, other than debts for goods, services, or taxes, or owing to an insider, exceed $5,000,000.***

2. **Duties of examiner:** Under § 1106(a)(3) and (4), the basic duties of the examiner are to conduct an investigation of the affairs of the debtor as may be appropriate, including any allegations of fraud, dishonesty, incompetence, misconduct, mismanagement, or irregularities in management. The examiner may also be asked to investigate any other matter relevant to the case or the plan and submit a report.

E. Rights, powers, and duties of debtor in possession — § 1107: As discussed, Chapter 11 usually proceeds with the debtor in possession, not a trustee, in control of the business. ***Under § 1107, the rights, duties and powers of the trustee are given to the debtor in possession.*** Consequently, it is the debtor in possession which must usually exercise the broad powers delegated by the Code to the trustee, including the avoiding powers listed in Chapter 5 (*supra*, p. 110).

1. **Duties:** The duties of the trustee enumerated in § 1106 are performed by the debtor in possession so long as there is no trustee. These include duties in § 704 prescribed for Chapter 7 cases (among them, the duty to be accountable for all property received, *supra*, p. 154). Certain § 1106 duties — the duty to investigate the operation of the debtor for example — are inappropriate and are not included.

2. **Rights and powers:** Because the rights and powers of a trustee are given to the debtor in possession, the debtor may, for example, assume or reject executory contracts and leases (§ 365 gives this power to the trustee, *supra*, p. 106) and avoid fraudulent transfers (§ 548 gives this power to the trustee, *supra*, p. 117). The debtor in possession does not have the power of the trustee to be compensated under § 330.

VI. CONVERSION OR DISMISSAL — § 1112

A. **Conversion by debtor:** The ability to convert from Chapter 11 to Chapter 7 is a much-used opportunity, since, as we have noted, Chapter 11 is only sparingly successful for rehabilitation of the debtor. ***Subject to three exceptions, the debtor is given the right under § 1112(a) to convert a case to Chapter 7. The debtor need not demonstrate any specific facts or conditions in order to transfer its case.*** The three exceptions are as follows:

1. **After appointment of trustee:** If the court has ordered the appointment of a trustee, the power to transfer out of Chapter 11 and into Chapter 7 is, along with other powers, removed from the debtor.

2. **Involuntary case:** If the Chapter 11 case was begun through an involuntary petition under § 303 (*supra*, p. 26), the debtor may not remove the case to Chapter 7 because the impetus for the case did not originate with the debtor.

3. **Previous Conversion to Chapter 11 by other than the debtor:** Where the case was previously converted to Chapter 11 by a party other than the debtor, it may not be converted out of Chapter 11 by the debtor. (Cases may be converted to Chapter 11 from

Chapter 7 and Chapter 13 by a party other than the debtor. See § 706(b), *supra*, p. 148 and § 1307(d), *supra*, p. 230.)

B. Conversion by other parties for cause: Under § 1112(b), *a Chapter 11 filing may be converted for cause to another chapter by parties other than the debtor.* Parties in interest, the United States Trustee, or the bankruptcy administrator (bankruptcy administrators serve in the few jurisdictions where United States Trustees are not available) may generally apply to convert a Chapter 11 case to Chapter 7 for cause. The meaning of "cause" is the same as the meaning of "cause" for dismissal (*infra*, p. 183). The United States Trustee is accorded this right because parties to a reorganization may have concern for the effect on their reputations in the business community if they come forward and request a move to liquidation. The United States Trustee need have no such concern.

1. **Notice and a hearing:** Under § 1112(b), *notice and a hearing are required if a conversion is requested by one other than the debtor.* As noted, the requirement for notice and a hearing generally means that notice must be given and that there must be an opportunity for a hearing, whether or not a hearing is actually held (§ 102(1) *supra*, p. 19). However, Rule 2002(a)(5) requires an actual hearing in the event of an application for conversion from one chapter to another.

2. **Farmers and charities:** The court may not convert a case to Chapter 7 if the debtor is a farmer or a charitable corporation unless the debtor requests the conversion.

C. Dismissal: We have dealt with dismissal in several contexts. First, we discussed it under the general provisions of § 305, which is used principally near the beginning of a case (*supra*, p. 29). We saw dismissal a second time under § 707 (*supra*, p. 148) and again under § 930 (*supra*, p. 171). Dismissal under Chapter 11 is similar.

1. **Who may request dismissal:** *Any party in interest and the United States Trustee may request dismissal of a Chapter 11 case.*

2. **Dismissal for "cause":** *The court may order dismissal for "cause" after notice and a hearing* (which, as with conversion, *supra*, requires an actual hearing under the Rules). "Cause" is broadly interpreted in § 1112(b) to include, but is not limited to, such events as:

    *   The likelihood of loss to the estate;
    *   Inability to effectuate a plan;
    *   Unreasonable delays by the debtor;

- Inability to effectuate substantial consummation of a confirmed plan.

3. **Dismissal and good faith:** *Although not specifically mentioned in the statute, if a petition is not filed in good faith, the court may dismiss the case under § 1112(b).* As we have noted, the Bankruptcy Code has deep roots in the law of equity and the requirement of good faith underlies all of its procedures (*supra,* p. 13). Good faith is occasionally mentioned specifically in the Code. (For example, see the third requirement for the court's confirmation of a plan under § 1129 (*infra,* p. 191)). However, it is still required even where it is not mentioned. One of the contexts in which it most frequently appears is in connection with the original petition for a Chapter 11 case. But, good faith is difficult to define. In the context of a Chapter 11 filing, the good faith requirement frequently is treated as the absence of good faith, i.e., bad faith.

   a. **Bad faith in operating the business:** Bad faith in connection with a business is frequently used to mean the creation or operation of a business in such a reckless manner that bankruptcy is the only likely result. If the initial capital was grossly insufficient, or if the business plan was so unrealistic or impractical that the wasting of creditors' money and ultimate bankruptcy were essentially inevitable, there may be a finding of bad faith. See *The Good Faith Principle in the Bankruptcy Code: A Case Study,* 38 The Bus. Law. 1795 (1983).

   b. **Bad faith and the filing:** Bad faith may be found where the filing was made to pervert rather than utilize the bankruptcy system. For example, the petition may have been filed principally to secure the § 362 automatic stay in order to slow down actions by legitimate creditors (*supra,* p. 36), or in order to evade an order properly made in a state court. An additional factor may be that there is simply no realistic likelihood of a successful reorganization.

   c. **Conduct during bankruptcy:** Bad faith may also relate to conduct in the bankruptcy itself. For example, inaccurate schedules may have been filed or the debtor may have been untruthful or evasive during examinations. A debtor's evasiveness in the Chapter 11 case, its feigned losses of memory, its failure to provide regular reports, its failure to recognize a tax liability, its continuing pattern of self-dealing, and its commingling of assets with an affiliated corporation, have all been found to support a finding of bad faith constituting cause for a Chapter 11 dismissal under § 1112. *In re Kerr,* 908 F.2d 400 (8th Cir. 1990).

4. **Later filings:** *If a case is dismissed, nothing in the Code prevents a subsequent filing, or even a series of subsequent filings, so long as they are done in good faith*. Subsequent filings have been recognized by the courts. Typically, a subsequent filing must represent a sufficiently different objective so that it will not be considered merely an effort to modify a previously confirmed plan. The clearest example of an acceptable new filing occurs when a Chapter 11 plan has failed and the debtor files anew in order to liquidate under Chapter 7 or Chapter 11. *In re Jartran, Inc.*, 886 F.2d 859 (7th Cir. 1989).

5. **Conversion or dismissal:** Sometimes, conversion of a Chapter 11 case to Chapter 7 would benefit some creditors, while dismissal of the entire case would benefit others. This was the situation in *In re Superior Siding & Window, Inc.*, 14 F.3rd 240 (4th Cir. 1994), where Chapter 11 was clearly inappropriate. In that case, seven of eight creditors obtained judgment liens before bankruptcy and would benefit if the case were dismissed so that they could then levy on their liens. The eighth creditor, who had no lien and was by far the largest creditor, would benefit from a conversion to Chapter 7 because the liens of the other creditors would be eliminated as voidable preferences. The Court of Appeals, in reversing the district court, decided in favor of conversion. The court looked to the general policy of equality among similar creditors in bankruptcy and held that enforcing the preference rule honored that policy. Where cases involve competing factors for dismissal or conversion, they must be worked out according to the merits of each case.

VIII. OPERATING THE BUSINESS — NEEDS OF DEBTOR IN POSSESSION

A. **Operating the business generally:** Assume at this point that the debtor is well established in its Chapter 11 case and is proceeding towards a reorganization of its affairs as a debtor in possession. Assume also there is no concern about a dismissal or a conversion to another chapter. The debtor in possession will find that it still has the basic needs and functions of any ongoing business: the use and control of property, money, and contracts.

B. **Use of property:** Several Code provisions are designed to ensure that the debtor in possession has property for its business purposes:

1. **Use, sale, and lease by debtor:** *The debtor is able to use, sell, or lease property of the estate* (§ 541 defines the property of the estate, *supra*, p. 95), *either in the ordinary course of its busi-*

ness or, with court approval, other than in the ordinary course (§ 363 *supra*, p. 103). This general rule is subject to certain limited rights by third parties which have continuing interests in the property of the debtor.

a. **Encumbered property:** The debtor in possession can continue to use property even though it is subject to liens. However, at the request of the secured creditor, the court can condition the use, sale, or lease of the property in order to provide adequate protection to the creditor (§ 363 *supra*, p. 104).

b. **After acquired property:** The Code generally does not recognize after-acquired property clauses in mortgages or lien documents; after acquired property of the debtor is thus protected from prepetition liens. However, if provided for in the security agreement, the liens generally do extend to ***proceeds***, such as rents or profits, ***from the use of the property*** (§ 552; see also §541(a)(6), *supra*, p. 98).

2. **Creditor's relief from stay in order to recover secured interests:** Third parties, generally secured creditors, may have interests in the debtor's property that entitle them to seek relief from the automatic stay. Under § 362(d), ***creditors have the right to request relief from the stay generally on two grounds: (1) for cause, including the lack of adequate protection, or (2) even where adequate protection is given, where the debtor does not have an equity in the property and the property is not necessary to an effective reorganization*** (*supra*, p. 44).

a. **Relief from stay for cause:** *Relief from the stay for cause is frequently established through failure of the debtor to give adequate protection* under § 361 (*supra*, p. 43). In one way or another, a secured creditor must be kept whole so that he does not lose the value of his security because of the stay. Also, the secured creditor gets a first priority under § 507(b) if adequate protection fails after it is promised (*supra*, p. 89).

i. **Adequate protection:** *The typical method of protecting the creditor is a series of cash payments equal to the value of depreciation of the property while the debtor is using it.* Other forms of adequate protection are permitted under § 361. For example, the debtor in possession may provide security through other available assets, may give a bond, or may make some other offer that the creditor can't refuse.

ii. **Measure of adequate protection:** The ultimate test of adequate protection under § 361(3) is whether the secured creditor receives "the indubitable equivalent of such entity's interest in such property."

      iii. Time value of money not included: The Supreme Court held in *United States v. Timbers of Inwood Forest*, 484 U.S. 365 (1988), that *the fact that the creditor is denied possession of its property for a period of time (and thus, during that time, loses the value of the use of the property, or the value of an investment of the proceeds from a sale of the property) is not a factor to be considered in establishing the value of adequate protection* (*supra*, p. 44).

  b. Relief from stay if there is lack of debtor equity and property not necessary to effective organization: *Even if adequate protection is supplied, the secured creditor may recover its security if, under § 362(d), the debtor (i) has no equity in the property and (ii) the property is not necessary to an effective reorganization.* The debtor has no equity in security if the security is worth less than the debt. The issue of value is usually resolved by appraisals submitted by outside experts. Whether the property is necessary to an effective reorganization is a more difficult question and one that the bankruptcy court must decide. What is clear, however, is that, if adequate protection is paid and the debtor needs the property to fulfill its Chapter 11 aspirations, the creditor cannot take the property back and the debtor may use, sell or lease it under § 363 (*supra*, p. 104).

  c. Relief from stay for single asset real estate: If substantially all of the gross income of a debtor is generated by the operation of a single piece or a single project of real property, other than residential property of three or fewer units, and the total secured debt does not exceed $4,000,000, then the debtor is a "single asset real estate" debtor under § 101(51B). With respect to such debtors, the court, under § 362(d)(3), will grant relief from the stay at the request of a secured creditor of the real estate, if the debtor, within 90 days after the order for relief, has not filed a feasible plan of reorganization, or has not begun monthly interest payments to each creditor whose claim is secured by the real estate. This special treatment for single-asset real estate was extended by amendment to the Code in 1994.

C. Use of cash and its equivalents: There are various sources that the debtor in possession or trustee in Chapter 11 can look to for its money needs.

1. **Debtor's own money:** Any unencumbered cash that the debtor has upon the bankruptcy, including, of course, money in the bank, becomes part of the estate. This may be used under the general powers in § 363 (*supra*, p. 102).

2. **Encumbered money — "cash collateral:"** Under §363(a), money, including bank accounts, may itself be subject to the interests of third parties. For example, a cash account can serve as collateral for borrowing or other credit extensions. *"Cash collateral" is the Code's term for cash and its equivalents (including negotiable instruments, securities, and documents of title) that are subject to liens.* Under § 552(b), the term "cash collateral" includes postpetition rents that fall within the perfected interest of a mortgagee under the mortgage agreement. Cash collateral also extends to postpetition proceeds, product, and profits of property that are perfectible under the security agreement *and* under state law.

    a. **Proceeds from sale of collateral:** Money is frequently the "proceeds" received when collateral is sold. The Uniform Commercial Code provides a system whereby proceeds from the sale of collateral, including money, may replace collateral. For example, inventory may be used to secure a loan; when the inventory is sold, money is often received in exchange. The money, as proceeds from the sale of the inventory, substitutes for the inventory as collateral for the loan. Under § 552(b), it is clear that proceeds received after bankruptcy in place of collateral that served as security before bankruptcy — cash collateral — can be subject to a secured creditor's lien.

    b. **Use of cash collateral:** Although court authorization is usually not needed for transactions in the ordinary course of business, § 363(c)(2) restricts the use of cash collateral. *The debtor or trustee may not use, sell, or lease cash collateral unless each entity that has an interest in the collateral consents, or, after notice and a hearing, authorization is given by the court.* Generally, the debtor in possession will negotiate a "cash collateral agreement" with its secured creditors providing for the collection and application of cash collateral, such as rents.

3. **Accounts subject to setoff:** *Where a debtor has money in the bank and, at the same time, owes money on a loan from the same bank, the bank is prohibited from making a set off* by § 362(a)(7) (*supra*, p. 40). The bank is only prohibited from making an actual setoff of the obligation from the debtor (resulting from the loan) against its obligation to the debtor (resulting from the

deposit). However, the bank is able to put an administrative hold (freeze) on the deposit account to the extent of the unpaid loan, thus preventing the debtor from getting access to that portion of the account. This action does not violate the automatic stay so long as the bank does not intend to permanently reduce the account balance by the amount of the defaulted loan. In many cases, the freeze is intended to last only so long as it takes for the bank to petition the court for relief from the stay or for other appropriate relief.

Example: Debtor D has money in Creditor C bank. C is also owed money resulting from D's default of a loan. Since, under general legal principles, the bank account may be setoff against the loan, C has rights in it and it constitutes "cash collateral" under § 363 (*supra*, p. 188). When, upon its Chapter 11 bankruptcy, D attempts to use its account, C puts an administrative hold on it to the extent of the defaulted loan, pending a determination of its petition for relief from the automatic stay. D asserts that C is guilty of contempt for applying the setoff in violation of the automatic stay.

Held: Because C's administrative freeze was not intended to be a permanent reduction of the account balance by the amount of the defaulted loan, it was not a setoff within the meaning of the automatic stay provision of § 362(a)(7). This conclusion is buttressed by the fact that § 542(b) requires that debts owed to the debtor be turned over to the estate except to the extent that the debt may be offset by a claim against the debtor. Further, § 553(a) provides as a general rule that the Bankruptcy Code does not affect a creditor's *right* of setoff. This general rule is, of course, modified by § 362(a)(7), which stays an actual setoff. *Citizens Bank of Maryland v. Strumpf*, No. 94-1340, 1995 U.S. LEXIS 7408 (1995).

D. Access to credit: In order to operate the business effectively, the debtor in possession or trustee must usually have access to new sources of cash and other credit. While undoubtedly not normally viewed as the most desirable loan prospect in view of its bankruptcy, it should not be assumed that a debtor in bankruptcy is a bad credit risk. *A debtor in Chapter 11 has certain positive qualities that should appeal to a proposed lender. These qualities are twofold: (1) the potential that prior obligations will be discharged through the bankruptcy, and (2) the ability to grant administrative expense priority under § 507(a)(1) to debts incurred after the petition* (*supra*, p. 86).

1. Availability of administrative expense priority — § 364(a) and (b): The special administrative expense priority, which confers the ability to reach the assets in the debtor's estate before most other claims, gives creditors a major incentive to lend or otherwise advance credit to debtors in Chapter 11 with a reasonable assurance of repayment.

   a. **Loans and credit in ordinary course of business:** Under § 364(a), a trustee (and, by virtue of § 1107, the debtor in possession) is granted the right to obtain a loan or credit in the debtor's ordinary course of business as an administrative expense (*supra*, p. 86). Typically, these credits will be for obligations to suppliers, known as "trade credit," where there is little question that they are in the ordinary course of business.

   b. **Loans/credits not in ordinary course of business:** Loans and credits not in the ordinary course of business, can be obtained under the procedure made available in § 364(b). This procedure allows the same administrative expense priority, but with court approval.

2. **Availability of super administrative expense priority — § 364(c)(1):** If the debtor in possession or trustee is unable to obtain credit through use of the administrative expense priority, § 364(c)(1) enables the court to raise a creditor's position to that of an administrative expense claimant ahead of all other administrative expense claimants (§ 503 *supra*, p. 86) and priorities (§ 507 *supra*, p. 86). This means that the claim will not only be ahead of other normal administrative expenses, but will also trump the special administrative expense allowed under § 507(c) for failed adequate compensation (*supra*, p. 89). However, it may not top other similar orders that a judge may issue under § 364(c)(1).

3. **Money or credit secured by liens — §§ 364(c)(2), (c)(3) and (d):** If the priorities just discussed are considered insufficient by a proposed creditor, the court may authorize that new credit be secured by new liens on the property of the estate. Under § 362(c)(2), the court may authorize a lien on property that is not encumbered by other liens. If that is not available, the court may even authorize junior or senior liens on encumbered property.

   a. **Junior liens:** If unencumbered property is not available, the court, under § 364(c)(3), may authorize a junior lien, behind existing liens, on property that is already encumbered.

   b. **Senior liens:** In limited situations, the court, under § 364(d), may grant an equal, or even a senior, lien on property of the estate that is already fully encumbered with a prior lien. The court may do this only if it is first satisfied that the debtor in possession is unable to obtain the needed credit without this unusual procedure. Typically, the court must also be convinced that the loan is crucial to the success of the reorganization.

    i. Fifth Amendment issue: By creating an equal or superior property right on property that is already encumbered, the prior lienholder could, of course, be deprived of its property rights; the imposition of the new lien could run afoul of the protection given to property generally by the Fifth Amendment. This potential problem is addressed by § 364(d)(1)(B), which provides that the equal or superior lien may be granted only if the prejudiced lienholder is given "adequate protection" (*supra*, p. 43).

    ii. Adequate protection for prior lienholders: The adequate protection necessary for prior lienholders is difficult to establish. In some cases, the new loan itself has been considered adequate protection to the old lienholder under the reasoning that, through the newly secured loan, there is a greater likelihood of a successful reorganization that will ultimately benefit the ousted lienholder. Another rationale is that the new loan may actually be used to enhance the value of the collateral — such as a loan enabling the construction of a valuable new building on property already subject to a mortgage.

4. Good faith protection: There is always a possibility that credit given under § 364, either as an administrative expense or supported by a new lien on collateral of the debtor, will be found on appeal from the bankruptcy court's decision to have been made in error. Under § 364(e), so long as the credit was given in good faith, the creditor will not lose whatever benefit it thought it had obtained under § 364.

E. Rights with respect to agreements — collective bargaining agreements: The Chapter 11 debtor in possession or trustee has the rights given by § 365 to review and confirm or to terminate its executory agreements and leases (see *supra*, p. 106.) Of signal importance here is the special procedure imposed by § 1113 on the right to assume or reject collective bargaining agreements with employees.

1. The *Bildisco* case: The enactment of § 1113 grew directly out of the controversial decision in *NLRB v. Bildisco & Bildisco*, 465 U.S. 513 (1984). The case arose from the conflict between Code § 365, which authorizes the rejection of executory contracts, and the National Labor Relations Act, which makes the interference with collective bargaining agreements an unfair labor practice. The Supreme Court held that the Bankruptcy Code was superior to the

National Labor Relations Act in this respect and authorized the rejection of collective bargaining agreements under standards not too different from those applicable to any executory agreement. Congress reacted almost immediately with the adoption of § 1113 as part of the 1984 amendments to the Code. This provision establishes a mini-collective bargaining procedure when an employer seeks to reject a collective bargaining agreement. The section is designed to enable debtors in possession to reject crippling labor contracts and still ensure employees an opportunity to renegotiate a new contract upon the best possible terms consistent with the reorganization.

2. **Procedures under § 1113:** *Before a debtor in possession or trustee may request the court to terminate a collective bargaining agreement, it must make a proposal to the employees for a new agreement that modifies the old only to the extent "necessary" to the "reorganization." The employees may reject this offer only for good cause.* The courts have recognized that the relatively simple bargaining procedure prescribed by § 1113 will actually be more complex in practice. *In re American Provision Co.,* 44 B.R. 907 (Bkrtcy. D. Minn. 1984) expanded the process into several steps.

   a. **Meaning of "necessary":** Faced with the statutory prescription that the debtor propose only those modifications that are "necessary" to the reorganization, the courts realized that, if only necessary modifications were made, there would be nothing for the employees to counter with and therefore no process of bargaining. Thus, the Second Circuit held that "necessary" means something less than "essential." Without attempting a definition, the court made it clear that it was looking for a good faith offer that would open the door to meaningful negotiations. *In re Carey Transportation, Inc.,* 816 F.2d 82 (2nd Cir. 1987).

   b. **Meaning of "reorganization":** In the *Carey Transportation* case, the Second Circuit also examined whether the "reorganization" for which the modifications are necessary is the short term prospect of survival or liquidation, or a more prolonged ability to succeed under the plan. It decided that the proposals must be those that are necessary to enable the debtor to complete the reorganization process successfully, not merely to stave off liquidation tomorrow. The courts have not reached an accord on the terms "necessary" or "reorganization," but *Carey Transportation* has had a considerable impact.

   c. **Burden of rejection on employer:** Under § 1113, there is clearly a heavy burden on the employer seeking to reject a collective bargaining agreement. The court can approve an application for termination of a collective bargaining agreement only if the court finds that the debtor in possession or trustee has made a proposal for modifications that assures that all creditors and affected parties are treated fairly and equitably, that it has provided the employee representative with the information necessary to evaluate the proposal, and that it has conferred with the representative in good faith in an attempt to reach mutually satisfactory modifications. Finally, the court must be satisfied that "the balance of the equities clearly favors rejection."

3. **Interim changes in collective bargaining agreement:** Under § 1113(e) and (f), it is clear that the debtor in possession or trustee cannot unilaterally terminate any provision in a collective bargaining agreement before complying with the mini collective bargaining provisions of § 1113. However, a court may permit interim changes in the terms, conditions, wages, benefits, or work rules "if essential to the continuation of the debtor's business."

VIII. CLASSES OF CLAIMS AND INTERESTS

A. **Purposes of classes:** The division of claims and interests into classes in a Chapter 11 plan serves two basic purposes. First, it establishes voting groups; *a class must either accept or reject a plan as a class*. Under § 1126, the votes of the individual members of a class establish the acceptance or rejection of the plan by that class (*infra*, p. 208). Also, under § 1129, the acceptance of the plan by the classes of claims forms the basis for the court's determination whether to confirm a plan (*infra*, p. 211). Second, the breakdown into classes determines the distributions made from the estate to the creditors and the interest (equity security) holders. For example, a class may be assigned a 15 percent recovery under the plan. If so, every member of the class must receive 15 percent of its claim (unless it specifically agrees otherwise). Different classes may be assigned different rates.

1. **Importance of class selection:** Principally because voting is conducted by classes, the creation of the classes (done by the drafter of the plan, which is usually the debtor in possession, *supra*, p. 176) is a subtle and complicated procedure that can have dramatic results on creditors.

   Example: One large unsecured creditor has a claim of $4 million resulting from a deficiency on a real estate mortgage loan and 25 small creditors have claims ranging from a few hundred to a few thousand dollars. The proposed plan deals generously with the small creditors but stingily with the large. If there is only one class of unsecured creditors, the large creditor can in effect force the class to reject the plan under the § 1126(c) voting rules. But if the large creditor is put into one class and the small creditors into another, the small class may accept the plan. The court in *In re Pine Lake Village Apartment Co.*, 19 B.R. 819 (Bkrtcy. S.D.N.Y. 1982), found that dividing creditors into two classes in this situation was not permissible. However, under the approach taken in *In re Northeast Dairy Co-op Federation, Inc.*, 73 B.R. 239 (Bkrtcy. N.D. N.Y. 1987), the division into two classes might have been permitted.

2. **Classification cannot be solely to influence voting:** An underlying policy of the classification process is that *classes may not be selected solely to influence voting results*. We will soon see that it is vital to the plan's proponent that at least one class approve the plan (*infra*, p. 212); however important this result may be, classes may not be gerrymandered to achieve this result. (See *Pine Lake, supra*.)

B. **Similar and dissimilar claims**:   Under § 1122, *all claims in a class must be similar to each other*. Although the statute does not define "similar," the courts have considered the term to mean at least that secured claims be kept separate from unsecured claims and that unsecured claims in the same class be of the same priority (priorities are discussed *supra*, p. 85). However, two similar claims need not be in the same class.

1. **Reasonable basis for separating similar claims:** *If there is a reasonable basis for separating similar claims into separate classes, it can be done.* For example, unsecured creditors that are, or represent, unionized employees may be in a separate class from unsecured creditors that are sellers or lenders. The reasonable basis for the separation is that the unionized employees have particular concerns under their collective bargaining agreements and their continuing relationship with the debtor. Tort claimants may also be in a separate class. Creditors whose claims are guaranteed may be in a different class from those without guarantees. On the other hand, similar claims cannot be put into different classes if the classifications are done for manipulative or discriminatory reasons.

2. **Small claims:**   Under § 1122(b), *a class can be created of all claims below an amount set by the court.* This grouping of small claims whose only common characteristic is size of claim is considered an appropriate administrative procedure in order to handle many minor matters together. It can in a specific case be an exception to the rule that claims in a class be similar.

3. **Secured creditors:** *Typically, each secured creditor will be in a different class because each item of security is different from all other items.* However, if the security for several secured creditors is essentially the same (for example, the security for different parcels of a subdivided lot), they may be put into the same class.

IX. UNDERSECURED CREDITORS — § 1111(b)

A. **Recourse rule for undersecured creditors:** In a Chapter 11 case, certain special rules apply to the rights of an undersecured creditor — the secured creditor whose loan to the debtor exceeds the value of the collateral securing the loan. *Under § 1111(b), with a few exceptions, non-recourse claims (those claims, as more fully described below, in which the creditor has no recourse against the debtor other than the property itself) are treated as recourse claims (those in which the creditor has a claim against the debtor for any deficiency that would result from foreclosure on the collateral).*

1. **Non-recourse claim defined:** A non-recourse claim is a secured claim under which the creditor, typically by agreement but occasionally by operation of a state law, can collect its claim only from the collateral and not "personally" from the debtor; i.e., there is no recourse against the debtor.

   Example: Creditor C loans Debtor D $100,000 secured by Blackacre alone (i.e., without recourse to D personally) and, at the time of default, Blackacre is worth only $80,000. C's ability to recoup on the loan is limited to the $80,000 value put on Blackacre. If C had made a recourse loan (i.e., it had insisted on recourse against D in addition to the amount of the claim secured by Blackacre), C would have a secured claim of $80,000 and an unsecured, deficiency claim of $20,000 against D.

2. **Conversion of non-recourse to recourse claims:** With two exceptions, a claim against a Chapter 11 debtor on a non-recourse loan will be treated as a recourse claim under § 1111(b), thereby establishing a deficiency claim against D for the undersecured portion of a loan.

B. **Exceptions from the recourse rule:** There are two exceptions as to which the rule for conversion of a secured loan from non-recourse to recourse status will not apply. *The exceptions apply when (1) the property is sold or will be sold, or (2) an election is made by the creditors of the class to treat the claims as fully secured loans.*

1. **Sale of property:** If the property is sold under § 363 (*supra*, p. 102), the recourse rule does not apply. In that event, C is able to get full value from Blackacre by buying it, using the amount of its claim as the purchase price. This is specifically permitted under § 363(k). Also, if Blackacre is to be sold under a Chapter 11 plan, the recourse rule is again inapplicable. C will again be able to get full value by buying it for his claim. (There is no provision like § 363(k) for using the claim to buy the property when it is sold under a plan, but many courts require this before the recourse rule is eliminated.)

2. **Election to be treated as a fully secured creditor:** *If the class of undersecured creditors so elects, the secured claim and the unsecured deficiency claim of each member of the class are combined into one fully secured claim.* (As noted *supra*, p. 195, each secured creditor is typically in a separate class because the security for each claim is usually different from all others.) To make the election, the affirmative vote of the class of claims must be two thirds in the amount of claims and more than half of the number of claims. In the Blackacre example above, by making the election under § 1111(b)(2), the creditor's claims for $80,000 secured and $20,000 unsecured, are changed to one claim for $100,000, all of which is secured by Blackacre.

   a. **When election cannot be made:** *The election cannot be made if: (1) the holder's interest in the property subject to the claim is of inconsequential value, or (2) the holder of the claim has recourse against the debtor and the property either is sold under § 363 or will be sold under a Chapter 11 plan.*

   b. **Reasons for making election:** The § 1111(b)(2) election is based on the expectation that Blackacre will continue to be held by D as it operates under the plan and on C's bet that Blackacre will rise in value during this period. Conceivably, C might feel that the $80,000 valuation that Blackacre received in the appraisal submitted to the Court under § 506 was too low. To whatever extent Blackacre's value increases (up to $100,000), C will benefit because Blackacre now secures the entire debt. C is also betting that the rise in value will be worth more to C than would its deficiency claim in the absence of the election. (We will see other ramifications of the § 1111(b)(2) election when we deal with confirmation of the Chapter 11 plan, *infra*, p. 214.)

   c. **Effect of making election:** In the example given, the election causes C to lose its $20,000 deficiency claim (and note that Blackacre is still worth no more than $80,000). C will also lose whatever leverage it might have in the case by voting its unsecured claim since it no longer has an unsecured claim. The election is also available to the full recourse lienholder who will also lose its deficiency rights. Without the election, the lienholder would (unless it were successful in amending the § 506(a) appraised valuation of the property at a later stage in the case) lose any appreciation in the value of Blackacre that might occur while D was holding and using the property.

X. THE PLAN

  A. General description: The central element in a Chapter 11 reorganization is the debtor's plan provided for by § 1123. ***The reorganization plan sets the debtor's future and establishes with particularity the financial relationship of the debtor, the creditors, and the other parties in interest.*** The plan describes the steps the debtor will take to accomplish its reorganization, including which debts will be paid, which will not, and which debts will be compromised and at what percentage. It describes the business operations that the debtor will undertake to see its way to ultimate financial revival.

  B. Who may file a plan and when — § 1121: The first formal step on the road to implementation of a plan is its filing with the bankruptcy court. After that, the plan will normally be widely discussed, particularly by the proponent and creditors' committees in the early stages of the reorganization.

  1. Filing by debtor: ***For the 120-day period after the order for relief, a plan may be filed only by the debtor.*** The debtor may also file a plan at any time later. In a voluntary case, the plan may be filed by the debtor at the same time as the filing of the petition.

  2. Filing by others: ***Any party in interest may file a plan, if (1) a trustee has been appointed, or (2) the debtor has not filed a plan within 120 days after the order for relief, or (3) if a plan filed by the debtor has not been accepted by all impaired classes*** (*infra*, p. 199) ***within 180 days after the order for relief.*** Parties in interest include the debtor, the trustee, a creditor or creditors' committee, an equity security holder or equity security holders' committee, and an indenture trustee (i.e., the trustee under an agreement governing an issue of debt securities, or under a mortgage or deed of trust, but excluding the trustee for a voting trust agreement).

  3. Changes in times of submission: The court, on request of a party in interest, may, for cause, reduce or increase the 120 and 180 day periods. Reduction of time periods is rare; increases in time periods, sometimes for years, is extremely common.

4. **Small business debtors:** If a debtor qualifies as a small business debtor and elects to be treated as such, shorter time periods apply.

   a. **"Small business" defined:** *A "small business", is defined under §101(51C) as a business whose total secured and unsecured debts on the date of the petition do not exceed $2,000,000.* The definition excludes businesses whose primary activity is related to owning or operating real estate.

   b. **Applicable time periods:** *During the first 100 days after the order for relief, only the small business debtor may file a plan. All plans must be filed within 160 days after the date of the order for relief.* On request by a party in interest (made within the relevant initial time period), the court may, under §1121(e), for cause, after notice and a hearing: (1) reduce the 100 and 160-day periods, or (2) increase the debtor's exclusive 100-day period, provided that the debtor can show that the need for the increase is not due to its own fault. There is no provision for an extension of the 160-day limit during which all plans must be filed.

C. **Prepackaged plans:** A major development in bankruptcy in the early 1990s was the development of the prepackaged plan. In some cases, a prepackaged plan is drafted and, frequently, acceptances are obtained, all before a petition is filed. While the Chapter 11 steps must nevertheless be taken, substantial amounts of time can be saved, since the debtor has accomplished a considerable part of the process on its own. Plans in Chapter 11 can frequently take years to spin out; a prepackaged plan can be confirmed in under two months.

D. **Mandatory contents of a plan — § 1123(a):** The statute governing the contents of a Chapter 11 plan is essentially divided between mandatory and permissive contents. The Code does not attempt to limit the scope of a plan, but it must address the following areas, as specified under § 1123(a).

1. **Classes of claims and interests:** *The plan must establish the classes of holders of claims and interests (equity security holders), which are the units into which votes for or against a plan are organized.* The writer of the plan has a great deal of discretion in selecting the classes, subject to the rules laid out in § 1122 (*supra*, p. 194).

   a. **Proof of claims:** A debt may be dealt with under the plan even if a proof of claim is not filed. Under § 1111(a), *for purposes of payment and inclusion in the plan, a claim is deemed* *filed if it is in the debtor's filed schedules* (unless it is disputed, contingent, or unliquidated); in contrast, for Chapter 7, a proof of claim must be filed by the creditor in order for it to participate in the distribution (*supra*, p. 72).

b. **Priority claims:** Under § 1129(a)(9), certain priority claimants must be paid their claims in cash or within 6 years, unless the holder of a particular priority claim has agreed otherwise. *There is no reason for creditors who receive their entire claims in this way to reject the plan; they don't have to vote and, consequently, don't have to be included in a class.*

2. **Unimpaired claims and interests:** Claims that are not impaired — those whose rights are not altered by the plan — must be identified. They will be *considered to have voted in favor of the plan*.

3. **Treatment of impaired claims and interests:** The proposed treatment of impaired claims — those whose rights are altered by the plan (*infra*) — must be identified. They have the right to vote on the plan.

   a. **Nature of impairment:** Impairment is dealt with by § 1124. Basically, it means that a claim or interest has been altered. If a claim is for $1,000 and the plan proposes to pay it $500, it is impaired; if the $1,000 was payable on June 1 and the plan proposes to pay it on July 1, the delay in payment means that the claim is impaired. Classes of claims or interests that are impaired vote on the plan (but, as we will see, even if they vote to reject the plan, they may yet be forced to accept it under the "cram down" provisions, *infra*, p. 212.)

   b. **Changes that are not impairments:** Certain changes in a creditor's or interest holder's rights are not deemed to justify the right to vote and, therefore, are not considered impairment. If a loan was in default, a curing of the default does change the rights of the claimant, but not in such a way as to constitute impairment. Even if an unpaid balance has been "accelerated" by the creditor pursuant to the terms of the contract (i.e., the remaining installments have been declared presently payable), there is no impairment if the plan proposes to reinstate the original payment terms.

4. **Equal treatment for each claim or interest in a class:** *Each claim or interest in a class must receive the same treatment as other claims or interests in the class, unless the holder of a particular claim agrees otherwise.* Thus, if one claim in a class will receive 20 percent of its amount, all claims in that class must

receive 20 percent (except as agreed otherwise). Claims in different classes need not receive the same treatment.

5. **Adequate means for plan's implementation:** Each plan must provide the means for its implementation. This fifth requirement is a broad-ranging provision giving a series of examples of acts, not meant to be exclusive, that may be undertaken by the debtor in possession in order to make the plan successful. Since more than three-quarters of Chapter 11 plans fail, this requirement has little impact. "Sincerity, honesty, and a willingness are not sufficient to make the plan feasible, and neither are any visionary promises. The test is whether the things which are to be done after confirmation can be done, as a practical matter under the facts." *Matter of Bergman*, 585 F.2d 1171, 1179 (2d Cir. 1978) (quoting Collier on *Bankruptcy*).

a. **Sale of property free of lien:** One provision suggested in the statute, which may be included in a plan as a means for its successful implementation, authorizes the sale of the debtor's property free of any lien. This is not meant to (nor could it constitutionally) destroy the rights of lienholders; a provision for lien protection is provided elsewhere in Chapter 11. (See § 1129, confirmation of plan, discussed *infra*, p. 211.)

b. **Other provisions:** Some of the other provisions for implementation of the plan suggested by the statute are:

- retention or sale of the debtor's property;
- mergers or consolidations;
- satisfaction or modification of liens;
- amendment of the debtor's charter.

c. **Preemption of state law:** As part of federal bankruptcy law, *this fifth requirement relating to implementation, preempts inconsistent areas of state law*. A typical inconsistency is a situation in which state law provides rights to parties or to a state supervisory agency that conflict with the goals of reorganization. For example, state laws guaranteeing stockholders preemptive rights that would interfere with a proposed stock distribution under a reorganization plan are considered preempted themselves and of no effect. *In re McCrory Stores Corporation*, 14 F.Supp. 739 (D.C.S.D. N.Y. 1935). Similarly, the statutory power of a public utility commission to give its approval to a reorganization has been negated. *In re Public Service Co. of New Hampshire*, 108 B.R. 854 (Bkrtcy. D.N.H. 1989). Preemption questions with respect to the fifth requirement deal principally with internal restructurings of the debtor that are needed for an effective plan. Other provisions of state or federal law must generally be complied with in the bankruptcy. (See, for example, § 1129(a)(3), *infra*, p. 210.)

6. **Amendment of corporate charter:** If new equity securities are to be issued, the plan may have to amend the debtor's charter to provide that the new securities have voting powers. Amendments may also be necessary to ensure that voting power for all securities is equitably distributed so as to give reasonable protection to the holders. The objective is to ensure that new equity holders under the plan have a say in the entity and that existing holders of voting stock are adequately represented. If the plan does not provide for the issuance of new securities, there may be no need to amend the charter. *In re Acequia*, 787 F.2d 1352 (9th Cir. 1986).

7. **Provision for fair representation:** The plan must provide that officers, directors, and trustees under the plan be selected in a manner that is consistent with the interests of creditors, equity security holders, and public policy.

   Example: A plan provided that debentures issued by the debtor would be outstanding for six years. However, directors representing the debenture holders would be appointed only for one year. The court refused approval of the plan, stating that the protection for the debenture holders was insufficient. *In re Romec Pump Co.*, 31 F. Supp. 389 (N.D. Ohio, 1939)

E. **Permissive contents of a plan — § 1123(b):** There are several provisions that the statute permits to be included in a plan. Under § 1123(b), the plan may contain the following elements, which should be contrasted with the mandatory elements contained in § 1123(a).

1. **Impair or not impair claims or interests:** This provision allows the plan to impair or not impair claims and interests. (For a full discussion of impairment, see *supra*, p. 199.) Essentially, this is a way of saying that the plan may vary the rights of claim holders, both secured and unsecured, and of equity interest holders, or it may leave them unchanged from what they were before the bankruptcy. (Secured claim holders are given certain protections in § 1129 to ensure that their property rights are not taken. *supra*, p. 196.) Note that this provision is closely related to the mandatory provisions requiring that unimpaired classes be identified as such and that the treatment of impaired classes be specified.

2. **Assume / reject / assign executory contracts & leases:** Under § 365(d)(2) (*supra*, p. 114), the debtor may accept or reject an executory contract or unexpired lease at any time up to the confirmation

of a Chapter 11 plan. The second permissive provision, which allows the plan to assume, reject, or assign executory contracts and leases, provides a vehicle in the plan for such action, assuming that it has not occurred at an earlier time.

3. **Settlement or retention of specified claim or interest:** The plan may provide for the settlement or adjustment of any claim or interest, or for the retention and enforcement of any claim or interest.

4. **Liquidation plans:** Under § 1123(b)(4), *the plan may provide for the sale of all or substantially all of the debtor's assets and the distribution of the proceeds among holders of claims or interests.*

   a. **Comparison to liquidation under Chapter 7:** We have previously observed that this authorization gives Chapter 11 a flavor similar to a liquidation under Chapter 7 (*supra*, p. 154). However, a Chapter 11 case typically takes longer than a case in Chapter 7, particularly since Chapter 11 requires creditor approval of the plan; but Chapter 7 does permit some delay in the process of liquidation. Because Chapter 11 requires a plan and creditor approval it is essentially different from Chapter 7. Whatever is done in Chapter 11 must conform to the plan as confirmed; Chapter 7 gives discretion for liquidation and distribution to the trustee. Also, note that, in our discussion of § 363 (*supra*, p. 154), the property of the estate can be sold with court approval, without creditor consent. This differs from the treatment under a Chapter 11 liquidation plan.

   b. **Limited flexibility of §363 under Chapter 11 liquidation plan:** Generally, there is very limited flexibility in selling substantially all of an estate's property under § 363 without first following all the requirements of a Chapter 11 plan. The courts will not make exceptions unless there is a compelling business reason.

      Example: The major asset of Debtor D in a Chapter 11 case is an 82 percent interest in a majority-owned subsidiary. The creditors' committee believes that the subsidiary should be sold even before acceptance of a plan of reorganization because D will come into a fund of cash that can be used to pay creditors. D's equity holders feel otherwise and believe that continued retention of the subsidiary can benefit D's long range health. The bankruptcy court and the district court agreed with the creditors' committee. The Second Circuit disagreed and reversed because there was no compelling need to sell. It was better, particularly in view of the disagreement between claims and interests, to go through the entire Chapter 11 procedure, get full consideration of all the options and the views of all parties on what was best to do. *In re Lionel Corp.*, 722 F.2d 1063 (2nd Cir. 1983).

    c. Refiling under Chapter 11 with a liquidation plan: Although the Code is silent on the subject, it has been held that, if a Chapter 11 reorganization attempt fails, even after its confirmation by the court (*infra*, p. 209), the debtor may refile for a Chapter 11 liquidation plan. It is not required to go into Chapter 7, although that option is also available to it. *In re Jartran, Inc.*, 886 F.2d 859 (7th Cir. 1989).

5. Modification or retention of creditor claims: The rights of holders of secured claims, other than on the individual debtor's principal residence, and of unsecured claims, may be modified or retained.

6. Other appropriate provisions in plan: The sixth permissive provision allows the inclusion of other appropriate plan provisions. Plans can become quite lengthy and complex, particularly when dealing with the future of large businesses.

XI.   DISCLOSURE AND SOLICITATION — § 1125

A. Importance of disclosure: Under § 1125, information concerning the plan must be disclosed to the holders of claims and interests who will vote on the plan. Congress has called the disclosure statement the "heart" of Chapter 11. ***The disclosure documents must be approved by the court, after notice and a hearing, as containing adequate information.***

B. The concept of "adequate information": The holders of claims and interests must receive "adequate information" in order to make an informed decision in voting for or against a plan. What constitutes adequate information turns on the complexity of the particular plan and the nature of the recipient. Generally, reorganizations of larger businesses will entail more complex plans and, consequently, will require that the voters get more information. One court prepared a list of 19 factors to test the adequacy of information. However, even these included such subjective standards as "information relevant to the risks posed to creditors under the plan." *In re Metocraft Publ. Services, Inc.*, 39 B.R. 567 (Bkrtcy. N.D.Ga. 1984). Most courts simply use their discretion based upon the situation before them.

1. **Usual criteria:** In most cases, the recipients should be told such things as:

   - what payment or property they will receive under the plan;

   - how that payment or property will be obtained and from what source;

   - how long the plan will take to be implemented;

   - what the business projections are and what they are based upon;

   - whether there are any major contingencies such as major lawsuits;

   - who will run the business; and

   - what the liquidation value of the business is (so that, under the best-interest-of-creditor test, a comparison can be made to the alternative results in Chapter 7 bankruptcy).

2. **Other sources of information:** The courts will also try to review the information the holders of claims and interests have received from other sources, such as, for example, proxy materials; the better informed the voters are and the better their access to alternative sources, the less information they must receive under § 1125.

C. **Documentation required to be sent:**   Under § 1125(b), *the plan, or a summary of the plan, and a written disclosure statement must be transmitted to the claims and interest holders.* In less complex cases, the disclosure statement may just parrot the plan itself. The requirement of distributing plan and statement must be fulfilled prior to solicitation of formal acceptances of a plan. However, communications just short of an actual solicitation of formal acceptance for a plan have been found permissible.

Example: Before solicitation documents are approved and sent, the debtor D and creditor C enter into a stipulation that binds them to use their best efforts to obtain confirmation as soon as practicable of a plan embodying their compromise of a $13 billion tort obligation. The stipulation is challenged by four creditors who assert that acceptance by C of the plan has been solicited by D without the proper documents. The court permitted the stipulation, holding that a stipulation to obtain acceptances was not the same thing as acceptance. *In re Texaco, Inc.*, 81 B.R. 813 (Bkrtcy. S.D.N.Y. 1988). (This case also illustrates the flexibility a court will apply to find its way out of a very difficult case.)

1. **Requirement of court approval:**   Under § 1125(b), the bankruptcy court must approve the adequacy of the information offered. Hearings on the adequacy of disclosure statements are typically held.

2. **Variations among classes:** The division into classes required by § 1123 has a bearing also on solicitations. Under § 1125(c), ***all members of a class must receive the same disclosure documents.*** However, documents may vary among classes. In actual practice, usually one set of documents goes to voters in all classes.

3. **Unimpaired claim and interest holders:** ***Holders of claims and interests that are not impaired, as well as those holders who receive nothing at all, don't vote.*** The policy of § 1125 would seem to indicate that holders of unimpaired claims and interests need not receive disclosure documents. However, the courts differ on this point. Some courts have held that unimpaired holders should be informed in order to participate actively in the proceedings and be able to influence others to vote either for or against the plan.

4. **Small business debtors:** In cases where the debtor qualifies as, and has elected to be treated as, a small business debtor (see *supra*, p. 198), the court is permitted to make a conditional approval of the disclosure statement, without notice and a hearing. Solicitations may be made with respect to a conditionally approved plan provided that adequate information is actually supplied to those who are solicited. The conditionally approved disclosure statement is subject to final approval at a hearing, which can be combined with the confirmation hearing. The conditionally approved disclosure statement must be mailed at least 10 days prior to the date of the confirmation hearing.

D. **Prepetition solicitation:** A plan proponent is permitted by § 1126(b) to attempt to obtain approval for its plan before the bankruptcy begins. ***If prepetition solicitation is conducted, targeted voters must get either whatever disclosures may be required by non-bankruptcy law or, if no other laws are applicable, "adequate information" as required under § 1125.*** Partly because it is difficult to be certain whether prepetition solicitations contain what will later be considered "adequate information," they are not frequently conducted.

1. **Application of securities laws:** The non-bankruptcy law applicable to prepetition solicitations is principally the laws applicable to the distribution of securities (the plan and disclosure statement may be considered a "security") under the Securities Act of 1933 or to proxy solicitations under the Securities Exchange Act of 1934. State securities laws may also be relevant. Although, as discussed (*infra*, p. 207), proceedings under bankruptcy law are largely exempt from federal securities law, prepetition solicitations are not exempt because bankruptcy law is not applicable until the petition is filed.

2. **Validity of prepetition solicitations:** Even if solicitations are properly made, there are additional requirements under Rule 3018(b) for determining whether the acceptances or rejections of the plan will be deemed valid.

E. **Communications by other than plan proponents:** Once adequate information has been supplied to the creditors with respect to a plan, there is generally no limit on communications among creditors for and against the plan. ***The opponents of the plan may actively solicit votes against the plan.*** The communications by opponents may include the draft of a different plan that has not received the approval of the court under the adequate information standard, provided an actual solicitation for votes for the unapproved plan is not made. This interpretation is based on the wording of § 1121(b), which provides for a 120 day exclusive period in which the debtor may file a plan; the statute does *not* provide that only the debtor can conduct solicitations with respect to that plan. In addition, the purpose of the Bankruptcy Code is to facilitate free negotiation among parties regarding a proposed plan; therefore, negotiations over the plan will not be readily construed as solicitations of an alternate plan. ***The term "solicitation" is given a narrow interpretation to mean the actual solicitation of an official vote for a plan.***

Example: Debtor D files a plan of reorganization. Creditor C1 announces at the disclosure hearing that it will file an alternate plan after D's exclusive period has expired. After D's disclosure statement is approved by the court, C1 successfully solicits the vote of another creditor C2 against D's plan. In the course of communications between C1 and C2, C2 requests a copy of C1's plan. D claims that C1 has improperly solicited and procured the rejection vote of C2. The court found that C1 had not violated D's exclusive period under § 1121(b), nor the requirement for an approved disclosure document under § 1125(b). Prior court approval of all solicitation materials was not required because the disclosure document with respect to D's plan had been approved by the court. C1 was held not to have solicited votes for its own plan in violation of § 1125(b) because the presentation of a draft plan for the purpose of negotiation was not the solicitation of an actual vote for C1's plan. *First American Bank of New York v. Century Glove,* 81 B.R. 274 (D.Del. 1988), aff'd in part, 860 F.2d 94 (1988).

F. **Good faith requirement:** Although the Code affords great latitude to the creditors to communicate among themselves, ***there is a general good faith requirement with respect to voting and the solicitation of votes.***

1. **Bad faith invalidation of votes:** Under § 1126(e), the court has the authority to invalidate votes that were not made in good faith,

or votes not solicited or procured in good faith or in accordance with bankruptcy law. This authority is exercised at the request of a party in interest and after notice and a hearing.

2. **Safe harbor protection:** *One who solicits in good faith and in accordance with the provisions of § 1125 will have no liability on account of any possible violation of other applicable law.* "Other law" refers mainly to federal and state securities laws. The safe harbor applies only in the event that the disclosure and solicitation requirements of § 1125 are fulfilled.

G. **Role of securities laws and the SEC:** The role of the securities laws and the Securities and Exchange Commission with respect to bankruptcy cases has markedly diminished with the enactment of the 1978 Code. The Chapter 11 plan that creditors and interest holders are solicited to accept would probably constitute a "security" under the federal securities laws except for provisions of the Code that provide their own controlling law. Under the old Act, Chapter 10, no longer in existence, required the SEC's participation in all cases. However, the SEC continues to be brought into the operation of the Code either explicitly or by implication in several ways.

1. **Relevant to prepetition solicitations:** If applicable, prepetition solicitations must be prepared under the requirements of laws other than the Code, usually federal securities laws (*supra*, p. 205).

2. **Participation by the Securities and Exchange Commission — § 1109:** *The SEC is explicitly invited by § 1109 to appear and be heard on any issue in a Chapter 11 case, but it is refused the right to appeal judgments, orders, or decrees of the court.*

3. **Exemption from securities laws — § 1145:** The exemption of offers and sales of securities in bankruptcy cases from federal and state securities laws is explicitly provided for in § 1145.

   a. **Offers and sales:** Under a reorganization plan, the offer of a security in exchange for a claim (the creditor relinquishes its claim and receives a security from the debtor in its place), or the offer of a security along with cash or property in exchange for a claim, does not require registration of the offer under the Securities Act of 1933 or under any state securities laws (generally called "blue sky" laws). Securities of an issuer other than the debtor in the Chapter 11 case may be offered or sold under the plan if (1) the debtor owned the securities when the bankruptcy petition was filed, (2) the issuer of the securities is itself in compliance with the securities laws, and (3) the securities represent only a small percentage, as defined in § 1145(a)(3), of the issuer's securities.

b. **Other transactions:** Other transactions that may bring the securities laws into play are exempted by § 1145. Among them are the offering of securities of the debtor for cash and the further distribution of securities of the debtor through purchase by a third party of securities issued under the plan. In addition, with respect to the issuance of debt securities under a plan, the Trust Indenture Act of 1939 does not apply to notes whose maturity is no later than one year after the effective date of the plan.

XII. ACCEPTANCE BY CREDITORS AND EQUITY SHAREHOLDERS — § 1126

Note: For purposes of the plan's acceptance or rejection, the class is the relevant voting unit. This section discusses acceptance as it applies to the several different types of classes. The extent to which all classes must accept a plan in order for it to be confirmed will be discussed in connection with confirmation by the court (*infra*, p. 211).

A. **Acceptance by class of claims:** Under § 1126(c), *a plan is accepted by a class if the plan has been approved by creditors in the class holding at least two-thirds in amount and more than one-half in number of the allowed claims.* If the voting results do not meet these requirements, the plan is rejected. Because of this requirement, it is apparent that the holder of a very large claim can prevent the class to which it belongs from accepting. The results of having even one non-accepting class will be seen in our discussion of confirmation (*infra*, p. 212).

B. **Acceptance by class of interests:** *A class of interests (equity security holders) accepts a plan if interest holders that hold at least two-thirds in amount of allowed interests approve.*

C. **Non-impaired classes deemed to approve:** *If a class of claims or interests is not impaired* (see *supra*, p. 199), *it is conclusively presumed to accept the plan.* The strategy of class selection again becomes evident: if a group of claims or interest holders whose claims and interests will not be impaired can be identified and, if they can be put in their own class, acceptance by that class is guaranteed. Under § 1126(f), since the acceptance of non-impaired claims is assumed, no solicitation for their votes is required. This does not mean that disclosure documents should not be provided to the non-impaired classes. We have noted the uncertainty on this point (*supra*, p. 205).

D. **Classes receiving nothing deemed to reject:** *If a class receives nothing under the plan, it is deemed under § 1126(f) to reject the plan.* Particularly with respect to equity interests, this raises the question of what will be considered nothing. For example, holders of partnership interests in a farm whose debts well exceeded its assets claimed that they had received nothing of value. The Supreme Court, in *Norwest Bank Worthington v. Ahlers*, 485 U.S. 197 (1988), disagreed and, consistent with most lower court decisions, held that ***an equity interest in a business necessarily had value because it gave the holders a potential opportunity to share in future profits and in increases in the worth of the business.***

XIII. CONFIRMATION BY THE COURT — §§ 1128, 1129

A. **Confirmation:** A plan becomes official and binding upon the parties when the court accepts it. The acceptance is called "confirmation" and the process of obtaining it is governed by § 1128 and § 1129. ***The bankruptcy court, after notice, must hold a hearing on whether the plan should be confirmed.***

B. **Requirements for confirmation — § 1129(a):** Under § 1129(a), there are 13 requirements that must be met for a plan to be confirmed. The only exception to these requirements is with respect to the eighth requirement, which need not be met if the plan and the votes satisfy the cramdown provision of § 1129(b) (*infra*, p. 211). The requirements for confirmation under § 1129 are as follows.

1. **Plan compliance:** The plan must comply with the requirements of the Code.

2. **Proponent of plan compliance:** The proponent of the plan must comply with the Code. If the plan satisfies the Code, it is not clear why there is a separate test for its proponent. If the proponent must separately satisfy the Code and the proponent need not be the debtor, it is also not clear why the other parties in interest do not have to satisfy the Code.

3. **Good faith proposal:** The plan must be proposed in good faith and not be in violation of any law. Under this third requirement, the courts generally agree that the meaning of good faith is different from the meaning defining other acts, such as the original filing of the Chapter 11 petition or the creditor's good faith in accepting or rejecting a plan under § 1126(e). ***Good faith in proposing a plan usually means that there exists a reasonable likelihood that the plan will achieve a result consistent with the objectives and purposes of the Code.*** Review of the debtor's behavior before the petition, its reasons for falling into bankruptcy, and its motives in filing the petition in the first place, are usually considered irrele-

vant to its good faith in proposing the plan. *Matter of Madison Hotel Associates*, 749 F.2d 410 (7th Cir. 1984). The courts are in disagreement on whether a bankruptcy filing made in bad faith should cause a court to reject a bankruptcy plan proposed in good faith.

    a. Not in violation of other laws: One provision in this third requirement for confirmation, i.e., that the plan not be proposed "by any means forbidden by law," has been interpreted to mean that ***the plan must abide by rules of state and federal law.*** If, for example, state corporation law requires cumulative voting and the plan provides otherwise, the plan cannot be confirmed in the absence of a compelling reason for violating the state law. *In re Mahoney*, 80 B.R. 197 (Bkrtcy. S.D.Cal. 1987). In this connection, note that the requirement that a reorganization plan provide adequate means for its implementation contemplates that state law may have to be preempted if it conflicts with the goals of the reorganization. Laws outside the Code are sometimes honored without reference to the provisions of § 1129 at all. *Board of Governors v. MCorp Financial, Inc.*, 502 U.S. 32 (1991). In one case, it was observed that the Code sometimes honors other laws and sometimes not. *In re Public Service Co. of New Hampshire*, *supra*, p. 200.

4. **Fees in connection with case must be reasonable:** *Payments made or to be made for costs in connection with the case or the plan must be approved by, or are subject to the approval of, the court as reasonable.* The payments may be made by the proponent of the plan, the debtor, or any other party issuing securities or acquiring property under the plan. Under § 327(a), the court is required to approve the employment of counsel, but most courts hold that the inclusion of counsel fees in a plan, even without such prior approval, will be permitted so long as the court has been aware of counsel's participation. *In re Tinsley and Groom*, 49 B.R. 94 (Bkrtcy. W.D. Ky. 1985).

5. **Identities of proposed directors and officers and other major persons:** The identity of those who are proposed to be directors, officers, affiliates participating in the plan, and successors under the terms of the plan, must be disclosed. Their appointment or continuation in office must be consistent with the interests of creditors, equity security holders, and public policy. The identity of insiders who will be employed and the nature of their compensation must also be disclosed.

6. **Regulatory rate commission approvals:** If publicly regulated rates are to be changed by the plan, appropriate regulatory approval must be obtained or the rate changes must be conditioned on such approval.

7. **Impaired interests:** *Assuming that a class is impaired, each member of that class must either have accepted the plan or receive sufficient property under the plan to satisfy the "best interests of creditor" test.*

   a. **Best interests of creditor test:** *The best interests of creditor test is a comparison between what creditors, both secured and unsecured, are to receive under the plan with what they would have received in a Chapter 7 liquidation.* The test discounts the value of what each creditor will receive in the future to the value of that amount on the plan's effective date. This means, for example, that, if a creditor is to receive $1,000 in the future, he may receive less than $1,000 if value is calculated back to the plan's effective date. The courts are not in agreement on what rate of interest should be applied to establish the discount. Some use the rate in the underlying credit agreement; some attempt to find a "market" rate; some use the state's usury limit. The value received on the plan's effective date must be at least what the creditor would receive under a Chapter 7 liquidation. This affords secured as well as unsecured creditors protection, since a secured creditor will receive the value of its security measured as it would have been in a Chapter 7 liquidation.

   b. **Exception for § 1111(b)(2) electors:** If a secured creditor has made the § 1111(b)(2) election (applicable to undersecured creditors and allowing the combination of a secured claim and the unsecured deficiency claim into one fully secured claim, *supra*, p. 196), the seventh requirement for confirmation requires that the creditor whose secured claim is no longer limited to the value of the collateral, receive property whose value is not less than the creditor's interest (the fully secured claim) in the secured property. Since § 1111(b)(2) is applicable only to Chapter 11 cases, there is no Chapter 7 equivalent.

8. **Acceptance by each class:** The eighth requirement for confirmation is that each class must either accept the plan or not be impaired. Since a class that is not impaired is deemed by the Code to accept the plan (*supra*, p. 208), this provision appears to require 100% acceptance of the plan. The burden of this requirement is lessened by the provision in § 1129(b) (*infra*, p. 212), which allows a plan to be crammed down on creditors who would otherwise reject and also provides protection to rejecting secured creditors.

9. **Priority claims:** The ninth requirement for confirmation deals with claims given priority under § 507 (*supra*, p. 85). ***Priority claims must be separated into groups: those who must receive 100% in cash as of the effective date; those who must receive cash or accept a plan providing for deferred payments valued in the amount of their claims at the effective date; and those to whom payments may be made over a period of not more than six years.*** Note that preferred creditors who are designated to receive cash or payments within six years are not put into classes under § 1123(a)(1) (*supra*, p. 199). The Code prescribes their treatment under the plan; they receive payment either immediately in cash or over a defined time period; and there is thus no need either for their votes or for their receipt of distributions as part of a class.

10. **Acceptance by one impaired class:** If any class of claims is impaired, which is the case in all but a very few bankruptcies, ***at least one class of impaired claims must accept the plan.*** The deemed acceptances by non-impaired classes are not counted for this purpose. The goal is to reduce the power of the plan's proponent to engineer acceptance through the manipulation of classes. At least one class whose rights are changed by the plan must decide affirmatively in its favor.

11. **Plan feasibility:** The eleventh requirement for confirmation is that the plan not be likely to result in liquidation of the debtor or the need for further reorganization unless liquidation or further reorganization is proposed in the plan. This is analogous to the requirement under § 1123(a)(5) that a plan contain an adequate means for the plan's success. Since most reorganization plans are followed by the liquidation of the debtor, the Code would seem to need some tightening in this area.

12. **Payment of fees:** All fees must be paid or the plan must provide that they will be paid on the effective date of the plan.

13. **Retiree benefits:** The thirteenth requirement for confirmation is that the retiree benefits for which a debtor is obligated, as established under § 1114, must continue to be paid.

C. **Cram down — § 1129(b):** On its face, the eighth requirement for plan acceptance appears to require the acceptance of 100% of the classes of claims and interests (*supra*, p. 211). Under § 1129(b), however, there is relief from this requirement by allowing, as bankruptcy practitioners say, that the plan be "crammed down" on certain of those who have rejected it. The idea underlying the cram down provision is that opposing creditors have received the best that they can get from this debtor and that their continuing opposition is irrational. *A plan may be crammed down if the court finds, on the request of the proponents of the plan, that two basic tests are met: first, that the plan "does not discriminate unfairly"; and, second, that it "is fair and equitable" with respect to each class of claims and interests that have not voted in favor of the plan.*

1. **Unfair discrimination test:** Unfair discrimination under Chapter 11 has a meaning that is similar to other areas of the law, i.e., disparate treatment of those similarly situated without a rational and acceptable reason. As one would expect, courts have taken different views of exactly what constitutes discrimination.

   a. **Unfair discrimination defined:** Since the Code provides that there may be more than one class of unsecured claims, it follows that there is likely to be some discrimination in the way in which the different classes are treated. But it is only discrimination that is unfair that is prohibited. The courts have frequently applied a four-part test to determine whether unfair discrimination exists:

      • Whether the discrimination is supported by a reasonable basis;

      • Whether the debtor can confirm and consummate a plan without the discrimination;

      • Whether the discrimination is proposed in good faith; and

      • Analysis of the treatment of the classes discriminated against.

      In re 11,111, Inc., 117 B.R. 471 (Bkrtcy. D. Minn. 1990).

   b. **Examples of discriminatory treatment:** To put a large creditor into a class by itself just because it is large may be discrimination. *In re Pine Lake Village Apartment Co. (supra*, p. 193). To lower the rate on one mortgage and leave the rate untouched on another mortgage on the same property is discrimination. *In re Dilts*, 100 B.R. 759 (Bkrtcy. W.D. Pa. 1989). On the other hand, where different unsecured creditors can be shown to have different rights against the debtor, it is not unfair discrimination to put them into different classes. Different views on whether claims are or are not sufficiently different to be put into different classes, and thus receive different treatment, are exemplified by the affirmance and reversal of several cases. *In re Greystone III Joint Venture*, 102 B.R. 560 (Bkrtcy. W.D.Tex.), aff'd, 127 B.R. 138 (W.D. Tex), rev'd, 948 F.2d 134 (5th Cir.), cert. denied, 113 S.Ct. 72 (1992).

2. **Fair and equitable test:** It is hardly possible to offer a succinct definition of what is meant by "fair and equitable", the second test under § 1129(b). First, the statute presents the test in general terms. Then it applies it mechanically to three specific groups — secured creditors, unsecured creditors, and interest holders. If the mechanical conditions set forth in the statute are met, a plan will be found to be fair and equitable as to the parties involved. Secured creditors must get full value out of their security. For unsecured creditors, a variation on the "absolute priority rule" applies.

a. **Factors in applying test:** As we shall see, the heart of the test of fairness is the ***"absolute priority rule," which decrees that one in a senior position must be paid in full before anyone in a junior position may receive anything.*** However, the rule is not the only test of "fair and equitable." Courts will also look to see whether the plan is fair and equitable to the impaired classes by looking at such common sense factors as:

- *the feasibility of the plan; In re Hallanger*, 15 B.R. 35 (Bkrtcy. W.D.La. 1981);

- *the treatment of creditors*, including the periods of time they will have to wait for payment; *In re Sanders Coal & Trucking, Inc.*, 129 B.R. 516 (Bkrtcy. E.D. Tenn. 1991); and

- *the rate of interest they are to receive* and how it relates to market rates; *In re Edgewater Motel, Inc.*, 85 B.R. 989 (Bkrtcy. E.D. Tenn. 1988).

Example: A plan provides for payments to a creditor of $178 thousand per month but the projected income is only $87 thousand per month. The plan was not fair and equitable. *In re Pine Lake Village Apartment Co. (supra*, p. 193).

b. **Secured creditors:** Impaired secured creditors have the right to reject the plan, but the plan's proponents have the opportunity to force the secured creditors to accept through cramdown. However, *a plan may not be forced on a secured creditor unless it is fair and equitable, which includes but is not limited to the requirement that the secured creditor retain the security interest or its equivalent.* If the § 1111(b)(2) election is made, the allowed amount of the creditor's secured claim will be the full claim, not restricted to the value of the collateral at the time of the bankruptcy, as it would have been had the § 506 division into secured and unsecured elements been retained (*supra*, p. 80). A plan will be considered fair and equitable to a secured claim holder if one of the following three conditions is met.

i. **Lien plus cash:** The holder retains its lien and also receives cash payments equalling the allowed amount of its secured claim (§ 502, *supra*, p. 75). These payments must have a present value as of the effective date of the plan equal to the collateral's value (note that this requires a valuation back from the actual payment date to the effective date of the plan to account for the time value of money); or

ii. **Lien on proceeds plus cash:** if the collateral is sold, the lien applies to the proceeds of the sale and the plan provides for the lienholder to receive what it would have received under (i) above or (iii) below; or

iii. **"Indubitable equivalent:"** The plan provides for the realization by the lienholder of the "indubitable equivalent" of its secured claim. The term "indubitable equivalent" is used both in § 1129(b) and in § 361 (*supra*, p. 43). Its meaning is probably the same in both sections. The best example of "indubitable equivalent" occurs where the secured property is abandoned to the secured party who then actually has its security in hand (§ 554 *supra*, p. 101). Where property of the same market value was proposed to be transferred from the debtor to a secured creditor, indubitable equivalence was not found because the cash flow from the new property was below that of the original property. *In re B.W. Alpha, Inc.*, 89 B.R. 592 (Bkrtcy. N.D. Tex.), aff'd, 100 B.R. 831 (N.D. Tex. 1988).

c. **Unsecured creditors:** The plan may be crammed down in situations where a class of unsecured creditors fail to vote in its favor, if the "absolute priority rule" is observed. The rule dictates that classes of senior rank must be paid in full before classes of junior rank receive anything. If all claim holders in a given class are paid in full under the plan (based upon the present value of the payments computed as of the time the plan becomes effective), they may be crammed down. *If they receive less than full payment, they may still be crammed down if all claims that are junior to them receive nothing.*

i. **Seniority of classes:** The seniority of classes in a cramdown is established by principles of law both inside and outside the Code. The most fundamental rule, and *the one most often raised in cram down disputes, is the rule applicable to corporations providing that creditors get paid before stockholders* (and are therefore senior in rank to stockholders). Seniority may be established by agreement, particularly subordination agreements, that are honored in bankruptcy through the application of § 510 (*supra*, p. 91). Corporate debt obligations titled "subordinated" have a level of seniority below those titled or referred to as "senior." The priority system under § 507 of the Code also creates levels of seniority with respect to distributions from the estate (*supra*, p. 85).

Example: A corporation has senior debt, subordinated debt, and equity stockholders. The plan grants the senior debt 90 percent of its claims; it is impaired but it accepts the plan. The subordinated debt is awarded only 50 percent and it rejects the plan. The stockholders are left with nothing. The plan fails the § 1129(a)(8) test of confirmation (because an impaired class, the subordinated debt, has not accepted), but is saved under the cram down provision in § 1129(b). The plan may be crammed down on the rejecting class so long as no class beneath it receives anything. The assumption is that, if in fact no class beneath it receives anything, the plan has done as well with the rejecting class as it can do; the class has no right to ask for more; and it cannot hold up the plan.

ii. **Definition of "nothing:"** A frequent question is what constitutes "nothing" for the stockholders, the only class lower in the pecking order than the subordinated debt. This question has already been addressed in connection with voting under § 1126(g) and the *Ahlers* case (*supra*, p. 208). *If the stockholders retain their stock and their ownership interests, even in a corporation with a zero net worth and questionable prospects of paying dividends, they still have something; a cram down cannot be accomplished.* Therefore, the stockholders must be eliminated. The question naturally arises: who owns the corporation if there are no stockholders? The answer is: ownership must be provided for in the plan. Perhaps some or all of the creditors will accept stock in exchange for their claims and become the new owners. Another possibility will be discussed in connection with the "new value exception," (*infra*, p. 217).

d. **Classes of interests:** A plan will be found to be fair and equitable with respect to a class of interests (principally the equity interests of stockholders or partners) if each member of the class receives either (1) the greatest of either the allowed amount of any liquidation preference, or the fixed redemption price to which it is entitled, or the value of the interest, or (2) as with unsecured claims, if any interest that is lower in the order of priorities receives nothing. For the typical stock corporation, all claims (which are necessarily senior to interests) must be paid in full under the plan or accept the plan before the issue of whether the stock interests are subject to cram down arises. (If claims are not paid in full or do not accept, they will have to be crammed down, which means that the stock interests must be eliminated under the *Ahlers* principle, *supra*, p. 208.)

3. **The new value exception:** To cram down a claim on unsecured claimants, the holders of equity interests must be eliminated. Whether those holders can retain their equity interests through a new infusion of capital is in some question. ***The Supreme Court, well before adoption of the Code in 1978, had held that the supply of new capital gave equity interests an exception from the absolute priority rule and enabled them to remain as stockholders.*** *Case v. Los Angeles Lumber Co.*, 308 U.S. 106 (1939). In the *Ahlers* case, the Court cast some doubt upon the *Los Angeles Lumber* rule in a footnote gratuitously questioning its continued vitality. (In *Ahlers*, the Court held that the services the owners of the farm in reorganization planned to supply, would not constitute new value under the *Los Angeles Lumber* principle.) Most of the courts considering the new value exception have held that it continues as good law. Typically, they have held that the new value must be real value, in money or money's worth, and that it must be substantial. In a recent Supreme Court case, *Bank of America National Trust and Savings Ass'n v. 203 N. LaSalle St.*, 526 U.S. 434 (1999), the Court did not rule out a possible reading of the Code that provides for the exception. However, it held that the exception could not apply to the facts of the particular case. There was no bidding for the stockholder position and the Court probably thought the new capital contributors had achieved an unfair benefit. More acceptable facts could yield a different result.

XIV. EFFECT OF CONFIRMATION — § 1141

A. **The plan binds the parties in interest:** By confirming a plan under § 1129, the bankruptcy court gives its seal of approval to the plan. ***Upon confirmation, the plan binds the debtor, the creditors, and the holders of equity security interests.*** It also binds any entity issuing securities under the plan and any entity acquiring property of the debtor under the plan. In so doing, it protects third parties against "successor liability" statutes, which are designed to prevent sellers (including debtors) who are responsible for a defective product from avoiding liability through the sale of assets. *In re White Motor Credit Corp.*, 75 B.R. 944 (Bkrtcy. N.D. Ohio 1987).

B. Vests property in debtor: Except as otherwise provided in the plan, confirmation vests all of the property remaining in the estate in the debtor. The debtor in possession thereupon disappears as a legal entity and the duties of a trustee end.

C. Effect upon liens: The property dealt with by the plan is free of all adverse claims, including liens, except as otherwise provided in the plan. As noted (*supra*, p. 211), the interests of lienholders are protected by § 1129(a)(7) and no property interest is lost that would violate the requirement for the payment of just compensation under the Constitution.

D. Discharge of debts: Confirmation of a plan *discharges all of the debtor's debts that arose before the date of the confirmation.*

    1. Contrast with Chapter 7: The discharge in Chapter 11 contrasts with a Chapter 7 discharge, which discharges only the debts (§ 727(b) *supra*, p. 163) that arose before the filing of the bankruptcy petition (with qualifications in § 502, *supra*, p. 77). For example, administrative claims, which typically arise after the petition, are discharged in Chapter 11; in Chapter 7, they generally are not (*supra*, p. 77).

    2. Contrast with Chapter 13: In Chapter 13, debts of an individual are generally not discharged until payments under the plan are completed (see § 1328 *infra*, p. 246). The earlier date for discharge upon confirmation of the plan in a Chapter 11 case is appropriate because the plan cannot be confirmed without creditor approval or the imposition of cramdown. Presumably, Chapter 11 matters know what they are getting into and accept the consequences.

    3. Necessity of proof of claim: Debts are discharged under § 1141(d)(1) whether or not a proof of claim is filed and whether or not the claim is "allowed" under § 502 (*supra*, p. 75). This is consistent with the approaches to discharge in other chapters of the Code.

    4. Exceptions for individuals: Under § 1141(d)(2), exceptions from discharge applicable to individuals under § 523 (*supra*, p. 75) are made applicable to discharges for individuals under Chapter 11.

    5. Exception for non-individual liquidations: We have noted that only individuals can obtain discharges in Chapter 7 since partnerships and corporations will dissolve as a consequence of their liquidation (*supra*, p. 53); discharges would be superfluous. However, *discharges are appropriate for partnerships and corporations under Chapter 11, since the essence of Chapter 11 is that they continue their existence and therefore need discharges from those obligations that are not assumed under the plan.* Because Chapter 11 also provides for liquidation plans, the statute contains a scheme compatible with the provisions of Chapter 7 for such plans. Under § 1141(d)(3), if: (i) the Chapter 11 plan is of the liquidation type; (ii) the debtor does not engage in business after its consummation; and (iii) the debtor would be denied a discharge under Chapter 7, then a discharge will be denied under Chapter 11. In this regard, note that only an individual can receive a discharge under Chapter 7.

6. **Supplemental injunctions:** In our discussion of §524, *supra*, p. 59-62, we noted that a discharge operates as an injunction. The court may issue additional injunctions in support of the discharge. These injunctions may, among other things, enjoin entities from taking legal action to collect or receive payment that would interfere with the effect of the discharge.

XV. IMPLEMENTATION OF PLAN — § 1142

A. **Debtor must carry out plan — § 1142:** The statute provides *"the debtor and any entity organized or to be organized for the purpose of carrying out the plan shall carry out the plan."* The plan becomes an order of the court and, as such, any effort to subvert it can be met with an action for contempt. Typically, the bankruptcy court can and does issue orders and injunctions in support of the plan. The court retains jurisdiction over the case for this purpose until it is closed by an order under § 350.

CHAPTER 12

FILING UNDER CHAPTER 12 — FAMILY FARMER WITH REGULAR ANNUAL INCOME

I. UNIQUE NEEDS OF FARMERS

A. Difficulty of filing under other Chapters: Although many farmers were hard hit by the events of the 1980s, few filed for bankruptcy. Congressional analysis revealed that no farmers were filing under the Code because neither Chapter 11 nor Chapter 13 of the Code met the particular needs of the family farmer.

  1. Difficulty in using Chapter 13: Farmers who ran into financial difficulties generally owed too much to qualify for consumer reorganization under Chapter 13 (*infra,* pp. 227-248). Also, certain procedures required of people who file under Chapter 13, such as the short time frame within which a plan must be proposed and within which payments must start after the plan is filed (*infra,* p. 245), dissuaded farmers from filing under Chapter 13.

  2. Difficulty in using Chapter 11: The only alternative for a farmer who wanted to reorganize — rather than just quit by filing under Chapter 7 of the Code — was the highly complex Chapter 11 (*supra,* p. 245), and few farmers took advantage of that avenue.

B. Creation of a new Chapter: Congress has always been sensitive to the unique needs of farmers, who have so much of their capital tied up in the land on which they live and work. ***The main impetus behind the creation of Chapter 12 in 1986 was the financial squeeze on farmers created by the rise in production costs and the accompanying reduction in commodity prices beginning in the early 1980s.*** Chapter 12 was adopted by Congress to fill the gap between Chapter 11 and Chapter 13.

II. WHO MAY BE A DEBTOR UNDER CHAPTER 12

A. Definition of family farmer: *A family farmer is defined under § 101(18) as an individual, or individual and spouse, or a corporation or partnership, more than half of which is owned by a family. There are also debt limitations — $1,500,000 in aggregate debts*, rather than Chapter 13's $1,000,000 ($250,000 in unsecured debt and $750,000 in secured debt) and other restrictions related to earnings and debt designed to ensure that the farm is of a family nature.

B. Need for regular income: Under § 109(f), *a debtor under Chapter 12 is limited to a "family farmer with regular annual income."* "Regular annual income" is defined in § 101(19) to mean *"sufficiently stable to enable such family farmer to make payments under a plan."*

III. ESTATE ADMINISTRATION

A. Applicability of general provisions of Code: Chapters 1, 3 and 5 of the Code apply to cases under Chapter 12, as they do to cases filed under other Chapters.

B. Stay of acts against co-debtor — § 1201: A stay is imposed under § 1201 against the collection of consumer debts from guarantors or co-signers of family farmer obligations, much as one is imposed under § 1301 for consumers.

C. Trustee and debtor in possession — §§ 1202 and 1207:
    Under § 1202, a trustee is appointed for all Chapter 12 cases, but its duties are largely ministerial.

    1. Debtor in possession: Under § 1207, *the debtor remains in possession of the property of the estate*; the trustee does not take over possession of the farm.

    2. Duties of trustee: The trustee's duties are as prescribed by § 704, except that it does not liquidate the estate, nor does it "investigate the financial affairs of the debtor," which is a duty imposed upon a Chapter 13 trustee. Otherwise, the trustee is much like a Chapter 13 trustee (*infra*, p. 232).

D. Special rules of adequate protection — § 1205: Under   § 1205, § 361 (dealing with what constitutes adequate protection) is made inapplicable to Chapter 12, largely to avoid the adverse effects upon farmers of *In re American Mariner Industries, Inc.*, 734 F.2d 426 (9th Cir. 1984) which gave a secured creditor monthly interest payments on its collateral as a means of providing adequate protection. However, since that case was overruled by *U.S. Savings Ass'n v. Timbers of Inwood Forest Associates, Ltd.*, 484 U.S. 365 (1988) (see *supra*, p. 44) the differences between § 361 and § 1205 now appear to be of little consequence.

E. Sale of farm property permitted — § 1206: If a family farmer is trying to reduce farm operations, equipment can be sold under the provisions of § 363 (*supra*, p. 102). If there is a lien on the equipment, then, in cases under Chapters other than Chapter 12, sale of the equipment is subject to § 363(f), under which either the sale price must cover the amount of the lien or the lienholder must consent. Under § 1206, these restrictions are liberalized in Chapter 12 cases and, subject to court supervision, a sale is permitted so long as the proceeds are held for the lienholder.

F. Property acquired after petition — § 1207: As in Chapter 13, *property acquired after the petition is filed is property of the estate*. In particular, earnings of the family farmer while in bankruptcy become property of the estate.

IV. THE PLAN — §§ 1221, 1222

A. Who may file a plan and when — § 1221: *Only the debtor farmer may file a plan. The plan must be filed within 90 days after the order for relief, except that the period may be extended for circumstances beyond the control of the debtor.*

B. Contents of plan — § 1222: The Chapter 12 plan is very similar to the Chapter 13 plan (*infra*, p. 236). The differences between them include the following:

1. **Modification by claim holders:** Under § 1222(a)(3), claim holders are allowed to agree to less favorable treatment than others in the same class. This is not allowed in a Chapter 13 plan.

2. **Modification of all secured claims:** Chapter 12 permits the modification of all secured claims including home mortgages.

3. **Extension of payments on secured claims:** Chapter 12 permits the modification of secured claims to allow their payment to extend beyond the period for payments that is provided for in the plan; Chapter 13 does not give this latitude.

C. Time of plans: *The time period over which a plan for payments may extend is normally three years*, which is the same as for Chapter 13. The court may extend the period, *not to exceed a total of five years*.

D. Confirmation — § 1224 and § 1225: The Chapter 12 plan becomes effective upon confirmation by the court. Under § 1224, the confirmation hearing must be concluded, except for cause, within 45 days after the filing of the plan. The requirements for confirmation under § 1225 are similar to those applicable to Chapter 13 (*infra*, p. 242).

E. Payments to creditors — § 1226: As with a Chapter 13 plan, *the trustee usually makes payments to creditors*; under § 1226, the plan may provide otherwise. A court, under appropriate circumstances, may order the debtor to start making payments himself.

1. **Funds received prior to confirmation or denial of plan:** Provision is made for the possibility that funds will be delivered to the trustee before confirmation is ordered, but this is less likely than under Chapter 13. Funds received are retained by the trustee until the plan is either confirmed or denied.

2. **Administrative expenses:** Under § 1226(b)(1), ***administrative expenses under § 507(a)(1)*** (*supra*, p. 86) ***must be paid in full before any creditor may receive a payment under the plan***. There is a similar provision in Chapter 13 (*infra*, p. 236).

F. **Effect of confirmation — § 1227:** The confirmed plan binds the parties in interest. ***To the extent that a trustee acquired any title to property, the title is revested in the debtor***. All liens are eliminated, except as provided for in the plan. (The property interests of lienholders are protected under the requirements for confirmation in § 1225. *In re Fenske*, 96 B.R. 244 (Bkrtcy. D.N.D. 1988).)

V.   DISCHARGE — § 1228

A. **Nature of discharge:** The discharge effected under Chapter 12 is the same as the discharge whose effects are described in § 524 (*supra*, p. 59). As with Chapter 13, discharge depends upon the debt's inclusion in the plan, not, as with Chapters 7 and 11, the time that the debt arose. There are two kinds of Chapter 12 discharge. They have been called the payment discharge and the hardship discharge.

B. **"Payment discharge":** ***As soon as practicable after payment of all debts under the plan, the court will grant the debtor a discharge of all allowed and disallowed debts provided for by the plan***, except as follows:

1. **Exclusion for long term debts:** Debts whose payment period extends beyond the period of the plan are not discharged.

2. **Exceptions from discharge:** The debts that are specified in § 523(a) as not dischargeable by individuals (*supra*, p. 54) are not discharged. In contrast, under § 1328, only certain of the debts specified in § 523(a) are not dischargeable in a Chapter 13 case.

C. **"Hardship discharge":** Chapter 12 has a rough equivalent of the hardship discharge that was created for Chapter 13 (*infra*, p. 247). ***If the Chapter 12 debtor's failure to complete payments was "due to circumstances for which the debtor should not justly be held accountable," a hardship discharge may be granted***.

1. **Terms of hardship discharge:** ***This discharge may be granted only if: (1) a "best interests of creditors" test*** (*supra*, p.

173) *is applied* and it is established that each creditor received property, valued as of the effective date of the plan, that was at least equal to what it would have received under a Chapter 7 liquidation, and (2) *modification of the plan is not practicable*.

2. **Debts discharged:** As with a payment discharge, the hardship discharge also will not discharge debts whose payment period extends beyond the time of the plan and also debts that are excluded from individual discharge under § 523(a).

CHAPTER 13

FILING UNDER CHAPTER 13 — INDIVIDUAL WITH REGULAR INCOME

I. OVERVIEW

A. Adjustment of debts for individuals: Chapter 13 provides a form of reorganization that is considerably simpler than Chapter 11 but is restricted to *relief for an individual, or an individual and spouse, with regular income*. The chapter is also *available to a small business conducted by an individual, provided that the business is a sole proprietorship*. Since, unlike Chapter 11, creditor approval is not required for a Chapter 13 reorganization plan, a strict debt ceiling is imposed upon Chapter 13 petitioners in order to ensure that the Chapter is used for smaller, less complicated debt situations.

B. Mandatory Chapter 13 rejected: *Resort to Chapter 13 is voluntary with the debtor*; no involuntary Chapter 13 relief is possible. We have in our early discussion of involuntary bankruptcy referred to creditor efforts to introduce a mandatory Chapter 13 (*supra*, p. 27). Creditor research over the years has indicated that individuals seeking liquidation in Chapter 7 often have a combination of assets and potential of future income to pay a sizable portion of their debts. It has, therefore, been proposed that liquidation not be permitted unless a debtor can demonstrate that debt payment under a plan, in whole or in substantial part, is not feasible. These proposals have consistently been rejected by Congress. Not only has Congress never been convinced of the social desirability of an involuntary Chapter 13, but, as mentioned earlier, it has had some concerns that such a law might run afoul of the 13th Amendment prohibition against involuntary servitude.

C. Encouragement of reasonable plans: As written for the 1978 Code, Chapter 13 embodies provisions which encourage individuals to devise plans that will do more than simply divert their non-exempt assets to their creditors over a period of time. Among these are: the composition of the Chapter 13 estate, which includes property and earnings acquired after the filing of the case (see § 1306, *infra*, p. 235); the relationship of Chapter 13 to § 727(a)(9), which prevents a discharge under Chapter 7 for an individual who has received a prior Chapter 13 discharge unless all prior obligations have been paid or a good faith/best efforts payment test in the Chapter 13 case has been met (*supra*, p. 164); and restrictions on use of a debtor's disposable income during the period of the plan under § 1325(b) (*infra*, p. 244).

II. WHO MAY ELECT CHAPTER 13 — § 109

A. Limitations on debt: To ensure that Chapter 13 will deal only with smaller bankruptcies, fairly restrictive ceilings on the amount of debt that may be owed are imposed by § 109. *An individual* (as defined *infra*) *may, either alone or with her spouse, owe no more than $250,000 in unsecured and $750,000 in secured debts*. The definition of debts in § 101 derives from the definition of claims (*supra*, p. 17). The scope of the term "debts" is therefore expansive, but the debts to which the tests apply must be both noncontingent and liquidated.

B. Scope of "individual" filings: An individual may file under 13 together with a spouse. Sole proprietorships may also file. Filing by an individual who is a stockbroker or commodities broker is not permitted.

1. **Sole proprietorships:** *Persons in "mom and pop" operations will qualify as individuals so long as they do not conduct the business as a separate legal entity, such as a partnership.* An individual and his spouse may be found to be a partnership by estoppel (i.e., although they are not a partnership, a third party is able to assert that they held themselves out to be partners with respect to a given transaction) and still be able to utilize Chapter 13 because they are, in fact, not a partnership.

2. **Partnerships:** If there is any evidence of an agreement, even an informal agreement, that the business is to be conducted as a partnership, then Chapter 13 is not available. Whether a debtor is an individual or a partner is a question of fact and turns on such matters as:

   - whether a certificate of partnership has been filed;

   - whether the assets of the business are used for the benefit of all creditors or only business creditors,

   - whether a separate business bank account exists and whether other parties are authorized to sign checks on that account;

   - whether there is a sharing of the management function over the business;

   - whether the debtor and his spouse have generally held themselves out to trade creditors as partners in a business.

   Example: Proposed debtor and his wife operate a small store. The wife began the business, but at the time of the petition was doing little work in the store. A certificate of partnership had been filed for the business and all the creditors were business creditors to whom both were liable as a result of the operation of the business. The debts were found to be partnership debts for which both husband and wife had legal liability. The debtor was not eligible for Chapter 13 relief. *In re Krokos*, 12 B.R. 520 (Bkrtcy. S.D.N.Y. 1981).

C. **"Regular income" defined:** *The term "individual with regular income" is defined in § 101(30), as an individual whose income is sufficiently stable and regular to enable him to make payments under a Chapter 13 plan.* It is clear that the debtor need not be employed. Whether income will be considered "regular" will depend on the facts in each case, including the skills, opportunities, and motivation of the debtor.

Example 1: A and B are divorced. A's total income is derived from the divorce decree. Whether A is an "individual with regular income" depends on the regularity of B's income.

Example 2: Before bankruptcy, debtor was employed first as a bus driver and then as a mechanic in a coal mine. After that, he was on unemployment insurance for a time and then earned money from a scattered series of odd jobs. The court held that his income was sufficiently regular to warrant Chapter 13 relief. "His skills are sufficient, his motivation seemingly adequate and the opportunities are apparently available." *In re Cole*, 3 B.R. 346, 350 (Bkrtcy. S.D. W.Va. 1980).

Example 3: Debtor is employed as a sprinkler system installer from October to April. Through the remainder of the year, he obtains odd jobs on a fairly regular basis but cannot predict with certainty the continuing availability of such jobs. His income was found *not* to be "regular." *In re Hickman*, 104 B.R. 374 (Bkrtcy. D.Col. 1989)

Example 4: Debtor's regular monthly expenses exceeded his income by eight dollars. He was found incapable of making payments under a plan. He had proposed a plan calling for zero payments, but that was also found unacceptable; see discussion of § 1325(a)(3) (*infra*, p. 242). *Tenney v. Terry*, 630 F.2d 634 (8th Cir. 1980).

III. CONVERSION OR DISMISSAL — § 1307

A. **Nature of conversion and dismissal:** With relatively minor variations, the rules on conversion and dismissal for Chapter 13 cases are comparable to analogous sections under other Chapters of the Code. The provision for dismissal under § 305 (*supra*, p. 29), generally used in the early stages of a case, overlaps with § 1307, the provision governing dismissal of Chapter 13 cases.

B. **Rights of debtor to convert or dismiss:** *The Chapter 13 debtor may at any time convert to Chapter 7 or have the case dismissed. Also, only a debtor may convert a case filed under another chap-*

ter to Chapter 13. This shows the high degree of control by the debtor in a Chapter 13 case.

C. **Rights of other parties to convert or dismiss:** *Parties   other than the debtor may request the court to either convert a Chapter 13 case to Chapter 7 or dismiss the case for cause, whichever is in the best interests of the creditors and the estate.* Ten grounds establishing cause are listed in the statute, although the list is not exclusive. Included in the list are such grounds as unreasonable delay, failure to file a timely plan, and failure to commence making timely payments. The list is similar to the lists under Chapter 7 (§ 707 *supra*, p. 148) and under Chapter 11 (§ 1112 *supra*, p. 183). (See also, the discussion under Chapter 11 concerning situations where there are competing reasons for conversion or dismissal, *supra*, p. 185.)

D. **Conversion to Chapters 11 and 12:** Under § 1307(d), *any party in interest may, before confirmation of the Chapter 13 plan, request the court to convert a case to Chapters 11 or 12.* No standards are given to the court to apply in this process, but presumably it would look to the procedures under Chapters 11 or 12 to see whether they afford some useful element for the case (for example, the discovery of new assets of the debtor, or ability of the creditors to participate more closely in Chapter 11).

E. **Consent of farmers:** If the debtor is a farmer, the court may not convert the case to Chapters 7, 11, or 12 unless the debtor consents.

IV. STAY OF ACTION AGAINST CO-DEBTOR — § 1301

A. **Expanded stay:** The automatic stay under § 362 (*supra*, p. 36) is expanded under § 1301 to protect parties who have acted in accommodation of the debtor. *The expanded stay applies to: (1) individuals who are liable on a debt with the debtor, such as guarantors or persons who co-signed promissory notes*, and *(2) persons who secured the debtor's obligations, such as one who gave a creditor a lien on his car to secure the debtor's obligation but did not himself assume personal responsibility. This expanded stay applies only to consumer debts*, defined by § 101 as debts for personal, family, or household purposes. A co-debtor upon a business obligation of the debtor would not be protected by § 1301.

1. **Operation of expanded stay:** The expanded automatic stay operates in a fashion similar to the basic stay in § 362. A creditor may not act in any way to collect the debt against the accommodation party; the prohibition includes civil actions for collection of the debt.

2. **Purpose of expanded stay:** Congress found that accommodation parties with respect to consumer debts are usually unsophisticated relatives or co-workers. To press claims against them would result in the kind of pressure upon the debtor as well as the co-debtor that the automatic stay was designed to prevent. The expanded stay is intended to make meaningful the respite from debt collection pressures while the debtor deals with the bankruptcy.

B. **Exceptions from the expanded stay:** *The stay against an individual who shares liability with a Chapter 13 debtor does not apply if (1) the individual became liable or gave security in the ordinary course of his business, or (2) the case is closed or dismissed or removed from Chapter 13.*

C. **Expanded relief from stay:** As the automatic stay is expanded, so the relief from the expanded stay is also expanded. Relief may be granted under § 1301(c) in the following three situations.

1. **Accommodation party received the consideration:** Relief from the stay will be granted where the property that gave rise to the debt was actually received by the accommodation party rather than the principal debtor.

   Example: A co-debtor co-signed a promissory note for the purchase of a car, and the co-debtor took possession of the car. Relief from the stay against the co-debtor will be granted.

2. **Plan would not pay claim:** To the extent that the plan proposed by the debtor in Chapter 13 does not propose to pay the guaranteed claim in full, relief will be granted to the creditor against the co-debtor guarantor.

   Example: Co-debtor CD guarantees Debtor D's obligation to Creditor C. D goes into Chapter 13 and defaults to C. When D's petition for Chapter 13 is filed, C may not attempt to collect from CD. But D proposes a plan that pays C only 15 percent of C's claim. The automatic stay preventing action by C against CD is lifted for 85 percent of the claim. *In re Jacobsen*, 20 B.R. 648 (9th Cir. Bkrtcy. App. 1982).

3. **Creditor would be irreparably harmed:** The stay will be lifted against the co-debtor if the creditor can demonstrate that it will be irreparably harmed by its continuation.

   Example: CD gave C a security interest in CD's car to secure D's debt to C. Knowing he will lose the car anyway because D's debts cannot be paid, CD enters it in a local demolition derby. The court should grant relief from the stay.

D. Timing of relief from stay: If a request for relief from the stay imposed by § 1301 is filed, the requested relief will be granted after 20 days unless there is an objection.

V.   TRUSTEE — § 1302

A. Appointment of trustees: ***Trustees are appointed in all Chapter 13 cases.*** The United States Trustee can appoint a "standing trustee" from the panel maintained by the U.S. Trustee (*supra*, p. 68), or another disinterested person in a particular case. The U.S. Trustee may also serve as trustee in the case. Under Chapter 13, management of the estate is divided between the debtor and the trustee, not always with a clear demarcation.

B. Duties of trustee — § 1302(b): The duties of a Chapter 13 trustee are not as significant as those of a trustee in Chapter 7 (who is appointed in all cases to oversee full liquidation of the estate) and not as extensive as those of a Chapter 11 trustee (who is appointed relatively rarely but, who upon appointment, assumes full management of the estate). The following duties of the Chapter 13 trustee are prescribed under § 1302(b).

  1. Duties prescribed by Chapter 7:   The Chapter 13 trustee performs all the duties assigned to a Chapter 7 trustee by § 704 (*supra*, p. 153), *except* for the duties to liquidate the estate (*supra*, p. 153), file tax returns, and submit regular periodic reports for the operation of a business (*supra*, p. 154). ***In general, the Chapter 13 trustee is required to serve as an overseer of the estate and report to the court.***

  2. Duty to appear and be heard: The trustee, consistent with its overseer duties, must appear and be heard at hearings that concern the value of property subject to a lien, the confirmation of the plan, and, where applicable, the modification of the plan.

  3. Duty to distribute payments: ***The trustee usually receives and distributes the moneys to be paid to creditors.*** This is generally considered to be the most important Chapter 13 trustee duty. The trustee's duties to receive and to pay monies are confirmed by the payment provisions of § 1326(a) and (c).

   a. Payments by the trustee: Under § 1326(a), the debtor must begin payments under the plan within 30 days after the plan is filed. Payments by the debtor must be retained by the trustee until the plan is either confirmed or denied. If a plan is confirmed, the trustee must distribute the payments as soon as practicable. If denied, the payments must be returned to the debtor after deducting administrative claims (*supra*, p. 86).

b. **Payments by the debtor:** Where business relationships dictate, the plan may provide that the debtor make payments directly to creditors. If circumstances warrant, payments may be made partially by the trustee and partially by the debtor. In the latter case, those who receive payments from the debtor automatically become a separate class of creditors and there may be a strong presumption that impermissible discrimination in favor of that class has been committed by the debtor. *In re Tatum*, 1 B.R. 445 (Bkrtcy. S.D. Ohio 1979). Some courts will look to all the facts to see if the debtor had good and valid reasons to make direct payments which belie an intent to discriminate. *In re Perskin*, 9 B.R. 626 (Bkrtcy. N.D. Texas 1981). If the debtor undertakes to make direct payments, the trustee still has a duty to ensure that the payments are made. *In re Case*, 4 C.B.C.2nd 978 (Bkrtcy. D. Utah 1981).

4. **Advise and assist debtor:** Part of the role of the trustee is to advise the debtor on matters, other than legal matters, concerning the bankruptcy and to assist the debtor in carrying out the plan.

5. **Ensure debtor payments:** The trustee must ensure the debtor makes timely payments under the plan.

6. **Investigate and report on business:** If the Chapter 13 debtor is engaged in a business, the trustee also performs the functions described in § 1106(a)(3) and (4), which require the investigation of the business, including the propriety of its operation, and the filing of reports that relate to the investigation.

C. **Avoiding and other powers of trustee:** Although they are not specifically stated in Chapter 13, there is general acknowledgment that the Chapter 13 trustee has the powers given in the Code to trustees generally. Primary among these are the avoiding powers in Chapter 5 of the Code, particularly § 544, 545, 547 and 548 (see Chapter 8, *supra*). However, due to the absence of specific language on the applicability of these powers in Chapter 13 cases, it is unclear just how and when the trustee is supposed to use the powers. *In re Walls*, 17 B.R. 701 (Bkrtcy. S.D.W.Va. 1982)

VI. RIGHTS AND POWERS OF DEBTOR — §§ 1303, 1304

A. General powers: Under § 1303, *the debtor is given most of the rights and powers of a trustee under § 363, which concerns the use, sale, or lease of the property of the estate* (*supra*, p. 102).

B. Avoidance powers: The bankruptcy courts are in disagreement on whether the debtor succeeds to the trustee's powers to avoid transfers under Chapter 5 of the Code. There is no statutory language supporting the use of those powers, but some courts, reasoning that the trustee has little incentive in Chapter 13 to pursue avoidances vigorously, hold that the debtor has these powers despite the lack of authorizing language. *In re Einoder*, 55 B.R. 319 (Bkrtcy. N.D. Ill. 1985). Some courts hold that the debtor has the right to avoid but only where he has a right to property that is exempt under § 522 (*supra*, p. 46). *In re Perry*, 90 B.R. 565 (Bkrtcy. S.D. Fla. 1988). A majority of the courts, relying on the words of the statute, have rejected any avoiding right in the debtor. *In re Houston*, 20 C.B.C.2d 755 (Bkrtcy. W.D.Texas 1989).

C. Debtor operating business: Under § 1304, *the debtor may operate his own business*, but is specifically subject to the limitations placed upon a trustee by § 363 with regard to the use, sale or lease of property (*supra*, p. 102) and by § 364 with regard to obtaining credit (*supra*, p. 189). The duty to file tax and other reports under § 704(8) (*supra*, p. 154) is assigned to the Chapter 13 debtor operating his own business. (As we have noted, this duty is not imposed on the Chapter 13 trustee. *supra*, p. 232)

VII. POSTPETITION CLAIMS — § 1305

A. Additional postpetition claims: Under § 502(b), a claim must, in the usual case, be in existence as of the date of the petition that begins the bankruptcy (*supra*, p. 75). As exceptions, certain claims that come into existence after the petition can also be allowed (*supra*, p. 77). Under § 1305, *postpetition claims for taxes and certain consumer debts are additional exceptions in Chapter 13 cases. If proofs of claims are filed for such debts and the claims are allowed, they will share in distributions from the estate.*

  1. **Tax obligations:** Taxes that become payable while the Chapter 13 case is pending are deemed claims that may be filed under § 501 and allowed under § 502.

  2. **Certain consumer debts:** *A claim may be filed for consumer debt arising after the order for relief for property or services*

that are necessary for the debtor's performance under Chapter 13, unless the holder of a claim knew or should have known that prior approval by the trustee was feasible. The goal of the restriction is to place some restraint upon the ability of the debtor to incur additional consumer debt after the petition.

Example: After entering into Chapter 13, Debtor D buys a car on time. The car is needed to transport D to his job. Since the income from the job is necessary for D's performance under the Chapter 13 plan, the claim for car payments may be filed.

B. Allowance of postpetition claims: Unlike prepetition claims, a postpetition claim must be allowed by the court in order to be provided for in a Chapter 13 plan. This has ramifications for the debtor as well as the creditor. *If a postpetition claim has not been allowed as provided by § 1305, it cannot be included in the Chapter 13 plan* (see discussion of § 1322(b)(6) *infra*, p. 241) *and, if not provided for in the plan, it cannot be discharged* (see discussion of § 1328(a) *infra*, p. 241). *In re Hester*, 63 B.R. 607 (Bkrtcy. E.D. Tenn. 1986).

VIII. PROPERTY OF THE ESTATE — § 1306

A. Debtor retains possession: Except as provided in a plan or in an order confirming a plan, *the Chapter 13 debtor remains in possession of the estate*. As mentioned (*supra*, p. 234), a debtor who has a business may continue to run the business.

B. Property acquired after petition: The rules as to what is property of the estate are generally established by § 541 (*supra*, p. 95). Under § 1306, *property of the estate in Chapter 13 also includes all property acquired by the debtor after the petition is filed. Most significantly, this includes income earned by the debtor while in bankruptcy.* (Contrast this with § 541(a)(6), *supra*, p. 98, which generally excludes post-petition earnings from the estate.) Typically, the income of a debtor in Chapter 13 will be his most significant asset. By making that asset part of the estate, the Code increases the likelihood that the plan will be adequately funded on a continuing basis. Although committing future income to the plan, the Chapter 13 debtor, may, by applying something less than 100% of his assets to the payment of creditors, escape the loss of all nonexempt assets as he would in a Chapter 7 bankruptcy. *The debtor's income will include revenues from pension plans and Social Security benefits*, unless the debtor elects to exempt such payments to the extent possible under § 522 (*supra*, p. 46). See *In re Buren*, 6 B.R. 744 (Bkrtcy. M.D.Tenn.), rev'd, 725 F.2d 1080 (6th Cir.), cert.denied, 469 U.S. 818 (1984).

IX.   THE PLAN — §§ 1321, 1322

A. **Only the debtor may file a plan:** Under § 1321, *only the debtor may file a plan in Chapter 13*. This is consistent with Chapter 12, but is in sharp contrast to Chapter 11, where creditors are given a significant say in the initiation of proceedings.

B. **Term of plan:** *The normal period of a Chapter 13 plan is three years, but the bankruptcy court may, for cause, approve plans that extend up to five years.* There is no definition of what constitutes "cause."

   1. **Terms longer than three years:** The courts will occasionally allow periods longer than three years where the debtor is trying to make larger payments to her creditors, particularly when the debtor is faced with unusual problems, such as heavy medical expenses. *In re Purdy*, 16 B.R. 847 (D.N.D. Ga. 1981). Where debts would not have been discharged under Chapter 7, but are discharged under the more expansive discharge rules of Chapter 13, a court may permit a longer plan to provide more money for the creditors; some courts may actually *require* longer plans for this purpose. *In re Todd*, 65 B.R. 249 (Bkrtcy. N.D. Ill. 1986).

   2. **Terms restricted to three years:** Courts will not permit longer plans where the proposed behavior of the debtor smacks of bad faith, as where he seeks the longer time to defer payment to creditors at the same time as he proposes to apply income from the earlier periods for his own purposes. *In re Lindsey*, 122 B.R. 157 (Bkrtcy. M.D. Fla. 1991).

C. **Mandatory contents of plan:**   Again, in contrast to Chapter 11 but consistent with Chapter 12, the Chapter 13 plan gives the debtor maximum flexibility to determine her financial future. Only a few elements are *required* to be contained in a Chapter 13 plan.

   1. **Allocate future income of the debtor:** *The plan must specify the extent to which the debtor's future income will be subjected to payments under the plan.* The court may order that income from the debtor's employer or other source be paid directly to the Chapter 13 trustee, who has the duty to distribute payments to the proper claim holders (*supra*, p. 232).

   2. **Pay priority claims under § 507:** *The plan must provide for the full payment of priority claims under § 507* (*supra*, p. 85), *unless the holder of such a claim agrees otherwise.* The plan may provide that payments for priority claims be deferred into the future.

3. **Provide the same treatment for claims within a class:** Contrary to a Chapter 11 plan, the Chapter 13 plan is not required to classify claims. However, *if a Chapter 13 plan does classify claims, each claim within a class must receive the same treatment*.

D. **Permissive contents of plan:** Under § 1322(b), there are ten items that *may be* included in a Chapter 13 plan. This reaffirms the high degree of discretion given to the Chapter 13 debtor.

1. **Designation of classes:** Under § 1322, *the debtor has the right to divide creditors into classes according to the provisions of § 1122, which require that similar claims be in the same class and, for administrative convenience, allow for a class of unrelated small claims* (*supra*, p. 194). The debtor "may not discriminate unfairly against any class so designated." Since there is no creditor vote, the debtor's division of creditors into classes has nothing to do with protecting a fair and equitable voting scheme, as is the case in a Chapter 11 plan, but is usually related to the debtor's desire to pay some creditors more than others to facilitate a fresh start.

   a. **Justification for separate classes:** The problems we have already seen in connection with § 1122 (*supra*, p. 193), in determining whether or not claims are sufficiently different to be put into different classes, with different payment terms for each class, appear again in Chapter 13. Separate classes in Chapter 13 have been sustained for creditors such as local tradespeople, landlords, and doctors. *Determinations on the validity of classes have been based upon such factors as whether the classification made is reasonable when related to the debtor's needs for rehabilitation and the extent to which distributions are withheld from some for the benefit of others. In re Terry*, 78 B.R. 171 (Bkrtcy. E.D.Tenn. 1987). The debtor is permitted to include as a separate class the claimholders whose obligations are guaranteed by another individual, much in the way that § 1122 permits a class of small claimholders whose obligations are below a court-approved amount.

   b. **Justification for discrimination in payments:** Whether different treatment of different classes is unfair discrimination has been determined by some courts under an analysis similar to that used in Chapter 11 cram down cases (*supra*, p. 212). Under this four-factor analysis, a determination is based on:

      • *Whether the discrimination has a reasonable basis;*

- ***Whether the debtor can carry out a plan without such discrimination;***

- ***Whether such discrimination is proposed in good faith;*** and

- ***The treatment of the class discriminated against.***

In re Storberg, 94 Bankr. 144 (Bktcy. D. Minn. 1988).

The test of a debtor's good faith is similar to the requirement of good faith for confirmation of a plan under § 1325(a)(3) (*infra*, p. 242). *In re Lawson*, 93 B.R. 979 (Bkrtcy. N.D. Ill. 1988). Fairness of a Chapter 13 plan has been held to turn on whether differences in the treatment of creditors accomplish the legitimate goals of the debtor. For example, a plan was found acceptable where more was allocated to child support than to a hairdresser. *In re Bowles*, 48 B.R. 502 (Bkrtcy. E.D.Va. 1985).

2. **Modify the rights of secured or unsecured claimants:** ***With one exception, the debtor has the right to change the rights of holders both of secured and unsecured claims***, subject to the Fifth Amendment protections accorded a secured claimant under the confirmation standards of § 1325 (*infra*, p. 244). Unlike a Chapter 11 plan, the plan does not require the consent of the unsecured claimholders, who are also protected along with the secured claimants by the confirmation provisions of § 1325. ***The one exception to the flexibility given the debtor is that the plan is limited to the extent it may change the rights of the holder of a mortgage on real estate that constitutes the debtor's principal residence.*** For the principal residence, the debtor may change the rights of a mortgage holder to the extent provided in §1325(a)(5): if the last payment of the original payment schedule of the claim is due before the date that the final payment under the plan is due, the mortgage holder's lien may be modified so long as its value as of the effective date of the plan is not less than the allowed amount of such claim. With this exception, a plan may provide for the payment of, for example, ten cents on the dollar to all creditors and, subject to the home mortgage exception and Fifth Amendment protections to other secured creditors, may also affect the liens of secured parties.

   a. **Home mortgage exception:** ***The home mortgage exception applies to claims secured "only" by such a mortgage.*** If a single mortgage document covers both the debtor's residence and other assets, the mortgage may be modified. *In re Caster*, 77 B.R. 8 (Bkrtcy. E.D. Pa. 1987.) In the case of undersecured home mortgages, the interaction of § 1322(b)(2) (prohibiting changes in a home mortgage) and § 506(a) (requiring a division between secured and unsecured portions of a debt, *supra*, p. 82), has created some problems for the courts. Some courts have held that the home mortgage exception applies to the entire amount of the debt, not just the secured portion. Other courts have held that the exception applies only to the secured portion, not to the unsecured portion, which may be modified. The following example illustrates the problem and the prevailing solution.

Example: Debtor D gives Creditor C a mortgage on D's residence to secure a $100,000 debt. At the time of bankruptcy, the residence is valued at $70,000. Under § 506(a), the debt is divided between a $70,000 secured portion and a $30,000 unsecured portion; however, § 1322(b)(2) requires that a home mortgage not be changed. It was held that only the secured portion of the debt after the § 506(a) division was subject to § 1322(b)(2) and could not be changed. Payment amounts and times and the interest rate were not changed as to the secured portion, but the maturity date of the mortgage could be reduced to coincide with the last payment sufficient to cover the secured portion of the claim. The unsecured portion could be varied in the same way as any unsecured obligation under Chapter 13. *In re Franklin*, 126 B.R. 702 (Bkrtcy. N.D. Miss. 1991).

b. **Claims not dealt with by plan:** *Although Chapter 13 does not require that all claims be dealt with in the plan, a discharge will be granted under § 1328 only for claims dealt with by the plan, claims disallowed under § 502* (*supra*, p. 75), *and administrative claims under § 503* (*supra*, p. 86). Therefore, a question is occasionally raised as to the right of a debtor to deal with claims entirely outside the plan. It is generally held that a debtor may deal with a wholly secured claim (where the creditor is assured of full repayment) outside the plan, but must deal with all of his unsecured claims in the plan. It has also been held that the debtor must at least disclose in the plan the existence of obligations that will be dealt with outside the plan so that the court will have a better perception of the debtor's full financial condition. *Matter of Foster*, 670 F.2d 478 (5th Cir. 1982).

3. **Curing or waiving of any default:** *The plan may provide for curing a default on an obligation and may also provide, in a proposal that will become firm when a plan is confirmed, for the waiver of a default by a creditor.* By curing a default and resuming regular payments on a secured loan, the debtor is able to remain in possession of the collateral (e.g., a car or a home).

a. **Default on home mortgage:** The curing of a default on a home mortgage is not considered to be a modification of a home mortgage, which, as we have discussed, is subject to the terms of the home mortgage exception to the permissive provisions of a plan. *In re Taddeo*, 685 F.2d 24 (2d Cir. 1982). The right to cure a default exists even if payment of the mortgage debt has been accelerated under the terms of the mortgage (i.e., all future payments are deemed to be due by virtue of a default). If a plan extends beyond the original payment schedule of a mortgage, the debtor may cure within the time allowed by the plan.

b. **Duration of right to cure:** Under § 1322(c), *a default on the debtor's principal residence may be cured at least until such time as the residence is sold at a foreclosure sale that is conducted in accordance with applicable nonbankruptcy law.* If a particular state law provides a longer cure period, such as a redemption period even after the foreclosure sale, the debtor may avail himself of the state law.

c. **Interest resulting from default:** Under a 1994 amendment to § 1322, *interest amounts owing only because of a default, such as interest on mortgage arrearages or other late charges and fees, will be paid in accordance with the underlying agreement and applicable nonbankruptcy law.* This provision has the effect of overruling the decision of the Supreme Court in *Rake v. Wade*, 113 S.Ct. 2187 (1993). In essence, that decision provided a windfall to secured creditors by providing for interest on mortgage arrears, including interest payments, late charges, or other fees, even where the applicable nonbankruptcy law prohibited such interest and even where that result was not contemplated in the original transaction.

4. **Arrange timing of payments:** Under this permissive provision, *the debtor has the right to arrange the timing of payments, which gives the debtor the flexibility to create the most feasible method of payment.* The plan may, but need not, provide priority in payments to any unsecured class and may arrange for payments to be made concurrently with any other payments, both to unsecured and secured claimholders. Even the holders of priority claims, which, as noted above, must be paid in full, need not be paid before ordinary unsecured claimants. However, note the duty under § 1326(b)(1) to pay administrative claims with or before other claims (*infra*, p. 245).

5. **Debts that extend beyond plan period:** Under the fifth permissive provision, *the debtor has the right to cure existing defaults on debts that extend beyond the plan period, the*

right to maintain regular payments during the period the plan is in effect, and the right to continue under such obligations after the plan expires. Most commonly, this provision is applicable to home mortgages, which typically extend beyond the usual plan period of three years and even the maximum plan period of five years (*infra*, p. 236). This provision does not grant the power to modify obligations, only to cure them or to continue under them. Obligations that extend beyond the plan length may be modified under the debtor's powers in the second permissive provision (*supra*, p. 238) (except for home mortgages, which may not be modified at all); but, if modified, they must be dealt with during the period of the plan. *Education Assistance Corp. v. Zellner*, 827 F.2d 1222 (8th Cir. 1987). With respect to the ability to cure a default in a long term mortgage, the powers granted by this provision and the third permissive provision, *supra*, appear to be interchangeable. *In re Taddeo* (*supra*, p. 240).

6. **Payment of postpetition claims:** ***This permissive provision allows the debtor to provide for the payment of allowed postpetition claims.*** It is unclear why there is a separate provision for option. One reason may be to remove any question concerning the term "allowed", since that term is not applied to prepetition claims. For a claim to be allowed, it must come within § 502 (*supra*, p. 75), which requires that a proof of claim be filed under § 501 (*supra*, p. 72). Thus, if a proof of claim is not filed with respect to postpetition claims, apparently the plan may not provide for them. If not provided for or improperly provided for in the plan, a significant consequence is that the discharge under § 1328 (*infra*, p. 235), which applies to claims "provided for by the plan," will not be available. *In re Hester*, 63 B.R. 607 (Bkrtcy. E.D. Tenn. 1986).

7. **Assumption, rejection, or assignment of executory contracts:** Subject to the requirements of § 365, ***this permissive provision allows for the assumption, rejection, or assignment of executory contracts and unexpired leases.*** Under § 365, there is an elaborate set of rules on how executory contracts and unexpired leases may be assumed, rejected, or assigned (*supra*, p. 106). Under § 365(d)(2), a contract or lease may be assumed or rejected in a Chapter 13 case up until the confirmation of the plan.

8. **Sources of payment:** ***This permissive provision allows the plan to provide for payment of a claim from property of the estate, or from property of the debtor that is outside the estate*** (for example, from exempted property). Most payments are made from the debtor's postpetition income, which, as we have seen, is made a part of the estate (§ 1306 discussed *supra*, p. 235).

9. **Vesting of estate upon confirmation:** *This permissive provision allows the plan, upon its confirmation or at a later point, to restore the property of the estate to the debtor or another entity.* Where the debtor's future income is an expected source for plan payments, the plan will normally provide that the income becomes part of the estate and will be paid to the trustee for distribution. Under the provisions of § 1327, unless the plan or the order confirming the plan provides otherwise, the estate vests in the debtor upon confirmation of the plan (*infra*, p. 246).

10. **Other provisions:** The tenth and final permissive provision states that the plan may include other appropriate provisions.

X. CONFIRMATION — §§ 1324, 1325

A. **Confirmation hearing — § 1324:** *After notice, the court will hold a confirmation hearing on the Chapter 13 plan.* At the hearing, the plan will be reviewed to establish whether it conforms to the prerequisites for confirmation set out in § 1325. Parties in interest may object to the plan, but, unlike a Chapter 11 plan (*supra*, p. 208), Chapter 13 creditors do not vote on plans. Objections, except those of unsecured creditors (which will be deal with under § 1325(b), *infra* p. 244), will simply be considered by the judge in the confirmation process.

B. **Confirmation — § 1325:** The bankruptcy court will ordinarily confirm the Chapter 13 plan, provided it complies with the following six factors.

1. **Compliance with the Code:** The first requirement is that the *plan comply with the dictates of Chapter 13 and the Code*. In particular, a plan must adhere to the mandatory and permissive provisions of a plan under § 1322 (*supra*, p. 236, et seq.).

2. **Fees paid:** The second requirement is that the *charges required to be paid prior to confirmation*, either by 28 U.S.C. § 1911 *et seq.* (filing fees, court costs, fees on appeals, witness fees, marshals fees, etc.) or by the plan, *must have been paid.*

3. **Good faith and legality:** The third requirement is that the *plan be proposed in good faith and not by any means forbidden by law.* At a minimum, good faith requires that the plan be based on accurate information. As good faith is largely fact-sensitive, the courts have employed different principles. Some courts have created a laundry list of factors, such as the list of eleven factors in *In re Carver*, 110 B.R. 305 (Bkrtcy. S.D. Ohio 1990). Other courts have relied on broad principles, such as, "[good faith must be viewed in] light of the totality of the circumstances surrounding confection of a

given Chapter 13 plan. This analysis must be accomplished mindful of the purpose of the Bankruptcy Code and its legislative predecessors. Debtors are to be given a reasonable opportunity to make a fresh start." *Public Finance v. Freeman*, 712 F.2d 219, 221 (5th Cir. 1983).

a. **Amount of payments:** While a zero payment plan was held to be indicative of bad faith, payments may be allocated in various ways, including payment only to secured and not to unsecured creditors, without a violation of the good faith requirement. *In re Harmon*, 72 B.R. 458 (Bkrtcy. E.D.Pa. 1987). A series of cases dealing with the issue whether good faith required that a minimum percentage of creditors' claims be paid, was largely replaced in 1984 by the adoption of § 1325(b) (discussed *infra*, p. 244).

b. **Multiple bankruptcies:** A bankruptcy following quickly after a prior dismissal may still be in good faith if the debtor's circumstances have changed. *In re Johnson*, 708 F.2d 865 (2d Cir. 1983). But a third filing by the same debtor will be harder to justify. *In re Hyman*, 82 B.R. 23 (Bkrtcy. D.S.C. 1987) (dealing with Chapter 12 cases).

c. **Not in violation of other laws:** As with the requirement for confirmation of a Chapter 11 plan (*supra*, p. 210), the Chapter 13 plan must not be in violation of other laws. Because Chapter 13 deals with consumer debt, plan provisions that provide for assignment of a debtor's pension benefits to a trustee sometimes conflict with anti-assignment provisions of the Veterans Administration and the Social Security laws. The courts have not been consistent in resolving these conflicts. *Matter of Roach*, 90 B.R. 286 (Bkrtcy. W.D.Mich.), aff'd, 94 B.R. 440 (D.W.D. Mich. 1988).)

4. **"Best interests of creditor" test:** As was the case in Chapter 11 (*supra*, p. 211) and Chapter 12 (*supra*, p. 224), ***a plan will be confirmed only if it can be demonstrated that the creditors will receive at least as much as they would receive under a Chapter 7 liquidation.*** The date as of which the comparison is made is the effective date of the Chapter 13 plan. As of that date, the bankruptcy court must compute what each creditor would receive under a hypothetical Chapter 7 liquidation. This process takes into account such aspects of Chapter 7 as claims found not allowable under § 502 (*supra*, p. 75) and exemptions claimed under § 522 (*supra*, p. 46). Comparisons of recovery under Chapter 7 will then be made for all creditors with what they are scheduled to receive under Chapter 13. The latter must be discounted back to the effective date of the plan at an appropriate rate of interest, in order for a mean-

ingful comparison to be made. (*See* discussion in connection with confirmation of Chapter 11 plans, *supra*, p. 200).

5. **Protection of secured creditors:** Since secured creditors do not vote on Chapter 13 plans, protection for their property interests under the Fifth Amendment (*supra*, p. 50) is provided for under this section, constituting the fifth requirement for confirmation. ***There are three alternatives under which the rights of secured creditors may be addressed.***

- ***First, the creditor may simply accept the plan.***

- ***Second, the creditor may retain its lien and receive property under the plan with a present value as of the effective date at least equal to its allowed claim.*** Under this option, should the debtor default under the plan, the creditor will have retained a right to the collateral and also receive adequate protection under § 361 (*supra*, p. 43) for so long as it is restrained from recovering the collateral by the § 362 automatic stay. In Chapter 13, the automatic stay lasts, unless modified by the court, until discharge.

- ***Third, the debtor may surrender the secured property to the creditor.***

6. **Ability to pay:** ***The sixth requirement for confirmation is that the court be satisfied that the debtor will be able to make the payments scheduled under the plan.*** The Chapter 13 trustee will usually play a central role in advising the Court on this task under the duty assigned in § 1302 to "investigate the financial affairs of the debtor" (§ 704(4), discussed *supra*, p. 154) and "to appear and be heard at any hearing" (§ 1302(b)(2), discussed *supra*, p. 232).

C. **Objections to confirmation:**   In the 1984 amendments to the Code, Congress enacted § 1325(b) to address the complaints of creditors that Chapter 13 plans were being confirmed with unduly low payment terms, while at the same time debtors were keeping disposable income that could be applied to pay creditors. The intent was to assure that all disposable income of the debtor would be applied for three years to payments under the plan. However, the provision is not used by creditors as much as anticipated because of the ability of a debtor to convert to Chapter 7 at any time and thereby force creditors to accept even less than they would receive under a Chapter 13 plan. However, under § 1325(b), ***if an unsecured creditor objects to confirmation, the court cannot approve the plan unless one of the following two tests is met***:

1. **Payment in amount of claim:** *As of the date of the plan, the value of the property to be distributed on account of the objecting claim is not less than the amount of the claim.*

2. **Disposable income applied to plan:** *The plan provides that all of the debtor's projected "disposable income" for three years be applied to payments under the plan.* "Disposable income" is defined to mean whatever income is left over after the debtor's (and her dependants') personal and business requirements are met. Personal requirements may include such modest luxury expenses as are appropriate for the debtor's income bracket. *In re Sutliff*, 79 B.R. 157 (Bkrtcy. N.D.N.Y. 1987). In 1998, Congress expanded the concept to include charitable contributions that would not be considered fraudulent transfers under §548, limited to 15 percent of the debtor's gross income in the year in which the transfer is made or, if more than that amount, an amount consistent with the practice of the debtor in making charitable contributions. By thus committing all surplus income to the plan, the provision essentially eliminated disputes about the percentage of income that must be provided for in order to meet the good faith requirement (*supra*, p. 242).

XI. PLAN PAYMENTS — § 1326

A. **When payments begin:** Payments by the debtor to the trustee normally begin within 30 days after the plan is filed. However, if the plan is not confirmed by that time, payments that are made will be held by the trustee. *If and when the plan is confirmed, the trustee begins making payment to creditors as soon as practicable; if confirmation is denied, payments are returned to the debtor after deducting any allowed administrative claims under § 503(b)* (*supra*, p. 86).

B. **Direct payment to trustee:** After a plan is confirmed, the court has the power to order anyone remitting income to the debtor to pay all or part of that income directly to the trustee.

C. **Administrative claims and fees:** *"Before or at the time of each payment to creditors,"* administrative costs and fees as specified in *§ 507(a)(1)* (*supra*, p. 86) *must be paid and, if a "standing trustee" has been appointed under 28 U.S.C. §586(b) (but not a trustee selected otherwise), the fees of such trustee.* Payments cannot be made to other creditors, even other priority creditors under § 507, until these expenses are paid.

D. Trustee makes payments: Unless the plan, or the court order confirming the plan, provides otherwise, the trustee receives payment funds from the debtor and then makes payments to creditors. Provision can be made for payments directly by the debtor or jointly by the debtor and the trustee (*supra*, p. 220).

XII. EFFECT OF CONFIRMATION — § 1327

A. Plan binds debtor and creditors: *The confirmed plan binds the debtor and all creditors, regardless of whether a creditor has objected to or rejected the plan, or has been provided for by the plan.*

B. Estate reverts to debtor: *Unless the plan or the order confirming the plan provides otherwise, the confirmation of the plan vests all of the property of the estate in the debtor* (*supra*, p. 169, p. 228). The plan may provide that property that is needed to effectuate the plan will remain property of the estate until a later date, usually the time of discharge. One result of this is that the property will continue to be subject to § 362(a)(4), the automatic stay provision that prevents creditors from enforcing liens against "property of the estate." *In re Elmore*, 94 B.R. 670 (Bkrtcy. C.D.Cal. 1988). (For duration of the stay, see discussion of § 362(c) *supra*, p. 42.)

C. Property vests free of claims: *Unless the plan or the order confirming the plan provides otherwise, the property of the estate reverts to the debtor free and clear of any claim or interest.* However, if property is not part of the plan, existing interests affecting the property, such as liens, continue in accordance with their terms. *In re Work*, 14 C.B.C.2d 935 (Bkrtcy. D.Ore. 1986).

XIII. DISCHARGE — § 1328

A. Scope of discharge: As an inducement for an individual to file under Chapter 13 rather than Chapter 7, the discharge under Chapter 13 is broader. The obligations discharged are more expansive than those discharged by § 727 (*supra* p. 164) and the exceptions from discharge are fewer than those under § 523 (*supra*, p. 54). Under § 1328, the following obligations are discharged:

1. Debts provided for by plan: *If the debt is provided for in some manner by the plan, even though not paid, it is discharged.* A reference to a debt in the plan will be sufficient for this purpose. *Matter of Gregory*, 705 F.2d 1118 (9th Cir. 1983). *This general rule does not apply to postpetition claims that have not* *been allowed because a proof of claim has not been filed* (*supra*, p. 228). *In re Hester*, 63 B.R. 607 (Bkrtcy. E.D. Tenn. 1986).

2. **Debts disallowed by § 502:** *Debts disallowed under § 502* (*supra*, p. 75) *are discharged.* To be disallowed, a proof of claim must obviously be filed first to permit the court to consider allowance or disallowance.

B. **Exceptions from discharge:**

1. **Debts extending beyond term of plan:** *Debts whose payment terms are longer than the three to five-year period of Chapter 13 plans* (called § 1322(b)(5) debts) *are not discharged* unless they are brought within the plan and dealt with within the time frame of the plan; since they are not discharged, payments must be made, as scheduled, after the plan terminates.

2. **Exceptions under § 523:** *Family obligations, educational loans, and drunk driving obligations, some of the items excepted from discharge under the general provisions of § 523, are excepted from a Chapter 13 discharge.* By contrast, all items under § 523(a) (*supra*, p. 54) are excepted from a Chapter 7 discharge.

3. **Restitution obligations:** Under § 1328, *restitution obligations included in a criminal sentence are not discharged.* This provision was added to the Code in 1990 to reverse the decision of the Supreme court in *Pennsylvania Public Welfare Dept. v. Davenport*, 495 U.S. 552 (1990). Four years previously, *Kelly v. Robinson*, 479 U.S. 36 (1986) (*supra*, p. 58) had decreed that, under the concepts of federalism, restitution obligations in criminal judgments are not discharged in Chapter 7. In *Davenport*, the court had held such obligations to be dischargeable in Chapter 13 because of the Chapter's broader discharge provisions.

C. **Time of discharge:** Chapter 7 provides an automatic discharge as of the time of the order for relief (*supra*, p. 163), while Chapter 11's discharge occurs upon confirmation of a plan (*supra*, p. 242). (Since the creditors have approved the plan under Chapter 11, they accept the risk of its being performed.) Under § 1328, *a Chapter 13 discharge occurs upon either of the following:*

1. **Completion of payments:** Upon completion of payments under the plan, the debtor is discharged.

2. **"Hardship":** *The court may grant a a discharge to a debtor who has not completed payments under a plan if:* (1) the debtor cannot be blamed for the failure, (2) the value of the distributions actually made to unsecured creditors as of the effective date

(discounted back from time of payment) is not less than would have been received under a Chapter 7 liquidation as of that date, and (3) modification of the plan under § 1329 is not practicable. In addition to the exceptions already noted (supra, p. 247), a hardship discharge excepts all of the obligations listed under § 523(a), making it like a Chapter 7 discharge.

XIV. MODIFICATION OF PLAN

A. **Modification of plan:** Under § 1329, *a plan may be modified if circumstances warrant upon application by the debtor, the holder of an allowed claim, or the trustee.*

Example: Debtor D's income is approximately $80,000 a year. His Chapter 13 plan is confirmed with payments of 800 dollars a month. During the course of the plan, D's income rises to $200,000 a year. Upon request of a creditor, the plan is modified to provide that payments be increased to $1,500 a month. *In re Arnold*, 869 F.2d 240 (4th Cir. 1989).

CHAPTER 14

JURISDICTION AND VENUE

I. OVERVIEW

A. Source of jurisdiction: Although Title 11 of the U.S. Code comprises all of the Bankruptcy Code, provisions governing jurisdiction and venue over bankruptcy matters are contained in Title 28, which deals with the federal judiciary.

1. **Bankruptcy judges:** Many jurisdictional questions have arisen from the fact that bankruptcy judges are not Article III judges like the judges of the district courts. *Bankruptcy judges are appointed under Article I of the Constitution and, as such, they have limited jurisdiction.* Questions have frequently arisen as to whether the bankruptcy courts have the power to hear matters that are governed by non-bankruptcy law, but nevertheless have an effect on a bankruptcy case.

2. **Jurisdiction of district courts:** *Original and exclusive jurisdiction over bankruptcy "cases" is conferred on the district courts by § 1334* (Title 28). A case is the adjudication of a bankruptcy filing under Chapter 7, 9, 11, 12, 13, or § 304. A proceeding is the adjudication of a specific dispute that arises within a case. This means that state courts may also, where they have jurisdiction under their own laws, adjudicate matters arising in bankruptcy proceedings.

3. **Relationship of bankruptcy courts to district courts:** *The bankruptcy courts exist as a part of the district courts and the district courts usually refer their bankruptcy matters to the bankruptcy courts. The bankruptcy courts are given their jurisdiction over bankruptcy matters by § 157 (Title 28).* They may hear and determine all cases. As to proceedings, § 157 divides them between "core" proceedings and non-core proceedings. The bankruptcy judge may hear and determine core proceedings, which are more closely related to the bankruptcy estate or to issues that relate directly to the Code. As to non-core proceedings, the bankruptcy judges, unless the parties consent to the judges' jurisdiction over them, may hear them but must submit their proposed findings to the district court for decision

II. BACKGROUND OF JURISDICTIONAL ISSUES

A. Pre-Code jurisdiction: Bankruptcy judges are appointed under Article 1 of the Constitution. In contrast to the requirements of the Constitution for Article III judges, the terms of bankruptcy judges are not for life "during good behavior" (instead they run for 14 years) and their salaries may be reduced. As Article I judges, their jurisdiction has traditionally been limited to the specific powers needed to deal with the assets of the bankruptcy estate. Through these powers, which extend to many *in rem* matters, the bankruptcy judges necessarily render many sophisticated decisions dealing with complicated issues of business and property law.

1. **Summary and plenary jurisdiction:** In hearing a bankruptcy case under the Bankruptcy Act, the law that preceded the 1978 Code, the judges of the bankruptcy courts first had to decide whether assets were part of the debtor's estate or the property of third persons. If the assets were in the estate, the bankruptcy court had, under its limited power known as "summary" jurisdiction, the authority to adjudicate ultimate disposition of the assets to creditors. Under the bankruptcy judges' summary jurisdiction, it was within their power to identify the creditors who were making claims upon those assets, determine whether their claims were legitimate, and answer most other issues that arose. If the estate did not have an interest in the property, or the parties to the property had not consented to the jurisdiction of the bankruptcy courts, the dispute could be dealt with only through the "plenary" jurisdiction of other federal or state courts. (Summary and plenary jurisdiction under pre-Code law are discussed in Collier on Bankruptcy, 15th Edition, Vol 2, Par. 23.02.)

B. Jurisdiction after the 1978 Code: With the enactment of the 1978 Bankruptcy Code, Congress expanded the powers of the bankruptcy court to something closer to those of the traditional Article III court and gave the bankruptcy courts jurisdiction over all "civil proceedings arising under Title 11 [the Bankruptcy Code] or arising in or related to cases under Title 11." This grant gave bankruptcy judges the power to hear and determine issues of any sort, whether or not a non-bankrupt party had submitted to the bankruptcy court's jurisdiction, so long as the issues were "related to" a bankruptcy case.

1. ***Northern Pipeline* facts:** In the case of *Northern Pipeline Const. Co. v. Marathon Pipe Line Co*, 458 U.S. 50 (1982), Northern Pipeline was in a Chapter 11 reorganization. Its trustee sued Marathon Pipe Line for breach of contract, misrepresentation, coercion and duress. Under the newly expanded bankruptcy court jurisdiction, Northern Pipeline brought its lawsuit in the bankruptcy court because the

suit was "related to" the Chapter 11 case. Marathon Pipe Line defended on the theory that there was no *in rem* jurisdiction by the bankruptcy court and Marathon had not submitted to the bankruptcy court's jurisdiction. It argued that Congress had given authority over ordinary non-bankruptcy cases to Article I bankruptcy judges in violation of the constitution and that this authority exceeded their powers under the Constitution.

2. **The *Northern Pipeline* holding:** The Supreme Court agreed with Marathon Pipe Line. The Article I bankruptcy judge had only limited powers. These included the *in rem* powers to deal with bankruptcy assets and the power to decide lawsuits *if* jurisdiction of the court was consented to by the parties. But the Court found the jurisdiction of the bankruptcy courts to be unconstitutional when extended to a common-law cause of action based on *in personam*, rather than *in rem* jurisdiction.

III. JURISDICTION OF DISTRICT COURTS

A. Jurisdiction in the district courts: After some delay, the 1984 amendments to the Code attempted to correct the constitutional problems raised by *Northern Pipeline*. The amendments established original jurisdiction in the district courts with respect to bankruptcy matters, with the power to refer cases and proceedings to the bankruptcy judges.

1. **Original and exclusive jurisdiction in bankruptcy cases:** The foundation of this corrective action lies in 28 U.S.C. §1334(a) which gives *the United States district courts original and exclusive jurisdiction of all bankruptcy cases.* This means that a case under Title 11 must be brought in a federal district court. (State courts may have jurisdiction over other forms of insolvency relief, such as in a state action based on a statute dealing with assignments for the benefit of creditors, but not over bankruptcy cases.)

2. **Original jurisdiction over proceedings:** The 1984 amendments also give *the district courts original, but not exclusive, jurisdiction over all civil proceedings arising under title 11, or arising in or related to cases under title 11.* A state court may have concurrent jurisdiction over *a proceeding, which is a specific dispute that arises during the pendency of a bankruptcy case* (*infra*).

3. ***In rem* jurisdiction:** Under § 1334(e), the district courts are given jurisdiction over the property of the debtor and property of the

estate. This serves to confirm *in rem* jurisdiction to the extent it is needed.

4. **Abstention:** Under § 1334(c), ***the district court may abstain from hearing a proceeding arising under Title 11, or arising in or related to a case under Title 11.*** This provision is to allow for abstention where, in the interests of justice, a matter is better handled in another court. ***With respect to proceedings that are only related to cases under Title 11*** (as contrasted with proceedings arising under cases in Title 11), ***conditions are set forth under which the court must abstain***. Note that this refers to ***proceedings***, not to entire ***cases*** within which proceedings may arise. Abstentions from cases are dealt with in § 305 (*supra,* p. 29) and in specific sections within each of the bankruptcy filing chapters.

B. **State court jurisdiction over proceedings:** Under § 1334(b), the district courts are given original "but not exclusive jurisdiction" of proceedings in and related to cases. ***The word "proceedings" is used to cover the various issues that may arise in a bankruptcy case.*** (Was the case begun in the right court; did the debtor choose the right chapter; was an exemption rightfully taken; should a creditor be paid; is a debt dischargeable, etc.?) A proceeding may, as contrasted with a case, be heard in a state court. The jurisdiction of a state court to hear and determine a bankruptcy proceeding depends entirely upon the jurisdictional powers given to that court by the law of the state in which it sits.

IV.   JURISDICTION OF BANKRUPTCY COURTS

A. **Status of bankruptcy courts:** The 1984 amendments coming as a result of *Northern Pipeline* established the present relationship between the district courts and the bankruptcy courts.

1. **Designation of bankruptcy courts and judges:** Under § 151 (title 28), ***bankruptcy courts are established as units of the district courts***. Bankruptcy judges, who serve as judicial officers of the district courts, are appointed by the circuit courts of appeals.

2. **Referral of bankruptcy cases to bankruptcy courts:** Under § 157 (title 28), the district courts, with their original and exclusive jurisdiction of bankruptcy cases, may provide that all Title 11 cases and all proceedings "arising under Title 11 or arising in or related to a case under Title 11" be referred to the bankruptcy judges. All district courts have adopted rules governing the referral of bankruptcy cases.

3. **Jury trials:** After years of considerable confusion on the issue of whether bankruptcy courts could conduct jury trials, the amendments to the Code in 1994 established the power of the bankruptcy court to conduct jury trials in limited circumstances. Under § 157(e), *if the right to a jury trial applies to a proceeding that a bankruptcy judge is empowered to hear*, whether by the Constitution or by statute, *a jury trial may be conducted, provided that the judge is empowered by the district court to do so and that express consent is given by the parties.*

B. **Bankruptcy cases; "core" and "non-core" proceedings:** *A bankruptcy judge is empowered under § 157 to hear and determine all Title 11 cases and all proceedings defined as "core."* In this way, Congress has dealt with the *Northern Pipeline* constitutionality problem. The bankruptcy judge, in deciding "core" matters only, is presumably limited to those issues that may be decided by an Article I judge.

1. **"Core" proceedings:** There are 15 kinds of core proceedings listed in § 157(b)(2). The list, which is not exclusive, includes issues that come within the pre-Code concept of "summary proceedings." These include such matters as the allowance of claims and proceedings affecting the liquidation of property. Also included are issues over which the adverse party has given its consent to the bankruptcy court's jurisdiction, as in the determination of counterclaims.

   a. **Matters concerning the administration of the estate:** The bankruptcy court is also given a power whose reach is uncertain — "matters concerning the administration of the estate." One would assume that almost every issue that arises in bankruptcy would concern to some degree the administration of the estate. However, this power has been construed to mean that, *the issue should be of substance or significance in the bankruptcy to be considered a "core" issue.* For example, whether the court should abstain from considering 1,000 lawsuits brought against a debtor in possession was deemed to be "core" when the effect of the lawsuits was "the heart of the reorganization process." *In re Hillsborough Holdings Corp.*, 123 B.R. 1004 (Bkrtcy. M.D. Fla.), aff'd, 123 B.R. 1018 (D.M.D. Fla. 1990).

   b. **Constitutionality:** In essence, most of the proceedings that will arise in a bankruptcy case are defined by Congress as core. Indeed, the Congressional history shows that Congress intended 95% of the issues that will arise to be core and to be decided by bankruptcy judges. *In re Arnold Print Works, Inc.*, 815 F.2d 165 (1st Cir. 1987). Some core proceedings, however, come perilously close to colliding with the *Northern Pipeline* rocks. While there has been some problem at the district court level with the bankruptcy judge's jurisdiction in certain proceedings construed as core, the Circuit Courts of Appeals have generally agreed that Congress acted constitutionally. *In re Harbour*, 840 F.2d 1165 (4th Cir. 1988).

2. **"Non-core" proceedings**: *As for "non-core" proceedings, the bankruptcy judge may hear them, but may not make a decision unless the parties consent* (*supra*, p. 22). Under §157(c), the judge may only refer his proposed findings of fact and conclusions of law to the district court for decision.

C. **Weakening vitality of *Northern Pipeline* holding**: The expansive view generally given to the concept of core proceedings as listed in § 157 suggests a departure from *Northern Pipeline*, which should probably not be given much weight today beyond the strictest reading. This departure is also suggested by the courts, which have been drawing away from the decision. For example, the Second Circuit Court of Appeals has allowed a contract action against a third party in bankruptcy court when the contract was entered into after the bankruptcy petition. *In re Ben Cooper*, 896 F.2d 1394 (2d Cir.), cert. denied, 111 S.Ct. 2041 (1991). This may be attributable to the fact that the *Northern Pipeline* decision was decided by a four justice plurality, with two other concurring justices and one justice in one dissent and three in another dissent (including the justice in the first dissent.) It is, therefore, difficult to be precise about its meaning.

V. VENUE

A. **Venue for cases**: The basic venue rule under § 1408 (title 28) is that *bankruptcy cases must be brought in the district in which "the domicile, residence, principal place of business in the United States, or principal assets in the United States" of the debtor were located for 180 days before the case is begun*. Since a partnership has no domicile or residence, the court will determine where the principal place of business is located; in one case, the court determined that the principal place of business was where major business decisions were made, not where the principal asset was located or where incidental ministerial functions were performed. *In re Peachtree Lane Associates, Ltd.*, 198 B.R. 272 (N.D. Ill. 1996). If there is a bankruptcy case pending concerning an affiliate, general partner, or partnership of the debtor, as defined in §101, the new case may be brought in the district court of the pending case.

B. **Venue for proceedings**: The proper venue for a proceeding (i.e., an issue in a case) is determined by § 1409.

1. **General rule**: *A proceeding may be brought in the district court where the case related to the proceeding is pending.*

2. **Special rule for certain consumer proceedings**: If the bankruptcy trustee is attempting to recover a money judgment or property worth less than $1,000 or a consumer debt of less than $5,000, it must proceed in the district court where the defendant resides. The purpose is to avoid for a defendant (e.g., the debtor) the inconvenience of going to a remote district court when the amount involved is small.

C. **Cases in the wrong district**: The statute does not prescribe what is to be done if a case is brought in the wrong district. Most courts have utilized the general judicial approach to issues of venue and have held that *the case may be heard where brought if it is in the interests of justice and is for the convenience of the parties.* For an opinion agreeing with the prevailing view and noting the minority view, see *In re Lazaro*, 128 B.R. 168 (Bkrtcy. W.D. Tex. 1991).

Example: A farm is located in Nebraska just south of the South Dakota border. It is considerably closer to the South Dakota bankruptcy court and the farm's major creditor is also in South Dakota. The debtor files in South Dakota. Although it was not proper venue, the court decided, for the convenience of the parties, to keep the case. *In re Boeckman*, 54 B.R. 110 (Bkrtcy. D.S.D. 1985).

D. **Cases in the right district**: Even if a case is brought in the right district, under § 1412, *a court may transfer it to another district "in the interest of justice or for the convenience of the parties."*

Example: A partnership with its official "principal place of business" in New York (the partnership and the senior partners are located in New York) files for bankruptcy in New York. The business of the partnership is the ownership of a hotel complex in Arizona. The land and buildings are in Arizona, as are most of the partnership's books and records; most of the creditors are in Arizona; appraisals would be made in Arizona; and, if a trustee were appointed to manage the properties, he would be in Arizona. The New York court could have the case moved to Arizona. *In re Landmark Capital Co.*, 20 B.R. 220 (D.S.D. N.Y. 1982).

TABLE OF CASES

TABLE OF REFERENCES TO THE BANKRUPTCY RULES

TABLE OF STATUTORY (U.S.C.) AND UNIFORM COMMERCIAL CODE (U.C.C.) REFERENCES

TABLE OF BANKRUPTCY CODE REFERENCES

SUBJECT MATTER INDEX

The Emanuel Law Outline Series

Each outline in the series is the work of Steven Emanuel. Each is packed with features that take you from next-day preparation to night-before-the-exam review. Outlines are available for all major law school subjects and many are revised annually. This year, Steve will prepare new editions of Evidence, Constitutional Law, Torts, Criminal Procedure and Property.

Available titles
Civil Procedure
Constitutional Law
Contracts
Corporations
Criminal Law
Criminal Procedure
Evidence
Property
Torts (General Edition)
Torts (Prosser Edition)

Law In A Flash Series

Flashcards add a dimension to law school study which cannot be matched by any other study aid, and these are the acknowledged leader in flashcards. They make legal issues and answers stick to your mind like glue. Each Law In a Flash card set contains 350-625 cards arranged to give you black-letter principles first. Then they teach you all the subtleties by taking you through a series of hypotheticals filled with mnemonics and checklists. Excellent for exam preparation.

Available titles
Civil Procedure 1
Civil Procedure 2
Constitutional Law
Contracts
Corporations
Criminal Law
Criminal Procedure
Evidence
Federal Income Taxation
Future Interests
Professional Responsibility
Real Property
Sales (UCC Article 2)
Torts
Wills & Trusts